P9-DEL-614

DATE DUE		

Voices of the
African American Experience

Voices of the African American Experience

VOLUME 1

Edited by Lionel C. Bascom

GREENWOOD PRESS
Westport, Connecticut • London

Library of Congress Cataloging-in-Publication Data

Voices of the African American experience / edited by Lionel C. Bascom.
   3 v. cm.
   Includes bibliographical references and index.
   ISBN 978-0-313-34347-6 (set) — ISBN 978-0-313-34349-0 (vol. 1) —
ISBN 978-0-313-34351-3 (vol. 2) — ISBN 978-0-313-34353-7
(vol. 3) 1. African Americans—History—Sources. I. Bascom, Lionel C.
   E184. 6. V65   2009
   973′.0496073—dc22   2008056155

British Library Cataloguing in Publication Data is available.

Library of Congress Catalog Card Number: 2008056155

ISBN: 978-0-313-34347-6 (set)
       978-0-313-34349-0 (vol 1)
       978-0-313-34351-3 (vol 2)
       978-0-313-34353-7 (vol 3)

First published in 2009

Greenwood Press, 88 Post Road West, Westport, CT 06881
An imprint of Greenwood Publishing Group, Inc.
www.greenwood.com

Printed in the United States of America

∞™

The paper used in this book complies with the
Permanent Paper Standard issued by the National
Information Standards Organization (Z39.48-1984).

10 9 8 7 6 5 4 3 2 1

Contents

VOLUME 2

Preface

Histories—compiled, written, and published with an intended audience and point of view—almost immediately become the natural targets of revisionists. *Voices of the African American Experience*, although a documents collection rather than a history, is no exception. This compiled document collection is an attempt at writing, shaping, and inventing earlier histories of Africans who came to the Americas more than five centuries ago.

This book is a compilation of documents that tell the stories of enslaved Africans and a race of people who eventually came to be seen as Americans, by themselves and by others. The facts surrounding the entire history of America are not as "self-evident" as they once seemed. One of those facts is that some of the so-called founding fathers were also slaveowners and hypocrites at the same time that they were seen and described as revolutionaries and patriots.

Voices of the African American Experience presents documents that begin with the importation of the first slaves to the English settlement of Jamestown in Virginia. The documents used in this book span across hundreds of years from around 1620 to 2008. Many histories covering this same period, based on primary documents and other reliable sources, ask us to believe an array of presumptions about this time period.

Almost from the very start of working to compile these volumes, the Greenwood editors and I began to debate the many issues surrounding publishing any book in today's changing market and the peculiar issues related to attempting to compile such an often unwieldy collection of primary documents, including oral histories, letters, interviews, speeches, legislation, essays, articles, first-person accounts, and more, all to represent the life and times of a people and an emerging culture we now call the African American Experience.

The title alone suggests a colossal undertaking that involved too many librarians to list here; institutions, whether electronic, virtual, or found in real places such as New Haven, Virginia, Cambridge, California, and Iowa; and bibliographies of bibliographies, all consulted in an attempt to compile the most complete book of books and source of sources possible, given the constraints of time, space, and the fair use of copyrighted materials. Every publishing venture has deadlines, dates that rightly define the beginning and absolute time allotted to the production of any book, and space restrictions. The number of volumes allotted for this work is generous by almost every known standard yet an infinite amount of space would be needed to adequately cover "the experience" of any culture. And finally, the restrictions, rights, and privileges of using material that rightfully belongs to others is always a knotty problem that can only be sorted out through a complicated process of obtaining copyright permission. It is at this juncture where the time, space, and the continuums of legal rights collide in the process of obtaining permissions. The rights to use work by the Reverend Dr. Martin Luther King Jr., for example, have proven quite difficult to obtain despite the fact that much of this material can be found freely enough by surfing the Internet. Finding it and obtaining permission to use it are not the same things. So, regrettably, many of the fine, iconic speeches made by King during his brief lifetime could not be included in this set. There are other omissions as well that could not be avoided.

At Western Connecticut State University in 2008, Professor Jeanne Lakatos and I spent months choosing and compiling these documents as a team, with the goal to present diverse types of documents through history and make them easily accessible for students and the general reader. We did not work alone, always continually discussing criteria for this project with colleagues, all seasoned historians, social scientists, journalists, and academics, along with the experienced editors at Greenwood Press. In the early 1980s, I studied what I now call literary archeology under Dr. Henry Louis Gates at Yale University who taught a course called Black Women and Their Fictions. Although its origin is still the debatable, it is believed that author Toni Morrison, the Nobel Prize winner, first taught the course at Yale. Throughout the more than twenty five years that I have been working and editing books, including discovering unpublished literary works for a variety of publishers, it has always been made particularly clear to me by feminist scholars, and by African American, Asian American, and Latino American scholars, that the term "primary document" is a loaded phrase. While we are using a liberal *Chicago Manual of Style* definition, primary documents can still mean many things to many people in a country where slavery, segregation; suffrage, ideas such as affirmative action and separate but equal, and the documents that liberally use these terms can still be used to skew every history of the United States ever written. Criticism in the form of questioning the reliability of sources is probably not a new complaint where minority histories or other histories regarding minority peoples and genders are concerns. There is an opposite, mirror complaint that popular histories have always excluded more obscure documents that are now gaining widespread use among academics and historians as primary sources. The oral history is just one example. Slave narratives as told to historians are another. Minority-owned and minority-operated newspapers started by W. E. B. Du Bois, Marcus Garvey, Frederick Douglass, A. Phillip Randolph and The Black Panther Party, and the National Association for the Advancement of Colored People are also important sources that have generally been ignored but contain much valuable information that historians are only recently rediscovering. Tens of thousands of African American newspapers (almost all defunct now) were the social critics of the times in which they were published, and, as such, they recorded primary events that otherwise would have been left unrecorded by mainstream society. Thousands of lynchings, for example, were recorded by newspapers, large and small, not by the town clerks who were the official keepers of primary documents where lynchings occurred. The Northern Star, the Afro-Am, The Liberator, and the New York Amsterdam News were newspapers that announced the arrival of abolitionists. The first person narratives of a federal writer's project launched in the 1930s recorded the stories about the life of a riverboat worker called Coonjine, which mirror the plight of a former slave who was made famous in the novel and play

Showboat and a song called *Old Man River*. We are just now finding some of these documents and are finally using them in the many new histories . They tell the stories of slaves, Negroes, the colored race, the New Negro, and African Americans over long periods of time that extend back across hundreds of years.

Just as it was presumed in the summer of 2008 that a mix-raced man from Chicago named Barack Obama would win the Democratic nomination for the presidency of the United States, the written history of America has always held up presumptions, masquerading them as facts. The ideal that all men in America were created equal is presumed to stem from the words of Thomas Jefferson, who was also a slave owner. No slave owner could possibly have really believed that all men were created equal. This book attempts to document how stating presumptions, such as Jefferson saying that all men are created equal, and believing them are sometimes mutually exclusive ideas. A close reading of the documents compiled in this reference book will hopefully lead the casual reader and scholarly researchers to new conclusions and new presumptions. For every leader like black activist Malcolm X, there is a movie director like Spike Lee and an FBI Director like J. Edgar Hoover who will each go to separate corners when asked to read and document some primary truths about the African American experience. To Hoover, Malcolm Little was a hustler and a villain whose militant movement posed a threat to the national security of the United States. Lee portrayed Malcolm X as a complicated, evolved visionary in the revolutionary wars of the twentieth century who helped to shape modern African American culture. These interpretations by people like Lee or Hoover are prisms of history, each viewable by some as fictions that we are merely calling history.

The nearly 150 documents are presented in chronological order. A brief introduction to each gives the reader some context. Further research value comes from the substantial chronology of African American history and the selected bibliography.

LIONEL C. BASCOM
Western Connecticut State University, 2008

Introduction

"Sails furled, flag drooping at her rounded stern, she rode the tide in from the sea. She was a strange ship, indeed, by all accounts, a frightening ship, a ship of mystery," wrote J. Saunders Redding, a black writer describing the landing of a slave ship to North America in 1619. Redding's observation documents the arrival of a slave ship to the English settlement called Jamestown. "Whether she was trader, privateer or man-of-war, no one knows. Through her bulwarks black mouth cannon yawned. The flag she flew was Dutch; her crew a motley [bunch]. She came, she traded, and shortly afterwards was gone. Probably no ship in modern history has carried a more portentous freight. Her cargo? Twenty slaves," Redding wrote in his book, *They Came in Chains* (1950). If accurate, Redding's narrative captures something larger than the arrival of the first slaves to the New World; it also marks the start of the African American and the experience of an evolving culture. Slavery and the indelible mark it left on that culture and on America are inseparable.

"There is not a country in world history in which racism has been more important, for so long a time as the United States," wrote historian Howard Zinn in the opening pages of his book, *A People's History of the United States, 1492-Present* (1980). "And the problem of 'the color line' as scholar W. E. B. Du Bois put it, is still with us. Slavery developed quickly into a regular institution, into the normal labor relation of blacks to whites in the New World. With it developed that special racial feeling—whether hatred, or contempt, or pity, or patronization that accompanied the inferior position of blacks in America for the next 350 years—that combination of inferior status and derogatory thought we call racism," Zinn posited.

Voices of the African American Experience is not a history or commentary on racism. The Greenwood Press title, *Encyclopedia of Racism in the United States* (2005), edited by Pyong Gap Min, adequately covers the subject. However, this set would not be thorough without noting, as Zinn notes, that "everything in the experience of the first white settlers acted as a pressure for the enslavement of blacks. That enslavement and the effects are the African-American experience."

Unshackled by civil war that freed millions of black slaves by the year 1865, living generations of former slaves, their children, and their grandchildren, then began an historic cultural migration to flee feudal America. It was a trek into the future that would take the greater part of the next century.

Stripped of their bonds, ex-slaves were left culturally, socially, and economically naked at the close of a war some ex-slaves described in first person narratives as the war between the white folks. When the civil strife between free states and slave states ended, slaves found themselves free but also stripped of the paternalism and protections against violence by masters who had valued them as personal property. Millions of emancipated slaves and their families suddenly became prey during reconstruction to widespread economic and social discrimination, vigilante violence, and a justice system that saw them as anything but equals. Laws that were passed in almost every southern state aimed to control and restrict the lives of blacks and almost immediately replaced the chains of slavery. The widespread segregation that ensued effectively barred Negroes from voting, purchasing property, and accessing adequate public schooling, employment, and the other necessities needed for the unfettered pursuit of happiness guaranteed by the U.S. Constitution.

By the end of World War I and decades after emancipation, millions of black tenant farmers and laborers who could not vote in Mississippi, Virginia, South Carolina, and other southern states, boarded railroad trains by the thousands each week, bound for new lives in northern cities. This move from life on the plantations of the south to futures in urban cities became one of the great sagas in modern American history. It was a tale of two countries, two Americas, one black, the other white, one free, the other perpetually seeking freedom. It was the Exodus transported to this side of the Atlantic, seemingly plucked whole from the pages of the second book of the Old Testament in the Bible, the universal story of the Israelites' escape from Egypt.

Shaking off the taint of slavery and the stench of a corrupt reconstruction, black men and women with their families set off to do for themselves what President Abe Lincoln's army and a nation of laws had failed to achieve for them through the Emancipation Proclamation. They left cotton fields in Georgia, orange groves in Florida, and tenant farms in Arkansas to begin the impossible task of reconstructing their lives at the turn of the twentieth century, just three decades after the emancipation. They took jobs in meatpacking plants, donned the uniforms of railroad porters and red-capped baggage handlers. Bean pickers from South Carolina became housemaids in Chicago, autoworkers in Detroit and sewing machine operators in the garment district of New York City. Calling themselves New Negroes, the participants of this great migration evolved into what would become the first generation of a soon-to-be assimilated group who eventually began calling themselves African Americans late in the same century.

Their exodus became known as the Great Migration and was first noted in the pages of a magazine called *Survey Graphic*, a journal that covered social change throughout the world. A special Harlem edition of the magazine was published in 1925, edited by Howard University Professor Alain Locke. "A railroad ticket and a suitcase, like a Baghdad carpet, transport the Negro peasant from the cotton-field and farm to the heart of the most complex urban civilization," Locke wrote. "Here in the mass, he must and does survive a jump of two generations in social economy and of a century and more in civilization. Like camp followers who traipsed from place to place behind an advancing army, the black poets, students, artists, professionals, and thinkers came too."

This migration of blacks was numerically smaller than the migration of European immigrants who had come to America from Ireland, Italy, Germany, Russia, and elsewhere. However, the impact these black migrants had on the cities where they landed was no less significant, Locke said. The influx of African Americans, he added, transformed sections of cities, into something more than city blocks that had suddenly become "unaccountably full of black people," Locke observed.

This represented a dramatic change in American demographics and transformed places such as Harlem in New York, Chicago's Southside, and numerous other places around America into communities of people who suddenly found themselves together and empowered by the strength of having common goals.

Freedom was an elusive ideal more than it was a reality. Nowhere was this more evident than in the rural south for those who stayed behind. During and after the reconstruction years between 1865 and 1897, every state in the south looked for ways to restrict African American citizens. These unofficial racial restrictions became virtual law and were bolstered [endorsed?] as the laws of the land when the U.S. Supreme Court institutionalized them in a famous Louisiana court decision, *Plessy v. Ferguson*, in 1896. Homer Plessy had been arrested in Louisiana for refusing to sit in a "colored" section of a train. He lost the case on appeal to the high court, which ruled in 1896 that separate but allegedly equal public facilities for blacks and whites were constitutional.

At the beginning of the twentieth century, blacks everywhere were refused service at restaurants, movie houses, public beaches, libraries, bathrooms, hotels, and public accommodations of all kinds. This deep-seated discrimination was practiced in the North as well as in the South. But it was most stringent in the South where laws based on the *Plessy* court decision were passed, legitimizing this kind of bigotry.

African Americans, who were forced to pay taxes in the communities where they lived, could be arrested for even trying use public bathrooms, train cars, schools, colleges, libraries, or movie houses that were reserved for "whites only." These prohibitions were generally called Jim Crow laws, named after a second-rate, white minstrel show actor named Thomas Dartmouth who popularized a slow-talking, ragged, blackface character in the 1830s. Appearing in black face with various foolish sidekicks like Jim Dandy, Zip Coon, and Sambo, Dartmouth's Jim Crow shows played in London and Dublin, and opened in New York in 1832. By 1838, the name "Jim Crow" itself became a racial slur for blacks in America that was as offensive as "nigger," "coon" or "darky."

By 1914, on the strength of the *Plessy* decision, every southern state had passed Black Codes, or Jim Crow laws. These laws did more than give comfort to an old southern aesthetic. They essentially made it legal to strip emancipated blacks and their heirs of their equal rights and protection of laws enacted to protect other Americans. By 1965, however, an array of political, social, and economic movements had started throughout the United States and the true assimilation of the so-called Negro began to take hold in America. The "darky" label and the colored man image of former slaves and their descendants started to fade.

I was born a colored person, almost always referred to by race before I became known by my surname, economic status, or even by gender as a boy growing up in New England and New York. I was a "Negro" or "colored" on my birth certificate, called "colored" throughout my school records, and, for all I know, my YMCA swim card noted my race before it determined whether I had passed a rigorous water safety course.

I grew up in a nation where apartheid was more widespread than almost anywhere else in the world. Black and white Americans were almost never seen together in public places. While blacks and whites attended schools together in many parts of the nation, most colleges still did not accept black students. The American Medical Association routinely discriminated against blacks and restricted its memberships to white doctors only, like almost all golf clubs, beach clubs, or fraternal organizations, such as the Elks and the American Legion and Veterans of Foreign Wars.

In the primary schools I attended in the late 1950s and early 1960s, I read the unrevised histories of the founding fathers of the American Revolution, at the same time that the spark of what we came to call "The Revolution," exploded in my neighborhood and in communities across America. What spewed forth was exhilarating, filled with new ideas about real emancipation and freedom that quickly spread like a wild fire all over the nation.

While I was still considered to be "a colored boy," men and women of all ages and races throughout America rose up to challenge long-standing racist policies everywhere. It was a revolution that was led by ministers and politicians, scholars and labor leaders. It was the era of civil rights, and suddenly the world began to listen to the speeches of people such as the Reverend Dr. Martin Luther King Jr., Minister Malcolm X, Presidents John F. Kennedy and Lynden B. Johnson, Attorney General Robert "Bobby" Kennedy, W. E. B. DuBois and Roy Wilkins, organizers and leaders of grassroots organizations such as the National Association for the Advancement of Colored People, the Congress Of Racial Equality, and many other people and groups. Together, they tried to put into practice the moral imperatives of equal protections under the law, defined by the founding fathers of a nation that was built with slavery as its foundation. In the 1960s, religious and political icons like Dr. Martin Luther King and brothers Robert and President John F. Kenndey led the movement. It was Martin, Bobby, John, and countless others who helped to chisel out new civil rights paradigms that transformed the life and experiences of a colored boy like me. Suddenly, the flowerings of an enchanted garden in an imaginary place called Camelot became imaginable in America after 1960.

This collection of documents illuminates the African American experience through history.

Chronology

1492   The first expedition to the New World by Christopher Columbus departs Europe. A black navigator named Pedro Alonso Nino is aboard one of the vessels.

1619   The first Africans in the New World, twenty indentured laborers, arrive in Jamestown, Virginia, aboard a Dutch ship on August 20. They are the first blacks to be forcibly settled as involuntary laborers in the North American British Colonies.

1641   Massachusetts becomes the first colony to legalize slavery by statute.

1663   The first documented slave rebellion takes place in Gloucester County, Virginia on September 13.

1664   Maryland becomes the first colony to discourage the marriage of white women to black men.

1688   The Quakers of Germantown, Pennsylvania, pass the first formal antislavery resolution on February 18.

1712   A slave insurrection is discovered on April 16 in New York City, resulting in the execution of twenty-one African Americans.

1739   The Stono Rebellion is the first serious insurrection to be implemented among slaves in North America on September 9. After they kill more than twenty-five whites, most of the rebels, led by a slave named Cato, are rounded up as they try to escape to Florida. More than thirty African Americans are executed.

1746   A poem called "Bar Fights," is recited by Lucy Terry, a slave who lived in Massachusetts. The poem was not published until 1855.

1758   The Bluestone Church is founded in Mecklenburg, Virginia, on the plantation of William Byrd near the Bluestone River. Many believe it was the first black church to be formed in North America.

1770   Escaped slave Crispus Attucks is one of the five victims in the Boston Massacre on March 5.

1773   Phillis Wheatley, a slave, publishes "Poems on Various Subjects, Religious and Moral." Her book is the first published work by an African American (in England).

1775 At Lexington and Concord, Massachusetts, on April 19, free blacks fight with the Minutemen in the initial skirmishes of the Revolutionary War. When some 5,000 join the ranks of white soldiers, the British governor in Virginia encourages slaves to join the British army with the promise of freedom.

1776 A little known passage in the Declaration of Independence condemning the slave trade is removed from the document when southern colonies objected.

1777 Vermont is the first state to abolish slavery on July 2.

The African Free School, designed to train African Americans for lives outside slavery, opens in New York City on November 1.

George Washington reverses previous policy and allows the recruitment of African Americans as soldiers on December 31. Approximately 5,000 will participate on the American side before the end of the Revolution.

1780 Brothers John and Paul Cuffe, both free blacks, petition the Massachusetts state legislature to grant them suffrage or to stop taxing them. Though the legislature denies the petition, it paves the way for the 1783 state constitution to grant equal rights to all citizens.

1787 The Free School is founded in New York City by free blacks.

Richard Allen and Absalom Jones organize the Free African Society, a mutual aid society in Philadelphia, Pennsylvania, on April 12.

With the Northwest Ordinance on July 13, the Continental Congress forbids slavery in the region northwest of the Ohio River. Slavery is, nonetheless, implicitly protected south of the Ohio River.

In September, the framers of the Constitution of the United States, in the so-called Three-Fifths Compromise, allow slaves to count as three-fifths of a person in determining representation in the House of Representatives. The recovery of runaway, fugitive slaves is aided by the U.S. Constitution when it is ratified. It provides for the continuation of the slave trade for at least another twenty years and requires states to assist slave owners in recovering fugitive slaves.

1791 The first almanac by an African American is published by Benjamin Banneker. He is subsequently appointed by President George Washington to help survey Washington, D.C.

1793 Congress passes the first Fugitive Slave Law, February 12.

Eli Whitney obtains a patent on March 14 for his cotton gin, a device that leads to the massive expansion of slavery in the South.

1794 Richard Allen founds the Bethel African Methodist Church in Philadelphia on June 10.

1797 On August 30, a slave revolt (often known as "Gabriel's Rebellion") near Richmond, Virginia, lead by Gabriel Prosser and Jack Bowley, is first postponed and then betrayed. More than forty blacks are eventually executed.

1804 The Ohio legislature on January 5 passes "Black Laws" designed to restrict the legal rights of free blacks. These laws are part of the trend toward increasingly severe restrictions on all African Americans in both the North and South before the Civil War.

1808   Federal law prohibiting the importation of African slaves takes effect on January 1. Nonetheless, illegal importation will continue for decades after the ban.

1809   The Abyssinian Baptist Church is founded in New York City.

1815   The resettlement of thirty-five African Americans in Sierra Leone is financed by Paul Cuffe.

1816   The African Methodist Episcopal Church is organized, April 9, as the first independent black denomination in the United States.

1818   General Andrew Jackson defeats a force of Native Americans and African Americans to end the First Seminole War on August 18.

1821   The African Company, believed to be the first black theater company in America, is formed.

1822   The Denmark Vesey conspiracy is betrayed in Charleston, South Carolina, on May 30. Some claims estimate that 5,000 African Americans were prepared to participate.

1827   *Freedom's Journal*, the first African American newspaper, is published in New York City by John Brown Russwurm and Samuel Cornish.

1829   In September, David Walker's militant antislavery pamphlet, *An Appeal to the Colored People of the World*, enters circulation in the South. This work is the first of its kind by an African American.

The first National Negro Convention meets in Philadelphia, September 20–24.

1831   The Nat Turner revolt, August 21–22, runs its course in Southampton County, Virginia, sending shockwaves of fear across the entire South.

The Liberator, an anti-slavery newspaper published in Boston, is launched by William Lloyd Garrisons.

1839   In July, the slaves carried on the Spanish ship, *Amistad*, take over the vessel and sail it to Montauk on Long Island. They eventually win their freedom in a case taken to the U.S. Supreme Court.

1845   *Narrative of the Life of Frederick Douglass: An American Slave*, is published and becomes an international bestseller.

1849   Harriet Tubman escapes from slavery in July. She will return to the South at least twenty times, leading over 300 slaves to freedom.

1850   Another Fugitive Slave Act is passed by the U.S. Congress requiring government support in the capture of escaped slaves. Passage prompts widespread protests in northern cities such as Boston and New York.

1851   Abolitionist Sojourner Truth appears at an anti-slavery rally in Akron, Ohio, where she delivers her famous "Ain't I A Woman" speech.

1852   The novel, *Uncle Tom's Cabin*, is published by Harriet Beecher Stowe. Her anti-slavery novel becomes an immediate bestseller and is used to fuel protests against the Fugitive Slave Act.

1854   The Ashmun Institute, later known as Lincoln University, is chartered in Oxford, Pennsylvania, becoming one of the first Negro colleges.

1857   The *Dred Scott* decision of the U.S. Supreme Court, March 6, denies that blacks are citizens of the United States and denies the power of Congress to restrict slavery in any federal territory.

1859   The first novel by an African American, *Our Nig; or Sketches from the Life of a Free Black*, is published.

   The slave ship, *Clothilde*, arrives in Mobile Bay, Alabama. It is believed to be the last known ship to bring slaves from Africa to the United States.

   Abolitionist John Brown and his men raid the federal arsenal at Harper's Ferry in Virginia on October 16–17 to obtain arms for a slave rebellion. Brown's plans are foiled and he is caught. He is hanged for treason on December 2.

1861   Confederate soldiers attack Fort Sumter in Charleston, South Carolina, starting the Civil War. Fought over the issue of slavery, the war rages on for four years. The U.S. victory laid the foundation for the end of formal slavery in the United States.

   James Stone of Ohio enlists on August 23, becoming the first black to fight for the Union during the Civil War. He is very light skinned and married to a white woman. His racial identity is revealed after his death in 1862.

1862   Congress allows the enlistment of blacks in the Union Army on July 17. Some black units precede this date, but they were disbanded as unofficial. Some 186,000 blacks will serve, and 38,000 of them will die.

   Slavery is abolished in the District of Columbia by the U.S. Congress, the first significant, legal end of slavery in American history.

1863   The Emancipation Proclamation on January 1 frees all slaves in states in rebellion against the United States and eventually shifts the goals of the war to include ending slavery.

   Anti-military draft riots break out in New York City where citizens object to being drafted in the federal army to abolish slavery. In the rioting, hundreds of blacks are killed by white rioters.

1864   The U.S. Congress passes legislation authorizing equal pay, equipment, arms, and health care for African American Union troops.

   The *New Orleans Tribune* begins publication on October 4, becoming the first daily newspaper in America produced by African Americans.

1865   Union Gen. William Sherman issues his now famous field order, allotting forty acres of land and a mule to former slaves in Georgia, South Carolina, and Florida.

The Thirteenth Amendment, outlawing slavery, is passed by Congress on December 18.

1866   Edward G. Walker and Charles L. Mitchell are the first blacks to sit in an American legislature, that of Massachusetts.

Legislatures throughout the former Confederate states pass "Black Code," bills severely limiting the freedoms of former slavess and essentially re-enslaving them in southern states.

President Johnson vetoes the Civil Rights Act of 1866 but the U.S. Congress overrides his veto, bestowing citizenship upon all black Americans and guaranteeing them equal rights.

The Ku Klux Klan, the white supremacist organization, is formed in Tennessee.

White civilians and police kill 46 African Americans and injure many others in a massacre that takes place in Memphis between May 1–3. The mob burns down ninety houses, twelve schools, and four churches.

Police in New Orleans storm a Republican meeting of blacks and whites on July 30, killing more than forty, wounding 150 others.

1867   The black citizens of the District of Columbia are granted the right to vote by the U.S. Congress, overriding a veto by President Johnson.

Five traditionally black colleges are founded: Howard University in Washington, D.C.; Morgan State College; Talladega College; St. Augustine's College; and Johnson C. Smith College.

1868   The South Carolina House on July 6 becomes the first and only legislature to have a black majority, eighty-seven blacks to forty whites. Whites continue to control the state senate and become a majority in the state house in 1874.

The Fourteenth Amendment is passed, July 28, making African Americans citizens of the United States.

1869   Ebenezer Don Carlos Bassett is appointed the minister to Haiti, making him the first black American diplomat and the first presidential appointee. For years thereafter this post and the diplomat to Liberia were black Americans, appointed by both Republican and Democratic administrations.

1870   Hiram R. Revels, a republican from Mississippi, becomes the first African American U.S. Senator, although he only serves one year.

The Fifteenth Amendment, which ensures suffrage to African Americans, is ratified on March 30.

1871   The Jubilee Singers of Fisk University begin their first national tour on October 6. They travel to earn the money necessary to build the university, and become world-renowned singers of black gospel music.

1872   The first African American governor elected by the state of Louisiana, P.B.S. Pinchback, is elected to the U.S. Congress, and the next year is elected to serve in the U.S. Senate in a disputed election.

1875   Congress passes a Civil Rights Bill, March 1, which bans discrimination in places of public accommodation. The U.S. Supreme Court overturns the bill in 1883.

        Blanche Kelso Bruce, a republican from Mississippi, is elected as the first African American U.S. senator to serve a full term. He serves six years in a seat not filled by another African American until 1969.

1877   Henry O. Flipper becomes the first black graduate of the United States Military Academy at West Point on June 15.

1881   The Tuskegee Institute is founded in Alabama to train African Americans in agriculture, industrial arts, and teaching.

        Booker Taliaferro Washington, a black leader of his time, becomes the first principal of Tuskegee Institute.

1890   The National Afro-American League is founded by Timothy Thomas Fortune and eventually becomes the model for a later organization called the National Association for the Advancement of Colored People.

1895   Booker T. Washington delivers the "Atlanta Compromise" speech at the Cotton States International Exposition in Atlanta, Georgia.

1896   With *Plessy v. Ferguson* on May 18, the U.S. Supreme Court gives legal backing to the concept of separate but equal public facilities for blacks.

1896   Poet Paul Lawrence Dunbar publishes *Lyrics of a Lowly Life*, a collection that contains some of his most important work. Dunbar is known as the poet laureate of the Negro race.

1898   *A Trip to Coontown* is produced by Robert Cole, the first full-length Broadway musical written, produced, and performed by African Americans.

1901   Negro leader Booker T. Washington has dinner at the White House with President Theodore Roosevelt, making Washington the first black American to ever dine with a sitting U.S. president at the White House.

1903   W. E. B. DuBois publishes *The Souls of Black Folk*.

        Publisher Robert S. Abbott launches the *Chicago Defender*, the city's first African American newspaper. It quickly becomes one of the largest and most influential black newspapers in the nation.

1905   W. E. B. DuBois and William Monroe Trotter are among the leaders of a meeting on July 11–13 from which springs the Niagara Movement, the forerunner of the National Association for the Advancement of Colored People.

1910   The National Urban League is established in April.

        The NAACP launches *Crisis Magazine*, edited by W. E. B. DuBois.

1912   On September 27, W. C. Handy publishes "Memphis Blues," perhaps the earliest commercially successful "Blues" song.

1915   Carter G. Woodson founds the Association for the Study of Negro Life and History on September 9.

1918   The First Pan-African Congress meets in Paris, France, under the guidance of W. E. B. DuBois, February 19–21.

1920   The national convention of Marcus Garvey's Universal Negro Improvement Society meets in New York City, August 1–2. Garvey will be charged with mail fraud in 1923, convicted in 1925, and deported in 1927 after serving time in prison.

1922–   The Harlem Renaissance, a cultural flowering of black literature and art,
1929   occurs.

1925   A. Philip Randolph organizes the Brotherhood of Sleeping Car Porters on May 8.

1926   Poet Langston Hughes publishes *The Weary Blues*, his first book of poetry.

1930   The Nation of Islam, a religious movement based on separatism, is founded in Detroit by W.D. Fard.

1931   Nine young blacks are accused of raping two white women in a boxcar on April 6. They are tried for their lives in Scottsboro, Alabama, and hastily convicted. The case attracts national attention.

1936   Jesse Owens, an African American athlete, wins four gold medals at the Summer Olympics in Berlin on August 9.

1937   Joe Louis, a cultural icon among African Americans, defeats James J. Braddock on June 22 to become heavyweight boxing champion of the world.

1939   Hattie McDaniel becomes the first African American actor to win an Academy Award as Best Supporting Actress in *Gone With the Wind*.

1939   Singer Marian Anderson is refused permission to sing by the Daughters of the American Revolution at their hall in Washington, D.C. In protest, she performs at the Lincoln Memorial before an audience of 75,000 people.

1940   Benjamin O. Davis, Sr., becomes the first black general in the United States Army, October 16.

       Writer Richard Wright publishes a fierce protest novel, *Native Son*, which becomes a bestseller.

1941   President Franklin D. Roosevelt issues an executive order, June 25, forbidding discrimination in defense industries after pressure from African Americans led by A. Philip Randolph.

       Tuskegee Institute in Alabama launches the first training program for African American pilots, who will go on to serve heroically during the fighting in World War II.

1942   Blacks and whites organize the Congress of Racial Equality (CORE) in Chicago in June. They led a sit-in at a Chicago restaurant.

1944   The United Negro College Fund is founded, April 24.

       The first working, production-ready model of a mechanical cotton picker is demonstrated on a farm near Clarksdale, Mississippi, on October 2.

1945   *Ebony* magazine, a general interest publication about African American life, is launched.

The pastor of the Abyssinian Baptist Church in Harlem, Adam Clayton Powell, Jr., is elected to the U.S. Senate and serves eleven consecutive terms.

1947   Jackie Robinson becomes the first black to play major league baseball, April 19.

1948   An executive order by President Truman desegregates the military.

1950   Gwendolyn Brooks becomes the first African American to win a Pulitzer Prize for her collection of poetry, Annie Allen.

Ralph J. Bunche becomes the first person of color to win the Nobel Peace Prize, September 22. He earns the distinction for his work as a mediator in Palestine.

1952   After keeping statistics kept for 71 years, Tuskegee reports that this was the first year with no lynchings of African Americans.

1953   Writer Ralph Ellison wins the National Book Award for his novel, *Invisible Man*.

1954   In *Brown v. Board of Education of Topeka, Kansas*, the U.S. Supreme Court completes the overturning of legal school segregation at all levels, May 17.

1955   Rosa Parks refuses to change seats in a Montgomery, Alabama, bus on December 1. On December 5, African Americans begin a boycott of the bus system which continues until shortly after December 13, 1956, when the U.S. Supreme Court outlaws bus segregation in the city.

1957   The Southern Christian Leadership Conference (SCLC) is formed with Martin Luther King, Jr., as president, February 14.

1957   Congress passes the Voting Rights Bill of 1957, the first major civil rights legislation in more than 75 years, August 29.

1959   Playwright Lorraine Hansberry's play, Raisin in the Sun, becomes the first dramatic play by an African American to be produced on Broadway.

Motown Records is founded in Detroit, Michigan by Berry Gordy.

1960   Sit-ins in Greensboro, North Carolina, on February 1 initiate a wave of similar protests throughout the South.

The Student Non-Violent Coordinating Committee (SNCC) is founded in Raleigh, North Carolina, April 15–17.

1963   Under the leadership of Martin Luther King, Jr., African Americans began a campaign against discrimination in Birmingham, April 3.

Civil rights protests take place in most major urban areas, June-August.

The March on Washington, August 28, is the largest civil rights demonstration in American history. Martin Luther King, Jr., delivers his "I Have a Dream" speech.

Martin Luther King Jr. writes his "Letter from a Birmingham Jail," a document that he began writing on the edges of an old newspaper and later became one of the most famous statements about the civil rights movement of the twentieth century.

1964   The Twenty-fourth Amendment forbids the use of the poll tax to prevent voting, January 23.

Malcolm X announces his split from Elijah Muhammad's Nation of Islam, March 12.

Beginning in Harlem, serious racial disturbances (often known as "race riots") occur in more than six major cities, July 18–August 30.

Civil rights groups, including the NAACP, CORE, the Student Nonviolent Coordinating Committee (SNCC), and others organize and carry out a massive voter registration drive in Mississippi during what became known as "Freedom Summer." During that summer, three CORE workers were murdered. Over a period of five summers, the number of black voters in Mississippi rose from 7 percent to more than 65 percent.

President Lyndon Johnson signs the Civil Rights Act on July 2, 1964, giving the federal government broad powers to prosecute discrimination in education, employment, and voting across the country.

Martin Luther King wins the Nobel Peace Prize

Boxer Cassius Clay becomes the World Heavyweight champion; announces his membership in the Nation of Islam and takes the name Muhammad Ali.

1965   The SCLC launches a voter drive in Selma, Alabama, which escalates into a nationwide protest movement, January 2.

Malcolm X is assassinated in Harlem by members of the Nation of Islam, February 21.

The Watts riots in Los Angeles, August 11–21, leave thirty-four dead, more than 3,500 arrested, and property damage of about $225 million dollars.

1966   The African American holiday, Kwanzaa, is invented by activist and scholar, Maulana Ron Karenga.

CORE endorses the concept "Black Power." SNCC also adopts it. SCLC does not, and the NAACP emphatically does not, July 1–9.

The Black Panther Party is founded in October by Huey P. Newton and Bobby Seale in Oakland, California.

1967   Thurgood Marshall becomes the first African American ever appointed to the U.S. Supreme Court.

This year witnesses the worst summer for racial disturbances in United States history. More than forty riots and 100 other disturbances occur, May 1–October 1,

1968   Shirley Chisholm of New York becomes the first African American woman to ever be elected to the U.S. Congress.

Martin Luther King, Jr., is assassinated in Memphis, Tennessee, April 4. In the following week riots occur in at least 125 places throughout the country.

1969   The U.S. Supreme Court rules that racial segregation in schools must end immediately and that unitary school systems are required, October 29.

1970   *Black Enterprise*, an African American business magazine, is launched and supported by a burgeoning black middle class.

Kenneth Gibson becomes the first black mayor of an Eastern city when he assumes the post in Newark, New Jersey, July 1.

1971   Operation Push, People United to Serve Humanity, a movement formed to bolster and stimulate African American economic advancement and education, is founded by the Reverend Jesse Jackson.

The Congressional Black Caucus is formed by fifteen members of the U.S. Congress, presenting a unified, powerful African American wing.

The Southern Regional Council reports March 24 that desegregation in Southern schools is the rule, not the exception. The report also points out that the dual school system is far from dismantled.

1972   Texas Democrat Barbara Jordan becomes the first African American woman to represent a southern state in the U.S. House of Representatives. She serves three terms.

1973   Thomas Bradley is elected the first black mayor of Los Angeles, May 29.

Maynard H. Jackson is elected the first black mayor of Atlanta, October 16.

1974   Henry ("Hank") Aaron hits his 715th home run, April 8, becoming the all-time leading hitter of home runs.

1977   Andrew Young becomes the first African American to serve as the U.S. ambassador to the United Nations.

February 3 marks the eighth and final night for the miniseries based on Alex Haley's *Roots*. This final episode achieves the highest ratings ever for a single program.

1978   The U.S. Supreme Court rules against universities using fixed racial quotas in making admissions decisions, a setback for affirmative action to offset past discrimination, in the landmark reverse discrimination case, *Regents of the University of California v. Bakke*.

1980   Racial disturbances beginning on May 17 result in fifteen deaths in Miami, Florida. This is the worst riot since those in Watts and Detroit in the 1960s.

1982   Lee P. Brown is named the first black police commissioner of Houston, Texas, May 23.

1983   Writer Alice Walker's novel, *The Color Purple*, wins a Pulitzer Prize and the National Book Award.

Vanessa Williams becomes to first African American to win the Miss America title.

Harold Washington wins the Democratic Party nomination for mayor of Chicago, February 23. On April 12, he wins the election for mayor.

The state legislature of Louisiana repeals the last racial classification law in the United States, June 22. The law had classified as "black" those with 1/32nd black ancestry.

Guion (Guy) S. Bluford, Jr., is the first black American astronaut to make a space flight on board the space shuttle *Challenger*, August 30.

President Ronald Reagan signs the bill establishing January 20 a federal holiday in honor of Martin Luther King, Jr., November 2.

1986 A bronze bust of Martin Luther King, Jr., is the first of any black American in the halls of Congress, January 16.

The first national Martin Luther King, Jr., holiday is celebrated, January 20.

1987 Frederick Drew Gregory is the first African American to command a space shuttle.

Playwright August Wilson wins a Pulitzer Prize for his play, *Fences*.

1988 Jesse L. Jackson receives 1,218 delegate votes at the Democratic National Convention, July 20. The number needed for the nomination, which goes to Michael Dukakis, is 2,082.

Bill Cosby announces his gift of $20,000,000 to Spelman College, November 4.

1989 General Colin L. Powell is named chair of the United States Joint Chiefs of Staff, August 10.

David Dinkins is elected mayor of New York, and L. Douglas Wilder, is elected governor of Virginia, marking two landmark achievements for African American political leaders, November 7.

1990 Playwright August Wilson wins a second Pulitzer Prize for his play, *The Piano Lesson*.

1992 *The Cosby Show* broadcasts the final original episode of its highly successful eight-season run, April 30.

Jackie Joyner-Kersee is the first woman to repeat as Olympic heptathlon champion, August 3.

Mae C. Jemison is the first black American woman in space on board the space shuttle *Endeavor*, September 12.

Carol Moseley Braun of Illinois is the first black woman ever elected to the U.S. Senate, November 3.

1993 M. Joycelyn Elders becomes the first black and the first woman U.S. Surgeon General, September 7.

Toni Morrison is the first black American to win the Nobel Prize in Literature, October 7.

1995 The Million Man March is held in Washington, D.C., October 16. The march is the idea of Nation of Islam leader Louis Farrakhan, who calls the event, "A Day of Atonement and Reconciliation." The march is described as a call to black men to take charge in rebuilding their communities and show more respect for themselves and devotion to their families.

1997   Black American women participate October 25 in the Million Woman March in Philadelphia, focusing on health care, education, and self-help.

1998   Civil rights veteran James Farmer is one of fifteen men and women awarded the Medal of Freedom from President Clinton, January 15. Born in Marshall, Texas, he was the national director of the Congress of Racial Equality during the 1960s and was one of the most influential leaders of the civil rights movement throughout its most turbulent decade.

Now an annual observance, the New York Stock Exchange closes, for the first time, in honor of the birthday of Dr. Martin Luther King, Jr., January 18.

Track star Florence Griffith Joyner dies September 21 at the age of 38. In the 1988 Seoul Olympic Games, Griffith had been the first American woman to win four track and field medals—three gold and one silver—in one Olympic competition.

1999   Alan Keyes announces his candidacy in the Republican presidential primaries for election 2000. Keyes, a radio talk show host and a leader of the conservative movement, also ran in the 1996 presidential elections.

2000   After thirteen seasons and six NBA championships, professional basketball star Michael Jordan retires from the game, January 13.

On February 25, Louis Farrakhan announces an end to the twenty-five-year-long rift between the Nation of Islam and the Moslem American Society headed by Wallace Deen Mohammed. The groups had split in 1975 following the death of Elijah Muhammad.

South Carolina governor Jim Hodges signs a bill on May 2 to make Martin Luther King Jr.'s birthday an official state holiday. South Carolina is the last state to recognize the day as a holiday.

At Wimbledon in July, tennis player Venus Williams beats her sister Serena Williams in the semifinals, and then becomes the first black woman to win the women's title since Althea Gibson did it in 1957–58.

In August the NAACP calls for a national boycott of vacation spots in South Carolina in an attempt to force the state government to remove the Confederate flag from the dome of its statehouse. Controversy on this issue grows, involving the flying of the Confederate flag in other southern states as well.

President-Elect George W. Bush announces in December the appointment of several African-Americans to his cabinet: Colin L. Powell will serve as Secretary of State, Condolezza Rice as foreign policy adviser, and Dr. Roderick Paige as Secretary of Education.

A location for a national monument to Martin Luther King, Jr., on the mall in Washington, D.C., between the Lincoln Memorial and the Washington Monument, is approved by the National Capital Planning Commission, December 2.

2001   Representative John Conyers of Michigan reintroduces legislation in January to create a commission to study the issue of slavery reparations.

Eight of the original "Freedom Riders" reenact their 1961 bus ride on May 12. In 1961, the civil rights protesters had ridden from Atlanta to Montgomery, stopping in facilities designated "white only," in order to test the U.S. Supreme Court ruling banning racial segregation in public facilities.

2002   Halle Berry becomes the first African American woman to receive an Academy Award for best actress, and Denzel Washington becomes only the second African American man to win in the best actor category, March 24.

President George W. Bush awards comedian and actor Bill Cosby and baseball player Hank Aaron the nation's highest civilian honor, the Presidential Medal of Freedom, July 9.

2003   The Montgomery bus on which Rosa Parks refused to give up her seat in 1955 is restored and put on display at the Henry Ford Museum in Dearborn, Michigan, in January.

The Cincinnati Bengals hire defensive coordinator Marvin Lewis as the football team's new head coach, January 14. Lewis, Tony Dungy, and Herman Edwards are the only African American coaches in the NFL.

The U.S. Supreme Court on June 23 issues decisions in two cases, *Grutter v. Bollinger* and *Gratz v. Bollinger*, which challenged the use of race in admissions policy at the University of Michigan's Law School and the undergraduate College of Literature, Science, and the Arts. The court upholds the concept of race as one of many factors in university admission, but rejects approaches that fail to examine each student's record on an individual basis.

2008   Barack Obama becomes the first African American to be the presidential nominee for one of the two major parties in August.

Obama becomes the first African American to be elected president of the United States.

Volume 1

1. A Narrative Of the Uncommon Sufferings, And Surprizing Delieverance Of Briton Hammon, A Negro Man,—Servant to General Winslow, Of Marshfield, in New-England; Who returned to Boston, after having been absent almost Thirteen Years. Containing An Account of the many Hardships he underwent from the Time he left his Master's House, in the Year 1747, to the Time of his Return to Boston.—How he was Cast away in the Capes of Florida;—the horrid Cruelty and inhuman Barbarity of the Indians in murdering the whole Ship's Crew;—the Manner of his being carry'd by them into Captivity. Also, An Account of his being Confined Four Years and Seven Months in a close Dungeon,—And the remarkable Manner in which he met with his good old Master in London; who returned to New-England, a Passenger, in the same Ship, 1760

BRITON HAMMON

This is an insightful narrative about the life and times of a Negro named Briton Hammon that was written in the style and form of many European writers of the eighteenth century. Accounts like Hammon's were rare in eighteenth-century America and Europe because black slaves, former slaves, and free men of color rarely had the opportunity to get an education. Accounts like this one by Hammon are extremely valuable in modern times because they are first-person accounts of the many hardships suffered by these men and women in a world where being black made them targets of immeasurable cruelties. This account recorded a daily experience that otherwise might be lost in the fog of time and history.

A **NARRATIVE** of the UNCOMMON SUFFERINGS, AND Surprizing DELIVERANCE OF Briton Hammon, A Negro Man,——

Servant to GENERAL **WINSLOW,** Of Marshfield, in NEW-ENGLAND; Who returned to *Boston,* after having been absent almost Thirteen Years.

CONTAINING An Account of the many Hardships he underwent from the Time he left his Master's House, in the Year 1747, to the Time of his Return to *Boston.*—How he was Cast away in the Capes of Florida;—the horrid Cruelty and inhuman Barbarity of the *Indians* in murdering the whole Ship's Crew;—the Manner of his being carry'd by them into Captivity. Also, An Account of his being Confined Four Years and Seven Months in a close Dungeon,—And the remarkable Manner in which he met with his good old Master in London; who returned to *New-England*, a Passenger, in the same Ship.

To THE READER,

As my Capacities and Condition of Life are very low, it cannot be expected that I should make those Remarks on the Sufferings I have met with, or the kind Providence of a good GOD for my Preservation, as one in a higher Station; but shall leave that to the Reader as he goes along, and so I shall only relate Matters of Fact as they occur to my Mind—

ON Monday, 25th Day of December, 1747, with the leave of my Master, I went from Marshfield, with an Intention to go a Voyage to Sea, and the next Day, the 26th, got to Plymouth, where I immediately ship'd myself on board of a Sloop, Capt. John Howland, Master, bound to Jamaica and the Bay.—We sailed from Plymouth in a short Time, and after a pleasant Passage of about 30 Days, arrived at Jamaica; we was detain'd at Jamaica only 5 Days, from whence we sailed for the Bay, where we arrived safe in 10 Days. We loaded our Vessel with Logwood, and sailed from the Bay the 25th Day of May following, and the 15th Day of June, we were cast away on Cape-Florida, about 5 Leagues from the Shore; being now destitute of every Help, we knew not what to do or what Course to take in this our sad Condition:— The Captain was advised, intreated, and beg'd on, by every Person on board, to heave over but only 20 Ton of the Wood, and we should get clear, which if he had done, might have sav'd his Vessel and Cargo, and not only so, but his own Life, as well as the Lives of the Mate and Nine Hands, as I shall presently relate.

After being upon this Reef two Days, the Captain order'd the Boat to be hoisted out, and then ask'd who were willing to tarry on board? The whole Crew was for going on Shore at this Time, but as the Boat would not carry 12 Persons at once, and to prevent any Uneasiness, the Captain, a Passenger, and one Hand tarry'd on board, while the Mate, with Seven Hands besides myself, were order'd to go on Shore in the Boat, which as soon as we had reached, one half were to be Landed, and the other four to return to the Sloop, to fetch the Captain and the others on Shore. The Captain order'd us to take with us our Arms, Ammunition, Provisions and Necessaries for Cooking, as also a Sail to make a Tent of, to shelter us from the Weather; after having left the Sloop we stood towards the Shore, and being within Two Leagues of the same, we espy'd a Number of Canoes, which we at first took to be Rocks, but soon found our Mistake, for we perceiv'd they moved towards us; we presently saw an English Colour hoisted in one of the Canoes, at the Sight of which we were not a little rejoiced, but on our advancing yet nearer, we found them, to our very great Surprize, to be Indians of which there were Sixty; being now so near them we could not possibly make our Escape; they soon came up with and boarded us, took away all our Arms Ammunition, and Provision.

The whole Number of CaRoes (being about Twenty,) then made for the Sloop, except Two which they left to guard us, who order'd us to follow on with them; the Eighteen which made for the Sloop, went so much faster than we that they got on board above Three Hours before we came along side, and had kill'd Captain Howland, the Passenger and the other hand; we came to the Larboard side of the Sloop, and they order'd us round to the Starboard, and as we were passing round the Bow, we saw the whole Number of Indians, advancing forward and loading their Guns, upon which the Mate said, "my Lads we are all dead Men," and before we had got round, they discharged their Small Arms upon us, and kill'd Three of our hands, viz. Reuben Young of Cape-Cod, Mate; Joseph Little and Lemuel Doty of Plymouth, upon which I immediately jump'd overboard, chusing rather to be drowned, than to be kill'd by those barbarous and inhuman Savages.

In three or four Minutes after, I heard another Volley which dispatched the other five, viz. John Nowland, and Nathaniel Rich, both belonging to Plymouth, and Elkanah Collymore, and James Webb, Strangers, and Moses Newmock, Molatto. As soon as they had kill'd the whole of the People, one of the Canoes padled after me, and soon came up with me, hawled me into the Canoe, and beat me most terribly with a Cutlass, after that they ty'd me down, then this Canoe stood for the Sloop again and as soon as she came along side, the Indians on board the Sloop betook themselves to their Canoes, then set the Vessel on Fire, making a prodigious shouting and hallowing like so many Devils. As soon as the Vessel was burnt down to the Water's edge, the Indians stood for the Shore, together with our Boat, on board of which they put 5 hands. After we came to the Shore, they led me to their Hutts, where I expected nothing but immediate death, and as they spoke broken English, were often telling me, while coming from the Sloop to the Shore, that they intended to roast me alive. But the Providence of God order'd it otherways, for He appeared for my Help, in this Mount of Difficulty, and they were better to me then my Fears, and soon unbound me, but set a Guard over me every Night. They kept me with them about five Weeks, during which Time they us'd me pretty well, and gave me boil'd Corn, which was what they often eat themselves. The Way I made my Escape from these Villains was this; A Spanish Schooner arriving there from St. Augustine, the Master of which, whose Name was Romond, asked the Indians to let me go on board his Vessel, which they granted. The Way I came to know this Gentleman was, by his being taken last War by an English Privateer, and brought into Jamaica, while I was there knowing me very well, weigh'd Anchor and carry'd me off to the Havanna, and after being there four Days the Indians came after me, and insisted on having me again, as I was their Prisoner;—They made Application to the Governor, and demanded me again from him; in answer to which the Governor told them, that as they had put the whole Crew to Death, they should not have me again, and so paid them Ten Dollars for me, adding, that he would not have them kill any person hereafter, but take as many of them as they could, of those that should be cast away, and bring them to him, for which he would pay them Ten Dollars a-head. At the Havanna I lived with the Governor in the Castle about a Twelve-month, where I was walking thro' the Street, I met with a Press-Gang who immediately prest me, and put me into Goal, and with a Number of others I was confin'd till next Morning, when we were all brought out, and ask'd who would go on board the King's Ships, four of which having been lately built, were bound to Old-Spain, and on my refusing to serve on board, they put me in a close Dungeon, where I was confin'd Four Years and seven months; during which Time I often made application to the Governor, by Persons who came to see the Prisoners, but they never acquainted him with it, nor did he know all this Time what became of me, which was the means of my being confin'd there so long. But kind Providence so order'd it, that after I had been in this Place so long as the Time mention'd above, the Captain of a Merchantman, belonging to Boston, having sprung a Leak was obliged to put into the Havanna to refit, and while he was at Dinner at Mrs. Betty Howard's, she told the Captain of my deplorable Condition, and said she would be glad, if he could by some means or other relieve me; The Captain told Mrs. Howard he would use his best Endeavours for my Relief and Enlargement.

Accordingly, after Dinner, came to the Prison, and ask'd the Keeper if he might see me; upon his Request I was brought out of the Dungeon, and after the Captain had Interrogated me, told me, he would intercede with the Governor for my Relief out of that miserable Place, which he did, and the next Day the Governor sent an Order to release me; I lived with the Governor about a Year after I was delivered from the Dungeon, in which Time I endeavour'd three Times to make my Escape, the last of which proved effectual; the first Time I got on board of Captain Marsh, an English Twenty Gun Ship, with a Number of others, and lay on board conceal'd that Night; and the next Day the Ship being under sail, I thought myself safe, and so made my Appearance upon Deck, but as soon as we were discovered the Captain ordered the Boat out, and sent us all on Shore—I intreated the Captain to let me, in particular, stay on board, begging, and crying to him, to commiserate my unhappy Condition, and added, that I had been confin'd almost five Years in a close Dungeon, but the Captain would not hearken to any Intreaties, for fear of having the Governor's Displeasure, and so was obliged to go on shore, after being on Shore another Twelve month, I endeavour'd to make my Escape the second Time, by trying to get on board of a Sloop bound to Jamaica, and as I was going from the City to the Sloop, was unhappily taken by the Guard, and ordered back to the Castle, and there confined.—However, in a short Time I was set at Liberty, and order'd with a Number of others to carry the He is carried (by Way of Respect) in a large Two-arm Chair; the Chair is lin'd with crimson Velvet, and supported by eight Persons.

Bishop from the Castle, thro' the Country, to confirm the old People, baptize Children, &c. for which he receives large Sums of Money.—I was employ'd in this Service about Seven Months, during which Time I lived very well, and then returned to the Castle again, where I had my Liberty to walk about the City, and do Work for my self;—The Beaver, an English Man of War then lay in the Harbour, and having been informed by some of the Ship's Crew that she was to sail in a few Days, I had nothing now to do, but to seek an Opportunity how I should make my Escape.

Accordingly one Sunday Night the Lieutenant of the Ship with a Number of the Barge Crew were in a Tavern, and Mrs. Howara who had before been a Friend to me, interceded with the Lieutenant to carry me on board: the Lieutenant said he would with all his Heart, and immediately I went on board in the Barge. The next Day the Spaniards came along side the Beaver, and demanded me again, with a Number of others who had made their Escape from them, and got on board the Ship, but just before I did; but the Captain, who was a true Englishman, refus'd them, and said he could not answer it, to deliver up any Englishmen under English Colours.—In a few Days we set Sail for Jamaica, where we arrived safe, after a short and pleasant Passage.

After being at Jamaica a short Time we sail'd for London, as convoy to a Fleet of Merchantmen, who all arrived safe in the Downs, I was turned over to another Ship, the Arcenceil, and there remained about a Month. From this Ship I went on board the Sandwich of 90 Guns; on board the Sandwich, I tarry'd 6 Weeks, and then was order'd on board the Hercules, Capt. John Porter, a 74 Gun Ship, we sail'd on a Cruize, and met with a French 84 Gun Ship, and had a very smart Engagement, A particular Account of this Engagement, has been Publish'd in the Boston News-Papers in which about 70 of our Hands were Kill'd and Wounded, the Captain lost his Leg in the Engagement, and I was Wounded in the Head by a small Shot. We should have taken this Ship, if they had not cut away the most of our Rigging; however, in about three Hours after, a 64 Gun Ship, came up with and took her.—I was discharged from the Hercules the 12th Day of May 1759 (having been on board of that Ship 3 Months) on account of my being disabled in the Arm, and render'd incapable of Service, after being honourably paid the Wages due to me. I was put into the Greenwich Hospital where I stay'd and soon recovered.—I then ship'd myself a Cook on board Captain Martyn, an arm'd Ship in the King's Service. I was on board this Ship almost Two Months, and after being paid my Wages, was discharg'd in the Month of October.— After my discharge from Captain Martyn, I was taken sick in London of a Fever, and was confin'd about 6 Weeks, where I expended all my Money, and left in very poor Circumstances; and unhappy for me I knew nothing of my good Master's being in London at this my very difficult Time. After I got well of my sickness, I ship'd myself on board of a large Ship bound to Guinea, and being in a publick House one Evening, I overheard a Number of Persons talking about Rigging a Vessel bound to New-England, I ask'd them to what Part of New-England this Vessel was bound? they told me, to Boston; and having ask'd them who was Commander? they told me, Capt. Watt; in a few Minutes after this the Mate of the Ship came in, and I ask'd him if Captain Watt did not want a Cook, who told me he did, and that the Captain would be in, in a few Minutes; and in about half an Hour the Captain came in, and then I ship'd myself at once, after begging off from the Ship bound to Guinea; I work'd on board Captain Watt's Ship almost Three Months, before she sail'd, and one Day being at Work in the Hold, I overheard some Persons on board mention the Name of Winslow, at the Name of which I was very inquisitive, and having ask'd what Winslow they were talking about? They told me it was General Winslow; and that he was one of the Passengers, I ask'd them what General Winslow? For I never knew my good Master, by that Title before; but after enquiring more particularly I found it must be Master, and in a few Days Time the Truth was joyfully verify'd by a happy Sight of his Person, which so overcome me, that I could not speak to him for some Time—My good Master was exceeding glad to see me, telling me that I was like one arose from the Dead, for he thought I had been Dead a great many Years, having heard nothing of me for almost Thirteen Years. I think I have not deviated from Truth, in any particular of this my Narrative, and tho' I have omitted a great many Things, yet what is wrote may suffice to convince the Reader, that I have been most grievously afflicted, and yet thro' the Divine Goodness, as miraculously preserved, and delivered out of many Dangers; of which I desire to retain a grateful Remembrance, as long as I live in the World.

And now, That in the Providence of that GOD, who delivered his Servant David out of the Paw of the Lion and out of the Paw of the Bear, I am freed from a long and dreadful Captivity, among worse Savages than they; And am return'd to my own Native Land, to Shew how Great Things the Lord hoth done for Me; I would call upon all Men, and Say, O Magnifie the Lord with Me, and let us Exalt his Name together!——O that Men would Praise the Lord for His Goodness, and for his Wonderful Works to the Children of Men!

Source: Boston: Printed and Sold by Green & Russell, in Queen-Street, 1760. Early American Imprints, 1st series, no. 8611. University of Virginia Library Electronic Text Center. Copyright © Readex.

2. A Narrative Of the Most Remarkable Particulars in the Life of James Albert Ukawsaw Gronniosaw, an African Prince, written by himself, 1774

This narrative was written by a woman in Europe who interviewed Gronniosaw. It is a biography, masked as an autobiography, and it enlightens us about the life of an African prince who was enslaved and lived in Europe and the United States. It is a curious narrative that falls into the category of what is now commonly called "creative nonfiction." Although the text claims that Gronniosaw wrote this account himself, such a claim is often used in the most general sense and rarely takes into account the point of view, impressions, and interpretations of a ghost writer who may have conducted an interview of the alleged writer and written the account on his behalf.

The authorship of this narrative is authentic in the sense that the true writer admits her role in the preface, although she does so in a clearly contradictory fashion by, saying both that she took down what Gronniosaw told her; and that it was penned by the subject himself. This was not uncommon for the period. Nevertheless, these types of accounts are vivid testimonies that in many ways are as accurate as any other form of memoir, meaning they, too, are subject to the editing, interpretation, and perspective of editors, no matter who authored the text. In this account, Gronniosaw's ghost writer relates a spiritual narrative in memoir form, depicting the European adventures of an African prince.

"I will bring the Blind by a Way that they know not, I will lead them in Paths that they have not known: I will make Darkness Light before them and crooked Things straight. These Things will I do unto them, and not forsake them," ISAI, xli,16.

TO THE RIGHT HONORABLE THE **Countess of** Huntingdon, THIS **NARRATIVE Of my LIFE**, And of GOD's wonderful Dealings with me, is, Through Her LADYSHIP's Permission, *Most Humbly Dedicated, By Her LADYSHIP's Most obliged And obedient Servant,*

James Albert.

THE PREFACE To the READER.

THIS account of the life and spiritual experience of James Albert, was taken from his own mouth, and committed to paper by the elegant pen of a young Lady of the town of Leominster, for her own private satisfaction, and without any intention, at first, that it should be made public. But she has now been prevailed on to commit it to the press, both with a view to serve Albert and his distressed family, who have the sole profits arising from the sale of it; and likewise, as it is apprehended, this little history contains matter well worthy the notice and attention of every Christian reader.

Perhaps we have here in some degree, a solution of that question that has perplex'd the minds of so many serious persons, viz. In what manner will God deal with those benighted parts of the world where the gospel of Jesus Christ hath never reached? Now, it appears, from the experience of this remarkable person, that God does not save without the knowledge of the truth; but, with respect to those whom he hath foreknown, though born under every outward disadvantage, and in the regions of the grossest darkness and ignorance, he most amazingly acts upon, and influences, their minds, and in the course of wisely and most wonderfuly appointed providence, he brings them to the means of spiritual information, gradually opens to their view the light of his truth, and gives them full possession and enjoyment of the inestimable blessings of his gospel. Who can doubt but that the suggestion so forcibly press'd upon the mind of Albert (when a boy) that there was a Being superior to the sun, moon, and stars (the objects of African idolatry) came from the Father of lights, and was, with respect to him, the first fruit of the display of gospel glory? His long and perilous journey to the coast of Guinea, where he was sold for a slave, and so brought into a Christian land; shall we consider this as the alone effect of a curious and inquisitive disposition? Shall we, in accounting for it refer to nothing higher than mere chance & accidental circumstances? Whatever Infidels & Deists may think, I trust the Christian reader will easily discern an all wise and omnipotent appointment and direction in these movements. He belonged to the Redeemer of lost sinners; he was the purchase of his cross; and therefore the Lord undertook to bring him by a way he knew not, out of darkness into his marvellous light, that he might lead him to a saving heart-acquaintance and union with the triune God in Christ, reconciling the world unto himself; and not imputing their trespasses. As his call was very extraordinary, so there are certain particulars exceedingly remarkable in his experience. God has put singular honor upon him in the exercise of his faith and patience, which, in the most distressing and pitiable trials and calamities, have been found to the praise and glory of God. How deeply must it affect a tender heart, not only to be reduc'd to the last extremity himself, but to have his wife and children perishing for want before his eyes! Yet his faith did not fail him; he put his trust in the Lord, and he was delivered. And, at this instant, though born in an exalted station of life, and now under the Pressure of various afflicting Providences, I am persuaded (for I know the man) he would rather embrace the dunghill, having Christ in his heart, than give up his spiritual possessions and enjoyment, to fill the throne of Princes. It perhaps may not be amiss to observe, that James Albert left his native country (as near as I can guess from certain circumstances) when he was about 15 years old. He now appears to be turn'd of 60; has a good natural understanding; is well acquainted with the scriptures, and the things of God; has an amiable and tender disposition; and his character can be well attested not only at Kidderminster, the place of his residence, but likewise by many creditable persons in London and other places. Reader, recommending this Narrative to your perusal, and him who is the subject of it, to your charitable regard,

I am your faithful and obedient servant, For Christ's sake,

W. Shirley.

AN ACCOUNT OF JAMES ALBERT, &C.

I WAS born in the city of *Baurnou*, my mother was the eldest daughter of the reigning King there. I was the youngest of six children, and particularly loved by my mother, and my grand-father almost doted on me. I had, from my infancy, a curious turn of mind; was more grave and reserved, in my disposition, than either of my brothers and sisters, I often teazed them with questions they could not answer; for which reason they disliked me, as they supposed that I was either foolish or insane. 'T was certain that I was, at times, very unhappy in myself: It being strongly impressed on my mind that there was some GREAT MAN of power which resided above the sun, moon and stars, the objects of our worship.—My dear, indulgent mother would bear more with me than any of my friends beside.—I often raised my hand to heaven, and asked her who lived there? Was much dissatisfied when she told me the sun, moon and stars, being persuaded, in my own mind, that there must be some SUPERIOR POWER.—I was frequently lost in wonder at the works of the creation: Was afraid, and uneasy, and restless, but could not tell for what. I wanted to be informed of things that no person could tell me; and was always dissatisfied.— These wonderful impressions began in my childhood, and followed me continually till I left my parents, which affords me matter of admiration and thankfulness. To this moment I grew more and more uneasy every day, insomuch that one Saturday (which is the day on which we kept our sabbath) I laboured under anxieties and fears that cannot be expressed; and, what is more extraordinary, I could not give a reason for it.—I rose, as our custom is, about three o'clock (as we are obliged to be at our place of worship an hour before the sun rise) we say nothing in our worship, but continue on our knees with our hands held up, observing a strict silence till the sun is at a certain height, which I suppose to be about 10 or 11 o'clock in *England*: When, at a certain sign made by the Priest, we get up (our duty being over) and disperse to our different houses.—Our place of meeting is under a large palm tree; we divide ourselves into many congregations; as it is impossible for the same tree to cover the inhabitants of the whole city, though they are extremely large, high and majestic; the beauty and usefulness of them are not to be described; they supply the inhabitants of the country with meat, drink and clothes; * the body of the palm tree is very large; at a certain season of the year they tap it, and bring vessels to receive the wine, of which they draw great quantities, the quality of which is very delicious: The leaves of this tree are of a silky nature; they are large and soft; when they are dried and pulled to pieces, it has much the same appearance as the English flax, and the inhabitants of BOURNOU manufacture it for clothing, &c. This tree likewise produces a plant, or substance, which has the appearance of a cabbage, and very like it, in taste almost the same: It grows between the branches. Also the palm tree produces a nut, something like a cocoa, which contains a kernel, in which is a large quantity of milk, very pleasant to the taste: The shell is of a hard substance, and of a very beautiful appearance, and serves for basons, bowls, &c.

I hope this digression will be forgiven.—I was going to observe, that after the duty of our sabbath was over (on the day in which I was more distressed and afflicted than ever) we were all on our way home as usual, when a remarkable black cloud arose and covered the sun; then followed very heavy rain and thunder, more dreadful than ever I had heard: The heavens roared, and the earth trembled at it: I was highly affected and cast down; insomuch that I wept sadly, and could not follow my relations & friends home.—I was obliged to stop, and felt as if my legs were tied, they seemed to shake under me: So I stood still, being in great fear of the MAN of POWER, that I was persuaded, in myself, lived above. One of my young companions (who entertained a particular friendship for me, and I for him) came back to see for me: He asked me why I stood still in such very hard rain? I only said to him that my legs were weak, and I could not come faster: He was much affected to see me cry, and took me by the hand, and said he would lead me home, which he did. My mother was greatly alarmed at my tarrying out in such terrible weather; she asked me many questions, such as what I did so for? And if I was well? My dear mother, says I, pray tell me who is the GREAT MAN of POWER that makes the thunder? She said, there was no power but the sun, moon and stars; that they made all our country.—I then inquired how all our people came? She answered me, from one another; and so carried me to many generations back.—Then says I, who made the *first man?* And who made the first cow, and the first lion, and where does the fly come from, as no one can make him? My mother seemed in great trouble; she was apprehensive that my senses were impaired, or that I was foolish. My father came in, and seeing her in grief asked the cause, but when she related our conversation to him he was exceedingly angry with me, and told me he would punish me severely if ever I was so troublesome again; so that I resolved never to say any thing more to him. But I grew very unhappy in myself; my relations and acquaintance endeavoured, by all the means they could think on, to divert me, by taking me to ride upon goats (which is much the custom of our country) and to shoot with a bow and arrow; but I experienced no satisfaction at all in any of these things; nor could I be easy by any means whatever: My parents were very unhappy to see me so dejected and melancholy.

About this time there came a merchant from the *Gold Coast* (the third city in GUINEA) he traded with the inhabitants of our country in ivory, &c. he took great notice of my unhappy situation, and inquired into the cause; he expressed vast concern for me, and said, if my parents would part with me for a little while, and let him take me home with him, it would be of more service to me than any thing they could do for me.—He told me that if I would go with him I should see houses with wings to them walk upon the water, and should also see the white folks; and that he had many sons of my age, which should be my companions; and he added to all this that he would bring me safe back again soon.—I was highly pleased with the account of this strange place, and was very desirous of going.—I seemed sensible of a secret impulse upon my mind, which I could not resist, that seemed to tell me I must go. When my dear mother saw that I was willing to leave them, she spoke to my father and grandfather and the rest of my relations, who all agreed that I should accompany the merchant to the Gold Coast. I was the more willing as my brothers and sisters despised me, and looked on me with contempt on the account of my unhappy disposition; and even my servants slighted me, and disregarded all I said to them. I had one sister who was always exceeding fond of me, and I loved her entirely; her name was LOGWY, she was quite white, and fair, with fine light hair, though my father and mother were black.—I was truly concerned to leave my beloved sister, and she cry'd most sadly to part with me, wringing her hands, and discovered every sign of grief that can be imagined. Indeed if I could have known when I left my friends and country that I should never return to them again my misery on that occasion would have been inexpressible. All my relations were sorry to part with me; my dear mother came with me upon a camel more than three hundred miles, the first of our journey lay chiefly through woods: At night we secured ourselves from the wild beasts by making fires all around us; we and our camels kept within the circle, or we must have been torn to pieces by the lions, and other wild creatures, that roared terribly as soon as night came on, and continued to do so till morning.—There can be little said in favour of the country through which we passed; only a valley of marble that we came through which is unspeakably beautiful.—On each side of this valley are exceedingly high and almost inaccessible mountains—Some of these pieces of marble are of prodigious length and breadth but of different sizes and colour, and shaped in a variety of forms, in a wonderful manner.—It is most of it veined with gold mixed with striking and beautiful colours; so that when the sun darts upon it, it is as pleasing a sight as can be imagined.— The merchant that brought me from BOURNOU was in partnership with another gentleman who accompanied us; he was very unwilling that he should take me from home, as, he said, he foresaw many difficulties that would attend my going with them.—He endeavoured to prevail on the merchant to throw me into a very deep pit that was in the valley, but he refused to listen to him, and said, he was resolved to take care of me: But the other was greatly dissatisfied; and when we came to a river, which we were obliged to pass through, he purposed throwing me in and drowning me; but the merchant would not consent to it, so that I was preserved.

We travel'd till about four o'clock every day, and then began to make preparations for night, by cutting down large quantities of wood, to make fires to preserve us from the wild beasts.—I had a very unhappy and discontented journey, being in continual fear that the people I was with would murder me. I often reflected with extreme regret on the kind friends I had left, and the idea of my dear mother frequently drew tears from my eyes. I cannot recollect how long we were in going from *Bournou* to the *Gold Coast*; but as there is no shipping nearer to *Bournou* than that city, it was tedious in travelling so far by land, being upwards of a thousand miles.— I was heartily rejoiced when we arrived at the end of our journey: I now vainly imagined that all my troubles and inquietudes would terminate here; but could I have looked into futurity, I should have perceived that I had much more to suffer than I had before experienced, and that they had as yet but barely commenced.

I was now more than a thousand miles from home, without a friend or any means to procure one. Soon after I came to the merchant's house I heard the drums beat remarkably loud, and the trumpets blow—the persons accustom'd to this employ, are oblig'd to go upon a very high structure appointed for that purpose, that the sound might be heard at a great distance: They are higher than the steeples are in *England.* I was mightily pleased with sounds so entirely new to me, and was very inquisitive to know the cause of this rejoicing, and asked many questions concerning it: I was answered that it was meant as a compliment to me, because I was grandson to the King of *Bournou.*

This account gave me a secret pleasure; but I was not suffered long to enjoy this satisfaction, for, in the evening of the same day, two of the merchant's sons (boys about my own age) came running to me, and told me, that the next day I was to die, for the King intended to behead me.—I reply'd, that I was sure it could not be true, for that I came there to play with them, and to see houses walk upon the water, with wings to them, and the white folks; but I was soon informed that their King imagined I was sent by my father as a spy, and would make such discoveries, at my return home, that would enable them to make war with the greater advantage to ourselves; and for these reasons he had resolved I should never return to my native country.—When I heard this, I suffered misery that cannot be described.—I wished, a thousand times, that I had never left my friends and country.—But still the Almighty was pleased to work miracles for me.

The morning I was to die, I was washed and all my gold ornaments made bright and shining, and then carried to the palace, where the King was to behead me himself (as is the custom of the place).—He was seated upon a throne at the top of an exceeding large yard, or court, which you must go through to enter the palace, it is as wide and spacious as a large field in *England*.—I had a lane of life-guards to go through.—I guessed it to be about three hundred paces. I was conducted by my friend, the merchant, about half way up; then he durst proceed no further: I went up to the King alone—I went with an undaunted courage, and it pleased God to melt the heart of the King, who sat with his scymitar in his hand ready to behead me; yet, being himself so affected, he dropped it out of his hand, and took me upon his knee and wept over me. I put my right hand round his neck, and prest him to my heart.—He set me down and blest me; and added that he would not kill me, and that I should not go home, but be sold for a slave, so then I was conducted back again to the merchant's house.

The next day he took me on board a French brig; the Captain did not chuse to buy me: He said I was too small; so the merchant took me home with him again. The partner, whom I have spoken of as my enemy, was very angry to see me return, and again purposed putting an end to my life; for he represented to the other, that I should bring them into troubles and difficulties, and that I was so little that no person would buy me.

The merchant's resolution began to waver, and I was indeed afraid that I should be put to death: But however he said he would try me once more. A few days after a *Dutch* ship came into the harbour, and they carried me on board, in hopes that the Captain would purchase me.—As they went, I heard them agree, that, if they could not sell me *then*, they would throw me overboard.—I was in extreme agonies when I heard this; and as soon as ever I saw the *Dutch* Captain, I ran to him, and put my arms round him, and said, "Father save me." (for I knew that if he did not buy me, I should be treated very ill, or, possibly murdered) And though he did not understand my language, yet it pleased the Almighty to influence him in my behalf, and he bought me *for two yards of check*, which is of more value *there*, than in *England*. When I left my dear mother I had a large quantity of gold about me, as is the custom of our country, it was made into rings, and they were linked into one another, and formed into a kind of chain, and so put round my neck, and arms and legs, and a large piece hanging at one ear almost in the shape of a pear. I found all this troublesome, and was glad when my new master took it from me.—I was now washed, & clothed in the *Dutch* or *English* manner.—My master grew very fond of me, and I loved him exceedingly. I watched every look, was always ready when he wanted me, and endeavoured to convince him, by every action, that my only pleasure was to serve him well.—I have since thought that he must have been a serious man. His actions corresponded very well with such a character.—He used to read prayers in public to the ship's crew every sabbath day; and when first I saw him read, I was never so surprised in my whole life as when I saw the book talk to my master; for I thought it did, as I observed him to look upon it, and move his lips.—I wished it would do so to me.—As soon as my master had done reading I follow'd him to the place where he put the book, being mightily delighted with it, and when nobody saw me, I open'd it and put my ear down close upon it, in great hope that it would say something to me; but was very sorry and greatly disappointed when I found it would not speak, this thought immediately presented itself to me, that every body and every thing despised me because I was black.

I was exceedingly sea-sick at first; but when I became more accustom'd to the sea, it wore off.—My master's ship was bound for *Barbados*. When we came there, he thought fit to speak of me to several gentlemen of his acquaintance, and one of them exprest a particular desire to see me.—He had a great mind to buy me; but the Captain could not immediately be prevail'd on to part with me; but however, as the gentleman seemed very solicitous, he at length let me go, and I was sold for fifty dollars (*four and six penny pieces in English.*) My new master's name was *Vanborn*, a young gentleman; his home was in *New-England*, in the city of *New-York*; to which place he took me with him. He dress'd me in his livery, & was very good to me. My chief business was to wait at table, and tea, & clean knives, & I had a very easy place; but the servants used to curse & swear surprizingly; which I learnt faster than any thing, 'twas almost the first English I could speak. If any of them affronted me, I was sure to call upon God to damn them immediately; but I was broke of it all at once, occasioned by the correction of an old black servant that lived in the family.—One day I had just clean'd the knives for dinner, when one of the maids took one to cut bread and butter with; I was very angry with her, and called upon God to damn her; when this old black man told me I must not say so: I ask'd him why? He replied there was a wicked man, call'd the Devil, that liv'd in hell, and would take all that said these words and put them in the fire and burn them.—This terrified me greatly, and I was entirely broke of swearing. Soon after this, as I was placing the china for tea, my mistress came into the room just as the maid had been cleaning it; the girl had unfortunately sprinkled the wainscot with the mop; at which my mistress was angry; the girl very foolishly answered her again, which made her worse, and she called upon God to damn her.—I was vastly concern'd to hear this, as she was a fine young lady, and very good to me, insomuch that I could not help speaking to her: Madam, says I, you must not say so: Why, says she? Because there is a black man, call'd the Devil, that lives in hell, and he will put you in the fire and burn you, and I shall be very sorry for that. Who told you this, replied my lady? Old Ned, says I. Very well was all her answer; but she told my master of it, who ordered that old Ned should be tied up and whipp'd, and was never suffered to come into the kitchen, with the rest of the servants, afterwards.—My mistress was not angry with me, but rather diverted at my simplicity, and, by way of talk, she repeated what I had said to many of her acquaintance that visited her; among the rest, *Freelandhouse*, a very gracious, good minister, heard it, and he took a great deal of notice of me, and desired my master to part with me to him. He would not hear of it at first, but, being greatly persuaded, he let me go; and Mr. *Freelandhouse* gave [pound sterling]50 for me.—He took me home with him, and made me kneel down, and put my two hands together, and prayed for me, and every night and morning he did the same.— I could not make out what it was for, nor the meaning of it, nor what they spoke to when they talked—I thought it comical, but I liked it very well.—After I had been a little while with my new master I grew more familiar, and asked him the meaning of prayer: (I could hardly speak *English* to be understood) he took great pains with me, and made me understand that he pray'd to God, who liv'd in Heaven; that he was my father and *best* friend.—I told him that this must be a mistake; that *my* father lived at *Bournou*, and I wanted very much to see him, and likewise my dear mother, and sister, and I wished he would be so good as to send me home to them; and I added, all I could think of to induce him to convey me back, I appeared in great trouble, and my good master was so much affected that the tears run down his face.

He told me that God was a great and good Spirit, that [he] created all the world, and every person and thing in it, *Ethiopia*, *Africa* and *America*, and every where. I was delighted when I heard this: There, says I, I always thought so when I lived at home! Now, if I had wings like an eagle, I would fly to tell my dear mother that God is greater than the sun, moon and stars; and that they were made by him.

I was exceedingly pleas'd with this information of my master's, because it corresponded so well with my own opinion; I thought now if I could but get home, I should be wiser than all my country-folks, my grandfather, or father, or mother, or any of them.—But though I was somewhat enlightened, by this information of my master's, yet I had no other knowledge of God than that he was a good Spirit, and created every body, and every thing.—I never was sensible, in myself, nor had any one ever told me, that he would punish the wicked, and love the just. I was only glad that I had been told there was a God, because I had always thought so.

My dear kind master grew very fond of me, as was his lady; she put me to school, but I was uneasy at that, and did not like to go; but my master and mistress requested me to learn in the gentlest terms, and persuaded me to attend my school without any anger at all; that, at last, I came to like it better, and learnt to read pretty well. My schoolmaster was a good man, his name was *Vanosdore*, and very indulgent to me.—I was in this state when, one Sunday, I heard my master preach from these words out of the *Revelations*, chap. i. v. 7. "*Behold, He cometh in the clouds and every eye shall see him and they that pierc'd Him.*" These words affected me excessively; I was in great agonies because I thought my master directed them to me only; and, I fancied, that he observed me with unusual earnestness—I was farther confirm'd in this belief as I looked round the church, and could see no one person beside myself in such grief and distress as I was; I began to think that my master hated me, and was very desirous to go home, to my own country; for I thought that if God did come (as he said) He would be sure to be most angry with *me*, as I did not know what He was, nor had ever heard of him before.

I went home in great trouble, but said nothing to any body.—I was somewhat afraid of my master; I thought he disliked me.—The next text I heard him preach from was, *Heb.* xii. 14. "*Follow peace with all men, and holiness, without which no man shall see the LORD.*" He preached the law so severely, that it made me tremble.—He said, that GOD would judge the whole world; *Ethiopia, Asia,* and *Africa,* and every where.—I was now excessively perplexed, and undetermined what to do; as I had now reason to believe that my situation would be equally bad to go as to stay.—I kept these thoughts to myself, and said nothing to any person whatever.

I should have complained to my good mistress of this great trouble of mind, but she had been a little strange to me for several days before this happened, occasioned by a story told of me by one of the maids. The servants were all jealous, and envied me the regard, and favour shewn me by my master and mistress; and the Devil being always ready, and diligent in wickedness, had influenced this girl to make a lie on me.—This happened about hay harvest, and one day, when I was unloading the waggon to put the hay into the barn, she watched an opportunity, in my absence, to take the fork out of the stick, and hide it: When I came again to my work, and could not find it, I was a good deal vexed, but I concluded it was dropt somewhere among the hay; so I went and bought another with my own money: When the girl saw that I had another, she was so malicious that she told my mistress I was very unfaithful, and not the person she took me for; and that she knew, I had, without my master's permission, ordered many things in his name, that he must pay for; and as a proof of my carelessnes produced the fork she had taken out of the stick, and said, she had found it out of doors—My Lady, not knowing the truth of these things, was a little shy to me, till she mentioned it, and then I soon cleared myself, and convinced her that these accusations were false.

I continued in a most unhappy state for many days. My good mistress insisted on knowing what was the matter. When I made known my situation, she gave me John Bunyan on the holy war, to read; I found his experience similar to my own, which gave me reason to suppose he must be a bad man; as I was convinced of my own corrupt nature, and the misery of my own heart: And as he acknowledged that he was likewise in the same condition, I experienced no relief at all in reading his work, but rather the reverse.—I took the book to my lady, and informed her I did not like it at all, it was concerning a wicked man as bad as myself; and I did not chuse to read it, and I desired her to give me another, wrote by a better man, that was holy, and without sin.—She assured me that John Bunyan was a good man, but she could not convince me; I thought him to be too much like myself to be upright, as his experience seemed to answer with my own.

I am very sensible that nothing but the great power and unspeakable mercies of the Lord could relieve my soul from the heavy burden it laboured under at that time.—A few days after my master gave me Baxter's *Call to the Unconverted*. This was no relief to me neither; on the contrary it occasioned as much distress in me as the other had before done, *as it* invited all to come to *Christ*; and I found myself so wicked and miserable that I could not come—This consideration threw me into ago-nies that cannot be described; insomuch that I even attempted to put an end to my life—I took one of the large case-knives, and went into the stable with an intent to destroy myself; and as I endeavoured with all my strength to force the knife into my side, it bent double. I was instantly struck with horror at the thought of my own rashness, and my conscience told me that had I succeeded in this attempt I should probably have gone to hell.

I could find no relief, nor the least shadow of comfort; the extreme distress of my mind so affected my health that I continued very ill for three days, and nights; and would admit of no means to be taken for my recovery, though my lady was very kind, and sent many things to me; but I rejected every means of relief and wished to die—I would not go into my own bed, but lay in the stable upon straw—I felt all the horrors of a troubled conscience, so hard to be born, and saw all the vengeance of God ready to overtake me—I was sensible that there was no way for me to be saved unless I came to *Christ*, and I could not come to Him: I thought that it was impossible He should receive such a sinner as me. The last night that I continued in this place, in the midst of my distress these words were brought home upon my mind, "*Behold the Lamb of God*," I was something comforted at this, and began to grow easier and wished for day that I might find these words in my bible—I rose very early the following morning, and went to my school-master, Mr. Vanosdore, and communicated the situation of my mind to him; he was greatly rejoiced to find me inquiring the way to Zion, and blessed the Lord who had worked so wonderfully for me a poor heathen.—I was more familiar with this good gentleman than with my master, or any other person; and found my self more at liberty to talk to him: He encouraged me greatly, and prayed with me frequently, and I was always bene-fited by his discourse.

About a quarter of a mile from my master's house stood a large, remarkably fine oak-tree, in the midst of a wood; I often used to be employed there in cutting down trees, (a work I was very fond of) I seldom failed going to this place every day; some-times twice a day if I could be spared. It was the highest pleasure I ever experienced to sit under this oak; for there I used to pour out all my complaints to the LORD: And when I had any particular grievance I used to go there, and talk to the tree, and tell my sorrows, as if it had been to a friend. Here I often lamented my own wicked heart, and undone state; and found more comfort and consolation than I ever was sensible of before.—Whenever I was treated with ridicule or contempt, I used to come here and find peace. I now began to relish the book my master gave me, Baxter's *Call to the Unconverted*, and took great delight in it. I was always glad to be employed in cutting wood, 'twas a great part of my business, and I followed it with delight, as I was then quite alone and my heart lifted up to GOD, and I was enabled to pray continually; and blessed for ever be his holy name, he faithfully answered my prayers. I can never be thankful enough to Almighty GOD for the many comfortable opportunities I experienced there

It is possible the circumstance I am going to relate will not gain credit with many; but this I know, that the joy and comfort it conveyed to me, cannot be expressed, and only conceived by those who have experienced the like.

I was one day in a most delightful frame of mind; my heart so overflowed with love and gratitude to the author of all my comforts:—I was so draw out of myself, and so fill'd and awed by the presence of God, that I saw (or thought I saw) light in-expressible dart down from heaven upon me, and shone around me for the space of a minute.—I continued on my knees, and joy unspeakable took possession of my soul.—The peace and serenity which filled my mind after this was wonderful, and cannot be told.—I would not have changed situations, or been any one but myself for the whole world. I blest God for my poverty, that I had no worldly riches or grandeur to draw my heart from him. I wished at that time, if it had been possible for me, to have continued on that spot forever. I felt an unwillingness in myself to have any thing more to do with the world, or to mix with society again. I seemed to possess a full assurance that my sins were forgiven me. I went home all my way rejoicing, and this text of scripture came full upon my mind. "*And I will make an everlasting covenant with them, that I will not turn away from them, to do them good; but I will put my fear in their hearts that they shall not depart from me.*" The first opportunity that presented itself, I went to my old schoolmaster, and made known to him the happy state of my soul who joined with me in praise to God for his mercy to me the vilest of sinners—I was now perfectly easy and had hardly a wish to make beyond what I possessed, when my temporal comforts were all blasted by the death of my dear and worthy master Mr. *Freelandhouse*, who was taken from this world rather suddenly: He had but a short illness, and died of a fever. I held his hand in mine when he departed; he told me he had given me my freedom. I was at liberty to go where I would.—He added that he had always prayed for me and hoped I should be kept unto the end. My master left me by his will ten pounds, and my freedom. I found that if he had lived twas his intention to take me with him to Holland, as he had often mentioned me to some friends of his there that were desirous to see me; but I chose to continue with my mis-tress who was as good to me as if she had been my mother.

The loss of Mr. *Freelandhouse* distressed me greatly, but I was rendered still more unhappy by the clouded and perplexed situation of my mind; the great enemy of my soul being ready to torment me, would present my own misery to me in such striking light, and distress me with doubts, fears, and such a deep sense of my own unworthiness, that after all the comfort and encouragement I had received, I was often tempted to believe I should be a cast-away at last.—The more I saw of the beauty and glory of God, the more I was humbled under a sense of my own vileness. I often repaired to my old place of prayer; I seldom came away without consolation. One day this scripture was wonderfully apply'd to my mind, *And ye are complete in him which is the head of all principalities and power*—The Lord was pleased to comfort me by the application of many gracious promises at times when I was ready to sink under my troubles. *Wherefore he is able also to save them to the uttermost that come unto God by him, seeing he ever liveth to make intercession for them*, Heb. x. xiv. *For by one offering he hath perfected forever them that are sanctified.*

My kind, indulgent mistress liv'd but two years after my master. Her death was a great affliction to me. She left five sons, all gracious young men, and ministers of the gospel.—I continued with them all, one after another, till they died; they lived but four years after their parents. When it pleased God to take them to himself. I was left quite destitute, without a friend in the world. But I, who had so often experienced the goodness of God, trusted in him to do what he pleased with me.—In this helpless condition I went in the wood to prayer as usual; and though the snow was a considerable height, I was not sensible of cold, or any other inconveniency.—At times, indeed, when I saw the world frowning round me, I was tempted to think that the LORD had forsaken me. I found great relief from the contemplation of these words in Isai. xlix. 16. *Behold I have graven thee on the palms of my hands; thy walls are continually before me.* And very many comfortable promises were sweetly applied to me. The 89th Psal. and 34th ver. *My covenant will I not break, nor alter the thing that is gone cut of my lips.* Heb. xvi. 17, 18. Phil i. 6. and several more. As I had now lost all my dear and valued friends, every place in the world was alike to me. I had for a great while entertained a desire to come to *England.*—I imagined that all the inhabitants of this island were *holy*; because all those that had visited my master from thence were good (Mr. Whitefield was his particular friend) and the authors of the books that had been given me were all English.—But, above all places in the world, I wish'd to see Kidderminster, for I could not but think that on the spot where Mr. Baxter had lived, and preach'd, the people must be all *righteous.*

The situation of my affairs required that I should tarry a little longer in *New York*, as I was something in debt, and was embarrassed how to pay it. About this time a young gentleman that was a particular acquaintance of my young master's, pretended to be a friend to me, and promis'd to pay my debts, which was three pounds; and he assured me he would never expect the money again.—But, in less than a month, he came and demanded it; and when I assured him I had nothing to pay, he threatened to sell me.—Though I knew he had no right to do that, yet, as I had no friend in the world to go to, it alarm'd me greatly.—At length he purpos'd my going a privateering, that I might, by these means, be enabled to pay him, to which I agreed.—Our Captain's name was——. I went in character of cook to him.—Near St. *Domingo* we came up to five French ships, merchantmen.—We had a very smart engagement, that continued from eight in the morning till three in the afternoon; when victory declared on our side.—Soon after this we were met by three English ships which join'd us, and that encouraged us to attack a fleet of 36 ships.—We boarded the three first, and then followed the others, and had the same success with twelve; but the rest escaped us.—There was a great deal of blood shed, and I was near death several times, but the LORD preserv'd me.

I met with many enemies, and much persecution, among the sailors; one of them was particularly unkind to me, and studied ways to vex and teaze me. I can't help mentioning one circumstance that hurt me more than all the rest, which was, that he snatched a book out of my hand, that I was very fond of, and used frequently to amuse myself with, & threw it into the sea.—But, what is remarkable, he was the first that was killed in our engagement.—I don't pretend to say that this happened because he was not my friend; but I thought 'twas a very awful providence, to see how the enemies of the LORD are cut off.

Our Captain was a cruel, hard-hearted man. I was excessively sorry for the prisoners we took in general: But the pitiable case of one young gentleman grieved me to the heart.—He appeared very amiable; was strikingly handsome.—Our Captain took four thousand pounds from him; but that did not satisfy him, as he imagined he was possessed of more, and had somewhere concealed it, so that the Captain threatened him with death, at which he appeared in the deepest distress, and took the buckles out of his shoes, and untied his hair, which was very fine, and long; and in which several very valuable rings were fastened. He came into the cabin to me, and in the most obliging terms imaginable asked for something to eat and drink; which when I gave him he was so thankful and pretty in his manner that my heart bled for him; and I heartily wished that I could have spoken in any language in which the ship's crew would not have understood me; that I might have let him know his danger; for I heard the Captain say he was resolved upon his death; and he put his barbarous design into execution, for he took him on shore with one of the sailors, and there they shot him. This circumstance affected me exceedingly. I could not put him out of my mind a long while.—When we returned to *New York* the Captain divided the prize-money among us, that we had taken. When I was called upon to receive my part, I waited upon Mr.—, (the gentleman that paid my debt and was the occasion of my going abroad) to know if he chose to go with me to receive my money, or if I should bring him what I owed.—He chose to go with me; and when the Captain laid my money on the table ('twas an hundred and thirty-five pounds) I desired Mr.—to take what I was indebted to him; and he swept it all into his handkerchief, and would never be prevailed on to give a farthing of money, nor any thing at all beside.—And he likewise secured a hogshead of sugar which was my due from the same ship. The Captain was very angry with him for this piece of cruelty to me, as was every other person that heard it.—But I have reason to believe (as he was one of the principal merchants in the city) that he transacted business for him and on that account did not chuse to quarrel with him. At this time a very worthy gentleman, a wine merchant, *Dunscum*, took me under his protection, and would have recovered my money for me if I had chose it; but I told him to let it alone; that I would rather be quiet.—I believed that it would not prosper with him, and so it happened, for by a series of losses and misfortunes he became poor, and was soon after drowned, as he was on a party of pleasure.—The vessel was driven out to sea, and struck against a rock by which means every soul perished. I was very much distressed when I heard it, and felt greatly for his family who were reduced to very low circumstances.—I never knew how to set a proper value on money, if I had but a little meat and drink to supply the present necessaries of life, I never wished for more; and when I had any I always gave it if ever I saw an object in distress. If it was not for my dear wife and children I should pay as little regard to money now as I did at any time.—I continued some time with Mr. *Dunscum* as his servant; he was very kind to me.—But I had a vast inclination to visit *England* and wished continually that it would please providence to make a clear way for me to see this island. I entertained a notion that if I could get to *England* I should never more experience either cruelty or ingratitude, so that I was very desirous to get among Christians. I knew Mr. *Whitefield* very well.—I had heard him preach often at *New-York*. In this disposition I listed in the twenty-eight regiment. We went in Admiral Pocock's fleet from *New York* to *Barbados*; from thence to *Martinico*.—When that was taken we proceeded to the *Havanna*, and took that place likewise.—There I got discharged.

I was then worth about thirty pounds, but I never regarded money in the least, nor would I tarry to receive my prize-money lest I should lose my chance of going to *England*.—I went with the *Spanish* prisoners to *Spain*; and came to *Old England* with the English prisoners.—I cannot describe my joy when we were within sight of *Portsmouth*. But I was astonished when we landed to hear the inhabitants of that place curse and swear, and otherwise profane. I expected to find nothing but goodness, gentleness and meekness in this Christian land, I then suffered great perplexities of mind.

I inquired if any serious Christian people resided there, the woman I made this inquiry of, answered me in the affirmative; and added that she was one of them.—I was heartily glad to hear her say so. I thought I could give her my whole heart: She kept a public house. I deposited with her all the money that I had not an immediate occasion for; as I thought it would be safer with her.—It was 25 guineas, but 6 of them I desired her to lay out to the best advantage, to buy me some shirts, hat, and some other necessaries. I made her a present of a very handsome large looking-glass, that I brought with me from Martinico, in order to recompence her for the trouble I had given her. I must do this woman the justice to acknowledge that she did lay out some little for my use, but the 19 guineas, and part of the 6, with my watch, she would not return, and denied that I ever gave it her. I soon perceived that I was got among bad people, who defrauded me of my money and watch; and that all my promis'd happiness was blasted, I had no friend but GOD, and I prayed to him earnestly. I could scarcely believe it possible that the place where so many eminent Christians had lived and preached could abound with so much wickedness and deceit. I thought it worse than *Sodom* (considering the great advantages they have) I cry'd like a child, and that almost continually: At length GOD heard my prayers and raised me a friend indeed. This publican had a brother who lived on *Portsmouth* common, his wife was a serious good woman. When she heard of the treatment I had met with, she came and inquired into my real situation, and was greatly troubled at the ill usage I had received, and took me home to her own house.—I began now to rejoice, and my prayer was turned into praise. She made use of all the arguments in her power to prevail on her who had wronged me, to return my watch and money, but it was to no purpose, as she had given me no receipt, and I had nothing to show for it, I could not demand it.—My good friend was excessively angry with her, and obliged her to give me back four guineas, which she said she gave me out of charity: Though in fact it was my own, and much more. She would have employed some rougher means to oblige her to give up my money, but I would not suffer her, let it go, says I, "My GOD is in heaven." Still I did not mind my loss in the least; all that grieved me was, that I had been disappointed in finding some Christian friends, with whom I hoped to enjoy a little sweet and comfortable society.

I thought the best method that I could take now, was to go to *London*, and find out Mr. *Whitefield*, who was the only living soul I knew in *England*, and get him to direct me to some way or other to procure a living without being troublesome to any person.—I took leave of my Christian friend at *Portsmouth*, and went in the stage to *London*.—A creditable tradesman in the city, who went up with me in the stage, offered to show me the way to Mr. *Whitefield*'s tabernacle. Knowing that I was a perfect stranger, I thought it very kind, and accepted his offer; but he obliged me to give him half-a-crown for going with me, and likewise insisted on my giving him five shillings more for conducting me to Dr. *Gifford*'s meeting.

I began now to entertain a very different idea of the inhabitants of *England* than what I had figured to myself before I came among them.—Mr. *Whitefield* received me very friendly, was heartily glad to see me, and directed me to a proper place to board and lodge in Petticoat-lane, till he could think of some way to settle me in, and paid for my lodging, and all my expences. The morning after I came to my new lodging, as I was at breakfast with the gentlewoman of the house, I heard the noise of some looms over our heads: I inquired what it was; she told me a person was weaving silk.—I expressed a great desire to see it, and asked if I might: She told me she would go up with me: She was sure I should be very welcome. She was as good as her word, and as soon as we entered the room, the person that was weaving looked about, and smiled upon us, and I loved her from that moment. She asked me many questions, and I in turn talked a great deal to her. I found she was a member of Mr. *Allen*'s meeting, and I began to entertain a good opinion of her, though I was almost afraid to indulge this inclination, least she should prove like all the rest I had met with at *Portsmouth* &c. and which had almost given me a dislike to all white women.—But after a short acquaintance I had the happiness to find she was very different, and quite sincere, and I was not without hope that she entertained some esteem for me. We often went together to hear Dr. *Gifford*, and as I had always a propensity to relieve every object in distress as far as I was able, I used to give to all that complained to me; sometimes half a guinea at a time, as I did not understand the real value of it.—This gracious, good woman took great pains to correct and advise me in that and many other respects. After I had been in *London* about six weeks I was recommended to the notice of some of my late master Mr. *Freeland-house*'s acquaintance, who had heard him speak frequently of me. I was much persuaded by them to go to *Holland*.

My master lived there before he bought me, and used to speak of me so respectfully among his friends there, that it raised in them a curiosity to see me; particularly the gentlemen engaged in the ministry, who expressed a desire to hear my experience and examine me. I found that it was my good old master's design that I should have gone if he had lived; for which reason I resolved upon going to *Holland*, and informed my dear friend Mr. *Whitefield* of my intention; he was much averse to my going at first, but after I gave him my reasons appeared very well satisfied. I likewise informed my *Betty* (the good woman that I have mentioned above) of my determination to go to *Holland*, and I told her that I believed she was to be my wife: That if it was the LORD's will I desired it, but not else.—She made me very little answer, but has since told me, she did not think it at that time.

I embarked at tower-wharf at four o'clock in the morning, and arrived at *Amsterdam* the next day by three o'clock in the afternoon. I had several letters of recommendation to my old master's friends, who received me very graciously. Indeed, one of the chief ministers was particularly good to me, he kept me at his house a long while, and took great pleasure in asking questions, which I answered with delight, being always ready to say, "*Come unto me all ye that fear GOD, and I will tell what he hath done for my soul.*" I cannot but admire the footsteps of *Providence*; astonished that I should be so wonderfully preserved ! Though the grandson of a King, I have wanted bread, and should have been glad of the hardest crust I ever saw. I who, at home, was surrounded and guarded by slaves, so that no indifferent person might approach me, and clothed with gold, have been inhumanly threatened with death; and frequently wanted clothing to defend me from the inclemency of the weather; yet I never murmured, nor was I discontented.—I am willing, and even desirous, to be counted as nothing, a stranger in the world, and a pilgrim here; for "*I know that my* REDEEMER *liveth,*" and I'm thankful for every trial and trouble that I've met with, as I am not without hope that they have been all sanctified to me. The Calvinist ministers desired to hear my experience from myself, which proposal I was very well pleased with: So I stood before 48 ministers every Thursday for seven weeks together, and they were all very well satisfied, and persuaded I was what I pretended to be.—They wrote down my experience as I spoke it; and the Lord almighty was with me at that time in a remarkable manner, and gave me words, and enabled me to answer them; so great was his mercy to take me in hand a poor blind Heathen.

At this time a very rich merchant at *Amsterdam* offered to take me into his family, in the capacity of his butler, and I very willingly accepted it.—He was gracious, worthy gentleman, and very good to me.—He treated me more like a friend than a servant.—I tarried there a twelvemonth, but was not thoroughly contented, I wanted to see my wife (that is now) and for that reason I wished to return to *England*. I wrote to her once in my absence, but she did not answer my letter; and I must acknowledge if she had, it would have given me a less opinion of her.—My master and mistress persuaded me not to leave them, and likewise their two sons, who entertained a good opinion of me; and if I had found my Betty married, on my arrival in *England*, I should have returned to them again immediately.

My lady proposed my marrying her maid; she was an agreeable young woman, had saved a good deal of money, but I could not fancy her, though she was willing to accept of me, but I told her my inclinations were engaged in *England*, and I could think of no other person.—On my return home I found my Betty disengaged.—She had refused several offers in my absence, and told her sister that she thought if ever she married I was to be her husband.

Soon after I came home I waited on Dr. Gifford, who took me into his family, and was exceedingly good to me. The character of this pious, worthy gentleman is well known; my praise can be of no use or signification at all.—I hope I shall ever gratefully remember the many favours I have received from him. Soon after I came to Dr. Gifford, I expressed a desire to be admitted into their church, and set down with them; they told me I must first be baptized; so I gave in my experience before the church, with which they were very well satisfied, and I was baptized by Dr. Gifford, with some others. I then made known my intentions of being married; but I found there were many objections against it, because the person I had fixed on was poor. She was a widow, her husband had left her in debt, and with a child, so that they persuaded me against it out of real regard to me. But I had promised, and was resolved to have her; as I knew her to be a gracious woman, her poverty was no objection to me, as they had nothing else to say against her. When my friends found that they could not alter my opinion, respecting her, they wrote to Mr. Allen, the minister she attended, to persuade her to leave me; but he replied that he would not interfere at all, that we might do as we would. I was resolved that all my wife's little debts should be paid before we were married; so that I sold almost every thing I had, and with all the money I could raise, cleared all that she owed; and I never did any thing with a better will in all my life, because I firmly believed that we should be very happy together, and so it proved, for she was given me from the Lord. And I have found her a blessed partner, and we have never repented, though we have gone through many great troubles and difficulties.

My wife got a very good living by weaving, and could do extremely well; but just at that time there was great disturbance among the weavers, so that I was afraid to let my wife work, least they should insist on my joining the rioters, which I could not think of, and, possibly, if I had refused to do so they would have knock'd me on the head. So that by these means my wife could get no employ, neither had I work enough to maintain my family. We had not yet been married a year before all these misfortunes overtook us.

Just at this time a gentleman, that seemed much concerned for us, advised me to go into *Essex* with him, and promised to get me employed. I accepted his kind proposal, and he spoke to a friend of his, a Quaker, a gentleman of large fortune, who resided a little way out of the town of *Colchester*, his name was *Handbarrar*, he ordered his steward to set me to work.

There were several employed in the same way with myself. I was very thankful and contented though my wages were but small. I was allowed but eight pence a day, and found myself; but after I had been in this situation for a fortnight, my master, being told that a Black was at work for him, had an inclination to see me. He was pleased to talk to me for some time, and at last inquired what wages I had; when I told him, he declared it was too little, and immediately ordered his steward to let me have eighteen pence a day, which he constantly gave me after; and I then did extremely well.

I did not bring my wife with me: I came first alone, and it was my design, if things answered according to our wishes, to send for her. I was now thinking to desire her to come to me, when I received a letter to inform me she was just brought to bed, and in want of many necessaries. This news was a great trial to me, and a fresh affliction: But my God, *faithful and abundant in mercy*, forsook me not in this trouble.

As I could not read English, I was obliged to apply to some one to read the letter I received, relative to my wife. I was directed by the good providence of God to a worthy young gentleman, a Quaker, and friend of my master.—I desired he would take the trouble to read my letter for me, which he readily complied with, and was greatly moved and affected at the contents; insomuch that he said he would undertake to make a gathering for me, which he did and was the first to contribute to it himself. The money was sent that evening to London, by a person who happened to be going there; nor was this all the goodness that I experienced from these kind friends, for as soon as my wife came about and was fit to travel, they sent for her to me, and were at the whole expence of her coming; so evidently has the love and mercy of God appeared through every trouble that ever I experienced. We went on very cordially all the summer. We lived in a little cottage near Mr. *Handbarrar*'s house, but when the winter came on I was discharged, as he had no further occasion for me. And now the prospect began to darken upon us again. We tho't it most adviseable to move our habitation a little nearer to the town, as the house we lived in was very cold and wet, and ready to tumble down.

The boundless goodness of God to me has been so very great, that, with the most humble gratitude, I desire to prostrate myself before him; for I have been wonderfully supported in every affliction.—My God never left me. I perceived light *still*, thro' the thickest darkness.

My dear wife and I were now both unemployed, we could get nothing to do. The winter proved remarkably severe, and we were reduced to the greatest distress imaginable.—I was always very shy of asking for any thing; I could never beg; neither did I chuse to make known our wants to any person, for fear of offending, as we were entire strangers; but our last bit of bread was gone, and I was obliged to think of something to do for our support. I did not mind for myself at all; but to see my dear wife and children in want, pierc'd me to the heart.—I now blam'd myself for bringing her from London, as doubtless had we continued there we might have found friends to keep us from starving. The snow was remarkably deep; so that we could see no prospect of being relieved. In this melancholy situation, not knowing what step to pursue, I resolved to make my case known to a gentleman's gardiner that lived near us, and entreat him to employ me; but when I came to him my courage fail'd me, and I was ashamed to make known our real situation.—I endeavoured all I could to prevail on him to set me to work, but to no purpose; he assured me it was not in his power: But just as I was about to leave him, he asked me if I would accept of some carrots? I took them with great thankfulness, and carried them home; he gave me four, they were very large and fine.—We had nothing to make fire with, so consequently could not boil them; but was glad to have them to eat raw. Our youngest child was quite an infant; so that my wife was obliged to chew it, and fed her in that manner for several days. We allowed ourselves but one every day, lest they should not last till we could get some other supply. I was unwilling to eat at all myself; nor would I take any the last day that we continued in this situation, as I could not bear the thought that my dear wife and children would be in want of every means of support. We lived in this manner till our carrots were all gone: Then my wife began to lament because of our poor babes; but I comforted her all I could; still hoping, and believing, that my God would not let us die; but that it would please him to relieve us, which he did by almost a miracle.

We went to bed, as usual, before it was quite dark (as we had neither fire nor candle) but had not been there long before some person knocked at the door, and inquired if *James Albert* lived there? I answer'd in the affirmative, and rose immediately; as soon as I opened the door I found it was the servant of an eminent attorney who resided at *Colchester*. He asked me how it was with me? If I was not almost starved? I burst out a crying, and told him I was indeed. He said his master suppos'd so, and that he wanted to speak with me, and I must return with him. This gentleman's name was *Daniel*, he was a sincere, good Christian. He used to stand and talk with me frequently, when I work'd in the road for Mr. *Handbarrar*, and would have employed me himself if I had wanted work.—When I came to his house he told me that he had thought a good deal about me of late, and was apprehensive that I must be in want, and could not be satisfied till he sent to inquire after me. I made known my distress to him, at which he was greatly affected; and generously gave me a guinea; and promised to be kind to me in future. I could not help exclaiming, *O the boundless mercies of my God* ! I prayed unto him, and he has heard me; I trusted in him, and he has preserv'd me: Where shall I begin to praise him? Or how shall I love him enough? I went immediately and bought some bread and cheese and coal and carried them home. My dear wife was rejoiced to see me return with something to eat. She instantly got up and dressed our babies, while I made a fire; and the first nobility in the land never made a more comfortable meal. We did not forget to thank the Lord for all his goodness to us. Soon after this, as the spring came on, Mr. *Peter Daniel* employed me in pulling down a house, and rebuilding it. I had then very good work, and full employ: He sent for my wife and children to *Colchester*, and provided us a house, where we lived very comfortably. I hope I shall always gratefully acknowledge his kindness to myself and family. I worked at this house for more than a year, till it was finished; and after that I was employed by several successively, and was never so happy as when I had something to do; but perceiving the winter coming on, and work rather slack, I was apprehensive that we should again be in want, or become troublesome to our friends.

I had at this time an offer made me of going to *Norwich*, and having constant employ. My wife seemed pleased with this proposal, as she supposed she might get work there in the weaving manufactory, being the business which she was brought up to, & more likely to succeed there than any other place; and we thought as we had an opportunity of moving to a town where we could both be employed, it was most adviseable to do so; and that probably we might settle there for our lives. When this step was resolved on, I went first alone to see how it would answer; which I very much repented after, for it was not in my power immediately to send my wife any supply, as I fell into the hands of a master that was neither kind nor considerate; and she was reduced to great distress, so that she was obliged to sell the few goods that we had, and when I sent for her was under the disagreeable necessity of parting with our bed.

When she came to *Norwich* I hired a room ready furnished—I experienced a great deal of difference in the carriage of my master from what I had been accustomed to from some of my other masters. He was very irregular in his payments to me.—My wife hired a loom and wove all the leisure time she had and we began to do very well, till we were overtaken by fresh misfortunes. Our three poor children fell ill of the small pox; this was a great trial to us; but still I was persuaded in myself we should not be forsaken.—And I did all in my power to keep my dear partner's spirits from sinking. Her whole attention now was taken up with the children, as she could mind nothing else, and all I could get was but little to support a family in such a situation, beside paying for the hire of our room, which I was obliged to omit doing for several weeks: But the woman to whom we were indebted would not excuse us, though I promised she should have the very first money we could get after my children came about, but she would not be satisfied, and had the cruelty to threaten us that if we did not pay her immediately, she would turn us all into the street.

The apprehension of this plunged me in the deepest distress, considering the situation of my poor babies: If they had been in health I should have been less sensible of this misfortune. But my God, *still faithful to his promise*, raised me a friend. Mr. *Henry Gurdney*, a Quaker, a gracious gentleman heard of our distress, he sent a servant of his own to the woman we hired the room of, paid our rent, and bought all the goods, with my wife's loom, and gave it us all. Some other gentlemen, hearing of his design, were pleased to assist him in these generous acts, for which we never can be thankful enough; after this my children soon came about; we began to do pretty well again; my dear wife worked hard and constant when she could get work, but it was upon a disagreeable footing, as her employ was so uncertain, sometimes she could get nothing to do, and at other times when the weavers of *Norwich* had orders from *London*, they were so excessively hurried, that the people they employed were often obliged to work on the Sabbathday: But this my wife would never do, and it was matter of uneasiness to us that we could not get our living in a regular manner, though we were both diligent, industrious, and willing to work. I was far from being happy in my master, he did not use me well. I could scarcely ever get my money from him; but I continued patient till it pleased GOD to alter my situation. My worthy friend Mr. *Gurdney* advised me to follow the employ of chopping chaff, and bought me an instrument for that purpose. There were but few people in the town that made this their business beside myself; so that I did very well indeed and we became easy and happy.—But we did not continue long in this comfortable state. Many of the inferior people were envious and ill-natur'd, and set up the same employ, and worked under price on purpose to get my business from me, and they succeeded so well that I could hardly get any thing to do, and became again unfortunate: Nor did this misfortune come alone, for just at this time we lost one of our little girls, who died of a fever; this circumstance occasioned us new troubles, for the Baptist minister refused to bury her because we were not their members. The parson of the parish denied us because she had never been baptized. I applied to the Quakers, but met with no success; this was one of the greatest trials I ever met with, as we did not know what to do with our poor baby—At length I resolved to dig a grave in the garden behind the hou'e, and bury her there; when the parson of the parish sent for me to tell me he would bury the child, but did not chuse to read the burial service over her. I told him I did not mind whether he would or not, as the child could not hear it.

We met with a great deal of ill treatment after this, and found it very difficult to live.—We could scarcely get work to do, and were obliged to pawn our clothes. We were ready to sink under our troubles.—When I proposed to my wife to go to *Kidderminster*, and try if we could do there. I had always an inclination for that place, and now more than ever, as I had heard Mr. *Fawcet* mentioned in the most respectful manner, as a pious worthy gentleman, and I had seen his name in a favourite book of mine, Baxter's *Saints Everlasting Rest*; and as the manufactory of *Kidderminster* seemed to promise my wife some employment, she readily came into my way of thinking.

I left her once more, and set out for *Kidderminster* in order to judge if the situation would suit us.—As soon as I came there I waited immediately on Mr. *Fawcet*, who was pleased to receive me very kindly and recommended me to Mr. *Watson*, who employed me in twisting silk and worsted together. I continued here about a fortnight, and when I thought it would answer our expectation, I returned to *Norwich* to fetch my wife; she was then near her time, and too much indisposed. So we were obliged to tarry until she was brought to bed, and as soon as she could conveniently travel we came to *Kidderminster*, but we brought nothing with us, as we were obliged to sell all we had to pay our debts, and the expences of my wife's illness, &c.

Such is our situation at present.—My wife, by hard labor at the loom, does every thing that can be expected from her towards the maintenance of our family; and God is pleased to incline the hearts of his people at times to yield us their charitable assistance; being myself through age and infirmity able to contribute but little to their support. As pilgrims, and very poor pilgrims we are traveling through many difficulties towards our heavenly home, and waiting patiently for his glorious call, when the Lord shall deliver us out of the evils of this present world, and bring us to the everlasting glories of the world to come.—To HIM be praise for ever and ever.

Amen.

Source: Bath printed: Newport, Rhode-Island, in Queen-Street 1774. Reprinted and sold by Solomon Southwick [1731–1797]. Early American Imprints, 1st series, no. 13311. University of Virginia Library Electronic Text Center. Copyright © Readex.

3. Notes on the State of Virginia, 1782
THOMAS JEFFERSON

Former President Thomas Jefferson has mostly been praised as one of the founding fathers of the American Republic. Yet he was also a slave owner who belonged to an elite group of Virginia planters who thought of themselves as "liberal slave owners." The following document presents a number of contradictions about the American patriot for historians to examine more closely. For example, Jefferson was behind a vigorous legislative effort to free all slaves born after passage of a law providing for the education or colonization of slaves "in a distant area." This sentiment can be found in several other movements aimed at deporting former slaves to countries and islands outside the United States, including the Caribbean and back to Africa.

From a slave's point of view Jefferson was no liberal when it came to slavery. He may have eventually realized it was wrong for a country that upheld freedom as its highest ideal to also condone slavery, but he also opposed assimilating the Negro into the general population. This dilemma does not necessarily constitute the thinking of a liberal. Jefferson supported educating some Negroes, "according to their geniuses," a position which may simply have been motivated by the fact that he, like many planters, had fathered children with his slaves. On the one hand, Jefferson advocated freeing slaves, but on the other, he shared the widely held belief that race mixing was dangerous in a nation built on the backs of slaves, not liberals. He is known to have supported racist claims that compared blacks to brutish looking animals and suggested that their dark skin may have been colored by bile.

Nor can Thomas Jefferson be considered a liberal by any modern standards held by African Americans. Jefferson is sometimes credited with urging caution and scientific investigation before reaching a final conclusions on racial potentialities. However, the following notes on slavery clearly contradict any of his expressions of sympathy for the so-called "Negro" of his period. To the contrary, inferior characteristics often attributed to blacks throughout the period of slavery and well into the twentieth century might easily be attributed to Jefferson himself. These include clichés such as claims that Negroes were shiftless, lazy, and savage, or that they prefer to associate with whites over members of their own race.

By the early 1800s, Virginian leaders looked to the organization of the American Colonization Society as a way of deporting emancipated slaves to off shore colonies that would be supported financially by American funds. This was a position Jefferson supported.

It will probably be asked, why not retain and incorporate the blacks into the state, and thus save the expense of supplying, by importation of white settlers, the vacancies they will leave? Deep rooted prejudices entertained by the whites; ten thousand recollections, by the blacks, of the injuries they have sustained; new provocations; the real distinctions which nature has made; and many other circumstances, will divide us into parties and produce convulsions, which will probably never end but in the extermination of the one or the other race.

To these objections, which are political, may be added others, which are physical and moral. The first difference which strikes us is that of colour. Whether the black of the Negro resides in the reticular membrane between the skin and scarf-skin, or in the scarf-skin itself; whether it proceeds from the colour of the blood, the colour of the bile, or from that of some other secretion, the difference is fixed in nature, and is as real as if its seat and cause were better known to us. And is this difference of no importance? Is it not the foundation of a greater or less share of beauty in the two races?

Are not the fine mixtures of red and white, the expressions of every passion by greater or less suffusions of colour in the one, preferable to that eternal monotony, which reigns in the countenances, that immovable veil of black which covers all the emotions of the other race?

Add to these, flowing hair, a more elegant symmetry of form, their own judgment in favour of the whites, declared by their preference of them, as uniformly as is the preference of the Oranootan for the black women over those of his own species. The circumstance of Superior beauty is thought worthy attention in the propagation of our horses, dogs, and other domestic animals; why not in that of man? Besides those of colour, figure, and hair, there are other physical distinctions proving a difference of race. They have less hair on the face and body. They secrete less by the kidneys, and more by the glands of the skin, which gives them a very strong and disagreeable odour. This greater degree of transpiration renders them more tolerant of heat, and less so of cold than the whites. Perhaps, too, a difference of structure in the pulmonary apparatus, which a late ingenious 1 experimentalist has discovered to be the principal regulator of animal heat, may have disabled them from extricating, in the act of inspiration, so much of that fluid from the outer air, or obliged them in expiration, to part with more of it. They seem to require less sleep. A black after hard labour through the day, will be induced by the slightest amusements to sit up till midnight, or later, though knowing he must be out with the first dawn of the morning. They are at least as brave, and more adventuresome. But this may perhaps proceed from a want of forethought, which prevents their seeing a danger till it be present.

When present, they do not go through it with more coolness or steadiness than the whites. They are more ardent after their female: but love seems with them to be more an eager desire, than a tender delicate mixture of sentiment and sensation. Their griefs are transient. Those numberless afflictions, which render it doubtful whether heaven has given life to us in mercy or in wrath, are less felt, and sooner forgotten with them. In general, their existence appears to participate more of sensation than reflection. To this must be ascribed their disposition to sleep when abstracted from their diversions, and unemployed in labour.

An animal whose body is at rest, and who does not reflect, must be disposed to sleep of course. Comparing them by their faculties of memory, reason, and imagination, it appears to me that in memory they are equal to the whites; in reason much inferior, as I think one could scarcely be found capable of tracing and comprehending the investigations of Euclid; and that in imagination they are dull, tasteless, and anomalous. It would be unfair to follow them to Africa for this investigation.

We will consider them here, on the same stage with the whites, and where the facts are not apocryphal on which a judgment is to be formed. It will be right to make great allowances for the difference of condition, of education, of conversation, of the sphere in which they move. Many millions of them have been brought to, and born in America. Most of them indeed have been confined to tillage, to their own homes, and their own society: yet many have been so situated, that they might have availed themselves of the conversation of their masters; many have been brought up to the handicraft arts, and from that circumstance have always been associated with the whites. Some have been liberally educated, and all have lived in countries where the arts and sciences are cultivated to a considerable degree, and have had before their eyes samples of the best works from abroad.

The Indians, with no advantages of this kind, will often carve figures on their pipes not destitute of design and merit. They will crayon out an animal, a plant, or a country, so as to prove the existence of a germ in their minds which only wants cultivation. They astonish you with strokes of the most sublime oratory; such as prove their reason and sentiment strong, their imagination glowing and elevated.

But never yet could I find that a black had uttered a thought above the level of plain narration; never saw even an elementary trait of painting or sculpture.

In music they are more generally gifted than the whites with accurate ears for tune and time... Whether they will be equal to the composition of a more extensive run of melody, or of complicated harmony, is yet to be proved. Misery is often the parent of the most affecting touches in poetry. Among the blacks is misery enough, God knows, but no poetry. Love is the peculiar oestrum of the poet. Their love is ardent, but it kindles the senses only, not the imagination. Religion indeed has produced a Phyllis Whately [sic] [Boston poet Phyllis Wheatley] but it could not produce a poet. The compositions published under her name are below the dignity of criticism. The heroes of the Dunciad are to her, as Hercules to the author of that poem.

Ignatius Sancho (c. 1729—14 December 1780) was a[n] Afro-British composer, actor) has approached nearer to merit in composition; yet his letters do more honour to the heart than the head. They breathe the purest effusions of friendship and general philanthropy, and show how great a degree of the latter may be compounded with strong religious zeal. He is often happy in the turn of his compliments, and his style is easy and familiar, except when he affects a Shandean fabrication of words.

But his imagination is wild and extravagant, escapes incessantly from every restraint of reason and taste, and, in the course of its vagaries, leaves a tract of thought as incoherent and eccentric, as is the course of a meteor through the sky. His subjects should often have led him to a process of sober reasoning: yet we find him always substituting sentiment for demonstration. Upon the whole, though we admit him to the first place among those of his own colour who have presented themselves to the public judgment, yet when we compare him with the writers of the race among whom he lived and particularly with the epistolary class, in which he has taken his own stand, we are compelled to enroll him at the bottom of the column.

This criticism supposes the letters published under his name to be genuine, and to have received amendment from no other hand; points which would not be of easy investigation. The improvement of the blacks in body and mind, in the first instance of their mixture with the whites, has been observed by every one, and proves that their inferiority is not the effect merely of their condition of life. We know that among the Romans, about the Augustan age especially, the condition of their slaves was much more deplorable than that of the blacks on the continent of America.

The two sexes were confined in separate apartments, because to raise a child cost the master more than to buy one. Cato, for a very restricted indulgence to his slaves in this particular, took from them a certain price. But in this country the slaves multiply as fast as the free inhabitants. Their situation and manners place the commerce between the two sexes almost without restraint. The same Cato, on a principle of economy, always sold his sick and superannuated slaves. He gives it as a standing precept to a master visiting his farm, to sell his old oxen, old wagons, old tools, old and diseased servants, and every thing else become useless....

The American slaves cannot enumerate this among the injuries and insults they receive.

With the Romans, the regular method of taking the evidence of their slaves was under torture. Here it has been thought better never to resort to their evidence. When a master was murdered, all his slaves, in the same house, or within hearing, were condemned to death. Here punishment falls on the guilty only, and as precise proof is required against him as against a freeman. Yet notwithstanding these and other discouraging circumstances among the Romans, their slaves were often their rarest artists. They excelled too in science, insomuch as to be usually employed as tutors to their masters' children. Epictetus, Terence, and Phaedrus, were slaves. But they were of the race of whites. It is not their condition then, but nature, which has produced the distinction.

The man, in whose favour no laws of property exist, probably feels himself less bound to respect those made in favour of others. When arguing for ourselves, we lay it down as a fundamental, that laws, to be just, must give a reciprocation of right; that, without this, they are mere arbitrary rules of conduct, founded in force, and not in conscience: and it is a problem which I give to the master to solve, whether the religious precepts against the violation of property were not framed for him as well as his slave? And whether the slave may not as justifiably take a little from one, who has taken all from him, as he may slay one who would slay him? That a change in the relations in which a man is placed should change his ideas of moral right or wrong, is neither new, nor peculiar to the colour of the blacks. Homer tells us it was so 2600 years ago.

Jove fix'd it certain, that whatever day
Makes man a slave, takes half his worth away.

But the slaves of which Homer speaks were whites. Notwithstanding these considerations which must weaken their respect for the laws of property, we find among them numerous instances of the most rigid integrity, and as many as among their better instructed masters, of benevolence, gratitude and unshaken fidelity. The opinion, that they are inferior in the faculties of reason and imagination, must be hazarded with great diffidence. To justify a general conclusion, requires many observations, even where the subject may be submitted to the anatomical knife, to optical classes, to analysis by fire, or by solvents. How much more then where it is a faculty, not a substance, we are examining; where it eludes the research of all the Senses; where the conditions of its existence are various and variously combined;

where the effects of those which are present or absent bid defiance to calculation; let me add too, as a circumstance of great tenderness, where our conclusion would degrade a whole race of men from the rank in the scale of beings which their Creator may perhaps have given them. To our reproach it must be said, that though for a century and a half we have had under our eyes the races of black and of red men, they have never yet been viewed by us as subjects of natural history.

I advance it therefore as a suspicion only, that the blacks, whether originally a distinct race, or made distinct by time and circumstances, are inferior to the whites in the endowments both of body and mind. It is not against experience to suppose, that different Species of the same genus, or varieties of the same species, may possess different qualifications. Will not a lover of natural history then, one who views the gradations in all the races of animals with the eye of philosophy, excuse an effort to keep those in the department of man as distinct as nature has formed them?

This unfortunate difference of colour, and perhaps of faculty, is a powerful obstacle to the emancipation of these people. Many of their advocates, while they wish to vindicate the liberty of human nature are anxious also to preserve its dignity and beauty. Some of these, embarrassed by the question 'What further is to be done with them?' join themselves in opposition with those who are actuated by sordid avarice only. Among the Romans emancipation required but one effort. The slave, when made free, might mix with, without staining the blood of his master. But with us a second is necessary, unknown to history. When freed, he is to be removed beyond the reach of mixture.

It is difficult to determine on the standard by which the manners of a nation may be tried, whether [C]atholic, or particular. It is more difficult for a native to bring to that standard the manners of his own nation, familiarized to him by habit. There must doubtless be an unhappy influence on the manners of our people produced by the existence of slavery among us. The whole commerce between master and slave is a perpetual exercise of the most boisterous passions, the most unremitting despotism on the one part, and degrading submissions on the other.

Our children see this, and learn to imitate it; for man is an imitative animal. This quality is the germ of all education in him. From his cradle to his grave he is learning to do what he sees others do. If a parent could find no motive either in his philanthropy or his self love, for restraining the intemperance of passion towards his slave, it should always be a sufficient one that his child is present. But generally it is not sufficient.

The parent storms, the child looks on, catches the lineaments of wrath, puts on the same airs in the circle of smaller slaves, gives a loose to the worst of passions, and thus nursed, educated, and daily exercised in tyranny, cannot but be stamped by it with odious pecularities. The man must be a prodigy who can retain his manners and morals undepraved by such circumstances. And with what execration should the statesman be loaded, who, permitting one half the citizens thus to trample on the rights of the other, transforms those into despots, and these into enemies, destroys the morals of the one part, and the amor patriae of the other. For if a slave can have a country in this world, it must be any other in preference to that in which he is born to live and labour for another; in which he must lock up the faculties of his nature, contribute as far as depends on his individual endeavours to the evanishment of the human race, or entail his own miserable condition on the endless generations proceeding from him. With the morals of the people, their industry also is destroyed. For in a warm climate, no man will labour for himself who can make another labour for him. This is so true, that of the proprietors of slaves a very small proportion indeed are ever seen to labour. And can the liberties of a nation be thought secure when we have removed their only firm basis, a conviction in the minds of the people that these liberties are of the gift of God? That they are not to be violated but with his wrath? Indeed I tremble for my country when I reflect that God is just: that his justice cannot sleep for ever: that considering numbers, nature and natural means only, a revolution of the wheel of fortune, an exchange of situation is among possible events: that it may become probable by supernatural interference! The almighty has no attribute which can take side with us in such a contest.

But it is impossible to be temperate and to pursue this subject through the various considerations of policy, of morals, of history natural and civil. We must be contented to hope they will force their way into every one's mind. I think a change already perceptible, since the origin of the present revolution. The spirit of the master is abating, that of the slave rising from the dust, his condition mollifying, the way I hope preparing, under the auspices of heaven, for a total emancipation, and that this is disposed, in the order of events, to be with the consent of the masters, rather than by their extirpation.

Source: The Avalon Project, Yale Law School, New Haven, CT. Copyright © 1996 The Avalon Project.

4. An Address to the Negroes in the State of New-York, 1787
JUPITER HAMMON

Jupiter Hammon is often referred to as "the first black poet in America." Records of his career as a poet are sketchy and records of his career are obscure, according to various accounts of his life. He was a slave on Long Island, New York, where he lived and worked for the Lloyd family in Lloyd's Neck, not far from Queen's Village, New York. There is speculation that Hammon was a minister before he became known as a poet, according to the Yale New Haven Teacher's Institute. His poetic work first began to appear in print in the 1760s.

"If we should ever get to Heaven, we shall find nobody to reproach us for being black, or for being slaves." By Jupiter Hammon, servant of John Lloyd,: jun, Esq; of the Manor of Queen's Village, Long-Island.

"Of a truth I perceive that God is no respecter of persons: But in every Nation, he that feareth him and worketh righteousness, is accepted with him."

Acts x. 34, 35.

To the Members of the African Society in the city of New York
Gentlemen,

I take the liberty to dedicate an address to my poor brethren to you. If you think it is likely to do good among them, I do not doubt but you will take it under your care. You have discovered so much kindness and good will to those you thought were oppressed, and had no helper, that I am sure you will not despise what I have wrote, if you judge it will be of any service to them. I have nothing to add, but only to wish that "the blessing of many ready to perish, may come upon you."

I am Gentlemen, Your Servant,

Jupiter Hammon

To the Public:

An Address to the Negroes of the State of New York

When I am writing to you with a design to say something to you for your good, and with a view to promote your happiness, I can with truth and sincerity join with the apostle Paul, when speaking of his own nation the Jews, and say, "That I have great heaviness and continual sorrow in my heart for my brethren, my kinsmen according to the flesh." Yes my dear brethren, when I think of you, which is very often, and of the poor, despised and miserable state you are in, as to the things of this world, and when I think of your ignorance and stupidity, and the great wickedness of the most of you, I am pained to the heart. It is at times, almost too much for human nature to bear, and I am obliged to turn my thoughts from the subject or endeavour to still my mind, by considering that it is permitted thus to be, by that God who governs all things, who seteth up one and pulleth down another. While I have been thinking on this subject, I have frequently had great struggles in my own mind, and have been at a loss to know what to do. I have wanted exceedingly to say something to you, to call upon you with the tenderness of a father and friend, and to give you the last, and I may say, dying advice, of an old man, who wishes our best good in this world, and in the world to come. But while I have had such desires, a sense of my own ignorance, and unfitness to teach others, has frequently discouraged me from attempting to say any thing to you; yet when I thought of your situation, I could not rest easy. When I was at Hartford in Connecticut, where I lived during the war, I published several pieces which were well received, not only by those of my own colour, but by a number of the white people, who thought they might do good among their servants. This is one consideration, among others, that emboldens me now to publish what I have written to you. Another is, I think you will be more likely to listen to what is said, when you know it comes from a negro, one your own nation and colour, and therefore can have no interest in deceiving you, or in saying any thing to you, but what he really thinks is your interest and duty to comply with. My age, I think, gives me some right to speak to you, and reason to expect you will hearken to my advice. I am now upwards of seventy years old, and cannot expect, though I am well, and able to do almost any kind of business, to live much longer. I have passed the common bounds set for man, and must soon go the way of all the earth. I have had more experience in the world than the most of you, and I have seen a great deal of the vanity, and wickedness of it. I have great reason to be thankful that my lot has been so much better than most slaves have had. I suppose I have had more advantages and privileges than most of you, who are slaves have ever known, and I believe more than many white people have enjoyed, for which I desire to bless God, and pray that he may bless those who have given them to me. I do not, my dear friends, say these things about myself to make you think that I am wiser or better than others; but that you might hearken, without prejudice, to what I have to say to you on the following particulars.

Ist. Respecting obedience to masters. Now whether it is right, and lawful, in the sight of God, for them to make slaves of us or not, I am certain that while we are slaves, it is our duty to obey our masters, in all their lawful commands, and mind them unless we are bid to do that which we know to-be sin, or forbidden in God's word. The apostle Paul says, "Servants be obedient to them that are your masters according to the flesh, with fear and trembling in singleness in your heart as unto Christ: Not with eye service, as men pleasers, but as the servants of Christ doing the will of God from the heart: With good will doing service to the Lord, and not to men: Knowing that whatever thing a man doeth the same shall he receive of the Lord, whether he be bond or free."—Here is a plain command of God for us to obey our masters. It may seem hard for us, if we think our masters wrong in holding us slaves, to obey in all things, but who of us dare dispute with God! He has commanded us to obey, and we ought to do it cheerfully, and freely. This should be done by us, not only because God commands, but because our own peace and comfort depend upon it. As we depend upon our masters, for what we eat and drink and wear, and for all our comfortable things in this world, we cannot be happy, unless we please them. This we cannot do without obeying them freely, without muttering or finding fault. If a servant strives to please his master and studies and takes pains to do it, I believe there are but few masters who would use such a servant cruelly. Good servants frequently make good masters. If your master is really hard, unreasonable and cruel, there is no way so likely for you to convince him of it, as always to obey his commands, and try to serve him, and take care of his interest, and try to promote it all in your power. If you are proud and stubborn and always finding fault, your master will think the fault lies wholly on your side, but if you are humble, and meek, and bear all things patiently, your master may think he is wrong, if he does not, his neighbours will be apt to see it, and will befriend you, and try to alter his conduct. If this does not do, you must cry to him, who has the hearts of all men in his hands, and turneth them as the rivers of waters are turned.

2d: The particular I would mention, is honesty and faithfulness. You must suffer me now to deal plainly with you, my dear brethren, for I do not mean to flatter, or omit speaking the truth, whether it is for you, or against you. How many of you are there who allow yourselves in stealing from your masters. It is very wicked for you not to take care of your masters goods, but how much worse is it to pilfer and steal from them, whenever you think you shall not be found out. This you must know is very wicked and provoking to God. There are none of you so ignorant, but that you must know that this is wrong. Though you may try to excuse yourselves, by saying that your masters are unjust to you, and though you may try to quiet your consciences in this way, yet if you are honest in owning the truth you must think it is as wicked, and on some accounts more wicked to steal from your masters, than from others.

We cannot certainly, have any excuse either for taking any thing that belongs to our masters without their leave, or for being unfaithful in their business. It is our duty to be faithful, not with eye service as men pleasers. We have no right to stay when we are sent on errands, any longer than to do the business we were sent upon. All the time spent idly, is spent wickedly, and is unfaithfulness to our masters. In these things I must say, that I think many of you are guilty. I know that many of you endeavour to excuse yourselves, and say that you have nothing that you can call your own, and that you are under great temptations to be unfaithful and take from your masters. But this will not do, God will certainly punish you for stealing and for being unfaithful. All that we have to mind is our own duty. If God has put us in bad circumstances that is not our fault and he will not punish us for it. If any are wicked in keeping us so, we cannot help it, they must answer to God for it. Nothing will serve as an excuse to us for not doing our duty. The same God will judge both them and us. Pray then my dear friends, fear to offend in this way, but be faithful to God, to your masters, and to your own souls.

The next thing I would mention, and warn you against, is profaneness. This you know is forbidden by God. Christ tells us, "swear not at all," and again it is said "thou shalt not take the name of the Lord thy God in vain, for the Lord will not hold him guiltless, that taketh his name in vain." Now though the great God has forbidden it, yet how dreadfully profane are many, and I don't know but I may say the most of you? How common is it to hear you take the terrible and awful name of the great God in vain?—To swear by it, and by Jesus Christ, his Son—How common is it to hear yon wish damnation to your companions, and to your own souls—and to sport with in the name of Heaven and Hell, as if there were no such places for you to hope for, or to fear. Oh my friends, be warned to forsake this dreadful sin of profaneness. Pray my dear friends, believe and realize, that there is a God—that he is great and terrible beyond what you can think—that he keeps you in life every moment—and that he can send you to that awful Hell, that you laugh at, in an instant, and confine you there for ever, and that he will certainly do it, if you do not repent. You certainly do not believe, that there is a God, or that there is a Heaven or Hell, or you would never trifle with them. It would make you shudder, if you heard others do it, if you believe them as much, as you believe any thing you see with your bodily eyes.

I have heard some learned and good men say, that the heathen, and all that worshiped false Gods, never spoke lightly or irreverently of their Gods, they never took their names in vain, or jested with those things which they held sacred. Now why should the true God, who made all things, be treated worse in this respect, than those false Gods, that were made of wood and stone. I believe it is because Satan tempts men to do it. He tried to make them love their false Gods, and to speak well of them, but he wishes to have men think lightly of the true God, to take his holy name in vain, and to scoff at, and make a jest of all things that are really good. You may think that Satan has not power to do so much, and have so great influence on the minds of men: But the scripture says, "he goeth about like a roaring Lion, seeking whom he may devour—That he is the prince of the power of the air—and that he rules in the hearts of the children of disobedience,—and that wicked men are led captive by him, to do his will." All those of you who are profane, are serving the Devil. You are doing what he tempts and desires you to do. If you could see him with your bodily eyes, would you like to make an agreement with him, to serve him, and do as he bid you. I believe most of you would be shocked at this, but you may be certain that all of you who allow yourselves in this sin, are as really serving him, and to just as good purpose, as if you met him, and promised to dishonor God, and serve him with all your might. Do you believe this? It is true whether you believe it or not. Some of you to excuse yourselves, may plead the example of others, and say that you hear a great many white-people, who know more, than such poor ignorant negroes, as you are, and some who are rich and great gentlemen, swear, and talk profanely; and some of you may say this of your masters, and say no more than is true. But all this is not a sufficient excuse for you. You know that murder is wicked. If you saw your master kill a man, do you suppose this would be any excuse for you, if you should commit the same crime? You must know it would not; nor will your hearing him curse and swear, and take the name of God in vain, or any other man, be he ever so great or rich, excuse you. God is greater than all other beings, and him we are bound to obey. To him we must give an account for every idle word that we speak. He will bring us all, rich and poor, white and black, to his judgment seat. If we are found among those who feared his name, and trembled at his word, we shall be called good and faithful servants. Our slavery will be at an end, and though ever so mean, low, and despised in this world, we shall sit with God in his kingdom as Kings and Priests, and rejoice forever, and ever. Do not then, my dear friends, take God's holy name in vain, or speak profanely in any way. Let not the example of others lead you into the sin, but reverence and fear that great and fearful name, the Lord our God. I might now caution you against other sins to which you are exposed; but as I meant only to mention those you were exposed to, more than others, by your being slaves, I will conclude what I have to say to you, by advising you to become religious, and to make religion the great business of your lives.

Now I acknowledge that liberty is a great thing, and worth seeking for, if we can get it honestly, and by our good conduct, prevail on our masters to set us free: Though for my own part I do not wish to be free, yet I should be glad, if others, especially the young negroes were to be free, for many of us, who are grown up slaves, and have always had masters to take care of us, should hardly know how to take care of ourselves; and it may be more for our own comfort to remain as we are. That liberty is a great thing we may know from our own feelings, and we may likewise judge so from the conduct of the white-people, in the late war. How much money has been spent, and how many lives has been lost, to defend their liberty. I must say that I have hoped that God would open their eyes, when they were so much engaged for liberty, to think of the state of the poor blacks, and to pity us. He has done it in some measure, and has raised us up many friends, for which we have reason to be thankful, and to hope in his mercy. What may be done further, he only knows, for known unto God are all his ways from the beginning. But this my dear brethren is by no means, the greatest thing we have to be concerned about. Getting our liberty in this world, is nothing to our having the liberty of the children of God. Now the Bible tells us that we are all by nature, sinners, that we are slaves to sin and Satan, and that unless we are converted, or born again, we must be miserable forever. Christ says, except a man be born again, he cannot see the kingdom of God, and all that do not see the kingdom of God, must be in the kingdom of darkness. There are but two places where all go after death, white and black, rich and poor; those places are Heaven and Hell. Heaven is a place made for those, who are born again, and who love God, and it is a place where they will be happy for ever. Hell is a place made for those who hate God, and are his enemies, and where they will be miserable to all eternity. Now you may think you are not enemies to God, and do not hate him: But if your heart has not been changed, and you have not become true Christians, you certainly are enemies to God, and have been opposed to him ever since you were born. Many of you, I suppose, never think of this, and are almost as ignorant as the beasts that perish. Those of you who can read I must beg you to read the Bible, and whenever you can get time, study the Bible, and if you can get no other time, spare some of your time from sleep, and learn what the mind and will of God is. But what shall I say to them who cannot read. This lay with great weight on my mind, when I thought of writing to my poor brethren, but I hope that those who can read will take pity on them and read what I have to say to them. In hopes of this I will beg of you to spare no pains in trying to learn to read. If you are once engaged you may learn. Let all the time you can get be spent in trying to learn to read. Get those who can read to learn you, but remember, that what you learn for, is to read the Bible. If there was no Bible, it would be no matter whether you could read or not. Reading other books would do you no good. But the Bible is the word of God, and tells you what you must do to please God; it tells you how you may escape misery, and be happy for ever. If you see most people neglect the Bible, and many that can read never look into it, let it not harden you and make you think lightly of it, and that it is a book of no worth. All those who are really good, love the Bible, and meditate on it day and night. In the Bible God has told us every thing it is necessary we should know, in order to be happy here and hereafter. The Bible is a revelation of the mind and will of God to men. Therein we may learn, what God is. That he made all things by the power of his word; and that he made all things for his own glory, and not for our glory. That he is over all, and above all his creatures, and more above them that we can think or conceive—that they can do nothing without him—that he upholds them all, and will over-rule all things for his own glory. In the Bible likewise we are told what man is. That he was at first made holy, in the image of God, that he fell from that state of holiness, and became an enemy to God, and that since the fall, all the imaginations of the thoughts of his heart, are evil and only evil, and that continually. That the carnal mind is not subject to the law of God, neither indeed can be. And that all mankind, were under the wrath, and curse of God, and must have been for ever miserable, if they had been left to suffer what their sins deserved. It tells us that God, to save some of mankind, sent his Son into this world to die, in the room and stead of sinners, and that now God can save from eternal misery, all that believe in his Son, and take him for their saviour, and that all are called upon to repent, and believe in Jesus Christ. It tells us that those who do repent, and believe, and are friends to Christ, shall have many trials and sufferings in this world, but that they shall be happy forever, after death, and reign with Christ to all eternity. The Bible tells us that this world is a place of trial, and that there is no other time or place for us to alter, but in this life. If we are Christians when we die, we shall awake to the resurrection of life; if not, we shall awake to the resurrection of damnation. It tells us, we must all live in Heaven or Hell, be happy or miserable, and that without end. The Bible does not tell us of but two places, for all to go to. There is no place for innocent folks, that are not Christians. There is no place for ignorant folks, that did not know how to be Christians. What I mean is, that there is no place besides Heaven and Hell. These two places, will receive all mankind, for Christ says, there are but two sorts, he that is not with me is against me, and he that gathereth not with me, scattereth abroad.—The Bible likewise tells us that this world, and all things in it shall be burnt up—and that "God has appointed a day in which he will judge the world, and that he will bring every secret thing whether it be good or bad into judgment—that which is done in secret shall be declared on the house top." I do not know, nor do I think any can tell, but that the day of judgment may last a thousand years. God could tell the state of all his creatures in a moment, but then every thing that every one has done, through his whole life is to be told, before the whole world of angels, and men. There, Oh how solemn is the thought! You, and I, must stand,

and hear every thing we have thought or done, however secret, however wicked and vile, told before all the men and women that ever have been, or ever will be, and before all the angels, good and bad.

Now my dear friends seeing the Bible is the word of God, and every thing in it is true, and it reveals such awful and glorious things, what can be more important than that you should learn to read it; and when you have learned to read, that you should study it day and night. There are some things very encouraging in God's word for such ignorant creatures as we are; for God hath not chosen the rich of this world. Not many rich, not many noble are called, but God hath chosen the weak things of this world, and things which are not, to confound the things that are: And when the great and the rich refused coming to the gospel feast, the servant was told, to go into the highways, and hedges, and compel those poor creatures that he found there to come in. Now my brethren it seems to me, that there are no people that ought to attend to the hope of happiness in another world so much as we do. Most of us are cut off from comfort and happiness here in this world, and can expect nothing from it. Now seeing this is the case, why should we not take care to be happy after death. Why should we spend our whole lives in sinning against God: And be miserable in this world, and in the world to come. If we do thus, we shall certainly be the greatest fools. We shall be slaves here, and slaves forever. We cannot plead so great temptations to neglect religion as others. Riches and honours which drown the greater part of mankind, who have the gospel, in perdition, can be little or no temptations to us.

We live so little time in this world that it is no matter how wretched and miserable we are, if it prepares us for heaven. What is forty, fifty, or sixty years, when compared to eternity. When thousands and millions of years have rolled away, this eternity will be no nigher coming to an end. Oh how glorious is an eternal life of happiness! And how dreadful, an eternity of misery. Those of us who have had religious masters, and have been taught to read the Bible, and have been brought by their example and teaching to a sense of divine things, how happy shall we be to meet them in heaven, where we shall join them in praising God forever. But if any of us have had such masters, and yet have lived and died wicked, how will it add to our misery to think of our folly. If any of us, who have wicked and profane masters should become religious, how will our estates be changed in another world. Oh my friends, let me entreat of you to think on these things, and to live as if you believed them to be true. If you become Christians you will have reason to bless God forever, that you have been brought into a land where you have heard the gospel, though you have been slaves. If we should ever get to Heaven, we shall find nobody to reproach us for being black, or for being slaves. Let me beg of you my dear African brethren, to think very little of your bondage in this life, for your thinking of it will do you no good. If God designs to set us free, he will do it, in his own time, and way; but think of your bondage to sin and Satan, and do not rest, until you are delivered from it. We cannot be happy if we are ever so free or ever so rich, while we are servants of sin, and slaves to Satan. We must be miserable here, and to all eternity. I will conclude what I have to say with a few words to those negroes who have their liberty. The most of what I have said to those who are slaves may be of use to you, but you have more advantages, on some accounts, if you will improve your freedom, as you may do, than they. You have more time to read God's holy word, and to take care of the salvation of your souls. Let me beg of you to spend your time in this way, or it will be better for you, if you had always been slaves. If you think seriously of the matter, you must conclude, that if you do not use your freedom, to promote the salvation of your souls, it will not be of any lasting good to you. Besides all this, if you are idle, and take to bad courses, you will hurt those of your brethren who are slaves, and do all in your power to prevent their being free. One great reason that is given by some for not freeing us, I understand is, that we should not know how to take care of ourselves, and should take to bad courses. That we should be lazy and idle, and get drunk and steal. Now all those of you, who follow any bad courses, and who do not take care to get an honest living by your labour and industry, are doing more to prevent our being free, than any body else. Let me beg of you then for the sake of your own good and happiness, in time, and for eternity, and for the sake of your poor brethren, who are still in bondage "to lead quiet and peaceable lives in all Godliness and honesty," and may God bless you, and bring you to his kingdom, for Christ's sake, Amen.

Finis

Source: New York, 1787. Published by Samuel Wood, 1806. American Memory Collection. Library of Congress Rare Book and Special Collections Division.

5. The Interesting Narrative of the Life of Olaudah Equiano, or Gustavus Vassa, the African, 1789

Captured in Africa at the age of 11, Olaudah Equiano was sold into slavery but later acquired his freedom. In 1789, he wrote his widely read autobiography that is excerpted here. The youngest son of a village leader, Equiano was born among the Ibo people in the kingdom of Benin, along the Niger River. His family expected him to follow in his father's footsteps and become a chief, an elder, and a judge. Slavery was an integral part of the Ibo culture, as it was with many other African peoples. Equiano's family owned slaves, but there was also a continual threat of being abducted and becoming someone else's slave. This is what happened, one day, while Equiano and his sister were at home alone.

Two men and a woman captured the children. Several days later Equiano and his sister were separated. Equiano continued to travel farther and farther away from home, day after day, month after month, exchanging masters along the way. As it was for all slaves, the Middle Passage (the term often used for the slave routes across the Atlantic Ocean) for Equiano was a long, arduous nightmare. In his autobiography he describes the inconceivable conditions of the slaves' hold: the "shrieks of the women," the "groans of the dying," the floggings, the wish to commit suicide, how those who somehow managed to drown themselves were envied.

The ship finally arrived at Barbados, where buyers purchased most of the slaves. There was no buyer, however, for the young Equiano. Less than two weeks after his arrival, he was shipped off to the English colony of Virginia, where he was purchased and put to work. Less than a month later, he had a new master—Michael Henry Pascal, a lieutenant in the Royal Navy. Under this master, who owned Equiano for the next seven years, Equiano would move to England, educate himself, and travel the world on ships under Pascal's command.

CHAPTER 2

I hope the reader will not think I have trespassed on his patience in introducing myself to him with some account of the manners and customs of my country. They had been implanted in me with great care, and made an impression on my mind, which time could not erase, and which all the adversity and variety of fortune I have since experienced, served only to rivet and record: for, whether the love of one's country be real or imaginary, or a lesson of reason, or an instinct of nature, I still look back with pleasure on the first scenes of my life, though that pleasure has been for the most part mingled with sorrow.

I have already acquainted the reader with the time and place of my birth. My father, besides many slaves, had a numerous family, of which seven lived to grow up, including myself and my sister, who was the only daughter. As I was the youngest of the sons, I became, of course, the greatest favorite with my mother, and was always with her; and she used to take particular pains to form my mind. I was trained up from my earliest years in the art of war: my daily exercise was shooting and throwing javelins, and my mother adorned me with emblems, after the manner of our greatest warriors. In this way I grew up till I had turned the age of eleven, when an end was put to my happiness in the following manner: Generally, when the grown people in the neighborhood were gone far in the fields to labor, the children assembled together in some of the neighboring premises to play; and commonly some of us used to get up a tree to look out for any assailant, or kidnapper, that might come upon us—for they sometimes took those opportunities of our parents' absence, to attack and carry off as many as they could seize. One day as I was watching at the top of a tree in our yard, I saw one of those people come into the yard of our next neighbor but one, to kidnap, there being many stout young people in it. Immediately on this I gave the alarm of the rogue, and he was surrounded by the stoutest of them, who entangled him with cords, so that he could not escape, till some of the grown people came and secured him. But, alas! Ere long it was my fate to be thus attacked, and to be carried off, when none of the grown people were nigh.

One day, when all our people were gone out to their works as usual, and only I and my dear sister were left to mind the house, two men and a woman got over our walls, and in a moment seized us both, and, without giving us time to cry out, or make resistance, they stopped our mouths, and ran off with us into the nearest wood. Here they tied our hands, and continued to carry us as far as they could, till night came on, when we reached a small house, where the robbers halted for refreshment, and spent the night. We were then unbound, but were unable to take any food; and, being quite overpowered by fatigue and grief, our only relief was some sleep, which allayed our misfortune for a short time. The next morning we left the house, and continued traveling all the day. For a long time we had kept the woods, but at last we came into a road which I believed I knew. I had now some hopes of being delivered; for we had advanced but a little way before I discovered some people at a distance, on which I began to cry out for their assistance; but my cries had no other effect than to make them tie me faster and stop my mouth, and then they put me into a large sack. They also stopped my sister's mouth, and tied her hands; and in this manner we proceeded till we were out of sight of these people. When we went to rest the following night, they offered us some victuals, but we refused it; and the only comfort we had was in being in one another's arms all that night, and bathing each other with our tears. But alas! We were soon deprived of even the small comfort of weeping together.

The next day proved a day of greater sorrow than I had yet experienced; for my sister and I were then separated, while we lay clasped in each other's arms. It was in vain that we besought them not to part us; she was torn from me, and immediately carried away, while I was left in a state of distraction not to be described. I cried and grieved continually; and for several days did not eat anything but what they forced into my mouth. At length, after many days' traveling, during which I had often changed masters, I got into the hands of a chieftain, in a very pleasant country. This man had two wives and some children, and they all used me extremely well, and did all they could do to comfort me; particularly the first wife, who was something like my mother. Although I was a great many days' journey from my father's house, yet these people spoke exactly the same language with us. This first master of mine, as I may call him, was a smith, and my principal employment was working his bellows, which were the same kind as I had seen in my vicinity. They were in some respects not unlike the stoves here in gentlemen's kitchens, and were covered over with leather; and in the middle of that leather a stick was fixed, and a person stood up, and worked it in the same manner as is done to pump water out of a cask with a hand pump. I believe it was gold he worked, for it was of a lovely bright yellow color, and was worn by the women on their wrists and ankles.

I was there I suppose about a month, and they at last used to trust me some little distance from the house. This liberty I used in embracing every opportunity to inquire the way to my own home; and I also sometimes, for the same purpose, went with the maidens, in the cool of the evenings, to bring pitchers of water from the springs for the use of the house. I had also remarked where the sun rose in the morning, and set in the evening, as I had travelled along; and I had observed that my father's house was towards the rising of the sun. I therefore determined to seize the first opportunity of making my escape, and to shape my course for that quarter; for I was quite oppressed and weighed down by grief after my mother and friends; and my love of liberty, ever great, was strengthened by the mortifying circumstance of not daring to eat with the free-born children, although I was mostly their companion.

While I was projecting my escape, one day an unlucky event happened, which quite disconcerted my plan, and put an end to my hopes. I used to be sometimes employed in assisting an elderly slave to cook and take care of the poultry; and one morning, while I was feeding some chickens, I happened to toss a small pebble at one of them, which hit it on the middle, and directly killed it. The old slave, having soon after missed the chicken, inquired after it; and on my relating the accident (for I told her the truth, for my mother would never suffer me to tell a lie), she flew into a violent passion, and threatened that I should suffer for it; and, my master being out, she immediately went and told her mistress what I had done. This alarmed me very much, and I expected an instant flogging, which to me was uncommoray dreadful, for I had seldom been beaten at home. I therefore resolved to fly; and accordingly I ran into a thicket that was hard by, and hid myself in the bushes. Soon afterwards my mistress and the slave returned, and, not seeing me, they searched all the house, but not finding me, and I not making answer when they called to me, they thought I had run away, and the whole neighborhood was raised in the pursuit of me.

In that part of the country, as in ours, the houses and villages were skirted with woods, or shrubberies, and the bushes were so thick that a man could readily conceal himself in them, so as to elude the strictest search. The neighbors continued the whole day looking for me, and several times many of them came within a few yards of the place where I lay hid. I expected every moment, when I heard a rustling among the trees, to be found out, and punished by my master; but they never discovered me, though they were often so near that I even heard their conjectures as they were looking about for me; and I now learned from them that any attempts to return home would be hopeless. Most of them supposed I had fled towards home; but the distance was so great, and the way so intricate, that they thought I could never reach it, and that I should be lost in the woods. When I heard this I was seized with a violent panic, and abandoned myself to despair. Night, too, began to approach, and aggravated all my fears. I had before entertained hopes of getting home, and had determined when it should be dark to make the attempt; but I was now convinced it was fruitless, and began to consider that, if possibly I could escape all other animals, I could not those of the human kind; and that, not knowing the way, I must perish in the woods. Thus was I like the hunted deer—

—Every leaf and every whispering breath, Convey'd a foe, and every foe a death.

I heard frequent rustlings among the leaves, and being pretty sure they were snakes, I expected every instant to be stung by them. This increased my anguish, and the horror of my situation became now quite insupportable. I at length quitted the thicket, very faint and hungry, for I had not eaten or drank anything all the day, and crept to my master's kitchen, from whence I set out at first, which was an open shed, and laid myself down in the ashes with an anxious wish for death, to relieve me from all my pains. I was scarcely awake in the morning, when the old woman slave, who was the first up, came to fight the fire, and saw me in the fireplace. She was very much surprised to see me, and could scarcely believe her own eyes. She now promised to intercede for me, and went for her master, who soon after came, and, having slightly reprimanded me, ordered me to be taken care of, and not ill treated.

Soon after this, my master's only daughter, and child by his first wife, sickened and died, which affected him so much that for sometime he was almost frantic, and really would have killed himself, had he not been watched and prevented. However, in a short time afterwards he recovered, and I was again sold. I was now carried to the left of the sun's rising, through many dreary wastes and dismal woods, amidst the hideous roarings of wild beasts. The people I was sold to used to carry me very often, when I was tired, either on their shoulders or on their backs. I saw many convenient well-built sheds along the road, at proper distances, to accommodate the merchants and travellers, who lay in those buildings along with their wives, who often accompany them; and they always go well armed.

From the time I left my own nation, I always found somebody that understood me till I came to the sea coast. The languages of different nations did not totally differ, nor were they so copious as those of the Europeans, particularly the English. They were therefore easily learned; and, while I was journeying thus through Africa, I acquired two or three different tongues. In this manner I had been traveling for a considerable time, when, one evening, to my great surprise, whom should I see brought to the house where I was but my dear sister! As soon as she saw me, she gave a loud shriek, and ran into my arms—I was quite over-powered; neither of us could speak, but, for a considerable time, clung to each other in mutual embraces, unable to do anything but weep. Our meeting affected all who saw us; and, indeed, I must acknowledge, in honor of those sable destroyers of human rights, that I never met with any ill treatment, or saw any offered to their slaves, except tying them, when necessary, to keep them from running away.

When these people knew we were brother and sister, they indulged us to be together; and the man, to whom I supposed we belonged, lay with us, he in the middle, while she and I held one another by the hands across his breast all night; and thus for a while we forgot our misfortunes, in the joy of being together; but even this small comfort was soon to have an end; for scarcely had the fatal morning appeared when she was again torn from me forever! I was now more miserable, if possible, than before. The small relief which her presence gave me from pain, was gone, and the wretchedness of my situation was redoubled by my anxiety after her fate, and my apprehensions lest her sufferings should be greater than mine, when I could not be with her to alleviate them. Yes, thou dear partner of all my childish sports! Thou sharer of my joys and sorrows! Happy should I have ever esteemed myself to encounter every misery for you and to procure your freedom by the sacrifice of my own. Though you were early forced from my arms, your image has been always riveted in my heart, from which neither time nor fortune have been able to remove it; so that, while the thoughts of your sufferings have damped my prosperity, they have mingled with adversity and increased its bitterness. To that Heaven which protects the weak from the strong, I commit the care of your innocence and virtues, if they have not already received their full reward, and if your youth and delicacy have not long since fallen victims to the violence of the African trader, the pestilential stench of a Guinea ship, the seasoning in the European colonies, or the lash and lust of a brutal and unrelenting overseer.

I did not long remain after my sister. I was again sold, and carried through a number of places, till after traveling a considerable time, I came to a town called Tinmah, in the most beautiful country I had yet seen in Africa. It was extremely rich, and there were many rivulets which flowed through it, and supplied a large pond in the centre of the town, where the people washed. Here I saw for the first time cocoanuts, which I thought superior to any nuts I had ever tasted before; and the trees, which were loaded, were also interspersed among the houses, which had commodious shades adjoining, and were in the same manner as ours, the insides being neatly plastered and whitewashed. Here I also saw and tasted for the first time, sugar-cane. Their money consisted of little white shells, the size of the finger nail. I was sold here for one hundred and seventy-two of them, by a merchant who lived and brought me there.

I had been about two or three days at his house, when a wealthy widow, a neighbor of his, came there one evening, and brought with her an only son, a young gentleman about my own age and size. Here they saw me; and, having taken a fancy to me, I was bought of the merchant, and went home with them. Her house and premises were situated close to one of those rivulets I have mentioned, and were the finest I ever saw in Africa: they were very extensive, and she had a number of slaves to attend her. The next day I was washed and perfumed, and when meal time came, I was led into the presence of my mistress, and ate and drank before her with her son. This filled me with astonishment; and I could scarce help expressing my surprise that the young gentleman should suffer me, who was bound, to eat with him who was free; and not only so, but that he would not at any time either eat or drink till I had taken first, because I was the eldest, which was agreeable to our custom. Indeed, every thing here, and all their treatment of me, made me forget that I was a slave.

The language of these people resembled ours so nearly, that we understood each other perfectly. They had also the very same customs as we. There were likewise slaves daily to attend us, while my young master and I, with other boys, sported with our darts and bows and arrows, as I had been used to do at home. In this resemblance to my former happy state, I passed about two months; and I now began to think I was to be adopted into the family, and was beginning to be reconciled to my situation, and to forget by degrees my misfortunes, when all at once the delusion vanished; for, without the least previous knowledge, one morning early, while my dear master and companion was still asleep, I was awakened out of my reverie to fresh sorrow, and hurried away even amongst the uncircumcised.

Thus, at the very moment I dreamed of the greatest happiness, I found myself most miserable; and it seemed as if fortune wished to give me this taste of joy only to render the reverse more poignant. The change I now experienced was as painful as it was sudden and unexpected. It was a change indeed, from a state of bliss to a scene which is inexpressible by me, as it discovered to me an element I had never before beheld, and till then had no idea of, and wherein such instances of hardship and cruelty continually occurred, as I can never reflect on but with horror.

All the nations and people I had hitherto passed through, resembled our own in their manners, customs, and language; but I came at length to a country, the inhabitants of which differed from us in all those particulars. I was very much struck with this difference, especially when I came among a people who did not circumcise, and ate without washing their hands. They cooked also in iron pots, and had European cutlasses and cross bows, which were unknown to us, and fought with their fists among themselves. Their women were not so modest as ours, for they ate, and drank, and slept with their men. But above all, I was amazed to see no sacrifices or offerings among them. In some of those places the people ornamented themselves with scars, and likewise filed their teeth very sharp. They wanted sometimes to ornament me in the same manner, but I would not suffer them; hoping that I might some time be among a people who did not thus disfigure themselves, as I thought they did. At last I came to the banks of a large river which was covered with canoes, in which the people appeared to live with their household utensils, and provisions of all kinds. I was beyond measure astonished at this, as I had never before seen any water larger than a pond or a rivulet; and my surprise was ningled with no small fear when I was put into one of these canoes, and we began to paddle and move along the river. We continued going on thus till night, and when we came to land, and made fires on the banks, each family by themselves; some dragged their canoes on shore, others stayed and cooked in theirs, and laid in them all night. Those on the land had mats, of which they made tents, some in the shape of little houses; in these we slept; and after the morning meal, we embarked again and proceeded as before. I was often very much astonished to see some of the women, as well as the men, jump into the water, dive to the bottom, come up again, and swim about.

Thus I continued to travel, sometimes by land, sometimes by water, through different countries and various nations, till, at the end of six or seven months after I had been kidnapped, I arrived at the sea coast. It would be tedious and uninteresting to relate all the incidents which befell me during this journey, and which I have not yet forgotten; of the various hands I passed through, and the manners and customs of all the different people among whom I lived—I shall therefore only observe, that in all the places where I was, the soil was exceedingly rich; the pumpkins, eadas, plantains, yams, &c. &c., were in great abundance, and of incredible size. There were also vast quantities of different gums, though not used for any purpose, and everywhere a great deal of tobacco. The cotton even grew quite wild, and there was plenty of red-wood. I saw no mechanics whatever in all the way, except such as I have mentioned. The chief employment in all these countries was agriculture, and both the males and females, as with us, were brought up to it, and trained in the arts of war.

The first object which saluted my eyes when I arrived on the coast, was the sea, and a slave ship, which was then riding at anchor, and waiting for its cargo. These filled me with astonishment, which was soon converted into terror, when I was carried on board. I was immediately handled, and tossed up to see if I were sound, by some of the crew; and I was now persuaded that I had gotten into a world of bad spirits, and that they were going to kill me. Their complexions, too, differing so much from ours, their long hair, and the language they spoke (which was very different from any I had ever heard), united to confirm me in this belief. Indeed, such were the horrors of my views and fears at the moment, that, if ten thousand worlds had been my own, I would have freely parted with them all to have exchanged my condition with that of the meanest slave in my own country. When I looked round the ship too, and saw a large furnace of copper boiling, and a multitude of black people of every description chained together, every one of their countenances expressing dejection and sorrow, I no longer doubted of my fate; and, quite overpowered with horror and anguish, I fell motionless on the deck and fainted. When I recovered a little, I found some black people about me, who I believed were some of those who had brought me on board, and had been receiving their pay; they talked to me in order to cheer me, but all in vain. I asked them if we were not to be eaten by those white men with horrible looks, red faces, and long hair. They told me I was not, and one of the crew brought me a small portion of spirituous liquor in a wine glass; but being afraid of him, I would not take it out of his hand. One of the blacks therefore took it from him and gave it to me, and I took a little down my palate, which, instead of reviving me, as they thought it would, threw me into the greatest consternation at the strange feeling it produced, having never tasted any such liquor before. Soon after this, the blacks who brought me on board went off, and left me abandoned to despair.

I now saw myself deprived of all chance of returning to my native country, or even the least glimpse of hope of gaining the shore, which I now considered as friendly; and I even wished for my former slavery in preference to my present situation, which was filled with horrors of every kind, still heightened by my ignorance of what I was to undergo. I was not long suffered to indulge my grief; I was soon put down under the decks, and there I received such a salutation in my nostrils as I had never experienced in my life: so that, with the loathsomeness of the stench, and crying together, I became so sick and low that I was not able to eat, nor had I the least desire to taste anything. I now wished for the last friend, death, to relieve me; but soon, to my grief, two of the white men offered me eatables; and, on my refusing to eat, one of them held me fast by the hands, and laid me across, I think, the windlass, and tied my feet, while the other flogged me severely. I had never experienced anything of this kind before, and, although not being used to the water, I naturally feared that element the first time I saw it, yet, nevertheless, could I have got over the nettings, I would have jumped over the side, but I could not; and besides, the crew used to watch us very closely who were not chained down to the decks, lest we should leap into the water; and I have seen some of these poor African prisoners most severely cut, for attempting to do so, and hourly whipped for not eating. This indeed was often the case with myself.

In a little time after, amongst the poor chained men, I found some of my own nation, which in a small degree gave ease to my mind. I inquired of these what was to be done with us? They gave me to understand, we were to be carried to these white people's country to work for them. I then was a little revived, and thought, if it were no worse than working, my situation was not so desperate; but still I feared I should be put to death, the white people looked and acted, as I thought, in so savage a manner; for I had never seen among any people such instances of brutal cruelty; and this not only shown towards us blacks, but also to some of the whites them-selves. One white man in particular I saw, when we were permitted to be on deck, flogged so unmercifully with a large rope near the foremast, that he died in conse-quence of it; and they tossed him over the side as they would have done a brute. This made me fear these people the more; and I expected nothing less than to be treated in the same manner. I could not help expressing my fears and apprehensions to some of my countrymen; I asked them if these people had no country, but lived in this hollow place (the ship)? They told me they did not, but came from a distant one. "Then," said I, "how comes it in all our country we never heard of them?" They told me because they lived so very far off. I then asked where were their women? had they any like themselves? I was told they had. "And why," said I, "do we not see them?" They answered, because they were left behind. I asked how the vessel could go? They told me they could not tell; but that there was cloth put upon the masts by the help of the ropes I saw, and then the vessel went on; and the white men had some spell or magic they put in the water when they liked, in order to stop the vessel. I was exceedingly amazed at this account, and really thought they were spirits. I therefore wished much to be from amongst them, for I expected they would sacrifice me; but my wishes were vain—for we were so quartered that it was impossi-ble for any of us to make our escape. While we stayed on the coast I was mostly on deck; and one day, to my great astonishment, I saw one of these vessels coming in with the sails up. As soon as the whites saw it, they gave a great shout, at which we were amazed; and the more so, as the vessel appeared larger by approaching nearer. At last, she came to an anchor in my sight, and when the anchor was let go, I and my countrymen who saw it, were lost in astonishment to observe the vessel stop— and were now convinced it was done by magic. Soon after this the other ship got her boats out, and they came on board of us, and the people of both ships seemed very glad to see each other. Several of the strangers also shook hands with us black people, and made motions with their hands, signifying I suppose, we were to go to their country, but we did not understand them.

At last, when the ship we were in, had got in all her cargo, they made ready with many fearful noises, and we were all put under deck, so that we could not see how they managed the vessel. But this disappointment was the least of my sorrow. The stench of the hold while we were on the coast was so intolerably loathsome, that it was dangerous to remain there for any time, and some of us had been permitted to stay on the deck for the fresh air; but now that the whole ship's cargo were confined together, it became absolutely pestilential. The closeness of the place, and the heat of the climate, added to the number in the ship, which was so crowded that each had scarcely room to turn himself, almost suffocated us. This produced copious perspirations, so that the air soon became unfit for respiration, from a variety of loathsome smells, and brought on a sickness among the slaves, of which many died—thus falling victims to the improvident avarice, as I may call it, of their purchasers. This wretched situation was again aggravated by the gaffing of the chains, now became insupportable, and the filth of the necessary tubs, into which the children often fell, and were almost suffocated. The shrieks of the women, and the groans of the dying, rendered the whole a scene of horror almost inconceivable. Happily perhaps, for myself, I was soon reduced so low here that it was thought necessary to keep me almost always on deck; and from my extreme youth I was not put in fetters. In this situation I expected every hour to share the fate of my companions, some of whom were almost daily brought upon deck at the point of death, which I began to hope would soon put an end to my miseries. Often did I think many of the inhabitants of the deep much more happy than myself. I envied them the freedom they enjoyed, and as often wished I could change my condition for theirs. Every circumstance I met with, served only to render my state more painful, and heightened my apprehensions, and my opinion of the cruelty of the whites.

One day they had taken a number of fishes; and when they had killed and satisfied themselves with as many as they thought fit, to our astonishment who were on deck, rather than give any of them to us to eat, as we expected, they tossed the remaining fish into the sea again, although we begged and prayed for some as well as we could, but in vain; and some of my countrymen, being pressed by hunger, took an opportunity, when they thought no one saw them, of trying to get a little privately; but they were discovered, and the attempt procured them some very severe floggings.

One day, when we had a smooth sea and moderate wind, two of my wearied countrymen who were chained together (I was near them at the time), preferring death to such a fife of misery, somehow made through the nettings and jumped into the sea; immediately, another quite dejected fellow, who, on account of his illness, was suffered to be out of irons, also followed their example; and I believe many more would very soon have done the same, if they had not been prevented by the ship's crew, who were instantly alarmed. Those of us that were the most active, were in a moment put down under the deck; and there was such a noise and confusion amongst the people of the ship as I never heard before, to stop her, and get the boat out to go after the slaves. However, two of the wretches were drowned, but they got the other, and afterwards flogged him unmercifully, for thus attempting to prefer death to slavery. In this manner we continued to undergo more hardships than I can now relate, hardships which are inseparable from this accursed trade. Many a time we were near suffocation from the want of fresh air, which we were often without for whole days together. This, and the stench of the necessary tubs, carried off many.

During our passage, I first saw flying fishes, which surprised me very much; they used frequently to fly across the ship, and many of them fell on the deck. I also now first saw the use of the quadrant; I had often with astonishment seen the mariners make observations with it, and I could not think what it meant. They at last took notice of my surprise; and one of them, willing to increase it, as well as to gratify my curiosity, made me one day look through it. The clouds appeared to me to be land, which disappeared as they passed along. This heightened my wonder; and I was now more persuaded than ever, that I was in another world, and that every thing about me was magic.

At last we came in sight of the island of Barbados, at which the whites on board gave a great shout, and made many signs of joy to us. We did not know what to think of this; but as the vessel drew nearer, we plainly saw the harbor, and other ships of different kinds and sizes, and we soon anchored amongst them, off Bridgetown. Many merchants and planters now came on board, though it was in the evening. They put us in separate parcels, and examined us attentively. They also made us jump, and pointed to the land, signifying we were to go there. We thought by this, we should be eaten by these ugly men, as they appeared to us; and, when soon after we were all put down under the deck again, there was much dread and trembling among us, and nothing but bitter cries to be heard all the night from these apprehensions, insomuch, that at last the white people got some old slaves from the land to pacify us. They told us we were not to be eaten, but to work, and were soon to go on land, where we should see many of our country people. This report eased us much. And sure enough, soon after we were landed, there came to us Africans of all languages.

We were conducted immediately to the merchant's yard, where we were all pent up together, like so many sheep in a fold, without regard to sex or age. As every object was new to me, everything I saw filled me with surprise. What struck me first, was, that the houses were built with bricks and stories, and in every other respect different from those I had seen in Africa; but I was still more astonished on seeing people on horseback. I did not know what this could mean; and, indeed, I thought these people were full of nothing but magical arts. While I was in this astonishment, one of my fellow prisoners spoke to a countryman of his, about the horses, who said they were the same kind they had in their country. I understood them, though they were from a distant part of Africa; and I thought it odd I had not seen any horses there; but afterwards, when I came to converse with different Africans, I found they had many horses amongst them, and much larger than those I then saw.

We were not many days in the merchant's custody, before we were sold after their usual manner, which is this: On a signal given (as the beat of a drum), the buyers rush at once into the yard where the slaves are confined, and make choice of that parcel they like best. The noise and clamor with which this is attended, and the eagerness visible in the countenances of the buyers, serve not a little to increase the apprehension of terrified Africans, who may well be supposed to consider them as the ministers of that destruction to which they think themselves devoted. In this manner, without scruple, are relations and friends separated, most of them never to see each other again.

I remember, in the vessel in which I was brought over, in the men's apartment, there were several brothers, who, in the sale, were sold in different lots; and it was very moving on this occasion, to see and hear their cries at parting. O, ye nominal Christians! might not an African ask you—Learned you this from your God, who says unto you, Do unto all men as you would men should do unto you? Is it not enough that we are torn from our country and friends, to toil for your luxury and lust of gain? Must every tender feeling be likewise sacrificed to your avarice? Are the dearest friends and relations, now rendered more dear by their separation from their kindred, still to be parted from each other, and thus prevented from cheering the gloom of slavery, with the small comfort of being together, and mingling their sufferings and sorrows? Why are parents to lose their children, brothers their sisters, or husbands their wives? Surely, this is a new refinement in cruelty, which, while it has no advantage to atone for it, thus aggravates distress, and adds fresh horrors even to the wretchedness of slavery.

Source: The Avalon Project, Yale Law School, New Haven, CT. Copyright © 1996 The Avalon Project.

6. The Fugitive Slave Act, 1793
U.S. CONGRESS

Enacted by Congress to ensure the right of slave owners to reclaim lost "property," the Fugitive Slave Act of 1793 opposed every ideal in the U.S. Constitution: free will, the right to happiness, and due process.

For the better security of the peace and friendship now entered into by the contracting parties, against all infractions of the same, by the citizens of either party, to the prejudice of the other, neither party shall proceed to the infliction of punishments on the citizens of the other, otherwise than by securing the offender, or offenders, by imprisonment, or any other competent means, till a fair and impartial trial can be had by judges or juries of both parties, as near as can be, to the laws, customs, and usage's of the contracting parties, and natural justice: the mode of such trials to be hereafter fixed by the wise men of the United States, in Congress assembled, with the assistance of such deputies of the Delaware nation, as may be appointed to act in concert with them in adjusting this matter to their mutual liking. And it is further agreed between the parties aforesaid, that neither shall entertain, or give countenance to, the enemies of the other, or protect, in their respective states, criminal fugitives, servants, or slaves, but the same to apprehend and secure, and deliver to the state or states, to which such enemies, criminals, servants, or slaves, respectively below [sic].

Source: Annals of Congress, 2nd Cong., 2nd sess., 1413 & 1414. Law Library of Congress.

7. Printed Letter, 1794
ANTHONY NEW

In this letter to President James Madison, U.S. government official Anthony New educates the chief executive about the slave trade from the West Indies. New advises Madison that this kind of activity does not coincide with progressive national policy of the United States.

PHILADELPHIA, February 27th, 1794.

DEAR SIR,

THE resolutions proposed by Mr. Madison, upon the principle of securing the advantages to the navigation and commerce of the United States, which of right belong to her, and which have been hitherto usurped by Britain, have been postponed to the first Monday in March, by which time, the public will may be tolerably ascertained, and foreign occurrences better known: A state like ours, whose prosperity depends upon the regular exportation of bulky commodities, to distant countries, must be deeply interested to secure the national means of doing it, independent of foreign revolutions and wars. The idea of a naval force (heretofore proposed) is yet progressing, attended with an additional tax; it is unfortunate that the benefits expected from the one, are by no means, so certain as the burthen upon the community, which will inevitably flow from the other, should it succeed.—Demands have been made from a French island, for aids of men, ammunition and provisions; but as these do not derive their origin from France itself, it is hardly probable that they will be persisted in, or productive of any degree of embarrassment.

The subject of the slave-trade, has been introduced by the Quakers, into Congress, and now stands upon the report of a committee, favorable to the object of the petitioners; this only extends to prevent a practice of some people, who have lately been employed, in transporting slaves from Africa to the West-India islands; and is not levelled in the remotest degree, against the rights of private property.

The Senate doors are to be opened at the next session; an event long desired, and from which the best predictions are deduced in favor of republicanism. It would be improper to conceal an apprehension, to meet which, the public mind ought to be prepared. It is not a secret, that prevarications have been resorted to by the British minister, to avoid a negociation for the fulfilment of the treaty, and that his court have almost peremptorily refused to surrender the western posts upon any event. Time only can develope the real motives of a conduct so unjust.

The late successes of France, against an unexampled combination of despots, will, I hope, clear away the clouds which had begun to darken our political horizon, and secure to us peace, the best pledge for liberty, safety and happiness. Should, however, these precious objects of society be unjustly assailed, contrary to my expectation, that the efforts in their defence may be commensurate to their importance, is the fervent hope of

Your most obedient-humble servant,

Anthony New

8. A Narrative of the Life and Adventures of Venture: A Native of Africa, but Resident above Sixty Years in the United States of America, Related by Himself, 1798

Kidnapped in Africa at the age of six, Venture Smith was sold to the steward on a slave ship and brought to Connecticut sometime in the early 1730s. At thirty-one years old, he purchased his freedom with money that he earned "cleaning muskrats and minks, raising potatoes and carrots and fishing."

Later, Smith himself became a slaveholder, owning at least three slaves. When he died at seventy-seven in 1805, he left a one-hundred-acre farm and three houses in East Haddam, Connecticut. This is his story, told in his own words.

I was born in Dukandarra, in Guinea, about the year 1729. My father's name was Saungm Furro, Prince of the tribe of Dukandara. My father had three wives. Polygamy was not uncommon in that country, especially among the rich, as every man was allowed to keep as many wives as he could maintain....

The first thing worthy of notice which I remember was, a contention between my father and mother, on account of my father marrying his third wife without the consent of his first and eldest, which was contrary to the custom generally observed among my countrymen. In consequence of this rupture, my mother left her husband and country, and traveled away with her three children to the eastward. I was then five years old....

After five days travel ... my mother was pleased to stop and seek a refuge for me. She left me at the house of a very rich farmer. I was then, as I should judge, not less than one hundred and forty miles from my native place, separated from all my relations and acquaintance....

My father sent a man and horse after me. After settling with my guardian for keeping me, he took me away and went for home. It was then about one year since my mother brought me here. Nothing remarkable occurred to us on our journey until we arrived safe home.

I found then that the difference between my parents had been made up previous to their sending for me. On my return, I was received both by my father and mother with great joy and affection, and was once more restored to my paternal dwelling in peace and happiness. I was then about six years old.

Not more than six weeks had passed after my return before a message was brought by an inhabitant of the place where I lived the preceding year to my father, that that place had been invaded by a numerous army from a nation not far distant, furnished with musical instrument, and all kinds of arms then in use; that they were instigated by some white nation who equipped and sent them to subdue and possess the country; that his nation had made no preparation for war, having been for a long time in profound peace; that they could not defend themselves against such a formidable train of invaders, and must therefore necessarily evacuate their lands to the fierce enemy, and fly to the protection of some chief; and that if he would permit them they would come under his rule and protection when they had to retreat from their own possessions. He was a kind and merciful prince, and therefore consented to these proposals....

He gave them every privilege and all the protection his government could afford. But they had not been there longer than four days before news came to them that the invaders had laid waste their country, and were coming speedily to destroy them in my father's territories. This affrighted them, and therefore they immediately pushed off to the southward, into the unknown countries there, and were never more heard of.

Two days after their retreat, the report turned out to be but too true. A detachment from the enemy came to my father and informed him, that the whole army was encamped not far out of his dominions, and would invade the territory and deprive his people of their liberties and rights, if he did not comply with the following terms. These were to pay them a large sum of money, three hundred fat cattle, and a great number of goats, sheep, asses, etc.

My father told the messenger he would comply rather than that his subjects should be deprived of their rights and privileges, which he was not then in circumstances to defend from so sudden an invasion. Upon turning out those articles, the enemy pledged their faith and honor that they would not attack him. On these he relied and therefore thought it unnecessary to be on his guard against the enemy. But their pledges of faith and honor proved no better than those of other unprincipled hostile nations; for a few days after a certain relation of the king came and informed him, that the enemy who sent terms of accommodation to him and received tribute to their satisfaction, yet meditated an attack upon his subjects by surprise and that probably they would commence their attack in less than one day, and concluded with advising him, as he was not prepared for war, to order a speedy retreat of his family and subjects. He complied with this advice.

The same night which was fixed upon to retreat, my father and his family set off about the break of day. The king and his two younger wives went in one company, and my mother and her children in another. We left our dwellings in succession, and my father's company went on first. We directed our course for a large shrub plain, some distance off, where we intended to conceal ourselves from the approaching enemy, until we could refresh ourselves a little. But we presently found that our retreat was not secure. For having struck up a little fire for the purpose of cooking victuals, the enemy who happened to be encamped a little distance off, had sent out a scouting party who discovered us by the smoke of the fire, just as we were extinguishing it, and about to eat. As soon as we had finished eating, my father discovered the party, and immediately began to discharge arrows at them. This was what I first saw, and it alarmed both me and the women, who being unable to make any resistance, immediately betook ourselves to the tall thick reeds not far off, and left the old king to fight alone. For some time I beheld him from the reeds defending himself with great courage and firmness, till at last he was obliged to surrender himself into their hands.

They then came to us in the reeds, and the very first salute I had from them was a violent blow on the back part of the head with the fore part of a gun, and at the same time a grasp round the neck. I then had a rope put about my neck, as had all the women in the thicket with me, and were immediately led to my father, who was likewise pinioned and haltered for leading. In this condition we were all led to the camp. The women and myself being pretty submissive, had tolerable treatment from the enemy, while my father was closely interrogated respecting his money which they knew he must have. But as he gave them no account of it, he was instantly cut and pounded on his body with great inhumanity, that he might be induced by the torture he suffered to make the discovery. All this availed not in the least to make him give up his money, but he despised all the tortures which they inflicted, until the continued exercise and increase of torment, obliged him to sink and expire. He thus died without informing his enemies where his money lay. I saw him while he was thus tortured to death. The shocking scene is to this day fresh in my mind, and I have often been overcome while thinking on it....

The army of the enemy was large, I should suppose consisting of about six thousand men. Their leader was called Baukurre. After destroying the old prince, they decamped and immediately marched toward the sea, lying to the west, taking with them myself and the women prisoners. In the march a scouting party was detached from the main army. To the leader of this party I was made waiter, having to carry his gun, etc. As we were a scouting we came across a herd of fat cattle, consisting of about thirty in number. These we set upon, and immediately wrested from their keepers, and afterwards converted them into food for the army. The enemy had remarkable success in destroying the country wherever they went. For as far as they had penetrated, they laid the habitations waste and captured the people. The distance they had now brought me was about four hundred miles. All the march I had very hard tasks imposed on me, which I must perform on pain of punishment. I was obliged to carry on my head a large flat stone used for grinding our corn, weighing as I should suppose, as much as twenty-five pounds; besides victuals, mat and cooking utensils. Though I was pretty large and stout at my age, yet these burdens were very grievous to me, being only six years and a half old.

We were then come to a place called Malagasco. When we entered the place we could not see the least appearance of either houses or inhabitants, but upon stricter search found, that instead of houses above ground they had dens in the sides of hillocks, contiguous to ponds and streams of water. In these we perceived they had all hid themselves, as I supposed they usually did on such occasions. In order to compel them to surrender, the enemy contrived to smoke them out with faggots. These they put to the entrance of the caves and set them on fire. While they were engaged in this business, to their great surprise some of them were desperately wounded with arrows which fell from above on them. This mystery they soon found out. They perceived that the enemy discharged these arrows through holes on top of the dens, directly into the air. Their weight brought them back, point downwards on their enemies heads, whilst they were smoking the inhabitants out. The points of their arrows were poisoned, but their enemy had an antidote for it, which they instantly applied to the wounded part. The smoke at last obliged the people to give themselves up. They came out of their caves, first putting the palms of their hands together, and immediately after extended their arms, crossed at their wrists, ready to be bound and pinioned....

The invaders then pinioned the prisoners of all ages and sexes indiscriminately, took their flocks and all their effects, and moved on their way towards the sea. On the march the prisoners were treated with clemency, on account of their being submissive and humble. Having come to the next tribe, the enemy laid siege and immediately took men, women, children, flocks, and all their valuable effects. They then went on to the next district which was contiguous to the sea, called in Africa, Anamaboo. The enemies provisions were then almost spent, as well as their strength. The inhabitants knowing what conduct they had pursued, and what were their present intentions, improve the favorable opportunity, attacked them, and took enemy, prisoners, flocks and all their effects. I was then taken a second time. All of us were then put into the castle [a European slave trading post], and kept for market. On a certain time I and other prisoners were put on board a canoe, under our master, and rowed away to a vessel belonging to Rhode Island, commanded by Captain Collingwood, and the mate Thomas Mumford. While we were going to the vessel, our master told us all to appear to the best possible advantage for sale. I was bought on board by one Robert Mumford, steward of said vessel, for four gallons of rum, and a piece of calico, and called Venture, on account of his having purchased me with his own private venture. Thus I came by my name. All the slaves that were bought for that vessel's cargo, were two hundred and sixty.

Source: New London: printed by C.Holt, at the BEE-Office, 1798. Reprinted—Middletown, Conn.: J. S. Stewart, printer, 1897.

9. The Confessions of Nat Turner, the Leader of the Late Insurrection in Southampton, Virginia, 1832

When lawyer Thomas R. Gray asked former slave Nat Turner why he led his revolt against slavery in an insurrection in Southampton, Virginia, Turner responded with the following:

Sir—You have asked me to give a history of the motives which induced me to undertake the late insurrection, as you call it—To do so I must go back to the days of my infancy.... In my childhood a circumstance occurred which made an indelible impression on my mind, and laid the groundwork of that enthusiasm, which has terminated so fatally to many, both white and black, and for which I am about to atone at the gallows.... Being at play with other children, when three or four years old, I was telling them something, which my mother overhearing, said it had happened before I was born ... others being called on were greatly astonished ... and caused them to say in my hearing, I surely would be a prophet....

For two years [I] prayed continually, whenever my duty would permit—and then again I had [a] ... revelation, which fully confirmed me in the impression that I was ordained for some great purpose, in the hands of the Almighty....

About this time [around 1825] I had a vision—and I saw white spirits and black spirits engaged in battle, and the sun was darkened—the thunder rolled in the Heavens, and blood flowed in streams ...

And on the 12th of May, 1828, I heard a loud noise in the heavens, and the Spirit instantly appeared to me and said the Serpent was loosened, and Christ had laid down the yoke he had borne for the sins of men, and that I should take it on and fight against the Serpent, for the time was fast approaching when the first should be last and the last should be first.

[Question] Do you not find yourself mistaken now?

[Answer] Was not Christ crucified? And by signs in the heavens that it would be made known to me when I should commence the great work—and until the first sign appeared, I should conceal if from the knowledge of men—And on the appearance of the sign (the eclipse of the sun last February), I should arise and prepare myself, and slay my enemies with their own weapons. And immediately on the sign appearing in the heavens, the seal was removed from my lips, and I communicated the great work laid out before me to do, to four in whom I had the greatest confidence (Henry, Hark, Nelson, and Sam)—It was intended by us to have begun the work of death on the 4th of July last—Many were the plans formed and rejected by us, and it affected my mind to such a degree, that I fell sick, and the time passed without our coming to any determination how to commence—Still forming new schemes and rejecting them, when the sign appeared again, which determined me not to wait longer.

Since the commencement of 1830, I had been living with Mr. Joseph Travis, who was to me a kind master, and placed the greatest confidence in me: in fact, I had no cause to complain of his treatment of me. On Saturday evening, the 20th of August, it was agreed between Henry, Hark, and myself, to prepare a dinner the next day for the men we expected, and then to concert a plan, as we had not yet determined on any. Hark, on the following morning, brought a pig, and Henry brandy, and being joined by Sam, Nelson, Will and Jack, they prepared in the woods a dinner, where, about three o'clock, I joined them ...

I saluted them on coming up, and asked Will how came he there, he answered, his life was worth no more than others, and his liberty as dear to him. I asked him if he thought to obtain it? He said he would, or lose his life. This was enough to put him in full confidence. Jack, I knew, was only a tool in the hands of Hark, it was quickly agreed we should commence at home (Mr. J. Travis') on that night, and until we had armed and equipped ourselves, and gathered sufficient force, neither age nor sex was to be spared (which was invariably adhered to). We remained at the feast, until about two hours in the night, when we went to the house and found Austin; they all went to the cider press and drank, except myself. On returning to the house Hark went to the door with an axe, for the purpose of breaking it open, as we knew we were strong enough to murder the family, if they were awakened by the noise; but reflecting that it might create an alarm in the neighborhood, we determined to enter the house secretly, and murder them whilst sleeping. Hark got a ladder and set it against the chimney, on which I ascended, and hoisting a window, entered and came down stairs, unbarred the door, and removed the guns from their places. It was then observed that I must spill the first blood. On which, armed with a hatchet, and accompanied by Will, I entered my master's chamber, it being dark, I could not give a death blow, the hatchet glanced from his head, he sprang from the bed and called his wife, it was his last word, Will laid him dead, with a blow of his axe, and Mrs. Travis shared the same fate, as she lay in bed. The murder of this family, five in number, was the work of a moment, not one of them awoke; there was a little infant sleeping in a cradle, that was forgotten, until we had left the house and gone some distance, when Henry and will returned and killed it; we got here, four guns that would shoot and several old muskets, with a pound or two of powder. We remained some time at the barn, where we paraded; I formed them in a line as soldiers, and ... marched them off to Mr. Salthul Francis', about six hundred yards distant. Sam and Will went to the door and knocked. Mr. Francis asked who was there, Sam replied it was him, and he had a letter for him, on which he got up and came to the door; they immediately seized him, and dragging him out a little from the door, he was dispatched by repeated blows on the head; there was no other white person in the family. We started from there for Mrs. Reese's, maintaining the most perfect silence on our march, where finding the door unlocked, we entered, and murdered Mrs. Reese in her bed, while sleeping; her son awoke, but it was only to sleep the sleep of death, he had only time to say who is that, and he was no more. From Mrs. Reese's we went to Mrs. Turner's, a mile distant, which we reached about sunrise, on Monday morning. Henry, Austin, and Sam, went to the still, where, finding Mr. Peebles, Austin shot him, and the rest of us went to the house; as we approached, the family discovered us, and shut the door. Vain hope! Will, with one stroke of his axe opened it, and we entered and found Mrs. Turner and Mrs. Newsome in the middle of a room, almost frightened to death. Will immediately killed Mrs. Turner, with one blow of his axe. I took Mrs. Newsome by the hand, and with the sword I had when I was apprehended, I struck her several blows over the head, but not being able to kill her, as the sword was dull. Will turning around and discovering it, dispatched her also. A general destruction of property and search for money and ammunition, always succeeded the murders. By this time my company amounted to fifteen, and nine men mounted, who started for Mrs. Whitehead's.... As we approached the house we discovered Mr. Richard Whitehead standing in the cotton patch, near the lane fence; we called him over into the lane, and Will, the executioner, was near at hand, with his fatal axe, to send him to an untimely grave.... As I came around to the door I saw Will pulling Mrs. Whitehead out of the house, and at the step he nearly severed her head from her body, with his broad axe. Miss Margaret, when I discovered her, had concealed herself in the corner ... on my approach she fled, but was soon overtaken, and after repeated blows with a sword, I killed her by a blow on the head, with a fence rail....

...'Twas my object to carry terror and devastation wherever we went.... I sometimes got in sight in time to see the work of death completed, viewed the mangled bodies as they lay, in silent satisfaction, and immediately started in quest of other victims—Having murdered Mrs. Waller and ten children, we started for

Mr. William Williams'—having killed him and two little boys that were there; while engaged in this, Mrs. Williams fled and got some distance from the house, but she was pursued, overtaken, and compelled to get up behind one of the company, who brought her back, and after showing her the mangled body of her lifeless husband, she was told to get down an lay by his side, where she was shot dead....

Our number amounted now to fifty or sixty, all mounted and armed with guns, axes, swords, and clubs.... We were met by a party of white men, who had pursued our blood- stained track.... The white men, eighteen in number, approached us in about one hundred yards, when one of them fired.... I then ordered my men to fire and rush them; the few remaining stood their ground until we approached within fifty yards, when they fired and retreated.... As I saw them re- loading their guns, and more coming up than I saw at first, and several of my bravest men being wounded, the other became panick struck and squandered over the field; the white men pursued and fired on us several times....

All deserted me but two, (Jacob and Nat,) we concealed ourselves in the woods until near night, when I sent them in search of Henry, Sam, Nelson, and Hark, and directed them to rally all they could, at the place where had had our dinner the Sunday before, where they would find me, and I accordingly returned there as soon as it was dark and remained until Wednesday evening, when discovering white men riding around the place as though they were looking for someone, and none of my men joining me, I concluded Jacob and Nat had been taken, and compelled to betray me. On this I gave up all hope for the present; and on Thursday night after having supplied myself with provisions from Mr. Travis' I scratched a hope under a pile of fence rails in a field, where I concealed myself for six weeks, never leaving my hiding place but for a few minutes in the dead of night to get water which was very near.... I know not how long I might have led this life, if accident had not betrayed me, a dog in the neighborhood passing by my hiding place one night while I was out, was attracted by some meat I had in my cave, and crawled in and stole it, and was coming out just as I returned. A few nights after, two Negroes having started to go hunting with the same dog, passed that way, the dog came again to the place, and having just gone out to walk about, discovered me and barked, on which thinking myself discovered, I spoke to them to beg concealment.

On making myself known they fled from me. Knowing when they would betray me, I immediately left my hiding place, and was pursued almost incessantly until I was taken a fortnight afterwards by Mr. Benjamin Phipps, in a little hole I had dug out with my sword, for the purpose of concealment, under the top of a fallen tree.

Source: Richmond: Thomas R. Gray, 1832. Library of Congress Rare Book and Special Collections Division, African American Odyssey Collection.

10. John Quincy Adams diary 41, 5 December 1836–4 January 1837, 29 July 1840–31 December 1841

A Spanish schooner called the *Amistad*, became the center of a major court case in the United States during the period of slavery in the Western hemisphere. The case was argued before United States Supreme Court in 1841 after slaves aboard the ship rebelled in 1839.

The rebellion broke out when the schooner, traveling along the coast of Cuba, was taken over by a group of captives who had earlier been kidnapped in Africa and sold into slavery. The Africans were later apprehended on the vessel near Long Island, New York, by the United States Navy and brought into the port of New Haven where the slaves were recaptured and jailed. The ensuing widely publicized court cases in the United States helped the abolitionist movement.

Former United States (sixth) President John Quincy Adams defended in federal court this group of slaves who had revolted aboard the Spanish schooner. In 1840, the federal trial court found that the initial transport of the Africans across the Atlantic (which did not involve the *Amistad*) had been illegal and that the Africans were not legally slaves but free. The U.S. Supreme Court affirmed this finding on March 9, 1841, and the Africans traveled home in 1842.

In the following excerpt, Adams describes his visit to the *Amistad* Africans in jail, which occurred after he met with Roger Sherman Baldwin to discuss trial tactics. This meeting took place with prisoner Cinque and the others.

At 1/2 past 5. A.M. I took the cars from Hartford to New Haven. My tavern bill at Hartford had been paid. The night had been frosty and the morning was bitter cold. But the sun rose bright and the whole day was fair. In the cars two passengers introduced themselves to me. Mr. Hopkins of Buffalo New York, and Mr. Curtis, the sheriff of the County of New Haven—I talked again too much. At 2 A.M. we arrived at New Haven, and I took lodgings at the Tontine Hotel—Breakfast—immediately after.

Mr. Roger Sherman Baldwin called on me, and invited me to his office in his house, whither I went with him. He read to me sundry papers, and gave me one containing an argument drawn up by him—all relating to the Negro prisoners taken in the Amistad. We had two hours of conversation upon the whole subject in which he exposed to me his views of the case. The points which had been taken beyond the District and Circuit Courts, and the motion to dismiss the appeal which he supposes the proper course to be taken before the Superior Court. He read to me numerous authorities on the several points which he proposes to urge at the trial, and said he hoped the Supreme Court would take up the case in the final or second week of the session.—I visited the prisoners with Mr. Baldwin, Rev. Wilcox, the Marshal of the District, Mr. Pendleton, his deputy, and Keeper of the house when they are confined together. The three girls are in a separate house, and I did not see them. They are, all but one, young men, under 30, and of small stature—none over 5 feet 6. Negro face, fleace, and form, but varying in shades of color from ebon black to dingy Brown—one or two of them are almost mulatto bright. Cinque and Grabow, the two chief conspirators, have very remarkable countenances. Three of them read to us part of a chapter in the English New Testament—very indifferently—one boy writes a tolerable hand—Mr. Ludlow teaches them; but huddled together as they are, and having no other person to talk with but themselves their learning must be very slow.

I dined at Mr. Baldwin's with 8 or 10 others—Mrs. Baldwin is a daughter of old Roger Sherman—Her mother and brother, Mr. Baldwin's father, Chauncey Goodrich and Mr. Ludlow were of the company. President Day, Professor Kingsley and Professor Silliman came in after dinner. I walked with Professor Silliman to his house to tea—his wife, son, 3 daughters—one married. Col. John Trumbull this day from New York—born in 1756—very unwell—said he was done up—worn out.

With Mr. Silliman I visited Mrs. Gerry—her 4 daughters—Went with Mr. White to Mr. Ludlow's Church. Delivered the lecture on Society and civilization. Full house. Attention—Applause.

Home to my lodgings at 9 P.M.

Source: John Quincy Adams diary 41, November 17, 1840.

December 12, 1840:

Summary: Adams worries over what tone he should strike in making his argument before the Supreme Court.

Rain great part of the day which confined me to the house. Mr. Force and Mr. Laurence came as a committee from the National Institution for the Promotion of Science, and stated that they proposed to hold a meeting of the society on the first Monday, the 4th of January next, when a discourse is to be delivered by Mr. Poinsett. The Society are desirous of obtaining the use of the Hall of the House of Representatives that evening for that purpose and wished me to offer the resolution that it be granted, which I promised to do. They said the Institution was likely to flourish, and that great interest was taken in it by the people here. Mr. Force left with me a memorandum of two books which I borrowed of him more than three years since and which I have not yet returned.

This day was fully occupied and quickly passed away. I made out my list of the persons to whom the documents of which extra copies are printed by order of the House are to be sent. My rule of distribution is: 1. One copy to each of the Editors of the newspapers published at Plymouth, the Old Colony Memorial, Hingham Patriot and Quincy Patriot, The Boston Courier and Evening Gazette. 2. To my son and a few other fraternal friends. 3. To the Senators in the Legislature of Massachusetts from the Counties of Plymouth and Norfolk. 4. To one representative from each of the 24 towns in the 12th Congressional District of Massachusetts. My portion of the extra documents is seldom sufficient for the whole of this supply, often for not half of them. My son, the Newspaper Editors and the County Senators are first served. The others are furnished according to the numbers of my allowance. I keep lists of the extra documents printed by order of the House of each session and of the names of the persons to whom I send them. I made out my lists for the present session; and dispatched by the mail 17 copies of the President's annual Message. But the lists are imperfect till the meeting of the Massachusetts Legislature shall ascertain the senators for the counties of Plymouth and Norfolk, and the Representatives from the 24 towns of the 12 Congregational districts.

I thought it necessary to look into this case of the Amistad captives to prepare for the argument before the Supreme Court in January; of which I dare scarcely to think. I read specially the Article in The American and Foreign Anti-Slavery Reporter of 1 October 1840, entitled the Amistad case, p. 48–51, with deep anguish of heart and a painful search of means to define and expose the abominable conspiracy of Executive and Judicial of this government against the lives of these wretched men—How shall the facts be brought out? How shall it be possible to comment upon them with becoming temper—with calmness—with moderation—with firmness—with address to avoid being silenced, and to escape the imminent danger of giving the adversary the advantage by overheated zeal. Of all the dangers before me, that of losing my self possession is the most formidable—I am yet unable to prepare the outline of the argument which I must be ready to offer the second week in January. Let me not forget my duty.

AMISTAD TRIAL BEGINS, FEBRUARY 23, 1841

With increasing agitation of mind, now little short of agony I rode in a hack to the Capitol, taking with me in confused order a number of books which I may have occasion to use. The very skeleton of my argument is not yet put together. When the Court met, Judge Wayne and Judge Story read in succession two decisions of the Court, and Mr. Baldwin occupied the remainder of the day, four hours, in closing his argument in behalf of the Amistad captives, and in the support of the discussion of the District and Circuit Courts. The point upon which he dwelt with most emphatic earnestness was the motion to dismiss the appeal of the United States, as the contest of their right to appear as parties in the cause they having no interest therein—His reasoning therein was powerful, and perhaps conclusive—But I am apprehensive there are precedents, and an Executive influence operating upon the courts which will turn the balance against us on that point.

Signed: John Quincy Adams, Former President of the United States

In commenting upon the insurrection of the blacks, Mr. Baldwin firmly maintained their right of self-emancipation, but spoke in cautious terms to avoid exciting Southern passions and prejudices, which it is our policy, as much as possible, to assuage and pacify. When he came to the point of questioning the validity of the Governor General's ladino passports he left a good deal still to be said. He closed at half past 3, and left the day open for me tomorrow. I went into the Congress Library, and took out for us the 37th volume of Niles's register containing the speech of James Madison, in the Virginia Convention on the double condition of slaves in that state as Persons and as property—I did not wait to attend the meeting of the House after the recess; but meeting as I was walking home Mr. Brockway, I enquired of him what had been done in the House. [H]e told me, that they had agreed to take the civil and diplomatic appropriation Bill out of the Committee of the whole on the State of the Union at 5 o'clock this afternoon. Mr. Trisby brought me this morning the new Edition in two large thick 8va Volumes of Noah Webster's Dictionary. The applicants for official appointments are gathering into a multitude—Mr. Whitcomb, heretofore a clerk in the general land office, is here and came to solicit my influence for himself and for his son to obtain an appointment as a cadet at West Point. Daniel Parkman is also here for an appointment to the marshal.

Source: John Quincy Adams diary 41, February 1841.

FORMER PRESIDENT CONCLUDES AMISTAD CASE

John Leavy was to have gone with the morning cars to Baltimore, but was by a few minutes belated, and went in the afternoon—He left in deposit with me 160 dollars 80 cents in gold for which I gave him a receipt and a promise to pay that sum to his order as demanded—I went and delivered at the orphans court the inventory and appraisement made by Jeremiah Pendergast and Thomas Dumphy of the goods and effects of Jeremy Leavy on Saturday Evening—Thence I went to the

Supreme Court and concluded my argument in the case of the Amistad captives—I spoke about four hours and then closed somewhat abruptly; leaving almost entirely untouched the review of the case of the Antelope, which I had intended and for which I was prepared—It would have required at least an hour, and I had barely reached it when the usual time of the Court's adjournment came.—I was unwilling to encroach upon the time of the Court for half of a third day, so that I cramped into a very brief summary what I had to say upon that case, and finished with a very short personal address to the Court. They immediately adjourned, and went into the hall of the House of Representatives.

Source: John Quincy Adams diary 41, March 1, 1841.

AMISTAD VERDICT RETURNED, MARCH 1, 1841

Judge Story delivered the opinions and decree of the Court in the case of the United States appellants vs. the Schooner Amistad. It affirms the decision of the District and Circuit Courts, excepting with regard to the Negroes—It reverses the decision below placing them at the disposal of the President of the United States to be sent to Africa; declares them to be free and directs the Circuit Court to order them to be discharged from the custody of the Marshal—Judge Baldwin expressed some dissent from the opinion which I did not hear nor did I learn what it was—I went to the chamber of the Committee of Manufacturers and wrote to Mr. Roger S. Baldwin at New Haven and to Mr. Lewis Tappan of New York to inform them of the decision of the Court, and gave the letters to Mr. McCormick, the Postmaster of the House.—The Court had adjourned.

—I went into the Senate chamber and heard a fiery debate ... Henry Clay closed a short and intemperate speech by declaring some personalities uttered against him by William A. King of Alabama false—untrue—and cowardly. The Senate shortly after adjourned ... and there was a rumour that King and Clay were both arrested by warrants from a magistrate. I went to the Office of the Clerk of the Supreme Court and wrote a motion for a mandate to the Marshall of the District of Connecticut to discharge forthwith the Amistad captives from custody—I called on Mr. Crittenden the new Attorney General to ask his consent to this motion. He said he saw no objection to it.

Source: Page 160, 185 [electronic edition]. The Diaries of John Quincy Adams: A Digital Collection. Boston: Massachusetts Historical Society, 2004. http://www.masshist.org/jqadiaries.

11. Illinois State Legislator Abraham Lincoln Opposes Slavery, March 3, 1837

At the age of 28, as an Illinois state legislator, Abraham Lincoln had already staked out what would become his signature stance on the slavery question: though he personally despised the institution, he also believed that the people of each state should determine whether the institution should exist in their state; Congress ought not interfere with the state's decision. Thus, when the Illinois legislature passed a resolution condemning slavery and arguing for its abolition, Lincoln argued that such an action merely served to whip up fervor in favor of slavery. Leaving the issue alone would allow it to die off, in time. Though Lincoln would be outvoted seventy-seven to six on this matter, the consistency of his position on slavery is quite remarkable.

Resolutions upon the subject of domestic slavery having passed both branches of the General Assembly at its present session, the undersigned hereby protest against the passage of the same.

They believe that the institution of slavery is founded on both injustice and bad policy; but that the promulgation of abolition doctrines tends rather to increase than to abate its evils.

They believe that the Congress of the United States has the power, under the constitution, to abolish slavery in the District of Columbia; but that that power ought not to be exercised unless at the request of the people of said District.

The difference between these opinions and those contained in the said resolutions, is their reason for entering this protest.

Dan Stone

Abraham Lincoln

March 3, 1837

Representatives from the county of Sangamon

Source: TeachingAmericanHistory.org © 2006 Ashbrook Center for Public Affairs.

12. The Church and Prejudice, November 4, 1841
FREDERICK DOUGLASS

Abolitionist Frederick Douglass delivered this speech before the Plymouth County Anti-Slavery Society, November 4, 1841, less than three months after he had attended the Anti-Slavery Convention on Nantucket Island, Massachusetts, at which he agreed to lecture for the Massachusetts Society. It is one of his first recorded anti-slavery speeches.

The Church and Prejudice
Fighting Rebels With Only One Hand
What the Black Man Wants

At the South I was a member of the Methodist Church. When I came north, I thought one Sunday I would attend communion, at one of the churches of my denomination, in the town I was staying. The white people gathered round the altar, the blacks clustered by the door. After the good minister had served out the bread and wine to one portion of those near him, he said, "These may withdraw, and others come forward;" thus he proceeded till all the white members had been served. Then he took a long breath, and looking out towards the door, exclaimed, "Come up, colored friends, come up! for you know God is no respecter of persons!" I haven't been there to see the sacraments taken since.

At New Bedford, where I live, there was a great revival of religion not long ago—many were converted and "received" as they said, "into the kingdom of heaven." But it seems, the kingdom of heaven is like a net; at least so it was according to the practice of these pious Christians; and when the net was drawn ashore, they had to set down and cull out the fish. Well, it happened now that some of the fish had rather black scales; so these were sorted out and packed by themselves. But among those who experienced religion at this time was a colored girl; she was baptized in the same water as the rest; so she thought she might sit at the Lord's table and partake of the same sacramental elements with the others. The deacon handed round the cup, and when he came to the black girl, he could not pass her, for there was the minister looking right at him, and as he was a kind of abolitionist, the deacon was rather afraid of giving him offense; so he handed the girl the cup, and she tasted. Now it so happened that next to her sat a young lady who had been converted at the same time, baptized in the same water, and put her trust in the same blessed Saviour; yet when the cup containing the precious blood which had been shed for all, came to her, she rose in disdain, and walked out of the church. Such was the religion she had experienced!

Another young lady fell into a trance. When she awoke, she declared she had been to heaven. Her friends were all anxious to know what and whom she had seen there; so she told the whole story. But there was one good old lady whose curiosity went beyond that of all the others—and she inquired of the girl that had the vision, if she saw any black folks in heaven? After some hesitation, the reply was, "Oh! I didn't go into the kitchen!"

Thus you see, my hearers, this prejudice goes even into the church of God. And there are those who carry it so far that it is disagreeable to them even to think of going to heaven, if colored people are going there too. And whence comes it? The grand cause is slavery; but there are others less prominent; one of them is the way in which children in this part of the country are instructed to regard the blacks.

"Yes!" exclaimed an old gentleman, interrupting him—"when they behave wrong, they are told, 'black man come catch you.'"

Yet people in general will say they like colored men as well as any other, but in their proper place! They assign us that place; they don't let us do it for ourselves, nor will they allow us a voice in the decision. They will not allow that we have a head to think, and a heart to feel, and a soul to aspire. They treat us not as men, but as dogs—they cry "Stu-boy!" and expect us to run and do their bidding. That's the way we are liked. You degrade us, and then ask why we are degraded—you shut our mouths, and then ask why we don't speak—you close our colleges and seminaries against us, and then ask why we don't know more.

But all this prejudice sinks into insignificance in my mind, when compared with the enormous iniquity of the system which is its cause—the system that sold my four sisters and my brothers into bondage—and which calls in its priests to defend it even from the Bible! The slaveholding ministers preach up the divine right of the slaveholders to property in their fellow- men. The southern preachers say to the poor slave, "Oh! if you wish to be happy in time, happy in eternity, you must be obedient to your masters; their interest is yours. God made one portion of men to do the working, and another to do the thinking; how good God is! Now, you have no trouble or anxiety; but ah! you can't imagine how perplexing it is to your masters and mistresses to have so much thinking to do in your behalf! You cannot appreciate your blessings; you know not how happy a thing it is for you, that you were born of that portion of the human family which has the working, instead of the thinking to do! Oh! how grateful and obedient you ought to be to your masters! How beautiful are the arrangements of Providence! Look at your hard, horny hands—see how nicely they are adapted to the labor you have to perform! Look at our delicate fingers, so exactly fitted for our station, and see how manifest it is that God designed us to be His thinkers, and you the workers—Oh! the wisdom of God!"—I used to attend a Methodist church, in which my master was a class leader; he would talk most sanctimoniously about the dear Redeemer, who was sent "to preach deliverance to the captives, and set at liberty them that are bruised"—he could pray at morning, pray at noon, and pray at night; yet he could lash up my poor cousin by his two thumbs, and inflict stripes and blows upon his bare back, till the blood streamed to the ground! all the time quoting scripture, for his authority, and appealing to that passage of the Holy Bible which says, "He that knoweth his master's will, and doeth it not, shall be beaten with many stripes!" Such was the amount of this good Methodist's piety.

Source: Speech delivered at the Plymouth County Anti-Slavery Society, November 4, 1841. Foner, Philip S., ed., *The Life and Writings of Frederick Douglass. Volume 1*, pgs. 102–105. New York: International Publishers, 1950. Permission of International Publishers/New York.

13. Narrative of the Life of Frederick Douglass, An American Slave, Written by Himself, 1845

From inauspicious beginnings, Frederick Douglass became the most well-known advocate of equal rights in the nineteenth century. Born into slavery on Maryland's eastern shore in 1818, he was the son of a slave woman and an unknown white man. While working as a ship caulker, he taught himself to read. He escaped slavery, fled to Europe, and became an abolitionist, orator, and publisher of an influential anti-slavery newspaper, *The North Star*. Years later, he wrote the following in a diary.

A mere look, word, or motion,—a mistake, accident, or want of power,—are all matters for which a slave may be whipped at any time. Does a slave look dissatisfied? It is said, he has the devil in him, and it must be whipped out. Does he speak loudly when spoken to by his master? Then he is getting high-minded, and should be taken down a button- hole lower. Does he forget to pull off his hat at the approach of a white person? Then he is wanting in reverence, and should be whipped for it. Does he ever venture to vindicate his conduct, when censured for it? Then he is guilty of impudence,—one of the greatest crimes of which a slave can be guilty. Does he ever venture to suggest a different mode of doing things from that pointed out by his master? He is indeed presumptuous, and getting above himself....

Source: Boston: Published at the Anti-Slavery Office, 1845. Project Gutenberg. Text retrieved from: http://www.gutenberg.org/catalog/world/readfile?fk_files=216491.

14. Farewell to the British People: An Address Delivered in London, England, March 30, 1847
FREDERICK DOUGLASS

Former slave Frederick Douglass traveled widely throughout the world in his effort to ensure that slavery in the United States was abolished. After a tour of Europe, Douglass gave this farewell speech before embarking on board the Cambria. Upon his return to America, it was delivered at the valedictory soiree given to him at the London Tavern, on March 30, 1847.

I do not go back to America to sit still, remain quiet, and enjoy ease and comfort.... I glory in the conflict, that I may hereafter exult in the victory. I know that victory is certain. I go, turning my back upon the ease, comfort, and respectability which I might maintain even here ... Still, I will go back, for the sake of my brethren. I go to suffer with them; to toil with them; to endure insult with them; to undergo outrage with them; to lift up my voice in their behalf; to speak and write in their vindication; and struggle in their ranks for the emancipation which shall yet be achieved.

Source: Foner, Philip S., ed., *The Life and Writings of Frederick Douglass. Volume 1*, pgs. 102–105. New York: International Publishers, 1950. Permission of International Publishers/New York.

15. Narrative of the life and adventures of Henry Bibb: an American slave, written by himself, 1849

Henry Walton Bibb was born in Kentucky to a slave mother and Kentucky state senator, James Bibb. Henry Bibb's master hired young Henry out to several neighboring plantations, where he often was treated inhumanely. As an adult, Bibb was traded frequently, and he lived in at least seven southern states. After trying to escape several times, he finally reached Canada in 1837, only to return shortly thereafter to see his wife. His many later attempts to escape from slavery with his family were unsuccessful, and they were permanently separated in 1840. Bibb's final experience in slavery was with a humane Cherokee owner in the "Indian Territory" of Kansas or Oklahoma. On the night of his owner's death, Bibb made a final, successful escape through Missouri and Ohio. He eventually settled in Detroit in 1841 and became an active abolitionist and lecturer. Bibb and his second wife, abolitionist Mary Miles, were married in 1848 and fled to Canada following the passing of the Fugitive Slave Act of 1850. Known as one of the most effective antislavery lecturers of his time, Bibb continued to be a leader in the black community in Canada.

Henry W. Bibb's autobiography, *Narrative of the Life and Adventures of Henry Bibb, An American Slave* (1849), elaborates on his life story, which he presented during his antislavery lectures. The text itself describes Bibb's childhood as a slave and his many experiences in slavery. It ends shortly after he secured his freedom.

CHAPTER 1

Henry Bibb writes an exquisitely eloquent personal memoir.

Sketch of my Parentage.—Early separation from my Mother.—Hard Fare.—First Experiments at running away.—Earnest longing for Freedom.—Abhorrent nature of Slavery.

I was born May 1815, of a slave mother, in Shelby County, Kentucky, and was claimed as the property of David White Esq. He came into possession of my mother long before I was born. I was brought up in the Counties of Shelby, Henry, Oldham, and Trimble. Or, more correctly speaking, in the above counties, I may safely say, I was flogged up; for where I should have received moral, mental, and religious instruction, I received stripes without number, the object of which was to degrade and keep me in subordination. I can truly say, that I drank deeply of the bitter cup of suffering and woe. I have been dragged down to the lowest depths of human degradation and wretchedness, by Slaveholders.

My mother was known by the name of Milldred Jackson. She is the mother of seven slaves only, all being sons, of whom I am the eldest. She was also so fortunate or unfortunate, as to have some of what is called the slaveholding blood flowing in her veins. I know not how much; but not enough to prevent her children though fathered by slaveholders, from being bought and sold in the slave markets of the South. It is almost impossible for slaves to give a correct account of their male parentage. All that I know about it is, that my mother informed me that my fathers name was James Bibb. He was doubtless one of the present Bibb family of Kentucky; but I have no personal knowledge of him at all, for he died before my recollection.

The first time I was separated from my mother, I was young and small. I knew nothing of my condition then as a slave. I was living with Mr. White whose wife died and left him a widower with one little girl, who was said to be the legitimate owner of my mother, and all her children. This girl was also my playmate when we were children.

I was taken away from my mother, and hired out to labor for various persons, eight or ten years in succession; and all my wages were expended for the education of Harriet White, my playmate. It was then my sorrows and sufferings commenced. It was then I first commenced seeing and feeling that I was a wretched slave, compelled to work under the lash without wages, and often without clothes enough to hide my nakedness. I have often worked without half enough to eat, both late and early, by day and by night. I have often laid my wearied limbs down at night to rest upon a dirt floor, or a bench, without any covering at all, because I had no where else to rest my wearied body, after having worked hard all the day. I have also been compelled in early life, to go at the bidding of a tyrant, through all kinds of weather, hot or cold, wet or dry, and without shoes frequently, until the month of December, with my bare feet on the cold frosty ground, cracked open and bleeding as I walked. Reader, believe me when I say, that no tongue, nor pen ever has or can express the horrors of American Slavery. Consequently I despair in finding language to express adequately the deep feeling of my soul, as I contemplate the past history of my life. But although I have suffered much from the lash, and for want of food and raiment; I confess that it was no disadvantage to be passed through the hands of so many families, as the only source of information that I had to enlighten my mind, consisted in what I could see and hear from others. Slaves were not allowed books, pen, ink, nor paper, to improve their minds. But it seems to me now, that I was particularly observing, and apt to retain what came under my observation. But more especially, all that I heard about liberty and freedom to the slaves,

I never forgot. Among other good trades I learned the art of running away to perfection. I made a regular business of it, and never gave it up, until I had broken the bands of slavery, and landed myself safely in Canada, where I was regarded as a man, and not as a thing.

The first time in my life that I ran away, was for ill treatment, in 1825. I was living with a Mr. Vires, in the village of Newcastle. His wife was a very cross woman. She was every day flogging me, boxing, pulling my ears, and scolding, so that I dreaded to enter the room where she was. This first started me to running away from them. I was often gone several days before I was caught. They would abuse me for going off, but it did no good. The next time they flogged me, I was off again; but after awhile they got sick of their bargain, and returned me back into the hands of my owners. By this time Mr. White had married his second wife. She was what I call a tyrant. I lived with her several months, but she kept me almost half of my time in the woods, running from under the bloody lash. While I was at home she kept me all the time rubbing furniture, washing, scrubbing the floors; and when I was not doing this, she would often seat herself in a large rocking chair, with two pillows about her, and would make me rock her, and keep off the flies. She was too lazy to scratch her own head, and would often make me scratch and comb it for her. She would at other times lie on her bed, in warm weather, and make me fan her while she slept, scratch and rub her feet; but after awhile she got sick of me, and preferred a maiden servant to do such business. I was then hired out again; but by this time I had become much better skilled in running away, and would make calculation to avoid detection, by taking with me a bridle. If any body should see me in the woods, as they have, and asked "what are you doing here sir? you are a runaway?"—I said, "no, sir, I am looking for our old mare;" at other times, "looking for our cows." For such excuses I was let pass. In fact, the only weapon of self defence that I could use successfully, was that of deception. It is useless for a poor helpless slave, to resist a white man in a slaveholding State. Public opinion and the law is against him; and resistance in many cases is death to the slave, while the law declares, that he shall submit or die. The circumstances in which I was then placed, gave me a longing desire to be free. It kindled a fire of liberty within my breast which has never yet been quenched. This seemed to be a part of my nature; it was first revealed to me by the inevitable laws of nature's God. I could see that the All-wise Creator, had made man a free, moral, intelligent and accountable being; capable of knowing good and evil. And I believed then, as I believe now, that every man has a right to wages for his labor; a right to his own wife and children; a right to liberty and the pursuit of happiness; and a right to worship God according to the dictates of his own conscience. But here, in the light of these truths, I was a slave, a prisoner for life; I could possess nothing, nor acquire anything but what must belong to my keeper. No one can imagine my feelings in my reflecting moments, but he who has himself been a slave. Oh! I have often wept over my condition, while sauntering through the forest, to escape cruel punishment.

"No arm to protect me from tyrants aggression;
No parents to cheer me when laden with grief.
Man may picture the bounds of the rocks and the rivers,
The hills and the valleys, the lakes and the ocean,
But the horrors of slavery, he never can trace."

The term slave to this day sounds with terror to my soul,—a word too obnoxious to speak—a system too intolerable to be endured. I know this from long and sad experience. I now feel as if I had just been aroused from sleep, and looking back with quickened perception at the state of torment from whence I fled. I was there held and claimed as a slave; as such I was subjected to the will and power of my keeper, in all respects whatsoever. That the slave is a human being, no one can deny. It is his lot to be exposed in common with other men, to the calamities of sickness, death, and the misfortunes incident to life. But unlike other men, he is denied the consolation of struggling against external difficulties, such as destroy the life, liberty, and happiness of himself and family. A slave may be bought and sold in the market like an ox. He is liable to be sold off to a distant land from his family. He is bound in chains hand and foot; and his sufferings are aggravated a hundred fold, by the terrible thought, that he is not allowed to struggle against misfortune, corporeal punishment, insults and outrages committed upon himself and family; and he is not allowed to help himself, to resist or escape the blow, which he sees impending over him.

This idea of utter helplessness, in perpetual bondage, is the more distressing, as there is no period even with the remotest generation when it shall terminate.

Source: With an introduction by Lucius C. Matlack. New York: Henry Bibb, 1849. Library of Congress Rare Book and Special Collections Division, African American Odyssey Collection.

16. Excerpted from "Uncle Tom's Story of His Life," an Autobiography of the Rev. Josiah Henson (Mrs. Harriet Beecher Stowe's "Uncle Tom"), from 1789 to 1876

Josiah Henson spent thirty years on a plantation in Montgomery County, Maryland, before he escaped slavery and became a Methodist preacher, abolitionist, lecturer, and founder of a cooperative colony of former slaves in Canada. His memoirs were published in 1849 and are said to have been the basis for the novel *Uncle Tom's Cabin* by Harriet Beecher Stowe. The following is an excerpt:

My earliest employments were, to carry buckets of water to the men at work, and to hold a horse-plough, used for weeding between the rows of corn. As I grew older and taller, I was entrusted with the care of master's saddle-horse. Then a hoe was put into my hands, and I was soon required to do the day's work of a man; and it was not long before I could do it, at least as well as my associates in misery.

A description of the everyday life of a slave on a southern plantation illustrates the character and habits of the slave and the slaveholder, created and perpetuated by their relative position. The principal food of those upon my master's plantation consisted of corn-meal and salt herrings; to which was added in summer a little buttermilk, and the few vegetables which each might raise for himself and his family, on the little piece of ground which was assigned to him for the purpose, called a truck- patch.

In ordinary times we had two regular meals in a day: breakfast at twelve o'clock, after laboring from daylight, and supper when the work of the remainder of the day was over. In harvest season we had three. Our dress was of tow-cloth; for the children, nothing but a shirt; for the older ones a pair of pantaloons or a gown in addition, according to the sex. Besides these, in the winter a round jacket or over-coat, a wool- hat once in two or three years, for the males, and a pair of coarse shoes once a year.

We lodged in log huts, and on the bare ground. Wooden floors were an unknown luxury. In a single room were huddled, like cattle, ten or a dozen persons, men, women, and children. All ideas of refinement and decency were, of course, out of the question. We had neither bedsteads, nor furniture of any description. Our beds were collections of straw and old rags, thrown down in the corners and boxed in with boards; a single blanket the only covering. Our favourite way of sleeping, how-ever, was on a plank, our heads raised on an old jacket and our feet toasting before the smouldering fire. The wind whistled and the rain and snow blew in through the cracks, and the damp earth soaked in the moisture till the floor was miry as a pig-sty. Such were our houses. In these wretched hovels were we penned at night, and fed by day; here were the children born and the sick—neglected.

Source: London, 1877.

17. The Meaning of July Fourth for the Negro, July 5, 1852
FREDERICK DOUGLASS

During the 1850s, abolitionist Frederick Douglass typically spent about six months of the year traveling extensively and giving lectures. During one winter—the winter of 1855–1856—he gave about seventy lectures during a tour that covered four to five thousand miles. And his speaking engagements did not halt at the end of a tour. From his home in Rochester, New York, he took part in local abolition-related events.

On July 5, 1852, Douglass gave a speech at an event commemorating the signing of the Declaration of Independence, held at Rochester's Corinthian Hall. The speech was full of biting oratory, in which Douglass told his audience, "This Fourth of July is *yours*, not *mine. You* may rejoice, I must mourn." And he asked them, "Do you mean, citizens, to mock me, by asking me to speak to-day?" Recognized as one of Douglass' most impassioned speeches, this address focuses on the evils of the con-troversial Fugitive Slave Law passed by Congress in 1850.

Fellow Citizens, I am not wanting in respect for the fathers of this republic. The signers of the Declaration of Independence were brave men. They were great men, too great enough to give frame to a great age. It does not often happen to a nation to raise, at one time, such a number of truly great men. The point from which I am compelled to view them is not, certainly, the most favorable; and yet I cannot con-template their great deeds with less than admiration. They were statesmen, patriots and heroes, and for the good they did, and the principles they contended for, I will unite with you to honor their memory....

... Fellow-citizens, pardon me, allow me to ask, why am I called upon to speak here to-day? What have I, or those I represent, to do with your national independ-ence? Are the great principles of political freedom and of natural justice, embodied in that Declaration of Independence, extended to us? and am I, therefore, called upon to bring our humble offering to the national altar, and to confess the benefits and express devout gratitude for the blessings resulting from your independence to us?

Would to God, both for your sakes and ours, that an affirmative answer could be truthfully returned to these questions! Then would my task be light, and my burden easy and delightful. For who is there so cold, that a nation's sympathy could not warm him? Who so obdurate and dead to the claims of gratitude, that would not thankfully acknowledge such priceless benefits? Who so stolid and selfish, that would not give his voice to swell the hallelujahs of a nation's jubilee, when the chains of servitude had been torn from his limbs? I am not that man. In a case like that, the dumb might eloquently speak, and the "lame man leap as an hart."

But such is not the state of the case. I say it with a sad sense of the disparity between us. I am not included within the pale of glorious anniversary! Your high independence only reveals the immeasurable distance between us. The blessings in which you, this day, rejoice, are not enjoyed in common. The rich inheritance of justice, liberty, prosperity and independence, bequeathed by your fathers, is shared by you, not by me. The sunlight that brought light and healing to you, has brought stripes and death to me. This Fourth July is yours, not mine. You may rejoice, I must mourn. To drag a man in fetters into the grand illuminated temple of liberty, and call upon him to join you in joyous anthems, were inhuman mockery and sacrilegious irony. Do you mean, citizens, to mock me, by asking me to speak to-day? If so, there is a parallel to your conduct. And let me warn you that it is dangerous to copy the example of a nation whose crimes, towering up to heaven, were thrown down by the breath of the Almighty, burying that nation in irrevocable ruin! I can to-day take up the plaintive lament of a peeled and woe-smitten people!

"By the rivers of Babylon, there we sat down. Yea! we wept when we remembered Zion. We hanged our harps upon the willows in the midst thereof. For there, they that carried us away captive, required of us a song; and they who wasted us required of us mirth, saying, Sing us one of the songs of Zion. How can we sing the Lord's song in a strange land? If I forget thee, O Jerusalem, let my right hand forget her cunning. If I do not remember thee, let my tongue cleave to the roof of my mouth."

Fellow-citizens, above your national, tumultuous joy, I hear the mournful wail of millions! whose chains, heavy and grievous yesterday, are, to-day, rendered more intolerable by the jubilee shouts that reach them. If I do forget, if I do not faithfully remember those bleeding children of sorrow this day, "may my right hand forget her cunning, and may my tongue cleave to the roof of my mouth!" To forget them, to pass lightly over their wrongs, and to chime in with the popular theme, would be treason most scandalous and shocking, and would make me a reproach before God and the world. My subject, then, fellow-citizens, is American slavery. I shall see this day and its popular characteristics from the slave's point of view. Standing there identified with the American bondman, making his wrongs mine, I do not hesitate to declare, with all my soul, that the character and conduct of this nation never looked blacker to me than on this 4th of July! Whether we turn to the declarations of the past, or to the professions of the present, the conduct of the nation seems equally hideous and revolting. America is false to the past, false to the present, and solemnly binds herself to be false to the future. Standing with God and the crushed and bleeding slave on this occasion, I will, in the name of humanity which is outraged, in the name of liberty which is fettered, in the name of the constitution and the Bible which are disregarded and trampled upon, dare to call in question and to denounce, with all the emphasis I can command, everything that serves to perpetuate slavery the great sin and shame of America! "I will not equivocate; I will not excuse"; I will use the severest language I can command; and yet not one word shall escape me that any man, whose judgment is not blinded by prejudice, or who is not at heart a slaveholder, shall not confess to be right and just.

But I fancy I hear some one of my audience say, "It is just in this circumstance that you and your brother abolitionists fail to make a favorable impression on the public mind. Would you argue more, and denounce less; would you persuade more, and rebuke less; your cause would be much more likely to succeed." But, I submit, where all is plain there is nothing to be argued. What point in the anti-slavery creed would you have me argue? On what branch of the subject do the people of this country need light? Must I undertake to prove that the slave is a man? That point is conceded already. Nobody doubts it. The slaveholders themselves acknowledge it in the enactment of laws for their government. They acknowledge it when they punish disobedience on the part of the slave. There are seventy-two crimes in the State of Virginia which, if committed by a black man (no matter how ignorant he be), subject him to the punishment of death; while only two of the same crimes will subject a white man to the like punishment. What is this but the acknowledgment that the slave is a moral, intellectual, and responsible being? The manhood of the slave is conceded. It is admitted in the fact that Southern statute books are covered with enactments forbidding, under severe fines and penalties, the teaching of the slave to read or to write. When you can point to any such laws in reference to the beasts of the field, then I may consent to argue the manhood of the slave. When the dogs in your streets, when the fowls of the air, when the cattle on your hills, when the fish of the sea, and the reptiles that crawl, shall be unable to distinguish the slave from a brute, then will I argue with you that the slave is a man!

For the present, it is enough to affirm the equal manhood of the Negro race. Is it not astonishing that, while we are ploughing, planting, and reaping, using all kinds of mechanical tools, erecting houses, constructing bridges, building ships, working in metals of brass, iron, copper, silver and gold; that, while we are reading, writing and ciphering, acting as clerks, merchants and secretaries, having among us lawyers, doctors, ministers, poets, authors, editors, orators and teachers; that, while we are engaged in all manner of enterprises common to other men, digging gold in California, capturing the whale in the Pacific, feeding sheep and cattle on the hill-side, living, moving, acting, thinking, planning, living in families as husbands, wives and children, and, above all, confessing and worshipping the Christian's God, and looking hopefully for life and immortality beyond the grave, we are called upon to prove that we are men!

Would you have me argue that man is entitled to liberty? that he is the rightful owner of his own body? You have already declared it. Must I argue the wrongfulness of slavery? Is that a question for Republicans? Is it to be settled by the rules of logic and argumentation, as a matter beset with great difficulty, involving a doubtful application of the principle of justice, hard to be understood? How should I look to-day, in the presence of Americans, dividing, and subdividing a discourse, to show that men have a natural right to freedom? speaking of it relatively and positively, negatively and affirmatively. To do so, would be to make myself ridiculous, and to offer an insult to your understanding. There is not a man beneath the canopy of heaven that does not know that slavery is wrong for him.

What, am I to argue that it is wrong to make men brutes, to rob them of their liberty, to work them without wages, to keep them ignorant of their relations to their fellow men, to beat them with sticks, to flay their flesh with the lash, to load their limbs with irons, to hunt them with dogs, to sell them at auction, to sunder their families, to knock out their teeth, to burn their flesh, to starve them into obedience and submission to their masters? Must I argue that a system thus marked with blood, and stained with pollution, is wrong? No! I will not. I have better employment for my time and strength than such arguments would imply.

What, then, remains to be argued? Is it that slavery is not divine; that God did not establish it; that our doctors of divinity are mistaken? There is blasphemy in the thought. That which is inhuman, cannot be divine! Who can reason on such a proposition? They that can, may; I cannot. The time for such argument is passed.

At a time like this, scorching irony, not convincing argument, is needed. O! Had I the ability, and could reach the nation's ear, I would, to-day, pour out a fiery stream of biting ridicule, blasting reproach, withering sarcasm, and stern rebuke. For it is not light that is needed, but fire; it is not the gentle shower, but thunder. We need the storm, the whirlwind, and the earthquake. The feeling of the nation must be quickened; the conscience of the nation must be roused; the propriety of the nation must be startled; the hypocrisy of the nation must be exposed; and its crimes against God and man must be proclaimed and denounced.

What, to the American slave, is your 4th of July? I answer; a day that reveals to him, more than all other days in the year, the gross injustice and cruelty to which he is the constant victim. To him, your celebration is a sham; your boasted liberty, an unholy license; your national greatness, swelling vanity; your sounds of rejoicing are empty and heartless; your denunciation of tyrants, brass fronted impudence; your shouts of liberty and equality, hollow mockery; your prayers and hymns, your sermons and thanksgivings, with all your religious parade and solemnity, are, to Him, mere bombast, fraud, deception, impiety, and hypocrisy—a thin veil to cover up crimes which would disgrace a nation of savages. There is not a nation on the earth guilty of practices more shocking and bloody than are the people of the United States, at this very hour.

Go where you may, search where you will, roam through all the monarchies and despotisms of the Old World, travel through South America, search out every abuse, and when you have found the last, lay your facts by the side of the everyday practices of this nation, and you will say with me, that, for revolting barbarity and shameless hypocrisy, America reigns without a rival....

... Allow me to say, in conclusion, notwithstanding the dark picture I have this day presented, of the state of the nation, I do not despair of this country. There are forces in operation which must inevitably work the downfall of slavery. "The arm of the Lord is not shortened," and the doom of slavery is certain. I, therefore, leave off where I began, with hope. While drawing encouragement from "the Declaration of Independence," the great principles it contains, and the genius of American Institutions, my spirit is also cheered by the obvious tendencies of the age. Nations do not now stand in the same relation to each other that they did ages ago. No nation can now shut itself up from the surrounding world and trot round in the same old path of its fathers without interference. The time was when such could be done. Long established customs of hurtful character could formerly fence themselves in, and do their evil work with social impunity. Knowledge was then confined and enjoyed by the privileged few, and the multitude walked on in mental darkness. But a change has now come over the affairs of mankind. Walled cities and empires have become unfashionable. The arm of commerce has borne away the gates of the strong city. Intelligence is penetrating the darkest corners of the globe. It makes its pathway over and under the sea, as well as on the earth. Wind, steam, and lightning are its chartered agents. Oceans no longer divide, but link nations together. From Boston to London is now a holiday excursion. Space is comparatively annihilated.— Thoughts expressed on one side of the Atlantic are distinctly heard on the other.

The far off and almost fabulous Pacific rolls in grandeur at our feet. The Celestial Empire, the mystery of ages, is being solved. The fiat of the Almighty, "Let there be Light," has not yet spent its force. No abuse, no outrage whether in taste, sport or avarice, can now hide itself from the all-pervading light. The iron shoe, and crippled foot of China must be seen in contrast with nature. Africa must rise and put on her yet unwoven garment. "Ethiopia, shall, stretch out her hand unto God." In the fervent aspirations of William Lloyd Garrison, I say, and let every heart join in saying it:

> God speed the year of jubilee
> The wide world o'er!
> When from their galling chains set free,
> Th' oppress'd shall vilely bend the knee,
> And wear the yoke of tyranny
> Like brutes no more.
> That year will come, and freedom's reign,
> To man his plundered rights again
> Restore.
> God speed the day when human blood
> Shall cease to flow!
> In every clime be understood,
> The claims of human brotherhood,
> And each return for evil, good,
> Not blow for blow;
> That day will come all feuds to end,
> And change into a faithful friend
> Each foe.
> God speed the hour, the glorious hour,
> When none on earth
> Shall exercise a lordly power,
> Nor in a tyrant's presence cower;
> But to all manhood's stature tower,
> By equal birth!
> That hour will come, to each, to all,
> And from his Prison-house, to thrall
> Go forth.
> Until that year, day, hour, arrive,
> With head, and heart, and hand I'll strive,
> To break the rod, and rend the gyve,
> The spoiler of his prey deprive—

So witness Heaven!
And never from my chosen post,
Whate'er the peril or the cost,
Be driven.

Source: The Life and Writings of Frederick Douglass, Volume II, Pre-Civil War Decade 1850–1860, Philip S. Foner. International Publishers Co. Inc.: New York, 1950. Permission of International Publishers/New York.

18. Choice Thoughts and Utterances of Wise Colored People

Centuries of conditioning left Americans, both black and white, unprepared to begin thinking of the millions of former slaves, their children, and the cultures they created, as full, able-bodied citizens. Theories touting racial inferiority and aimed at stripping African Americans' equal rights reigned throughout the nation. Racial segregation was a fact of life for decades after slavery officially ended. The de facto poverty experienced by a majority of blacks in America was like a tattoo that branded every black citizen as inferior near the end of the nineteenth century.

Erasing this negative image became the work of emerging black figures such as W. E. B. DuBois, Booker T. Washington, union leader A. Philip Randolph, Marcus Garvey, and many others at the start of the twentieth century. In their own ways, newspaper editors, political thinkers, and social thinkers all sought ways to create a deeper understanding of race and how it impacted the daily lives of African Americans. Their task was to ignite self-awareness in African Americans who still thought of themselves as second-class American citizens and to confront a tangled web of racial issues that confronted all Americans.

These issues became the centerpieces for the rhetoric delivered by newly formed groups such as the National Association for the Advancement of Colored People, the Urban League, union organizations, and nationalistic movements which sprang up as these issues sparked debate everywhere. Phrases and slogans aimed at raising self awareness and self esteem were common in newspapers, church bulletins, and other means of communication. Hundreds of African American newspapers were published in major cities and small towns across the nation as the African American press grew and flourished in this racially charged atmosphere.

Thoughtless Bondage: To make a contented slave you must make a thoughtless one.

Source: Frederick Douglass, My Bondage, My Freedom, Part I. Life as a Slave. Part II. Life as a Freeman. New York: Miller, Orton & Mulligan, 1855.

Angelic Train: Christian Negroes, black as Cain, may be refined and join the angelic train.

Source: Phillis Wheatley, On being brought from Africa to America, Poems on Various Subjects, Religious and Moral, 1773.

Sizing Up: A man who wants to know his own strength, he need not measure himself. He needs only to size up the fellows who are pulling against him to find out how strong he is.

Source: Bishop Grant, (Abraham L. Grant) 1847–1911, bishop of the African Methodist Episcopal Church.

Ignorance and Poverty: We cannot go to Africa and succeed with all our ignorance and poverty. Let our big men set out to break down immorality among Negroes and white folks. Get Negroes to have more refinement and race pride, use Negro books and papers, hang Negro pictures on their walls; get up Negro industries and give deserving colored men and women employment; break down superstition and mistrust. Get Negroes to act decently both publicly and privately.

Source: Anon. quote, *Athen's* (GA) *Clipper*, edited and published by S. A. Davis, 1887–1912.

Truth: Flirting with the truth is the modest way of calling a man a liar without making him mad.

Source: Editor, *The Gazette*, Texas. 19th Century.

Station in Life: Christian education and wealth is the colored man's only savior. Those two things acquired will do more to adjust his station in life than any two acquisitions imaginable.

Source: Editor, *Knoxville Gleaner*, 19th Century.

Negroes: Negroes are more religious than white folks. They are more emotional. Emotion is not a virtue, for some emotionalists are sadly wanting in all the virtues.

Source: Editor, *Nashville Citizen*, 19th Century.

Pagans and Christians: I am exceedingly anxious that every young colored man and woman should keep a hopeful and cheerful spirit as to the future. Despite all of our disadvantages and hardships, ever since our fore-fathers set foot upon American soil as slaves, our pathway has been marked by progress. Think of it. We went into slavery pagans; we came out Christians. We went into slavery a piece of property; we came out American citizens. We went into slavery without a language; we came out speaking the proud Anglo-Saxon tongue. We went into slavery with slave chains clanking about our wrists; we came out with the American ballot in our hands.

Source: Quote from Booker T. Washington, lecture at Fisk University, Nashville, TN. Spring, 1895.

Silent Voices: There is not a single Negro in the United States on the road to practical truth, so far as his race is concerned. He feels something in him; his instincts point to it, but he cannot act out what he feels. And when he has made up his mind to remain in America, he has also made up his mind to surrender his race integrity; for he sees no chance of its preservation.

Source: Quote from Edward Wilmot Blyden, *Christianity, Islam and the Negro Race*. London: W. B. Whittingham & Co., 1888.

Prohibition: "Give the women a free use of the ballot and the Upas tree of intemperance will be hewn down by the axe of prohibition."

Source: Quote from Mrs. M.A. McCurdy, 19th century.

Earnest Purpose: Influences may be set at work in your life and in mine, supported by an earnest purpose, which, like a mighty anthem, shall swell and expand, increasing in volume and sweetness as it makes its way adown the years—drawing men through the power of that Christian education which has been emphasized in us, to recognize the beauty of knowledge and wisdom, "whose ways are ways of pleasantness and all her paths are peace."

Source: Quote from Rev. George C. Rowe Clinton, 19th century.

On Culture: "There is a mistaken idea that 'culture' means to paint a little, sing a little, dance a little, put on haughty airs, and to quote passages from popular books. It means nothing of the kind. Culture means politeness, charity, fairness, good temper and good conduct. Culture is not a thing to make a display of; it is something to use so moderately that people do not discover all at once that you have it."

Source: Quote from Editor, *Colored American*, 19th century.

On Women: While man can boast of great physical strength, skill and bull dog courage, woman carries in her weak frame a moral courage very seldom found among men. If our race is to be a great race in this great nation of races, our women must be largely instrumental in making it so.

Source: Quote from *American Baptist*, 19th century.

On Reading: Reading is to the mind what eating is to the body. So to eat without giving nature time to assimilate is to rob her, first of health, then life; so to read without reflecting is to cram the intellect and paralyze the mind. In all cases, dear friends, reflect more than you read, in order to present what you read to your hearers.

Source: Quote from S. A. Wesson, Lincolnville, S. C., 19th century.

On Being Negro: Let us as Negroes educate; let us survive; let us live up to our opportunities of doing good to ourselves and to others, so shall we work out a glorious destiny upon earth, and contribute our share of the good and great immorals out of every nation, that shall take their places among "the spirits of just men made perfect who are without fault before the throne."

Source: Quote from Rev. Wm. D. Johnson, D.D., Athens, GA, 19th century.

Back to Africa: "It will be a serious step for Africa, the emigrants themselves and the cause of Christianity for any great number of Negroes who do not know the primary principles of the Christian religion, and the rudiments of self-government to migrate to that dark continent. None but the very best people should go to Africa— none but wise and industrious Christians should be encouraged nor induced to go to that benighted land."

Source: Quote from Professor Floyd, 19th century.

Exiled: The exiled Negro in the Western Hemisphere, in spite of slavery, in spite of bitter prejudices, the dark passions of which he has been the victim, has come under influences which have given him the elements of a noble civilization. The seed of a spiritual, intellectual, industrial life has been planted in his bosom, which, when he is transferred to the land of his fathers, will grow up into beauty, expand into flower, and develop into fruit which the world will be glad to welcome.

Source: Quote from Edward Wilmot Blyden, 19th century.

On Debate: A potent factor for the elevation of the Negro that can be wielded to better advantage in literary and debating societies than by any other channel in the disseminating and encouragement of Negro literature among the masses, for there is no intermediate agency that will instill race pride, race confidence and race co-operation in the Negro faster than reading race books and race papers.

Source: Quote from Chas. V. Monk, Philadelphia, 19th century.

On Character: "Character possession is as essential to a people as to an individual. That is to say, the race without a greater percentage of moral worth on its side is as helpless and hopeless as the man or woman devoid of the same attribute of strength and greatness. Those nations and peoples with centuries of history behind them need not be so careful in the matter of virtuous conduct as those who have made none or but little headway on the road to civilization and race grandeur. The Afro-American youth therefore would do well to rid himself of the delusions that he can afford to follow in the wake of his dominant Caucasian companion so far as vice and immorality are involved. Japhet has reveled in success so long and maintains such a grasp on the reins of universal mastery at present, that he can with more propriety afford to take a day off than can his unfortunate brother of Hamitic descent. From pulpits, lecture stands, lyceums, tracts, books, papers, club rooms and every other medium of reaching them, our young men should be given to understand that they can ignore the claims of morality, virtue and religion only at the greatest peril. Cards, dice, drink and dissipation in numberless forms may be indulged in by the weak ones of the stronger race, but those of our weaker race who would be strong must avoid these vices as they would shun poison."

Source: Quote from Rev. H. T. Johnson, Editor, *Christian Recorder*, 19th century.

All quotations listed above were also published in: *Afro-American encyclopedia, or, the thoughts, doings, and sayings of the race: embracing addresses, lectures, biographical sketches, sermons, poems, names of universities, colleges, seminaries, newspapers, books, and a history of the denominations, giving the numerical strength of each. In fact, it teaches every subject of interest to the colored people, as discussed by more than one hundred of their wisest and best men and women.* Compiled and arranged by James T. Haley. Nashville, Tenn.: Haley & Florida, 1895. Source: Documenting the American South, University of North Carolina at Chapel Hill, 2000. Electronic edition available at: http://docsouth.unc.edu/church/haley/haley.html.

19. Essay on Slavery Conditions, 1856
FRANCIS HENDERSON

In 1841, Francis Henderson was 19 when he escaped from a slave plantation outside of Washington, D.C. In this essay fifteen years later, he describes the conditions he encountered on a plantation so close to the seat of government for a land where freedom had always been the most cherished ideal—except for millions of men like Henderson.

"MY BEDSTEAD CONSISTED OF A BOARD WIDE ENOUGH TO SLEEP ON"

Our houses were but log huts—the tops partly open—ground floor—rain would come through. My aunt was quite an old woman, and had been sick several years; in rains I have seen her moving from one part of the house to the other, and rolling her bedclothes about to try to keep dry—everything would be dirty and muddy. I lived in the house with my aunt. My bed and bedstead consisted of a board wide enough to sleep on—one end on a stool, the other placed near the fire. My pillow consisted of my jacket—my covering was whatever I could get. My bedtick was the board itself. And this was the way the single men slept—but we were comfortable in this way of sleeping, being used to it. I only remember having but one blanket from my owners up to the age of nineteen, when I ran away.

Our allowance was given weekly—a peck of sifted corn meal, a dozen and a half herrings, two and a half pounds of pork. Some of the boys would eat this up in three days—then they had to steal, or they could not perform their daily tasks. They would visit the hog- pen, sheep- pen, and granaries. I do not remember one slave but who stole some things—they were driven to it as a matter of necessity. I myself did this—many a time have I, with others, run among the stumps in chase of a sheep, that we might have something to eat.... In regard to cooking, sometimes many have to cook at one fire, and before all could get to the fire to bake hoe cakes, the overseer's horn would sound: then they must go at any rate. Many a time I have gone along eating a piece of bread and meat, or herring broiled on the coals—I never sat down at a table to eat except at harvest time, all the time I was a slave. In harvest time, the cooking is done at the great house, as the hands they have are wanted in the field. This was more like people, and we liked it, for we sat down then at meals. In the summer we had one pair of linen trousers given us—nothing else; every fall, one pair of woolen pantaloons, one woolen jacket, and two cotton shirts.

My master had four sons in his family. They all left except one, who remained to be a driver. He would often come to the field and accuse the slave of having taken so and so. If we denied it, he would whip the grown- up ones to make them own it. Many a time, when we didn't know he was anywhere around, he would be in the woods watching us—first thing we would know, he would be sitting on the fence look- ing down upon us, and if any had been idle, the young master would visit him with blows. I have known him to kick my aunt, an old woman who had raised and nursed him, and I have seen him punish my sisters awfully with hickories from the woods.

The slaves are watched by the patrols, who ride about to try to catch them off the quarters, especially at the house of a free person of color. I have known the slaves to stretch clothes lines across the street, high enough to let the horse pass, but not the rider; then the boys would run, and the patrols in full chase would be thrown off by running against the lines. The patrols are poor white men, who live by plundering and stealing, getting rewards for runaways, and setting up little shops on the public roads. They will take whatever the slaves steal, paying in money, whiskey, or whatever the slaves want. They take pigs, sheep, wheat, corn—any thing that's raised they encourage the slaves to steal: these they take to market next day. It's all speculation—all a matter of self- interest, and when the slaves run away, these same traders catch them if they can, to get the reward. If the slave threatens to expose his traffic, he does not care—for the slave's word is good for nothing—it would not be taken.

Source: Benjamin Drew, *A North-Side View of Slavery.* Boston: J. P. Jewett and Company, 1856.

20. Supreme Court of the United States in Dred Scott v. John F. Sanford, March 6, 1857

Dred Scott and his lawyers claimed that the U.S. Constitution protected his rights to freedom as a citizen in an appeal of a lower court ruling to the U.S. Supreme Court. In Scott v. Sanford the Court states that Scott should remain a slave, that as a slave he is not a citizen of the United States and thus not eligible to bring suit in a federal court, and that as a slave he is personal property and thus has never been free. U.S. Supreme Court Chief Justice Roger B. Taney, speaking for the majority, stated the following:

"… We think they [people of African ancestry] are … not included, and were not intended to be included, under the word "citizens" in the Constitution, and can therefore claim none of the rights and privileges which that instrument provides for and secures to citizens of the United States.…"

Source: TeachingAmericanHistory.org © 2006 Ashbrook Center for Public Affairs.

21. Speech by Abraham Lincoln on the Dred Scott Decision and Slavery, June 26, 1857

In one of the most telling speeches regarding his position on slavery, Abraham Lincoln's address on the *Dred Scott* decision explains his view of what was known as "popular sovereignty"; this concept was that each territory or state would determine whether slavery would exist within its boundaries.

Lincoln's speech was well received, catapulting him into a famous campaign for the U.S. Senate against Stephen Douglas in 1858. Though Lincoln would lose that election, his campaigning and speaking skills would distinguish him as a possible presidential candidate for the Republican Party in 1860.

Fellow Citizens: I am here tonight, partly by the invitation of some of you, and partly by my own inclination. Two weeks ago Judge Douglas spoke here on the several subjects of Kansas, the Dred Scott decision, and Utah. I listened to the speech at the time, and have read the report of it since.

Abraham Lincoln
June 26, 1857
Speech at Springfield, Illinois

It was intended to controvert opinions which I think just, and to assail (politically, not personally,) those men who, in common with me, entertain those opinions. For this reason I wished then, and still wish, to make some answer to it, which I now take the opportunity of doing.

I begin with Utah. If it prove to be true, as is probable, that the people of Utah are in open rebellion to the United States, then Judge Douglas is in favor of repealing their territorial organization, and attaching them to the adjoining States for judicial purposes. I say, too, if they are in rebellion, they ought to be somehow coerced to obedience; and I am not now prepared to admit or deny that the Judge's mode of coercing them is not as good as any. The Republicans can fall in with it without taking back anything they have ever said. To be sure, it would be a considerable backing down by Judge Douglas from his much vaunted doctrine of self-government for the territories; but this is only additional proof of what was very plain from the beginning, that that doctrine was a mere deceitful pretense for the benefit of slavery. Those who could not see that much in the Nebraska act itself, which forced Governors, and Secretaries, and Judges on the people of the territories, without their choice or consent, could not be made to see, though one should rise from the dead to testify.

But in all this, it is very plain the Judge evades the only question the Republicans have ever pressed upon the Democracy in regard to Utah. That question the Judge well knows to be this: "If the people of Utah shall peacefully form a State Constitution tolerating polygamy, will the Democracy admit them into the Union?" There is nothing in the United States Constitution or law against polygamy; and why is it not a part of the Judge's "sacred right of self-government" for that people to have it, or rather to keep it, if they choose? These questions, so far as I know, the Judge never answers. It might involve the Democracy to answer them either way, and they go unanswered.

As to Kansas. The substance of the Judge's speech on Kansas is an effort to put the free State men in the wrong for not voting at the election of delegates to the Constitutional Convention. He says: "There is every reason to hope and believe that the law will be fairly interpreted and impartially executed, so as to insure to every bona fide inhabitant the free and quiet exercise of the elective franchise."

It appears extraordinary that Judge Douglas should make such a statement. He knows that, by the law, no one can vote who has not been registered; and he knows that the free State men place their refusal to vote on the ground that but few of them have been registered. It is possible this is not true, but Judge Douglas knows it is asserted to be true in letters, newspapers and public speeches, and borne by every mail, and blown by every breeze to the eyes and ears of the world. He knows it is boldly declared that the people of many whole counties, and many whole neighborhoods in others, are left unregistered; yet, he does not venture to contradict the declaration, nor to point out how they can vote without being registered; but he just slips along, not seeming to know there is any such question of fact, and complacently declares: "There is every reason to hope and believe that the law will be fairly and impartially executed, so as to insure to every bona fide inhabitant the free and quiet exercise of the elective franchise."

I readily agree that if all had a chance to vote, they ought to have voted. If, on the contrary, as they allege, and Judge Douglas ventures not to particularly contradict, few only of the free State men had a chance to vote, they were perfectly right in staying from the polls in a body.

By the way since the Judge spoke, the Kansas election has come off. The Judge expressed his confidence that all the Democrats in Kansas would do their duty— including "free state Democrats" of course. The returns received here as yet are very incomplete; but so far as they go, they indicate that only about one sixth of the registered voters, have really voted; and this too, when not more, perhaps, than one half of the rightful voters have been registered, thus showing the thing to have been altogether the most exquisite farce ever enacted. I am watching with considerable interest, to ascertain what figure "the free state Democrats" cut in the concern. Of course they voted—all democrats do their duty—and of course they did not vote for slave-state candidates. We soon shall know how many delegates they elected, how many candidates they had, pledged for a free state; and how many votes were cast for them.

Allow me to barely whisper my suspicion that there were no such things in Kansas "as free state Democrats"—that they were altogether mythical, good only to figure in newspapers and speeches in the free states. If there should prove to be one real living free state Democrat in Kansas, I suggest that it might be well to catch him, and stuff and preserve his skin, as an interesting specimen of that soon to be extinct variety of the genus, Democrat.

And now as to the Dred Scott decision. That decision declares two propositions—first, that a negro cannot sue in the U.S. Courts; and secondly, that Congress cannot prohibit slavery in the Territories. It was made by a divided court—dividing differently on the different points. Judge Douglas does not discuss the merits of the decision; and, in that respect, I shall follow his example, believing I could no more improve on McLean and Curtis, than he could on Taney.

He denounces all who question the correctness of that decision, as offering violent resistance to it. But who resists it? Who has, in spite of the decision, declared Dred Scott free, and resisted the authority of his master over him?

Judicial decisions have two uses—first, to absolutely determine the case decided, and secondly, to indicate to the public how other similar cases will be decided when they arise. For the latter use, they are called "precedents" and "authorities."

We believe, as much as Judge Douglas, (perhaps more) in obedience to, and respect for the judicial department of government. We think its decisions on Constitutional questions, when fully settled, should control, not only the particular cases decided, but the general policy of the country, subject to be disturbed only by amendments of the Constitution as provided in that instrument itself. More than this would be revolution. But we think the Dred Scott decision is erroneous. We know the court that made it, has often over-ruled its own decisions, and we shall do what we can to have it to over-rule this. We offer no resistance to it.

Judicial decisions are of greater or less authority as precedents, according to circumstances. That this should be so, accords both with common sense, and the customary understanding of the legal profession.

If this important decision had been made by the unanimous concurrence of the judges, and without any apparent partisan bias, and in accordance with legal public expectation, and with the steady practice of the departments throughout our history, and had been in no part, based on assumed historical facts which are not really true; or, if wanting in some of these, it had been before the court more than once, and had there been affirmed and re-affirmed through a course of years, it then might be, perhaps would be, factious, nay, even revolutionary, to not acquiesce in it as a precedent.

But when, as it is true we find it wanting in all these claims to the public confidence, it is not resistance, it is not factious, it is not even disrespectful, to treat it as not having yet quite established a settled doctrine for the country—But Judge Douglas considers this view awful. Hear him:

"The courts are the tribunals prescribed by the Constitution and created by the authority of the people to determine, expound and enforce the law. Hence, whoever resists the final decision of the highest judicial tribunal, aims a deadly blow to our whole Republican system of government—a blow, which if successful would place all our rights and liberties at the mercy of passion, anarchy and violence. I repeat, therefore, that if resistance to the decisions of the Supreme Court of the United States, in a matter like the points decided in the Dred Scott case, clearly within their jurisdiction as defined by the Constitution, shall be forced upon the country as a political issue, it will become a distinct and naked issue between the friends and the enemies of the Constitution—the friends and the enemies of the supremacy of the laws."

Why this same Supreme court once decided a national bank to be constitutional; but Gen. Jackson, as President of the United States, disregarded the decision, and vetoed a bill for a re-charter, partly on constitutional ground, declaring that each public functionary must support the Constitution, "as he understands it." But hear the General's own words. Here they are, taken from his veto message:

"It is maintained by the advocates of the bank, that its constitutionality, in all its features, ought to be considered as settled by precedent, and by the decision of the Supreme Court. To this conclusion I cannot assent. Mere precedent is a dangerous source of authority, and should not be regarded as deciding questions of constitutional power, except where the acquiescence of the people and the States can be considered as well settled. So far from this being the case on this subject, an argument against the bank might be based on precedent. One Congress in 1791, decided in favor of a bank; another in 1811, decided against it. One Congress in 1815 decided against a bank; another in 1816 decided in its favor. Prior to the present Congress, therefore the precedents drawn from that source were equal. If we resort to the States, the expressions of legislative, judicial and executive opinions against the bank have been probably to those in its favor as four to one. There is nothing in precedent, therefore, which if its authority were admitted, ought to weigh in favor of the act before me."

I drop the quotations merely to remark that all there ever was, in the way of precedent up to the Dred Scott decision, on the points therein decided, had been against that decision. But hear Gen. Jackson further—

"If the opinion of the Supreme court covered the whole ground of this act, it ought not to control the co-ordinate authorities of this Government. The Congress, the executive and the court, must each for itself be guided by its own opinion of the Constitution. Each public officer, who takes an oath to support the Constitution, swears that he will support it as he understands it, and not as it is understood by others."

Again and again have I heard Judge Douglas denounce that bank decision, and applaud Gen. Jackson for disregarding it. It would be interesting for him to look over his recent speech, and see how exactly his fierce philippics against us for resisting Supreme Court decisions, fall upon his own head. It will call to his mind a long and fierce political war in this country, upon an issue which, in his own language, and, of course, in his own changeless estimation, was "a distinct and naked issue between the friends and the enemies of the Constitution," and in which war he fought in the ranks of the enemies of the Constitution.

I have said, in substance, that the Dred Scott decision was, in part, based on assumed historical facts which were not really true; and I ought not to leave the subject without giving some reasons for saying this; I therefore give an instance or two, which I think fully sustain me. Chief Justice Taney, in delivering the opinion of the majority of the Court, insists at great length that negroes were no part of the people who made, or for whom was made, the Declaration of Independence, or the Constitution of the United States.

On the contrary, Judge Curtis, in his dissenting opinion, shows that in five of the then thirteen states, to wit, New Hampshire, Massachusetts, New York, New Jersey and North Carolina, free negroes were voters, and, in proportion to their numbers, had the same part in making the Constitution that the white people had. He shows this with so much particularity as to leave no doubt of its truth; and, as a sort of conclusion on that point, holds the following language:

"The Constitution was ordained and established by the people of the United States, through the action, in each State, of those persons who were qualified by its laws to act thereon in behalf of themselves and all other citizens of the State. In some of the States, as we have seen, colored persons were among those qualified by law to act on the subject. These colored persons were not only included in the body of 'the people of the United States,' by whom the Constitution was ordained and established; but in at least five of the States they had the power to act, and, doubtless, did act, by their suffrages, upon the question of its adoption."

Again, Chief Justice Taney says: "It is difficult, at this day to realize the state of public opinion in relation to that unfortunate race, which prevailed in the civilized and enlightened portions of the world at the time of the Declaration of Independence, and when the Constitution of the United States was framed and adopted." And again, after quoting from the Declaration, he says: "The general words above quoted would seem to include the whole human family, and if they were used in a similar instrument at this day, would be so understood."

In these the Chief Justice does not directly assert, but plainly assumes, as a fact, that the public estimate of the black man is more favorable now than it was in the days of the Revolution. This assumption is a mistake. In some trifling particulars, the condition of that race has been ameliorated; but, as a whole, in this country, the change between then and now is decidedly the other way; and their ultimate destiny has never appeared so hopeless as in the last three or four years. In two of the five States—New Jersey and North Carolina—that then gave the free negro the right of voting, the right has since been taken away; and in a third—New York—it has been greatly abridged; while it has not been extended, so far as I know, to a single additional State, though the number of the States has more than doubled. In those days, as I understand, masters could, at their own pleasure, emancipate their slaves; but since then, such legal restraints have been made upon emancipation, as to amount almost to prohibition. In those days, Legislatures held the unquestioned power to abolish slavery in their respective States; but now it is becoming quite fashionable for State Constitutions to withhold that power from the Legislatures. In those days, by common consent, the spread of the black man's bondage to new countries was prohibited; but now, Congress decides that it will not continue the prohibition, and the Supreme Court decides that it could not if it would. In those days, our Declaration of Independence was held sacred by all, and thought to include all; but now, to aid in making the bondage of the negro universal and eternal, it is assailed, and sneered at, and construed, and hawked at, and torn, till, if its framers could rise from their graves, they could not at all recognize it. All the powers of earth seem rapidly combining against him. Mammon is after him; ambition follows, and philosophy follows, and the Theology of the day is fast joining the cry. They have him in his prison house; they have searched his person, and left no prying instrument with him. One after another they have closed the heavy iron doors upon him, and now they have him, as it were, bolted in with a lock of a hundred keys, which can never be unlocked without the concurrence of every key; the keys in the hands of a hundred different men, and they scattered to a hundred different and distant places; and they stand musing as to what invention, in all the dominions of mind and matter, can be produced to make the impossibility of his escape more complete than it is.

It is grossly incorrect to say or assume, that the public estimate of the negro is more favorable now than it was at the origin of the government.

Three years and a half ago, Judge Douglas brought forward his famous Nebraska bill. The country was at once in a blaze. He scorned all opposition, and carried it through Congress. Since then he has seen himself superseded in a Presidential nomination, by one indorsing the general doctrine of his measure, but at the same time standing clear of the odium of its untimely agitation, and its gross breach of national faith; and he has seen that successful rival Constitutionally elected, not by the strength of friends, but by the division of adversaries, being in a popular minority of nearly four hundred thousand votes. He has seen his chief aids in his own State, Shields and Richardson, politically speaking, successively tried, convicted, and executed, for an offense not their own, but his. And now he sees his own case, standing next on the docket for trial.

There is a natural disgust in the minds of nearly all white people, to the idea of an indiscriminate amalgamation of the white and black races; and Judge Douglas evidently is basing his chief hope, upon the chances of being able to appropriate the benefit of this disgust to himself. If he can, by much drumming and repeating, fasten the odium of that idea upon his adversaries, he thinks he can struggle through the storm. He therefore clings to this hope, as a drowning man to the last plank. He makes an occasion for lugging it in from the opposition to the Dred Scott decision. He finds the Republicans insisting that the Declaration of Independence includes ALL men, black as well as white; and forth-with he boldly denies that it includes negroes at all, and proceeds to argue gravely that all who contend it does, do so only because they want to vote, and eat, and sleep, and marry with negroes! He will have it that they cannot be consistent else. Now I protest against that counterfeit logic which concludes that, because I do not want a black woman for a slave I must necessarily want her for a wife. I need not have her for either, I can just leave her alone. In some respects she certainly is not my equal; but in her natural right to eat the bread she earns with her own hands without asking leave of any one else, she is my equal, and the equal of all others.

Chief Justice Taney, in his opinion in the Dred Scott case, admits that the language of the Declaration is broad enough to include the whole human family, but he and Judge Douglas argue that the authors of that instrument did not intend to include negroes, by the fact that they did not at once, actually place them on an equality with the whites. Now this grave argument comes to just nothing at all, by the other fact, that they did not at once, or ever afterwards, actually place all white people on an equality with one or another. And this is the staple argument of both the Chief Justice and the Senator, for doing this obvious violence to the plain unmistakable language of the Declaration. I think the authors of that notable instrument intended to include all men, but they did not intend to declare all men equal in all respects. They did not mean to say all were equal in color, size, intellect, moral developments, or social capacity. They defined with tolerable distinctness, in what respects they did consider all men created equal—equal in "certain inalienable rights, among which are life, liberty, and the pursuit of happiness." This they said, and this meant. They did not mean to assert the obvious untruth, that all were then actually enjoying that equality, nor yet, that they were about to confer it immediately upon them. In fact they had no power to confer such a boon. They meant simply to declare the right, so that the enforcement of it might follow as fast as circumstances should permit. They meant to set up a standard maxim for free society, which should be familiar to all, and revered by all; constantly looked to, constantly labored for, and even though never perfectly attained, constantly approximated, and thereby constantly spreading and deepening its influence, and augmenting the happiness and value of life to all people of all colors everywhere. The assertion that "all men are created equal" was of no practical use in effecting our separation from Great Britain; and it was placed in the Declaration, nor for that, but for future use. Its authors meant it to be, thank God, it is now proving itself, a stumbling block to those who in after times might seek to turn a free people back into the hateful paths of despotism. They knew the proneness of prosperity to breed tyrants, and they meant when such should re-appear in this fair land and commence their vocation they should find left for them at least one hard nut to crack.

I have now briefly expressed my view of the meaning and objects of that part of the Declaration of Independence which declares that "all men are created equal."

Now let us hear Judge Douglas' view of the same subject, as I find it in the printed report of his late speech. Here it is:

"No man can vindicate the character, motives and conduct of the signers of the Declaration of Independence except upon the hypothesis that they referred to the white race alone, and not to the African, when they declared all men to have been created equal—that they were speaking of British subjects on this continent being equal to British subjects born and residing in Great Britain—that they were entitled to the same inalienable rights, and among them were enumerated life, liberty and the pursuit of happiness. The Declaration was adopted for the purpose of justifying the colonists in the eyes of the civilized world in withdrawing their allegiance from the British crown, and dissolving their connection with the mother country."

My good friends, read that carefully over some leisure hour, and ponder well upon it—see what a mere wreck—mangled ruin—it makes of our once glorious Declaration.

"They were speaking of British subjects on this continent being equal to British subjects born and residing in Great Britain!" Why, according to this, not only negroes but white people outside of Great Britain and America are not spoken of in that instrument. The English, Irish and Scotch, along with white Americans, were included to be sure, but the French, Germans and other white people of the world are all gone to pot along with the Judge's inferior races. I had thought the Declaration promised something better than the condition of British subjects; but no, it only meant that we should be equal to them in their own oppressed and unequal condition. According to that, it gave no promise that having kicked off the King and Lords of Great Britain, we should not at once be saddled with a King and Lords of our own.

I had thought the Declaration contemplated the progressive improvement in the condition of all men everywhere; but no, it merely "was adopted for the purpose of justifying the colonists in the eyes of the civilized world in withdrawing their allegiance from the British crown, and dissolving their connection with the mother country." Why, that object having been effected some eighty years ago, the Declaration is of no practical use now—mere rubbish—old wadding left to rot on the battle-field after the victory is won.

I understand you are preparing to celebrate the "Fourth," tomorrow week. What for? The doings of that day had no reference to the present; and quite half of you are not even descendants of those who were referred to at that day. But I suppose you will celebrate; and will even go so far as to read the Declaration. Suppose after you read it once in the old fashioned way, you read it once more with Judge Douglas' version. It will then run thus: "We hold these truths to be self-evident that all British subjects who were on this continent eighty-one years ago, were created equal to all British subjects born and then residing in Great Britain."

And now I appeal to all—to Democrats as well as others,—are you really willing that the Declaration shall be thus frittered away?—thus left no more at most, than an interesting memorial of the dead past? thus shorn of its vitality, and practical value; and left without the germ or even the suggestion of the individual rights of man in it?

But Judge Douglas is especially horrified at the thought of the mixing blood by the white and black races: agreed for once—a thousand times agreed. There are white men enough to marry all the white women, and black men enough to marry all the black women; and so let them be married. On this point we fully agree with the Judge; and when he shall show that his policy is better adapted to prevent amalgamation than ours we shall drop ours, and adopt his. Let us see. In 1850 there were in the United States, 405,751, mulattoes. Very few of these are the offspring of whites and free blacks; nearly all have sprung from black slaves and white masters. A separation of the races is the only perfect preventive of amalgamation but as an immediate separation is impossible the next best thing is to keep them apart where they are not already together. If white and black people never get together in Kansas, they will never mix blood in Kansas. That is at least one self-evident truth. A few free colored persons may get into the free States, in any event; but their number is too insignificant to amount to much in the way of mixing blood. In 1850 there were in the free states, 56,649 mulattoes; but for the most part they were not born there—they came from the slave States, ready made up. In the same year the slave States had 348,874 mulattoes all of home production. The proportion of free mulattoes to free blacks—the only colored classes in the free states—is much greater in the slave than in the free states. It is worthy of note too, that among the free states those which make the colored man the nearest to equal the white, have, proportionably the fewest mulattoes the least of amalgamation. In New Hampshire, the State which goes farthest towards equality between the races, there are just 184 Mulattoes while there are in Virginia—how many do you think? 79,775, being 23,126 more than in all the free States together. These statistics show that slavery is the greatest source of amalgamation; and next to it, not the elevation, but the degeneration of the free blacks. Yet Judge Douglas dreads the slightest restraints on the spread of slavery, and the slightest human recognition of the negro, as tending horribly to amalgamation.

This very Dred Scott case affords a strong test as to which party most favors amalgamation, the Republicans or the dear Union-saving Democracy. Dred Scott, his wife and two daughters were all involved in the suit. We desired the court to have held that they were citizens so far at least as to entitle them to a hearing as to whether they were free or not; and then, also, that they were in fact and in law really free. Could we have had our way, the chances of these black girls, ever mixing their blood with that of white people, would have been diminished at least to the extent that it could not have been without their consent. But Judge Douglas is delighted to have them decided to be slaves, and not human enough to have a hearing, even if they were free, and thus left subject to the forced concubinage of their masters, and liable to become the mothers of mulattoes in spite of themselves—the very state of case that produces nine tenths of all the mulattoes—all the mixing of blood in the nation.

Of course, I state this case as an illustration only, not meaning to say or intimate that the master of Dred Scott and his family, or any more than a percentage of masters generally, are inclined to exercise this particular power which they hold over their female slaves.

I have said that the separation of the races is the only perfect preventive of amalgamation. I have no right to say all the members of the Republican party are in favor of this, nor to say that as a party they are in favor of it. There is nothing in their platform directly on the subject. But I can say a very large proportion of its members are for it, and that the chief plank in their platform—opposition to the spread of slavery—is most favorable to that separation.

Such separation, if ever effected at all, must be effected by colonization; and no political party, as such, is now doing anything directly for colonization. Party operations at present only favor or retard colonization incidentally. The enterprise is a difficult one; but "when there is a will there is a way;" and what colonization needs most is a hearty will. Will springs from the two elements of moral sense and self-interest. Let us be brought to believe it is morally right, and, at the same time, favorable to, or, at least, not against, our interest, to transfer the African to his native clime, and we shall find a way to do it, however great the task may be. The children of Israel, to such numbers as to include four hundred thousand fighting men, went out of Egyptian bondage in a body.

How differently the respective courses of the Democratic and Republican parties incidentally bear on the question of forming a will—a public sentiment—for colonization, is easy to see. The Republicans inculcate, with whatever of ability they can, that the negro is a man; that his bondage is cruelly wrong, and that the field of his oppression ought not to be enlarged. The Democrats deny his manhood; deny, or dwarf to insignificance, the wrong of his bondage; so far as possible, crush all sympathy for him, and cultivate and excite hatred and disgust against him; compliment themselves as Union-savers for doing so; and call the indefinite outspreading of his bondage "a sacred right of self-government."

The plainest print cannot be read through a gold eagle; and it will be ever hard to find many men who will send a slave to Liberia, and pay his passage while they can send him to a new country, Kansas for instance, and sell him for fifteen hundred dollars, and the rise.

Source: Speech at Springfield, Illinois. June 26, 1857. TeachingAmericanHistory.org © 2006 Ashbrook Center for Public Affairs.

22. Our Nig; or, Sketches from the Life of a Free Black, in a Two-Story White House, North, 1859
HARRIET E. WILSON

Harriet Wilson writes a narrative of the life experiences of a free black woman pre–Emancipation Proclamation. The vocabulary and style of this novel is Romantic, indicating the literary background of the writer. *Our Nig* made headlines in the 1980s when the text was rediscovered by Henry Louis Gates, a professor at Yale University at the time, who declared that this novel appeared to be the first literary work written and published by an African American. This proclamation, made in the pages of scholarly journals and the *New York Times*, made Harriet Wilson and this work a landmark in the annals of American literature.

CHAPTER I.

MAG SMITH, MY MOTHER.
Oh, Grief beyond all other griefs, when fate
First leaves the young heart lone and desolate
In the wide world, without that only tie
For which it loved to live or feared to die;
Lorn as the hung-up lute, that ne'er hath spoken
Since the sad day its master-chord was broken!
MOORE.

LONELY MAG SMITH! See her as she walks with downcast eyes and heavy heart. It was not always thus. She *had* a loving, trusting heart. Early deprived of parental guardianship, far removed from relatives, she was left to guide her tiny boat over life's surges alone and inexperienced. As she merged into womanhood, unprotected, uncherished, uncared for, there fell on her ear the music of love, awakening an intensity of emotion long dormant. It whispered of an elevation before unaspired to; of ease and plenty her simple heart had never dreamed of as hers. She knew the voice of her charmer, so ravishing, sounded far above her. It seemed like an angel's, alluring her upward and onward. She thought she could ascend to him and become an equal. She surrendered to him a priceless gem, which he proudly garnered as a trophy, with those of other victims, and left her to her fate. The world seemed full of hateful deceivers and crushing arrogance. Conscious that the great bond of union to her former companions was severed, that the disdain of others would be insupportable, she determined to leave the few friends she possessed, and seek an asylum among strangers. Her offspring came unwelcomed, and before its nativity numbered weeks, it passed from earth, ascending to a purer and better life.

"God be thanked," ejaculated Mag, as she saw its breathing cease; "no one can taunt *her* with my ruin."

Blessed release! may we all respond. How many pure, innocent children not only inherit a wicked heart of their own, claiming life-long scrutiny and restraint, but are heirs also of parental disgrace and calumny, from which only long years of patient endurance in paths of rectitude can disencumber them.

Mag's new home was soon contaminated by the publicity of her fall; she had a feeling of degradation oppressing her; but she resolved to be circumspect, and try to regain in a measure what she had lost. Then some foul tongue would jest of her shame, and averted looks and cold greetings disheartened her. She saw she could not bury in forgetfulness her misdeed, so she resolved to leave her home and seek another in the place she at first fled from.

Alas, how fearful are we to be first in extending a helping hand to those who stagger in the mires of infamy; to speak the first words of hope and warning to those emerging into the sunlight of morality! Who can tell what numbers, advancing just far enough to hear a cold welcome and join in the reserved converse of professed reformers, disappointed, disheartened, have chosen to dwell in unclean places, rather than encounter these "holier-than-thou" of the great brotherhood of man!

Such was Mag's experience; and disdaining to ask favor or friendship from a sneering world, she resolved to shut herself up in a hovel she had often passed in better days, and which she knew to be untenanted. She vowed to ask no favors of familiar faces; to die neglected and forgotten before she would be dependent on any. Removed from the village, she was seldom seen except as upon your introduction, gentle reader, with downcast visage, returning her work to her employer, and thus providing herself with the means of subsistence. In two years many hands craved the same avocation; foreigners who cheapened toil and clamored for a livelihood, competed with her, and she could not thus sustain herself. She was now above no drudgery. Occasionally old acquaintances called to be favored with help of some kind, which she was glad to bestow for the sake of the money it would bring her; but the association with them was such a painful reminder of by-gones, she returned to her hut morose and revengeful, refusing all offers of a better home than she possessed. Thus she lived for years, hugging her wrongs, but making no effort to escape. She had never known plenty, scarcely competency; but the present was beyond comparison with those innocent years when the coronet of virtue was hers.

Every year her melancholy increased, her means diminished. At last no one seemed to notice her, save a kind-hearted African, who often called to inquire after her health and to see if she needed any fuel, he having the responsibility of furnishing that article, and she in return mending or making garments.

"How much you earn dis week, Mag?" asked he one Saturday evening.

"Little enough, Jim. Two or three days without any dinner. I washed for the Reeds, and did a small job for Mrs. Bellmont; that's all. I shall starve soon, unless I can get more to do. Folks seem as afraid to come here as if they expected to get some awful disease. I don't believe there is a person in the world but would be glad to have me dead and out of the way."

"No, no, Mag! don't talk so. You shan't starve so long as I have barrels to hoop. Peter Greene boards me cheap. I'll help you, if nobody else will."

A tear stood in Mag's faded eye. "I'm glad," she said, with a softer tone than before, "if there is *one* who isn't glad to see me suffer. I b'lieve all Singleton wants to see me punished, and feel as if they could tell when I've been punished long enough. It's a long day ahead they'll set it, I reckon."

After the usual supply of fuel was prepared, Jim returned home. Full of pity for Mag, he set about devising measures for her relief. "By golly!" said he to himself one day—for he had become so absorbed in Mag's interest that he had fallen into a habit of musing aloud–"By golly! I wish she'd *marry* me."

"Who?" shouted Pete Greene, suddenly starting from an unobserved corner of the rude shop.

"Where you come from, you sly nigger!" exclaimed Jim.

"Come, tell me, who is't?" said Pete; "Mag Smith, you want to marry?"

"Git out, Pete! and when you come in dis shop again, let a nigger know it. Don't steal in like a thief."

Pity and love know little severance. One attends the other. Jim acknowledged the presence of the former, and his efforts in Mag's behalf told also of a finer principle.

This sudden expedient which he had unintentionally disclosed, roused his thinking and inventive powers to study upon the best method of introducing the subject to Mag.

He belted his barrels, with many a scheme revolving in his mind, none of which quite satisfied him, or seemed, on the whole, expedient. He thought of the pleasing contrast between her fair face and his own dark skin; the smooth, straight hair, which he had once, in expression of pity, kindly stroked on her now wrinkled but once fair brow. There was a tempest gathering in his heart, and at last, to ease his pent-up passion, he exclaimed aloud, "By golly!" Recollecting his former exposure, he glanced around to see if Pete was in hearing again. Satisfied on this point, he continued: "She'd be as much of a prize to me as she'd fall short of coming up to the mark with white folks. I don't care for past things. I've done things 'fore now I's 'shamed of. She's good enough for me, any how."

One more glance about the premises to be sure Pete was away.

The next Saturday night brought Jim to the hovel again. The cold was fast coming to tarry its apportioned time. Mag was nearly despairing of meeting its rigor.

"How's the wood, Mag?" asked Jim.

"All gone; and no more to cut, any how," was the reply.

"Too bad!" Jim said. His truthful reply would have been, I'm glad.

"Anything to eat in the house?" continued he.

"No," replied Mag.

"Too bad!" again, orally, with the same *inward* gratulation as before.

"Well, Mag," said Jim, after a short pause, "you's down low enough. I don't see but I've got to take care of ye. 'Sposin' we marry!"

Mag raised her eyes, full of amazement, and uttered a sonorous "What?"

Jim felt abashed for a moment. He knew well what were her objections.

"You's had trial of white folks any how. They run off and left ye, and now none of 'em come near ye to see if you's dead or alive. I's black outside, I know, but I's got a white heart inside. Which you rather have, a black heart in a white skin, or a white heart in a black one?"

"Oh, dear!" sighed Mag; "Nobody on earth cares for *me*—"

"I do," interrupted Jim.

"I can do but two things," said she, "beg my living, or get it from you."

"Take me, Mag. I can give you a better home than this, and not let you suffer so."

He prevailed; they married. You can philosophize, gentle reader, upon the impropriety of such unions, and preach dozens of sermons on the evils of amalgamation. Want is a more powerful philosopher and preacher. Poor Mag. She has sundered another bond which held her to her fellows. She has descended another step down the ladder of infamy.

Source: Our Nig; pseud. Harriet E. Wilson, Editor Henry Louis Gates, Jr. Boston: G. C. Rand & Avery, 1859. © 2000, Rector and Visitors of the University of Virginia. Courtesy of The University of Virginia Library.

23. Letters on American slavery from Victor Hugo, de Tocqueville, Emile de Girardin, Carnot, Passy, Mazzini, Humboldt, O. Lafayette—&c, 1860

These are letters written by Victor Hugo, Alexis de Tocqueville, Emile de Girardin, Carnot, Passy, Mazzini, Humboldt, and O. Lafayette to the editor of the *London News* in regard to the American Tract Society. These letters are in response to a decision not to publish a tract that touched upon slavery. They were later published by the American Anti-Slavery Society.

VICTOR HUGO ON JOHN BROWN

To The Editor Of *The London News*:

Sir: When our thoughts dwell upon the United States of America, a majestic form rises before the eye of imagination. It is a Washington!

Look, then, to what is taking place in that country of Washington at this present moment.

In the Southern States of the Union there are slaves; and this circumstance is regarded with indignation, as the most monstrous of inconsistencies, by the pure and logical conscience of the Northern States. A white man, a free man, John Brown, sought to deliver these negro slaves from bondage. Assuredly, if insurrection is ever a sacred duty, it must be when it is directed against Slavery. John Brown endeavored to commence the work of emancipation by the liberation of slaves in Virginia. Pious, austere, animated with the old Puritan spirit, inspired by the spirit of the Gospel, he sounded to these men, these oppressed brothers, the rallying cry of Freedom. The slaves, enervated by servitude, made no response to the appeal. Slavery afflicts the soul with weakness. Brown, though deserted, still fought at the head of a handful of heroic men; he was riddled with balls; his two young sons, sacred martyrs, fell dead at his side, and he himself was taken. This is what they call the affair at Harper's Ferry.

John Brown has been tried, with four of his comrades, Stephens, Cowpoke, Green and Copeland.

What has been the character of his trial? Let us sum it up in a few words:—

John Brown, upon a wretched pallet, with six hal gaping wounds, a gun-shot wound in his arm, another in its loins, and two in his head, scarcely conscious of surrounding sounds, bathing his mattress in blood, and with the ghastly presence of his two dead sons ever beside him; his four fellow-sufferers wounded, dragging themselves along by his side; Stephens bleeding from four sabre wounds; justice in a hurry, and over-leaping all obstacles; an attorney, Hunter, who wishes to proceed hastily, and a judge, Parker, who suffers, him to have his way; the hearing cut short, almost every application for delay refused, forged and mutilated documents produced, the witnesses for the defense kidnapped, every obstacle thrown in the way of the prisoner's counsel, two cannon loaded with canister stationed in the Court, orders given to the jailers to shoot the prisoners if they sought to escape, forty minutes of deliberation, and three men sentenced to die! I declare on my honor that all this took place, not in Turkey, but in America!

Such things cannot be done with impunity in the face of the civilized world. The universal conscience of humanity is an ever-watchful eye. Let the judges of Charlestown, and Hunter and Parker, and the slaveholding jurors, and the whole population of Virginia, ponder it well: they are watched! They are not alone in the world. At this moment, America attracts the eyes of the whole of Europe.

John Brown, condemned to die, was to have been hanged on the 2d of December—this very day.

But news has just reached us. A respite has been granted to him. It is not until the 16th that he is to die. The interval is a brief one. Before it has ended, will a cry of mercy have had time to make itself effectually heard?

No matter! It is our duty to speak out.

Perhaps a second respite may be granted. America is a noble nation. The impulse of humanity springs quickly into life among a free people. We may yet hope that Brown will be saved.

If it were otherwise, if Brown should die on the scaffold on the 16th of December, what a terrible calamity! The executioner of Brown, let us avow it openly (for the day of the kings is past, and the day of the peoples dawns, and to the people we are bound frankly to speak the truth)—the executioner of Brown would be neither the attorney Hunter, nor the judge Parker, nor the Governor Wise, nor the State of Virginia; it would be, though we can scarce think or speak of it without a shudder, the whole American Republic.

The more one loves, the more one admires, the more one venerates that Republic, the more heart-sick one feels at the contemplation of such a catastrophe. A single State ought not to have the power to dishonor all the rest, and in this case there is an obvious justification for a federal intervention. Otherwise, by hesitating to interfere when it might prevent a crime, the Union becomes a participator in its guilt. No matter how intense may be the indignation of the generous Northern States, the Southern States force them to share the opprobrium of this murder. All of us, no matter who we may be, who are bound together as compatriots by the common tie of a democratic creed, feel ourselves in some measure compromised. If the scaffold should be erected on the 16th of December, the incorruptible voice of history would thenceforward testify that the august Confederation of the New World, had added to all its rites of holy brotherhood a brotherhood of blood, and the *fasces* of that splendid Republic would be bound together with the running noose that hung from the gibbet of Brown!

This is a bond that kills.

When we reflect on what Brown, the liberator, the champion of Christ, has striven to effect, and when we remember that he is about to die, slaughtered by the American Republic, the crime assumes an importance co-extensive with that of the nation which commits it—and when we say to ourselves that this nation is one of the glories of the human race; that like France, like England, like Germany, she is one of the great agents of civilization; that she sometimes even leaves Europe in the rear by the sublime audacity of some of her progressive movements; that she is the Queen of an entire world, and that her brow is irradiated with a glorious halo of freedom, we declare our conviction that John Brown will not die; for we recoil horror-struck from the idea of so great a crime committed by so great a people.

Viewed in a political light, the murder of Brown would be an irreparable fault. It would penetrate the Union with a gaping fissure which would lead in the end of its entire disruption. It is possible that the execution of Brown might establish slavery on a firm basis in Virginia, but it is certain that it would shake to its centre the entire fabric of American democracy. You preserve your infamy, but you sacrifice your glory. Viewed in a moral light, it seems to me that a portion of the enlightenment of humanity would be eclipsed, that even the ideas of justice and injustice would be obscured on the day which should witness the assassination of Emancipation by Liberty.

As for myself, though I am but a mere atom, yet being, as I am, in common with all other men, inspired with the conscience of humanity, I fall on my knees, weeping before the great starry banner of the New World; and with clasped hands, and with profound and filial respect, I implore the illustrious American Republic, sister of the French Republic, to see to the safety of the universal moral law, to save John Brown, to demolish the threatening scaffold of the 16th of December, and not to suffer that beneath its eyes, and I add, with a shudder, almost by its fault a crime should be perpetrated surpassing the first fratricide in iniquity.

For—yes, let America know it, and ponder on it well—there is something more terrible than Cain slaying Abel: It is Washington slaying Spartacus!

Victor Hugo.
Hauteville House, Dec. 2d, 1859.

VICTOR HUGO ON AMERICAN SLAVERY

To Mrs. Maria Weston Chapman.

Madame: I have scarcely anything to add to your letter. I would cheerfully sign every line of it. Pursue your holy work. You have with you all great souls and all good hearts.

You are pleased to believe, and to assure me, that my voice, in this august cause of Liberty, will be listened to by the great American people, whom I love so profoundly, and whose destinies, I am fain to think, are closely linked with the mission of France. You desire me to lift up my voice.

I will do it at once, and I will do it on all occasions. I agree with you in thinking that, within a definite time—that, within a time not distant—the United States will repudiate Slavery with horror! Slavery in such a country! Can there be an incongruity more monstrous? Barbarism installed in the very heart of a country, which is itself the affirmation of civilization; liberty wearing a chain; blasphemy echoing from the altar; the collar of a negro chained to the pedestal of Washington! It is a thing unheard of. I say more, it is impossible. Such a spectacle would destroy itself. The light of the Nineteenth Century alone is enough to destroy it.

What! Slavery sanctioned by law among that illustrious people, who for seventy years have measured the progress of civilization by their march, demonstrated democracy by their power, and liberty by their prosperity! Slavery in the United States! It is the duty of this republic to set such an example no longer. It is a shame, and she was never born to bow her head.

It is not when Slavery is taking leave of old nations, that it should be received by the new. What! When Slavery is departing from Turkey, shall it rest in America? What! Drive it from the hearth of Omar, and adopt it at the hearth of Franklin? No! No! No!

There is an inflexible logic which develops more or less slowly, which fashions, which redresses according to a mysterious plan, perceptible only to great spirits, the facts, the men, the laws, the morals, the people; or better, under all human things, there are things divine.

Let all those great souls who love the United States, as a country, be re-assured. The United States must renounce Slavery, or they must renounce Liberty. They cannot renounce Liberty. They must renounce Slavery, or renounce the Gospel. They will never renounce the Gospel.

Accept, Madame, with my devotion to the cause you advocate, the homage of my respect.

Victor Hugo.
6 Juillet, 1851, Paris.

LETTER FROM ALEXIS DE TOCQUEVILLE

I do not think it is for me, a foreigner, to indicate to the United States the time, the measures, or the men by whom Slavery shall be abolished.

Still, as the persevering enemy of despotism everywhere, and under all its forms, I am pained and astonished by the fact that the freest people in the world is, at the present time, almost the only one among civilized and Christian nations which yet maintains personal servitude; and this, while serfdom itself is about disappearing, where it has not already disappeared, from the most degraded nations of Europe.

An old and sincere friend of America, I am uneasy at seeing Slavery retard her progress, tarnish her glory, furnish arms to her detractors, compromise the future career of the Union which is the guaranty of her safety and greatness, and point our beforehand to her, to all her enemies, the spot where they are to strike. As a man too, I am moved at the spectacle of man's degradation by man, and I hope to see the day when the law will grant equal civil liberty to all the inhabitants of the same empire, as God accords the freedom of the will, without distinction, to the dwellers upon earth.

France, 1855.

LETTER FROM EMILE DE GIRARDIN

I seize the occasion now offered me to accuse myself of having too long believed, on the faith of American citizens and French travellers, that the slavery of the blacks neither could nor ought, for their own sakes, to be abolished, without a previous initiation to liberty, by labor, instruction, economy, and redemption—an individual purchase of each one by himself.

But this belief I end by classing among those inveterate errors, which are like the rings of a chain, that even the freest of men drag after them, and even the strongest find it difficult to break.

What I once believed, I believe no longer.

Of all the existing proofs that Liberty is to be conquered or gained, not given, or dealt out by halves, the strongest proof is that, in the United States, the freest of all countries, the maintenance of Slavery is not made a question of time, but of race. Now if the reasons there alleged for the perpetuating and the legalizing of Slavery are true, they will be no less true a thousand years hence than to-day; if they are false, they have no right to impose themselves for a day, for an hour, for a moment. Error has no right against truth; iniquity has no right against equity, for the same reason that the dying have no right against death.

I hold, then, as false—incontestably and absolutely false,—all that blind self-interest and limping common-place are continually repeating, in order to perpetuate and legalize Slavery in the United States; just as I hold as false all that was said and printed before 1789, to perpetuate and legitimate serfdom; and all that is still said in Russia, in favor of the same outrage of men against the nature of man. The slavery of the blacks is the opprobrium of the whites. Thus every wrong brings its own chastisement.

The punishment of the American people is to be the last of the nations, while it is also the first. It is the first, by that Liberty of which it has rolled back the limits, and it is the last by that Slavery whose inconsistency it tolerates; for there are no slaves without tyrants. What matter whether the tyrant be *regal* or *legal*?

Paris, (Office of La Presse,) 1855.

LETTER FROM M. CARNOT

The question of Slavery is intimately connected with questions of general policy.

The Pagan republics had Slavery for their basis. They were so organized that they could not subsist without it; and so when Slavery was shaken down, they perished. Liberty for the few, on condition of keeping the many in servitude—such was the principle of the ancient societies.

Christianity bids another morality triumph,—that of human brotherhood. Modern societies recognize the principle that each citizen increases the domain of his own liberty by sharing it with his fellows. Republican France put this principle in practice; at her two great epochs of emancipation, she hastened to send Liberty to her colonial possessions.

North America presents a sad anomaly—a contradiction to the general rule with which we have prefaced these reflections, and thence the enemies of Liberty try to justify their departure from it.

They pretend to believe that the Republic of the United States rests on a basis analogous to that of the Pagan republics; and that the application of the new morality will be dangerous to it. But it is not so. Liberty in the United States is founded on reason, on custom, on patriotism, and on experience already old. She can but gain by diffusion even to prodigality. In the United States, Slavery is more than elsewhere a monstrosity, protected only by private interests. It is a source of corruption and barbarism which delays America in the path of European civilization. It is a fatal example that she presents to Europe, to turn her from the pursuit of American independence.

Paris, 1855.

LETTER FROM M. PASSY

Humanity is governed by laws which continually impel it to extend, without ceasing, the sphere of its knowledge. There is no discovery which does not conduct it to new discoveries; each generation adds its own to the mass which it has received from the past, and thus from age to age are the strength and riches of civilization augmented.

Now it is one of the numerous proofs of the benevolent purposes of the Creator, that every step of mental progress strengthens the ideas of duty and justice, of which humanity makes application in its acts. Human society, as it gains light, does not merely learn thereby the better to profit by its labors. It gains, at the same time, clearer and surer notions of moral order. It discerns evil where it did not at first suspect its existence; and no sooner does it perceive the evil than it seeks the means to suppress it.

This is what, in our day, has awakened so much opposition to Slavery. Thanks to the flood of light already received, society begins to comprehend, not only its iniquity in principle, but all the degradation and suffering it scatters in the lands where it exists. A cry of reprobation arises, and associations are formed to hasten its abolition.

We may, without fear, assert that it will be with Slavery as with all the other remnants of ignorance and original barbarism. The day will come when it must disappear, with the rest of the institutions which have been found inconsistant with the moral feelings to which the development of human reason gives the mastery.

Let those reflect who, at this day, constitute themselves the defenders of Slavery. They have against them the most irresistible of all powers—that of moral truth becoming more and more distinct—that of human conceptions necessarily rising with the growth in knowledge of the divine will. Their defeat is, sooner or later, inevitable.

How much wiser would they be, did they resign themselves to the preparation for a reform, the necessity for which presents itself with such inflexible urgency. It is, doubtless, a work of difficulty. Freemen require other conditions than those to which they were subjected by the lash; but the requisite changes may be effected. Wise precautions and temporary arrangements, united with the injunctions of authority, will not fail of success. Proprietors who dread emancipation! show to your people a little of that benevolence which so promptly subdues those who are unaccustomed to it, and you will find them docile and industrious as freemen. It is Slavery which corrupts and deteriorates the faculties which God has given to all for the amelioration of their destinies and the enjoyment of existence. Liberty, on the contrary, animates and develops them. Human activity rises to extend its conquests, more ingenious and energetic at her reviving breath.

May such assertions as these, conformable as they are to the experience of all ages, no longer meet in America the contradictions which are long extinct in Europe. May those States of the Union where Slavery still counts its partizans, hasten to prepare for its abolition. Storms are gathering over the seat of injustice. Prosperity, gained at the expense of humanity, flows from a source which time will necessarily dry up. There can exist no durable prosperity on earth, but in consistency with the laws of God; and his laws command men to love and serve each other as brethren.

Nice, January 28th, 1855.

LETTER FROM MAZZINI

London, May 1, 1854.

Dear Sir: I have delayed to the present moment my answering your kind invitation, in the hope that I should, perhaps, be enabled to give a better answer than a written one; but I find that neither health nor business will allow me to attend. I must write, and express to you, and through you to your friends, how much I feel grateful for your having asked me to attend the first meeting of the "North of England Anti-Slavery Association;" how earnestly I sympathize with the noble aim you are going to pursue; how deeply I shall commune with your efforts, and help, if I can, their success. No man ought ever to inscribe on his flag the sacred word "Liberty," who is not prepared to shake hands cordially with those, whoever they are, who will attach their names to the constitution of your association. Liberty may be the godlike gift of all races, of all nations, of every being who bears on his brow the stamp of Man, or sink to the level of a narrow and mean self-interest, unworthy of the tears of good and the blood of the brave. I am yours, because I believe in the unity of God; yours, because I believe in the unity of mankind; yours, because I believe in the educatibility of the whole human race, and in a heavenly law of infinite progression for all; yours, because the fulfilment of the law implies the consciousness and the responsibility of the agent, and neither consciousness nor responsibility can exist in slavery; yours, because I have devoted my life to the emancipation of my own country. And I would feel unequal to this task, a mean rebel, not an apostle of truth and justice, had I not felt from my earliest years that the right and duty of revolting against lies and tyranny were grounded on a far higher sphere than that of the welfare of one single nation; that they must start from belief in a principle, which will have sooner or later to be universally applied: "*One God, one humanity, one law, one love from all for all.*" Blessed be your efforts, if they start from this high ground of a common faith; if you do not forget, whilst at work for the emancipation of the black race, the millions of white slaves, suffering, struggling, expiring in Italy, in Poland, in Hungary, throughout all Europe; if you always remember that free men only can achieve the work of freedom, and that Europe's appeal for the abolition of slavery in other lands will not weigh all-powerful before God and men, whilst Europe herself shall be desecrated by arbitrary, tyrannical power, by czars, emperors, and popes.

Every faithfully yours,
Joseph Mazzini

ANOTHER LETTER FROM MAZZINI

Rev. Dr. Beard, Manchester.
London, March 21st, 1859.

Dear Sir: I beg to apologize for being so late in acknowledging the receipt of $112.09, subscribed by you and others at the end of the lecture delivered at your institution by my friend, Mm. Jessie M. White Mario, toward our Italian school, &c.

I am very much pleased at my honored friend's first success and response to her efforts in the United States, coming from Young America, to whom Young Italy looks for sympathy and support in her approaching struggle, and my thanks are the thanks of all the members both teachers and pupils, of our Italian school.

We are fighting the same sacred battle for freedom and the emancipation of the oppressed—you, Sir, against *negro*, we against *white* slavery. The cause is truly identical; for, depend upon it, the day in which we shall succeed in binding to one freely accepted pact twenty-six millions of Italians, we shall give what we cannot now, an active support to the cause you pursue. We are both the servants of the God who says, "Before Me there is no Master, no Slave, no Man, No Woman, but only Human Nature, which must be everywhere responsible, therefore free."

May God bless your efforts and ours! May the day soon arrive in which the word *bondage* will disappear from our living languages, and only point out a historical record! And, meanwhile, let the knowledge that we, all combatants under the same flag, do, through time and space, commune in love and faith, and strengthen one another against the unavoidable suffering which we must meet on the way.

Believe me, my dear Sir,

Very gratefully yours,
Joseph Mazzini

LETTER FROM N. TOURGUENEFF

Paris, September 29, 1885.

Madame,—seeing you on the point of departing for America, I cannot forbear entreating you to be the bearer of my tribute of respect and admiration to one of your compatriots. Need I add that I have in view our holy cause of human freedom, and one of its most eminent defenders, Mr. Garrison? Every word he utters is dictated by the deepest sense of justice; but his recent discourse on the anniversary of British Colonial Emancipation is distinguished not only by its profound feeling of sympathy for the emancipated, but by that rigorously just reasoning, and that clear, firm, and above all, moral logic which leads him to prefer the separation of the States to the continuance of Slavery. It is by this trait that I recognize the true Abolitionist, and the truly worthy man. It was with the truest joy that I read those strong and noble words, each going straight to its end, acknowledging no law superior to the sentiment of right engraven in the human conscience by its divine Creator, and disdaining all the common-place sophistry of weakness and hypocrisy that is so often employed in these discussions.

Deeply touched by this discourse of Mr. Garrison, I feel that a Cause so holy, defended by such advocates, could not fail to triumph, if urged forward without delay. Every action, every work, which brings nearer the time of this triumph, is a blessing to millions of unfortunate beings.

May Almighty God crown with success the generous labors of all these noble men, who, after all, are but following the commands and walking in the ways traced by his holy will!

May I entreat of you, Madame, the kindness of presenting to Mr. Garrison the accompanying copy of my work, by which he will see that a co-laborer in another hemisphere has long wrought in the same vineyard of the Lord; if not with the same renown, I may, at least, venture to say with the same disinterestedness, with the same self-abnegation, with the same love for the oppressed. Even the efforts I made in their behalf they could never directly know, for exile and proscription have compelled me to live far from my own land, and to plead the cause of human rights in a language which is neither theirs nor mine. I am thoroughly persuaded that all success obtained in America in the cause of the colored race will be eminently serviceable to my poor countrymen in Russia. It is then, first as a man, and secondly as a Russian, that I hail the efforts of Mr. Garrison and his fellow-laborers for the deliverance of their country from the hideous plague-spot of Slavery.

Receive, Madame, my earnest good wishes for your voyage. May Heaven grant that in again beholding your native country, you may there find new consolations and fresh encouragements to persevere in the great Cause which you have made the principal object of your life.

Accept, at the same time, the expression of my high respect.

N. TOURGUENEFF. To Mrs. Henry Grafton Chapman.

LETTER FROM HUMBOLDT

In 1856, Baron von Humboldt caused the following letter to be inserted in the *Spenersche Zeitung*:—

"Under the title of *Essai Politique sur l' Isle de Cuba*, published in Paris in 1826, I collected together all that the large edition of my *Voyage aux Regions Equinoxiales du Nouveau Continent* contained upon the state of agriculture and slavery in the Antilles. There appeared at the same time an English and a Spanish translation of this work, the latter entitled *Ensayo Politico sobre la Isle de Cuba*, neither of which omitted any of the frank and open remarks which feelings of humanity had inspired. But there appears just now, strangely enough, translated from the Spanish translation, and not from the French original, and published by Derby and Jackson, in New York, an octavo volume of 400 pages, under the title of *The Island of Cuba*, by Alexander Humboldt; with notes and a preliminary essay by J. S. Thrasher. The translator, who has lived a long time on that beautiful island, has enriched my work by more recent *data* on the subject of the numerical standing of the population, of the cultivation of the soil, and the state of trade, and, generally speaking, exhibited a charitable moderation in his discussion of conflicting opinions. I owe it, however, to a moral feeling, that is now as lively in me as it was in 1826, publicly to complain that in a work which bears my name, the entire seventh chapter of the Spanish translation, with which my *essai politique* ended, has been arbitrarily omitted. To this very portion of my work I attach greater importance than to any astronomical observations, experiments of magnetic intensity, or statistical statements. I have examined with frankness (I here repeat the words I used thirty years ago) whatever concerns the organization of human society in the colonies, the unequal distribution of the rights and enjoyments of life, and the impending dangers which the wisdom of legislators and the moderation of freemen can avert, whatever may be the form of government.

"It is the duty of the traveller who has been an eye-witness of all that torments and degrades human nature to cause the complaints of the unfortunate to reach those whose duty it is to relieve them. I have repeated, in this treatise, the fact that the ancient legislation of Spain on the subject of slavery is less inhuman and atrocious than that of the slave States on the American continent, north or south of the equator.

"A steady advocate as I am for the most unfettered expression of opinion in speech or in writing, I should never have thought of complaining if I had been attacked on account of my statements; but I do think I am entitled to demand that in the free States of the continent of America, people should be allowed to read what has been permitted to circulate from the first year of its appearance in a Spanish translation.

ALEXANDER VON HUMBOLDT

"Berlin, July, 1856."

HUMBOLDT ON WEBSTER.

"For thirty years—for thirty years (and he counted them on his fingers)—you have made no progress about slavery; you have gone backward—very far backward in any respects about that. I think especially of your law of 1850, that law by which a man in a free State, where he ought to be free, can be made a slave of. That I always call the *Webster* law.

"I always before liked Mr. Webster. He was a great man. I knew him, and always till then liked him. But, ever after that, I hated him. He was the man who made it. If he wanted to prevent it, he could have done it. That is the reason why I call it the Webster law. And ever after that, I hated him."

I made some remarks about Mr. Webster's influence on that point not being confined to a political sphere, but of his also carrying with him that circle of literary men with whom he was connected. "Yes," said he, "it was he who did it all; and those very men not connected with politics, who ought to have stood against it, as you say, he moved with it. You came from New England, where there is so much anti-slavery feeling, and where you have learned to think slavery is bad. While you are here in Europe, you may see things which you think bad; but I know Europe, and I tell you that you will find nothing here that is one half so bad as your slavery is."

These were the opinions of Baron Humboldt, a Christian philosopher of world-wide renown, whose views of men and of nations went further to establish their character, than any man now living. As Humboldt thought, the Christian world would think. Mr. Webster, as one of Fillmore's Cabinet, approved the Fugitive Act, and lent his personal and official influence to sustain it. By doing that, he let down his own moral nature. He not only disgraced himself, but the nation who placed him in that conspicuous position. We would not speak unkindly of any man; but that reads and reflects can be ignorant of the fact, that all who sustain or sanction that infamous enactment must tarnish their own characters, and degrade themselves in their own opinion, and in the opinion of all good men?

LETTER FROM O. LAFAYETTE

Paris, April 26 1851.
To M. Victor Schaelcher, Representative of the People.
My Dear Colleague,—you have been so obliging as to ask for my views and impressions respecting one of the most important events of our epoch,—the Aboli-tion of Slavery in the French Colonies. I know well that you have an almost pater-nal interest in this question. You have contributed more than any one to the emancipation of the blacks, in our possessions beyond the seas, and you have enjoyed the double pleasure of seeing the problem completely resolved, and resolved by the Government of the Republic. At the present time, wearied by controversy, the mind loves to repose upon certain and solid progress, which future events can neither alter nor destroy, and which are justly considered as the true conquests of civilization and humanity. In examining the Emancipation of the Slaves in the French Antilles, from the point of view of the material interests of France, it may be variously appreciated; but the immense moral benefit of the act of Emancipation cannot be contested.

In one day, and as by the stroke of a wand, one hundred and fifty thousand of human beings were snatched from the degradation in which they had been held by former legislation, and resumed their rank in the great human family. And we should not omit to state, that this great event was accomplished without our wit-nessing any of those disorders and struggles which had been threatened, in order to perplex the consciences of the Friends of Abolition.

Will the momentary obstruction of material interests be opposed to these great results? When has it ever been possible in this world to do much good, without seeming at the same time to do a little harm?

I have sometime heard it said that the conditions labor in the Colonies would have been less disturbed, if the preparation and the accomplishment of the Emanci-pation had been left to the colonists themselves; but you know better than I, my dear Colleague, that these assertions are hardly sincere.

We cannot but recollect with what unanimity and what vehemence the colonial councils opposed, in 1844 and 1845, the Ameliorations that we sought to introduce into the condition of the Slaves.

Is it not evident that this disposition would have rendered impossible the time of a system of transition, which indeed was attempted without success in the English colonies? For myself, I am quite convinced that it would have been impossible to effect the emancipation otherwise than as it was effected, that is to say, in one day, and by a single decree. I would add also, that in my opinion the Abolition of Slavery in our colonies would have remained a long time unaccomplished, if France had not been in Revolution: and if it be easy to understand why all men of the white race do not consent to the Revolution of 1848, I cannot conceive that a single man of color can be found, who does not regard it with benedictions.

Furthermore, my dear colleague, this great question of the Abolition of Negro Slavery, which has my entire sympathy, appears to me to have established its importance throughout the world. At the present time, the States of the Peninsula, if I do not deceive myself, are the only European powers who still continue to possess Slaves; and America, while continuing to uphold Slavery, feel daily more and more how heavily this plague weighs upon her destinies.

In expressing to you, my dear colleague, how much I rejoice in these results, I do not gratify my personal feelings alone. I obey also my family traditions.

You know the interest which my grandfather, General LaFayette, took in the emancipation of the negroes. You know what he had begun to do at the Habitation de la Gabrielle, and what he intended to do there. It was not among the least regrets of his life, that he was stopped in that enterprise.

Pardon, my dear colleague, the details into which I have been led. I know well that I can hardly be indiscreet in speaking on this subject to you. I rely upon those sentiments of friendship which you have always testified for me, and which differences of opinion respecting other political questions cannot weaken.

With fresh assurances of my friendship and consideration,

Your obedient servant and devoted Colleague,

O. LAFAYETTE, Representative of the People, (Seine et Maine.)

Testimony Of Gen. LaFayette. 'When I am indulging in my views of American liberty, it is mortifying to be reminded that a large portion of the people in that very country are SLAVES. It is a dark spot on the face of the nation.' 'I never would have drawn my sword in the cause of American, If I could have conceived that thereby I was helping to found A NATION OF SLAVES.'

LETTER FROM EDWARD BAINES

To what source shall we trace the heroic deeds and immortal productions of the ancient Greeks, but to the fount of Liberty? In what mould were those men cast who made Rome the mistress of Italy, and the world but the mould of Liberty? Among whom did art, letter, and commerce revive, after the sleep of the dark ages, but among the citizens of free republics? Where was the Reformation cradled but among the sons of Liberty? What passages of the history of England are held in the fondest remembrance, if not Magna Charta, the Bill of Rights, and the charters and statutes which secure civil and religious freedom? In the history of the United States, what event yet awakens the proud enthusiasm of a whole people, in comparison with the Declaration of Independence? Among the colonies of England, what Act arouses a joy the deepest and most universal but that of Slave Emancipation?

Does not every oppressed nation groan in its bondage? Does not every free nation exult in its freedom? Would not every slave leap to break his chains?

If in any nation, slavery is the most monstrous of inconsistencies, it is in a free republic; and if in any community it is the most flagrant of sins, it is in a Christian community.

Nothing is more notorious than the tendency of self-interest to blind the judgment; and it is, therefore, the part of wisdom for those who are interested, to ask in any question of difficulty the judgment of those who are disinterested. If American Christians will accept the opinion of English Christians they will learn that it is unanimously and unhesitatingly adverse to slavery. Without distinction of party or sect, Englishmen condemn the system of slaveholding; but if any are more earnest than others in expressing this condemnation, it is those who rejoice in the establishment of American Independence, and who have most sympathy with free institutions. It is not assumed that all masters are cruel, or all miserable. But it is known that masters may be cruel with impunity, and that slaves are, to the last hour of life, devoid of security for person, property, home, wife, or children. To reflect on these things shocks the understanding and heart of all English Christians. They feel deeply for their Christian brethren and sisters in bondage, and it is difficult for them to believe that other Christian brethren can be the means of so great an injustice. A Christian inflicting the lash, as it is inflicted in the Slave States of America, or selling his fellow man for money, seems to them an incomprehensible thing. Be it remembered, there is no national or political prejudice in this. English Christians felt the same when the slave owners were their own countrymen, and so strongly did they feel it as to buy the freedom of the slaves at a great price. May they not, then, appeal to the Christians of the United States, to declare uncompromising hostility against the slave system? Let slavery be abolished, and the United States would rise higher in the estimation of the Old World, than if all the New World were embraced in their Union, and all were one golden California.

Edward Baines.
Leeds Mercury Office, Nov. 9th, 1856.

TESTIMONY OF DANIEL O'CONNELL.

I will now turn to a subject of congratulation: I mean the Anti-Slavery Societies of America—those noble-hearted men and women, who through difficulties and dangers, have proved how hearty they are in the cause of abolition. I hail them all as my friends, and wish them to regard me as a brother. I wish for no higher station in the world; but I do covet the honor of being a brother with these American Abolitionists. In this country, the abolitionists are in perfect safety; here we have fame and honor; we are lauded and encouraged by the good; we are smiled upon and cheered by the fair; we are bound together by godlike truth and charity; and though we have our differences as to points of faith, we have no differences as to this point, and we proceed in our useful career esteemed and honored. But it is not so with our anti-slavery friends in America: there they are vilified, there they are insulted. Why, did not very lately a body of men—of gentlemen, so called—of persons who would be angry if you denied them that cognomen, and would even be ready to call you out to share a rifle and a ball—did not such "gentlemen" break in upon an Anti-Slavery Society in America; aye, upon a ladies' Anti-Slavery Society, and assault them in a America; aye, upon a ladies' Anti-Slavery Society, and assault them in a most cowardly manner? And did they not denounce the members of that Society? And where did this happen? Why, in Boston—in enlightened Boston, the capital of a non-slaveholding State. In this country, the abolitionist have nothing to complain of; but in America, they are met with the bowie-knife and lynch law! Yes! in America, you have had martyrs; your cause has been stained with blood; the voice of your brethren's blood crieth from the ground, and riseth high, not, I trust, for vengeance, but for mercy upon those who have thus treated them. But you ought not be discouraged, nor relax in your efforts. Here you have honor. A human being cannot be placed in a more glorious position than to take up such a cause under such circumstances. I am delighted to be one of a Convention in which are so many of such great and good men. I trust that their reception will be such as that their zeal may be greatly strengthened to continue their noble struggle. I have reason to hope that, in this assembly, a voice will be raised which will roll back in thunder to America, which will mingle with her mighty waves, and which will cause one universal shout of liberty to be heard throughout the world. O, there is not a delegate from the Anti-Slavery Societies of America, but ought to have his name, aye, her name, written in characters of immortality. The Anti-Slavery Societies in America are deeply persecuted, and are deserving of every encouragement which we can possibly give them. I would that I had the eloquence to depict their character aright; but my tongue falters, and my powers fail, while I attempt to describe them. They are the true friends of humanity, and would that I had a tongue to describe aright the mighty majesty of their undertaking!—[*Extract from a speech of Daniel o'Connell, at the World's Anti-Slavery Convention in London, 1840.*]

Source: Boston: American Anti-slavery Society, 1860. Library of Congress, Rare Book and Special Collections Division, Daniel A. P. Murray Pamphlets Collection.

24. Correspondence between Lydia Maria Child and Gov. Wise and Mrs. Mason, of Virginia, 1860

In 1860, Virginia abolitionist Lydia Maria Child wrote to Governor Henry A. Wise of Virginia regarding the arrest and execution of abolitionist John Brown. In the fall of 1859 (October 16), Brown and twenty-one men had arrived under the cover of night in the Virginia town of Harpers Ferry. The abolitionist had captured scores of local officials as hostages and seized arms from an arsenal. Dubbing themselves part of an "army of emancipation," Brown and his men had hoped to spark a rebellion that would eventually overturn slavery. Instead, the rebels were captured by Col. Robert E. Lee. Brown was tried, convicted of murder and slave insurrection, and promptly hanged.

In her correspondence with Wise, Child criticizes Virginia's laws on race and draws a rebuke from Wise. Also included is a letter from John Brown to Child asking for financial help for his family, and an exchange of (hostile) letters between Child and another Virginia woman, Mrs. Mason, over the issues of Brown's tactics and slavery.

Wayland, Mass., Oct. 26th, 1859.

Governor Wise: I have heard that you were a man of chivalrous sentiments, and I know you were opposed to the iniquitous attempt to force upon Kansas a

Constitution abhorrent to the moral sense of her people. Relying upon these indications of honor and justice in your character, I venture to ask a favor of you. Enclosed is a letter to Capt. John Brown. Will you have the kindness, after reading it yourself, to transmit it to the prisoner?

I and all my large circle of abolition acquaintances were taken by surprise when news came of Capt. Brown's recent attempt; nor do I know of a single person who would have approved of it, had they been apprised of his intention. But I and thousands of others feel a natural impulse of sympathy for the brave and suffering man. Perhaps God, who sees the inmost of our souls, perceives some such sentiment in your heart also. He needs a mother or sister to dress his wounds, and speak soothingly to him. Will you allow me to perform that mission of humanity? If you will, may God bless you for the generous deed!

I have been for years an uncompromising Abolitionist, and I should scorn to deny it or apologize for it as much as John Brown himself would do. Believing in peace principles, I deeply regret the step that the old veteran has taken, while I honor his humanity towards those who became his prisoners. But because it is my habit to be as open as the daylight, I will also say, that if I believed our religion justified men in fighting for freedom, I should consider the enslaved every where as best entitled to that right. Such an avowal is a simple, frank expression of my sense of natural justice.

But I should despise myself utterly if any circumstances could tempt me to seek to advance these opinions in any way, directly or indirectly, after your permission to visit Virginia has been obtained on the plea of sisterly sympathy with a brave and suffering man. I give you my word of honor, which was never broken, that I would use such permission solely and singly for the purpose of nursing your prisoner, and for no other purpose whatsoever.

Yours, respectfully,
L. Maria Child

REPLY OF GOV. WISE

Richmond, Va., Oct. 29th, 1859

Madam: Yours of the 26th was received by me yesterday, and at my earliest leisure I respectfully reply to it, that I will forward the letter for John Brown, a prisoner under our laws, arraigned at the bar of the Circuit Court for the country of Jefferson, at Charlestown, Va., for the crimes of murder, robbery and treason, which you ask me to transmit to him. I will comply with your request in the only way which seems to me proper, by enclosing it to the Commonwealth's attorney, with the request that he will ask the permission of the Court to hand it to the prisoner. Brown, the prisoner, is now in the hands of the judiciary, not of the executive, of this Commonwealth.

You ask me, further, to allow you to perform the mission "of mother or sister, to dress his wounds, and speak soothingly to him." By this, of course, you mean to be allowed to visit him in his cell, and to minister to him in the offices of humanity. Why should you not be so allowed, Madam? Virginia and Massachusetts are involved in no civil war, and the Constitution which unites them in one confederacy guarantees to you the privileges and immunities of a citizen of the United States in the State of Virginia. That Constitution I am sworn to support, and am, therefore, bound to protect your privileges and immunities as a citizen of Massachusetts coming into Virginia for any lawful and peaceful purpose.

Coming, as you propose, to minister to the captive in prison, you will be met, doubtless, by all our people, not only in a chivalrous, but in a Christian spirit. You have the right to visit Charlestown. Va., Madam; and your mission being merciful and humane, will not only allowed, but respected if not welcomed. A few unenlightened and inconsiderate persons, fanatical in their modes of thought and action, to maintain justice and right, might molest you, or be disposed to do so; and this might suggest the imprudence of risking any experiment upon the peace of a society very much excited by the crimes with whose chief author you seem to sympathize so much. But still, I repeat, your motives and avowed purpose are lawful and peaceful, and I will, as far as I am concerned, do my duty in protecting your rights in our limits. Virginia and her authorities would be weak indeed—weak in point of folly, and weak in point of power—if her State faith and constitutional obligations cannot be redeemed in her own limits to the letter of morality as well as of law; and if her chivalry cannot courteously receive a lady's visit to a prison, every arm which guards Brown from rescue on the one hand, and from Lynch law on the other, will be ready to guard your person in Virginia.

I could not permit an insult even to woman in her walk of charity among us, though it to be to one who whetted knives of butchery for our mothers, sisters, daughters and babes. We have no sympathy with your sentiments of sympathy with Brown, and are surprised that you were "taken by surprise when news came of Capt. Brown's recent attempt." His attempt was a natural consequence of your sympathy, and the errors of that sympathy ought to make you doubt its virtue from the effect on his conduct. But it is not of this I should speak. When you arrive at Charlestown, if you go there, it will be for the Court and its officers, the Commonwealth's attorney, sheriff and jailer, to say whether you may see and wait. On the prisoner. But whether you are thus permitted or not, (and you will be, if my advice can prevail) you may rest assured that he will be humanely, lawfully and mercifully dealt by in prison and on trial.

Respectfully,
Henry A. Wise

MRS. CHILD TO GOV. WISE

In your civil but very diplomatic reply to my letter, you inform me that I have a constitutional right to visit Virginia, for peaceful purposes, in common with every citizen of the United States. I was perfectly well aware that such was the *theory* of constitutional obligation in the Slave States; but I was also aware of what you omit to mention, viz.; that the Constitution has, in reality, been completely and systematically nullified, whenever it suited the convenience or the policy of the Slave Power. Your constitutional obligation, for which you profess so much respect, has never proved any protection to citizens of the Free States, who happened to have a black, brown, or yellow complexion; nor to any white citizen whom you even suspected of entertaining opinions opposite to your own, on a question of vast importance to the temporal welfare and moral example of our common country. This total disregard of constitutional obligation has been manifested not merely by the Lynch Law of mobs in the Slave States, but by the deliberate action of magistrates and legislators. What regard was paid to constitutional obligation in South Carolina, when Massachusetts sent the Hon. Mr. Hoar there as an envoy, on a purely legal errand? Mr. Hedrick, Professor of Political Economy in the University of North Carolina, had a constitutional right to reside in that State. What regard was paid to that right, when he was driven from his home, merely for declaring that he considered Slavery an impolitic system, injurious to the prosperity of States? What respect for constitutional rights was manifested by Alabama, when a bookseller in Mobile was compelled to flee for his life, because he had, at the special request of some of the citizens, imported a few copies of a novel that every body was curious to read? Your own citizen, Mr. Underwood, had a constitutional right to live in Virginia, and vote for whomsoever he pleased. What regard was paid to his rights, when he was driven from your State for declaring himself in favor of the election of Fremont? With these, and a multitude of other examples before your eyes, it would seem as if the less that was said about respect for constitutional obligations at the South, the better. Slavery is, in fact, an infringement of all law, and adheres to no law, save for its own purposes of oppression.

You accuse Captain John Brown of "whetting knives of butchery for the mothers, sisters, daughters and babes" of Virginia; and you inform me of the well-known fact that he is "arraigned for the crimes of murder, robbery and treason." I will not here stop to explain why I believe that old hero to be no criminal, but a martyr to righteous principles which he sought to advance by methods sanctioned by his own religious views, though not by mine. Allowing that Capt. Brown did attempt a scheme in which murder, robbery and treason were, to his own consciousness, involved, I do not see how Gov. Wise can consistently arraign him for crimes he has himself commended. *You* have threatened to trample on the Constitution, and break the Union, if a majority of the legal voters in these Confederated States dared to elect a President unfavorable to the extension of Slavery. Is not such a declaration proof of premeditated treason? In the Spring of 1842, you made a speech in Congress, from which I copy the following:—

"Once set before the people of the Great Valley the conquest of the rich Mexican Provinces, and you might as well attempt to stop the wind. This Government might send its troops, but they would run over them like a herd of buffalo. Let the work once begin, and I do not know that this House would hold *me* very long. Give me five millions of dollars, and I would undertake to do it myself. Although I do not know how to set a single squadron in the field, I could find men to do it. Slavery should pour itself abroad, without restraint, and find no limit but the Southern Ocean. The Camanches should no longer hold the richest mines of Mexico. Every golden image which had received the profanation of a false worship, should soon be melted down into good American eagles. I would cause as much gold to cross the Rio del Norte as the mules of Mexico could carry; aye, and I would make better use of it, too, than any lazy, bigoted priesthood under heaven."

When you thus boasted that you and your "booted loafers" would overrun the troops of the United States "like a herd of buffalo," if the Government sent them to arrest your invasion of a neighboring nation, at peace with the United States, did you not pledge yourself to commit treason? Was it not by robbery, even of churches, that you proposed to load the mules of Mexico with gold for the United States? Was it not by the murder of unoffending Mexicans that you expected to advance those schemes of avarice and ambition? What humanity had you for Mexican "mothers and babes," whom you proposed to make childless and fatherless? And for what purpose was this wholesale massacre to take place? Not to right the wrongs of any oppressed class; not to sustain any great principles of justice, or of freedom; but merely to enable "Slavery to pour itself forth without restraint."

Even if Captain Brown were as bad as you paint him, I should suppose he must naturally remind you of the words of Macbeth:

"We but teach
Bloody instructions, which, being taught, return
To plague the inventor: This even-handed justice
Commends the ingredients of our poisoned chalice
To our own lips."

If Captain Brown intended, as you say, to commit treason, robbery and murder, I think I have shown that he could find ample authority for such proceedings in the public declarations of Gov. Wise. And if, as he himself declares, he merely intended to free the oppressed, where could he read a more forcible lesson than is furnished by the State Seal of Virginia? I looked at it thoughtfully before I opened your letter; and though it had always appeared to me very suggestive, it never seemed to me so much so as it now did in connection with Captain John Brown. A liberty-loving hero stands with his foot upon a prostrate despot; under his strong arm, manacles and chains lie broken; and the motto is, *"Sic Semper Tyrannis"*; "Thus be it ever done to Tyrants." And this is the blazon of a State whose most profitable business is the Internal Slave-Trade!—in whose highways coffles of human chattels, chained and manacled, are frequently seen! And the Seal and the Coffles are both looked upon by other chattels, constantly exposed to the same fate! What if some Vezey, or Nat Turner, should be growing up among those apparently quiet spectators? It is in no spirit if taunt or of exultation that I ask this question. I never think of it but with anxiety, sadness, and sympathy. I know that a slave-holding community necessarily lives in the midst of gunpowder; and, in this age, sparks of free thought are flying in every direction. You cannot quench the fires of free thought and human sympathy by any process of cunning or force; but there is a method by which you can effectually wet the gunpowder. England has already tried it, with safety and success. Would that you could be persuaded to set aside the prejudices of education, and candidly examine the actual working of that experiment! Virginia is so richly endowed by nature that Free Institutions alone are wanting to render her the most prosperous and powerful of the States.

In your letter, you suggest that such a scheme as Captain Brown's is the natural result of the opinions with which I sympathize. Even if I thought this to be a correct statement, though I should deeply regret it, I could not draw the conclusion that humanity ought to be stifled, and truth struck dumb, for fear that long-successful despotism might be endangered by their utterance. But the fact is, you mistake the source of that strange outbreak. No abolition arguments or denunciations, however earnestly, loudly, or harshly proclaimed, would have produced that result. It was the legitimate consequence of the continual and constantly increasing aggressions of the Slave Power. The Slave States, in their desperate efforts to sustain a bad and dangerous institution, have encroached more and more upon the liberties of the Free States. Our inherent love of law and order, and our superstitious attachment to the

Union, you have mistaken for cowardice; and rarely have you let slip any opportunity to add insult to aggression.

The manifested opposition to Slavery began with the lectures and pamphlets of a few disinterested men and women, who based their movements upon purely moral and religious grounds; but their expostulations were met with a storm of rage, with tar and feathers, brickbats, demolished houses, and other applications of Lynch Law. When the dust of the conflict began to subside a little, their numbers were found to be greatly increased by the efforts to exterminate them. They had become an influence in the State too important to be overlooked by shrewd calculators. Political economists began to look at the subject from a lower point of view. They used their abilities to demonstrate that slavery was a wasteful system, and that the Free States were taxed, to an enormous extent, to sustain an institution which, at heart, two-thirds of them abhorred. The forty millions, or more, of dollars, expended in hunting Fugitive Slaves in Florida, under the name of the Seminole War, were adduced, as one item in proof, to which many more were added. At last, politicians were compelled to take some action on the subject. It soon became known to all the people that the Slave States had always managed to hold in their hands the political power of the Union, and that while they constituted only one-third of the white population of these States, they held more than two-thirds of all the lucrative, and once honorable offices; an indignity to which none but a subjugated people had ever submitted. The knowledge also became generally diffused, that while the Southern States *owned* their Democracy at home, and voted for them, they also systematically *bribed* the nominally Democratic party, at the North, with the offices adroitly kept at their disposal.

Through these, and other instrumentalities, the sentiments of the original Garrisonian Abolitionist became very widely extended, in forms more or less diluted. But by far the most efficient co-labors we have ever had have been the Slave States themselves. By denying us the sacred Right of Petition, they roused the free spirit of the North, as it never could have been roused by the loud trumpet of Garrison, or the soul-animating bugle of Phillips. They bought the great slave, Daniel, and according to their established usage, paid him no wages for his labor. By his cooperation, they forced the Fugitive Slave Law upon us, in violation of all our humane instincts and all our principles of justice. And what did they procure for the Abolitionist by that despotic process? A deeper and wider detestation of Slavery throughout the Free States, and the publication of Uncle Tom's Cabin, an eloquent outburst of moral indignation, whose echoes wakened the world to look upon their shame.

By fillibustering and fraud, they dismembered Mexico, and having thus obtained the soil of Texas, they tried to introduce it as a Slave State into the Union. Failing to effect their purpose by constitutional means, they accomplished it by a most open and palpable violation of the Constitution, and by obtaining the votes of Senators on the false pretences.*

[Note: *The following Senators, Mr. Niles, of Connecticut, Mr. Dix, of New York, and Mr. Tappan, of Ohio, published statements that their votes had been obtained by false representations; and they declared that the case was the same with Mr. Heywood, of North Carolina.]

Soon afterward, a Southern Slave Administration ceded to the powerful monarchy of Great Britain several hundred thousands of square miles, that must have been made into Free States, to which that same Administration had declared that the United States had "an unquestionable right;" and then they turned upon the weak Republic of Mexico, and, in order to make more Slave States, wrested from her twice as many hundred thousands of square miles, to which we had not a shadow of right.

Notwithstanding all these extra efforts, they saw symptoms that the political power so long held with a firm grasp was in danger of slipping from their hands, by reason of the extension of Abolition sentiments, and the greater prosperity of Free States. Emboldened by continual success in aggression, they made use of the pretence of "Squatter Sovereignty" to break the league into which they had formerly cajoled the servile representatives of our blinded people, by which all the territory of the United States south of 36 ° 30' was guaranteed to Slavery, and all north of it to Freedom. Thus Kansas became the battle-ground of the antagonistic elements in our Government. Ruffians hired by the Slave Power were sent thither temporarily, to do the voting, and drive from the polls the legal voters, who were often murdered in the process. Names, copied from the directories of cities in other States, were returned by thousands as legal voters in Kansas, in order to establish a Constitution abhorred by the people. This was their exemplification of Squatter Sovereignty. A Massachusetts Senator, distinguished for candor, courtesy, and stainless integrity, was half murdered by slaveholders, merely for having the manliness to state these facts to the assembled Congress of the nation. Peaceful emigrants from the North, who went to Kansas for no other purpose than to till the soil, erect mills, and establish manufactories, schools, and churches, were robbed, outraged, and murdered. For many months, a war more ferocious than the warfare of wild Indians was carried on against a people almost unresisting, because they relied upon the Central Government for aid. And all this while, the power of the United States, wielded by the Slave Oligarchy, was on the side of the aggressors. They literally tied the stones, and let loose the mad dogs. This was the state of things when the hero of Osawatomie and his brave sons went to the rescue. It was he who first turned the tide of Border-Ruffian triumph, by showing them that blows were to be taken as well as given.

You may believe it or not, Gov. Wise, but it is certainly the truth that, because slaveholders so recklessly sowed the wind in Kansas, they reaped a whirlwind at Harper's Ferry.

The people of the North had a very strong attachment to the Union; but, by your desperate measures, you have weakened it beyond all power of restoration. They are not your enemies, as you suppose, but they cannot consent to be your tools for any ignoble task you may choose to propose. You must not judge of us by the crawling sinuosities of an Everett; or by our magnificent hound, whom you trained to hunt your poor cripples, and then sent him sneaking into a corner to die—not with shame for the base purposes to which his strength had been applied, but with vexation because you withheld from him the promised bone. Not by such as these must you judge the free, enlightened ycomanry of New England. A majority of them would rejoice to have the Slave States fulfil their oft-repeated threat of withdrawal from the Union. It has ceased to be a bugbear, for we begin to despair of being able, by any other process, to give the world the example of a real republic. The moral sense of these States is outraged by being accomplices in sustaining an institution vicious in all its aspects; and it is now generally understood that we purchase our disgrace at great pecuniary expense. If you would only make the offer of a separation in serious earnest, you would here the hearty response of millions, "Go, gentlemen, and 'stand not upon the order of your going, But go at once!'"

Yours, with all due respect,
L. Maria Child

EXPLANATORY LETTER

To The Editor Of The New York Tribune:

Sir: I was much surprised to see my correspondence with Governor Wise published in your columns. As I have never given any person a copy, I presume you must have obtained it from Virginia. My proposal to go and nurse that brave and generous old man, who so willingly gives his life a sacrifice for God's oppressed poor, originated in a very simple and unmeritorious impulse of kindness. I heard his friends inquiring, "Has he no wife, or sister, that can go to nurse him? We are trying to ascertain, for he needs some one." My niece said she would go at once, if her health were strong enough to be trusted. I replied that my age and state of health rendered me a more suitable person to go, and that I would go most gladly. I accordingly wrote to Captain Brown, and enclosed the letter to Governor Wise. My intention was to slip away quietly, without having the affair made public. I packed my trunk and collected a quantity of old linen for lint, and awaited tidings from Virginia. When Governor Wise answered, he suggested the "imprudence of trying any experiment upon the peace of a society already greatly excited," &c. My husband and I took counsel together, and we both concluded that, as the noble old veteran was said to be fast recovering from his wounds, and as my presence might create a popular excitement unfavorable to such chance as the prisoner had for a fair trial, I had better wait until I received a reply from Captain Brown himself. Fearing to do him more harm than good by following my impulse, I waited for his own sanction. Meanwhile, his wife, said to be a brave-hearted Roman matron, worthy of such a mate, has gone to him, and I have received the following reply.

Respectfully yours,
L. Maria Child
Boston, Nov. 10, 1859.

MRS. CHILD TO JOHN BROWN

Wayland, Mass., Oct. 26, 1859

Dear Capt. Brown: Though personally unknown to you, you will recognize in my name an earnest friend of Kansas, when circumstances made that Territory the battle-ground between the antagonistic principles of slavery and freedom, which politicians so vainly strive to reconcile in the government of the United States.

Believing in peace principles, I cannot sympathize with the method you chose to advance the cause of freedom. But I honor your generous intentions—I admire your courage, moral and physical. I reverence you for the humanity which tempered your zeal. I sympathize with you in your cruel bereavement, your sufferings, and your wrongs. In brief, I love you and bless you.

Thousands of hearts are throbbing with sympathy as warm as mine. I think of you night and day, bleeding in prison, surrounded by hostile faces, sustained only by trust in God and your own heart. I long to nurse you—to speak to you sisterly words of sympathy and consolation. I have asked permission of Governor Wise to do so. If the request is not granted, I cherish the hope that these few words may at least reach your hands, and afford you some little solace. May you be strengthened by the conviction that no honest man ever sheds blood for freedom in vain, however much he may be mistaken in his efforts. May God sustain you, and carry you through whatsoever may be in store for you!

Yours, with heartfelt respect, sympathy and affection,

L. Maria Child

REPLY OF JOHN BROWN

Mrs. L. Maria Child:

My Dear Friend—Such you prove to be, though a stranger—your most kind letter has reached me, with the kind offer to come here and take care of me. Allow me to express my gratitude for your great sympathy, and at the same time to propose to you a different course, together with my reasons for wishing it. I should certainly be greatly pleased to become personally acquainted with one so gifted and so kind, but I cannot avoid seeing some objections to it, under present circumstances. First, I am in charge of a most humane gentleman, who, with his family, has rendered me every possible attention I have desired, or that could be of the least advantage; and I am so recovered of my wounds as no longer to require nursing. Then, again, it would subject you to great personal inconvenience and heavy expense, without doing me any good. Allow me to name to you another channel through which you may reach me with your sympathies much more effectually. I have at home a wife and three young daughters, the youngest but little over five years old, the oldest nearly sixteen. I have also two daughters-in-law, whose husbands have both fallen near me here. There is also another widow, Mrs. Thompson, whose husband fell here. Whether she is a mother or not, I cannot say. All these, my wife included, live at North Elba, Essex county, New York. I have a middle-aged son, who has been, in some degree, a cripple from his childhood, who would have as much as he could well do to earn a living. He was a most dreadful sufferer in Kansas, and lost all he had laid up. He has not enough to clothe himself for the winter comfortably. I have no living son, or son-in-law, who did not suffer terribly in Kansas.

Now, dear friend, would you not as soon contribute fifty cents now, and a like sum yearly, for the relief of those very poor and deeply afflicted persons, to enable them to supply themselves and their children with bread and very plain clothing, and to enable the children to receive a common English education? Will you also devote your own energies to induce others to join you in giving a like amount, or any other amount, to constitute a little fund for the purpose named?

I cannot see how your coming here can do me the least good; and I am quite certain you can do immense good where you are. I am quite cheerful under all my afflicting circumstances and prospects; having, as I humbly trust, "the peace of God which passeth all understanding" to rule in my heart. You may make such use of this as you see it fit. God Almighty bless and reward you a thousand fold!

Yours in sincerity and truth,

John Brown

LETTER OF MRS. MASON

Alto, King George's Co., Va., Nov. 11th, 1859

Do you read your Bible, Mrs. Child? If you do, read there, "Woe unto you, hypocrites," and take to yourself with two-fold damnation that terrible sentence; for, rest assured, in the day of judgment it shall be more tolerable for those thus scathed by the awful denunciation of the Son of God, than for you. *You* would soothe with sisterly and motherly care the hoary-headed murderer of Harper's Ferry! A man whose aim and intention was to incite the horrors of a servile war—to condemn women of your own race, ere death closed their eyes on their sufferings from violence and outrage, to see their husbands and fathers murdered, their children butchered, the ground strewed with the brains of their babes. The antecedents of Brown's band proved them to have been the offscourings of the earth; and what would have been our fate had they found as many sympathizers in Virginia as they seem to have in Massachusetts?

Now, compare yourself with those your "sympathy" would devote to such ruthless ruin, and say, on that "word of honor, which never has been broken," would *you* stand by the bedside of an old negro, dying of a hopeless disease, to alleviate his sufferings as far as human aid could? Have *you* ever watched the last, lingering illness of a consumptive, to soothe, as far as in you lay, the inevitable fate? Do *you* soften the pangs of maternity in those around you by all the care and comfort you can give? Do *you* grieve with those near you, even though the sorrows resulted from their own misconduct? Did *you* ever sit up until the "wee hours" to complete a dress for a motherless child, that she might appear on Christmas day in a new one, along with her more fortunate companions? We do these and more for our servants, and why? Because we endeavor *to do our duty in that state of life it has pleased God to place us.* In his revealed word we read our duties to them—theirs to us are there also—"Not only to the good and gentle, but to the forward."—(Peter 2:18.) Go thou and do likewise, and keep away from Charlestown. If the stories read in the public prints be true, of the sufferings of the poor of the North, you need not go far for objects of charity. "Thou hypocrite! take first the beam out of thine own eye, then shalt thou see clearly to pull the mote out of thy neighbor's." But if, indeed, you do lack objects of sympathy near you, go to Jefferson county, to the family of George Turner, a noble, true-hearted man, whose devotion to his friend (Col. Washington) causing him to risk his life, was shot down like a dog. Or to that of old Beckham, whose grief at the murder of his negro subordinate made him needlessly expose himself to the aim of the assassin Brown. And when you can equal in deeds of love and charity to those *around* you, what is shown by nine-tenths of the Virginia plantations, then by your "sympathy" whet the knives for our throats, and kindle the torch that fires our homes. *You* reverence Brown for his clemency to his prisoners! Prisoners! and how taken? Unsuspecting workmen, going to their daily duties; unarmed gentlemen, taken from their beds at the dead hour of the night, by six men doubly and trebly armed. Suppose he had hurt a hair of their heads, do you suppose one of the band of desperadoes would have left the engine-house alive? And did he not know that his treatment of them was only hope of life then, or of clemency afterward? Of course he did. The United States troops could not have prevented him from being torn limb from limb.

I will add, in conclusion, no Southerner ought, after your letter to Governor Wise and to Brown, to read a line of your composition, or to touch a magazine which bears your name in its lists of contributors; and in this we hope for the "sympathy," at least of those at the North who deserve the name of woman.

M. J. C. Mason

REPLY OF MRS. CHILD

Wayland, Mass., Dec. 17th, 1859.

Prolonged absence from home has prevented my answering your letter so soon as I intended. I have no disposition to retort upon you the "two-fold damnation" to which you consign me. On the Contrary, I sincerely wish you well, both in this world and the next. If the anathema proved a safety valve to your own boiling spirit, it did some good to you, while it fell harmless upon me. Fortunately for all of us, the Heavenly Father rules His universe by laws, which the passions or the prejudices of mortals have no power to change.

As for John Brown, his reputation may be safety trusted to the impartial pen of History; and his motives will be righteously judged by Him who knoweth the secrets of all hearts. Men, however great they may be, are of small consequence in comparison with principles; and the principle for which John Brown died is the question issue between us.

You refer me to the Bible, from which you quote the favorite text of slaveholders:—"Servants, be subject to your masters with all fear; not only to the good and gentle, but also to the forward."—1 Peter, 2:18.

Abolitionists also have favorite texts, to some of which I would call your attention:—

"Remember those that are in bonds as bound with them."—Heb. 13:3. "Hide the outcasts. Bewray not him that wandereth. Let mine outcasts dwell with thee. Be thou a convert to them from the face of the spoiler."—Isa. 16:3, 4.

"Thou shalt not deliver unto his master the servant which is escaped from his master unto thee. He shall dwell with thee where it liketh him best. Thou shalt not oppress him."—Deut. 23:15, 16.

"Open thy mouth for the dumb, in the cause of all such are appointed to destruction. Open thy mouth judge righteously, and plead the cause of the poor and needy."—Prov. 29:8, 9.

"Cry aloud, spare not, lift up thy voice like a trumpet, and show my people their transgression, and the house of Jacob their sins."—Isa. 58:1.

I would especially commend to slaveholders the following portions of that volume, wherein you say God has revealed the duty of masters:—

"Masters, give unto your servants that which is just and equal, knowing that ye also have a Master in heaven."—Col. 4:1.

"Neither be ye called masters; for one is your master, even Christ; and all ye are brethren."—Matt. 23: 8, 10.

"Whatsoever ye would that men should do unto you, do ye even so unto them."—Matt. 7: 12.

"Is not this the fast that I have chosen, to loose the bands of wickedness, to undo the heavy burdens and to let the oppressed go free, and that ye break every yoke?"—Isa. 58:6.

"They have given a boy for a harlot, and sold a girl for wine, that they might drink."—Joel 3:3.

"He that oppresseth the poor, reproacheth his Maker."—Prov. 14:31.

"Rob not the poor, because he is poor; neither oppress the afflicted. For the Lord will plead their cause, and spoil the soul of those who spoiled them."—Prov. 22:22, 23.

"Woe unto him that useth his neighbor's service without wages, and giveth him not for his work."—Jer. 22:13.

"Let him that stole, steal no more, but rather let him labor, working with his hands."—Eph. 4:28.

"Woe unto them that decree unrighteous decrees, and that write grievousness which they have prescribed; to turn aside the needy from judgment, and to take away the right from the poor, that widows may be their prey, and that they may rob the fatherless."—Isa. 10:1, 2.

"If I did despise the cause of my man-servant or my maid-servant, when they contend with me, what then shall I do when God riseth up? and when he visiteth, what shall I answer Him?"—Job 31:13, 14.

"Thou hast sent widows away empty, and the arms of the fatherless have been broken. Therefore snares are round about thee, and sudden fear troubleth thee; and darkness, that thou canst not see."—Job 22:9, 10, 11.

"Behold, the hire of your laborers, who have reaped down your fields, which is of you kept back by fraud, crieth; and the cries of them which have reaped are entered into the ears of the Lord of saboath. Ye have lived in pleasure on the earth, and been wanton; ye have nourishes your hearts as in a day of slaughter; ye have condemned and killed the just."—James 5:4.

If the appropriateness of these texts is not apparent, I will try to make it so, by evidence drawn entirely from *Southern* sources. The Abolitionists are not such an ignorant set of fanatics as you suppose. They *know* whereof they affirm. They are familiar with the laws of the Slave States, which are alone sufficient to inspire abhorrence in any humane heart or reflecting mind not perverted by the prejudices of education and custom. I might fill many letters with significant extracts from your statue-books; but I have space only to glance at a few, which indicate the *leading* features of the system you cherish so tenaciously.

The universal rule of the slave State is, that "the child follows the condition of its *mother*." This is an index to many things. Marriages between white and colored people are forbidden by law; yet a very large number of the slaves are brown or yellow. When Lafayette visited this country in his old age, he said he was very much struck by the great change in the colored population of Virginia; that in the time of the Revolution, nearly all the household slaves were black, but when he returned to America, he found very few of them black. The advertisements in Southern newspapers often describe runaway slaves that "pass themselves for white men." Sometimes they are descibed as having straight, light hair blue eyes, and clear complexion." This could not be, unless their fathers, grandfathers, and great-grandfathers had been white men. But as their *mothers* were slaves, the law pronounces *them* slaves, subject to be sold on the auction-block whenever the necessities or convenience of their masters or mistresses required it. The sale of one's own children, brother, or sisters, has an ugly aspect to those who are unaccustomed to it; and, obviously, it cannot have a good moral influence, that law and custom should render licentiousness a *profitable* vice.

Throughout the Slave States, the testimony of no colored person, bond or free, can be received against a white man. You have some laws, which, on the face of them, would seem to restrain inhuman men from murdering or mutilating slaves; but they are rendered nearly null by the law I have cited. Any drunken master, overseer, or patrol, may go into the negro cabins, and commit what outrages he pleases, with perfect impunity, if no white person is present who chooses to witness against him. North Carolina and Georgia leave a large loophole for escape, even if white persons present, when murder is committed. A law to punish persons for "maliciously killing a slave" has this remarkable qualification: "Always provided that this act shall not extend to any dying of moderate correction." We at the North find it difficult to understand how *moderate* punishment can cause *death*. I have read several of your law books attentively, and I find no cases of punishment for the murder of a slave, except by fines paid to the *owner*, to indemnify him for the loss of his *property*: the same as if his horse or cow had been killed. In South Carolina Reports is a case where the State had indicted Guy Raines for the murder of slave Isaac. It was proved that William Gray, the owner of Isaac, had given him a *thousand lashes*. The poor creature made his escape, but was caught, and delivered to the custody of Raines, to be carried to the county jail. Because he refused to go, Raines gave him five hundred lashes, and he died soon after. The counsel for Raines proposed that he should be allowed to acquit himself by his *own oath*. The Court decided against it, because *white witnesses* had testified; but the Court of afterward decided he *ought* to have been exculpated by his own oath, and he was *acquitted*. Small indeed is the chance for justice to a slave, when his own color are not allowed to testify, if they see him maimed or his children murdered; when he has slaveholders for Judges and Jurors; when the murderer can exculpate himself by his own oath; and when the law provides that it is no murder to kill a slave by "moderate correction"!

Your laws uniformly declare that "slave shall be deemed a chattel personal in the hands of his master, to all intents, constrictions, and purposes whatsoever." This, of course, involves the right to sell his children, as if they were pigs; also, to take his wife from him "for any intent or purpose whatsoever." Your laws also make it death for him to resist a white man, however brutally he may be treated, or however much his family may be outraged before his eyes. If he attempts to run away, your laws allow any man to shoot him.

By your laws, all a slave's earnings belong to his master. He can neither receive donations or transmit property. If his master allows him some hours to work for himself, and by great energy and perseverance he earns enough to buy his own bones and sinews, his master may make him pay two or three times over, and he has no redress. Three such cases have come within my knowledge. Even a written promise from his master has no legal value, because slave can make no contracts.

Your laws also systematically aim at keeping the minds of the colored people in the most abject state of ignorance. If white people attempt to teach them to read or write, they are punished by imprisonment or fines; if they attempt to teach each other, they are punished with from twenty to thirty-nine lashes each. It cannot be said that the anti-slavery agitation produced such laws, for they date much further back; many of them when we were Provinces. They are the *necessities* of the system, which, being itself an outrage upon human nature, can be sustained only by perpetual outrages.

The next reliable source of information is the advertisements in the Southern papers. In the North Carolina (Raleigh) *Standard*, Mr. Mieajah Ricks advertises,

"Runaway, a negro woman and her two children. A few days before went off, I burned her with a hot iron on the left side of her face. I tried to make the letter M." in the Natchez *Courier*, Mr. J.P. Ashford advertises a runaway negro girl, with "a good many teeth missing, and the letter A branded on her cheek and forehead." In the Lexington (Ky.) *Observer*, Mr. William Overstreet advertises a runaway negro with "his left eye out, scars from a drik on his left arm, and much scarred with the whip." I might quote from hundreds of such advertisements, offering rewards for runaways, "dead or alive," and describing them with "cars cut off," "jaws broken," scarred by rifle-balls," &c.

Another source of information is afforded by your "Fugitives from Injustice," with many of whom I have conversed freely. I have seen scars o of the whip and marks of the branding-iron, and I have listened to their heart-breaking sobs, while they told of "piccaninnies" torn from their arms and sold.

Another source of information is furnished by emancipated slaveholders Sarah M. Grimké, daughter of the late Judge Grimke, of the Supreme Court of South Carolina, testifies as follows: "As I left my native State on account of Slavery, and deserted the home of my fathers to escape the sound of the lash and the shrieks of tortured victims, I would gladly bury in oblivion the recollection of those seens with which I have been familiar. But this cannot be. They come over my memory like gory sceptres, and implore me, with resistless power, in the name of a God of mercy, in the name of a crucified Saviour, in the name of humanity, for the sake of the slaveholder, as well as the slave, to bear witness to the horrors of the Southern prison-house." She proceeds to describe dreadful tragedies, the actors in which she says were "men and women of the families in South Carolina;" and that their cruelties did not, in the slightest degree, affect their standing in society. Her sister, Angelina Grimké, declared: "While I live, and Slavery lives, I *must* testify against it. Not merely for the sake of my poor brothers and sisters in bonds; for even were Slavery no curse to its victims, the exercise of arbitrary power works such fearful ruin upon the hearts of slaveholders, that I should feel impelled to labor and pray for its overthrow with my latest breath." Among the horrible barbarities she enumerates is the case of a girl thirteen years old, who was flogged to death by her master. She says: "I asked a prominent lawyer, who belonged to one of the first families in the State, whether the murderer of this helpless child could not be indicted, and he coolly replied that the slave was Mr.—'s property, and if he chose to suffer the *loss*, no one else had any thing to do with it." She proceeds to say: "I felt there could be for me no rest in the midst of such outrages and pollutions. Yet I saw nothing of Slavery in its most vulgar and repulsive forms. I saw it in the city, among the fashionable and the honorable, where it was garnished by refinement and decked out for show. It is my deep, solemn, deliberate conviction, but this is a cause worth dying for. I say so from what I have seen, and heard, and known, in a land of Slavery, whereon rest the darkness of Egypt and the sin of Sadom." I once asked Miss Angelina if she thought Abolitionists exaggerated the horrors of Slavery. She replied, with earnest emphasis: "They *cannot* be exaggerated. It is impossible for imagination to go beyond the fact." To a lady who observed that the time had not yet come for agitating the subject, she answered: "I apprehend if thou wert a *slave*, toiling in the fields of Carolina, thou wouldst think the time had *fully* come."

Mr. Thome, of Kentucky, in the course of his eloquent lectures on this subject, said: "I breathed my first breath in an atmosphere of Slavery. But though I am heir to a slave inheritance, I am bold to denounce the whole system as an outrage, a complication of crimes, and wrongs, and cruelties, that make angels weep." Mr. Allen, of Alabama, in a discussion with the students at Lane Seminary, in 1834, told of a slave who was tied up and beaten all day, with a paddle full of holes. "At night, his flesh was literally pounded to a jelly. The punishment was inflicted within hearing of the Academy and the Public Green. But no one took any notice of it. No one thought any wrong was done. At our house, it is so common to hear screams from a neighboring plantation, that we think nothing of it. Lest any one should think that the slaves are *generally* well treated, and that the cases I have mentioned are exceptions, let me be distinctly understood that cruelty is the *rule*, and kindness is the exception."

In the same discussion, a student from Virginia, after relating cases of great cruelty, said: "Such things are common all over Virginia; at least, so far as I am acquainted. But the planters generally avoid punishing their slaves before *strangers*."

Miss Mattie Griffith, of Kentucky, whose entire property consisted in slaves, emancipated them all. The noble-hearted girl wrote to me: "I shall go forth into the world penniless; but I shall work with a heart, and, best of all, I shall live with an easy consience." Previous to this generous resolution, she had never read any Abolition document, and entertained the common Southern prejudice against them. But her own observation so deeply impressed her with the enormities of Slavery, that she was impelled to publish a book, called "The Autobiography of a Female Slave." I read it with thrilling interest; but some of the scenes made my nerves quiver so painfully, that told her I hoped they were too highly colored. She shook her head sadly, and replied: "I am sorry to say that every incident in the book has come within my own knowledge."

St. George Tucker, Judge and Professor of Law in Virginia, speaking of the legalized murder of runaways, said: "Such are the cruelties to which a state of Slavery gives birth—such the horrors to which the human mind is capable of being reconciled by its adoption." Alluding to our struggle in '76, he said: "While we proclaimed our resolution to live free or die, we imposed on our fellow-men, of different complexion, a Slavery ten thousand times worse than the utmost extremity of the oppressions of which we complained."

Governor Giles, in a Message to the Legislature of Virginia, referring to the custom of selling free colored people into Slavery, as a punishment for offences not capital, said: "Slavery must be admitted to be a *punishment of the highest order*; and, according to the just rule for the apportionment of punishment to crimes, it ought to be applied only to *crimes of the highest order*. The most distressing reflection in the application of this punishment to female offenders, is that it extends to their offspring; and the innocent are thus punished with the guilty." Yet one hundred and twenty thousand innocent babies in this country are annually subjected to a punishment which your Governor declared "ought to be applied only to crimes of the highest order."

Jefferson said: "*One day* of American Slavery is worse than a *thousand years* of that which we rose in arms to oppose." Alluding to insurrections, he said: "The Almighty has no attribute that can take side with us in such a contest."

John Randolph declared: "Every planter is a sentinel at his own door. Every Southern mother, when she hears an alarm of fire in the night, instinctively presses her infant closer to her bosom."

Looking at the system of slavery in the light of all this evidence, do you candidly think we deserve "two-fold damnation" for detesting it? Can you not believe that we may hate the system, and yet be truly your friends? I make allowance for the excited state of your mind, and for the prejudices induced by education. I so not care to change your opinion of me; but I so wish you could be persuaded to examine this subject dispassionately, for the sake of the prosperity of Virginia, and the welfare of unborn generations, both white and colored. For thirty years, Abolitionists have been trying to reason with slaveholders, through the press, and in the halls of Congress. Their efforts, though directed to the *masters only*, have been met with violence and abuse almost equal to that poured on head of John Brown. Yet surely we, as a portion of the Union, involved in the expense, the degeneracy, the danger, and the disgrace, of the inquitious and fatal system, have a *right* to speak about it, and a right to be *heard* also. At the North, we willingly publish pro-slavery arguments, and ask only a fair field and no favor for the other side. But you will not even allow your own citizens a chance to examine this important subject. Your letter to me is published in Northern papers, as well as Southern; my reply will not be allowed to appear in any Southern paper. The despotic measures you take to silence investigation, and shut out the light from your own white population, prove how little reliance you have on the strength of your cause. In this enlightened age, all despotisms *ought* to come to an end by the agency of moral and rational means. But if they resist such agencies, it is in the order of Providence that they must *come* to an end by violence. History is full of such lessons.

Would that the evil of prejudice could be removed from your eyes. If you would candidly examine the statements of Governor Hincks of the British West Indies, and of the Rev. Mr. Bleby, long time a Missionary in those Islands, both before and after emancipation, you could not fail to be convinced that Cash is a more powerful incentive to labor than the Lash, and far safer also. One fact in relation to those Islands is very significant. While the working people were slaves, it was always necessary to order out the military during the Christmas holidays; but since emancipation, not a soldier is to be seen. A hundred John Browns might land there, without exciting the slightest alarm.

To the personal questions you ask me, I will reply in the name of all the women of New England. It would be extremely difficult to find any woman in our villages who does *not* sew for the poor, and watch with the sick, whenever occasion requires. We pay our domestic generous wages, with which they can purchase as many Christmas gown as they please; a process far better for their characters, as well as our own, than to receive their clothing as a charity, after being deprived of just payment for their labor. I have never known an instance where the "pangs of maternity " did not meet with requisite assistance; and here at the North, after we have helped the mothers, *we do not sell the babies*.

I readily believe what you state concerning the kindness of many Virginia matrons. It is creditable to their hearts: but after all, the best that can be done in that way is a poor equivalent for the perpetual wrong done to the slaves, and the terrible liabilities to which they are always subject. Kind masters and mistresses among you are merely lucky accidents.

If any one *chooses* to be a brutal despot, your laws and customs give him complete power to do so. And the lot of those slaves who have the kindest masters is exceedingly precarious. In case of death, or pecuniary difficulties, or marriages in the family, they may at any time be suddenly transferred from protection and indulgence to personal degradation, or extreme severity; and if they should try to escape from such sufferings, any body is authorized to shoot them down like dogs.

With regard to your declaration that "no Southerner ought henceforth to read a line of my composition," I reply that I have great satisfaction in the consciousness of having nothing to loose in that quarter. Twenty-seven years ago, I published a book called "An Appeal in behalf of that class of Americans called Africans." It influenced the minds of several young men, afterward conspicuous in public life, through whose agency the cause was better served than it could have been by me. From that time to this, I have labored too earnestly for the slave to be agreeable to slaveholders. Literary popularity was never a paramount object with me, even in my youth; and, now that I am old, I am utterly indifferent to it. But, if I cared for the exclusion you threaten I should at least have the consolation of being exiled with honorable company. Dr. Channing's writings, mild and candid as they are, breathe what you would call arrant treason. William C. Bryant, in his capacity of editor, is openly on our side. The inspired muse of Whittier has incessantly sounded the trumpet for moral warfare with your iniquitous institution; and his stirring tones have been answered, more or less loudly, by Pierpont, Lowell, and Longfellow. Emerson, the Plato of America, leaves the scholastic seclusion he love so well, and disliking noise with all his poetic soul, bravely takes his stand among the trumpeters. George W. Curtis, the brilliant wealth of his talent on the altar of Freedom, and makes common cause with rough-shod reformers.

The genius of Mrs. Stowe carried the outworks of your institution at one dash, and left the citadel open to besiegers, who are pouring in amain. In the church, on the ultra-liberal side, it is assailed by the powerful battering-ram of Theodore Parker's eloquence. On the extreme orthodox side is set a huge fire, kindled by the burning words of Dr. Cheever. Between them is Henry Ward Beecher, sending a shower of keen arrows into your entrenchments; and with him ride a troop of sharp-shooters from all sects. If you turn to the literature of England or France, you will find your institution treated with as little favor. The fact is, the whole civilized world proclaims Slavery an outlaw, and the best intellect of the age is active in hunting it down.

L. Maria Child

THE TOUGHSTONE

BY WILLIAM ALL I. GU AMK

A man there came, whence none could tell,
Bearing a touchstone in his hand,
And tested all things in the land
By its unerring spell.
A thousand transformations rose,
From fair to foul, from foul to fair;
The golden crown he did not share,
Nor scorn the beggar's clothes.
Of heirloom jewels, prized so much,
Were many changed to chips and clods,
And even statues of the gods
Crumbled beneath its touch.
Then angrily the people cried,

"The loss outweighs the profit far,
Our goods suffice us as they are,
We will not have them tried."
But since they could not so avail
To check his unrelenting quest,
They seized him, saying, "Let him test
How real is our jail."
But though they slew him with their swords,
And in the fire the touchstone burned,
Its doings could not be o'erturned,
Its undoings restored.
And when, to stop all future harm,
They strewed his ashes to the breeze,
They little guessed each grain of these
Conveyed the perfect charm.

Source: New York: American Anti-slavery Society, 1860. Library of Congress, Rare Book and Special Collections Division, Daniel A. P. Murray Pamphlets Collection.

25. The Constitution of the United States: Is It Pro-Slavery or Anti-Slavery? March 26, 1860
FREDERICK DOUGLASS

This is an excerpt of a speech given by Frederick Douglass in Glasgow, Scotland on the issue of slavery. Douglass addressed whether or not the Constitution of the United States was pro- or anti-slavery. He delivered this speech in the winter of 1860, five years before the Civil War ended the debate.

The Constitution of the United States: Is It Pro-Slavery or Anti-Slavery?

I proceed to the discussion. And first a word about the question. Much will be gained at the outset if we fully and clearly understand the real question ... Indeed, nothing is or can be understood. This are often confounded and treated as the same, for no better reason than that they resemble each other, even while they are in their nature and character totally distinct and even directly opposed to each other. This jumbling up of things is a sort of dust-throwing which is often indulged in by small men who argue for victory rather than for truth.

Signed: Frederick Douglass

THE GLASGOW SPEECH

The American Government and the American Constitution are spoken of in a manner which would naturally lead the hearer to believe that one is identical with the other; when the truth is, they are distinct in character as is a ship and a compass. The one may point right and the other steer wrong. A chart is one thing, the course of the vessel is another. The Constitution may be right, the Government is wrong. If the Government has been governed by mean, sordid, and wicked passions, it does not follow that the Constitution is mean, sordid, and wicked.

What, then, is the question? I will state it. It is not whether slavery existed in the United States at the time of the adoption of the Constitution; it is not whether slaveholders took part in the framing of the Constitution; it is not whether those slaveholders, in their hearts, intended to secure certain advantages in that instrument for slavery; it is not whether the American Government has been wielded during seventy-two years in favour of the propagation and permanence of slavery; it is not whether a pro-slavery interpretation has been put upon the Constitution by the American Courts—all these points may be true or they may be false, they may be accepted or they may be rejected, without in any wise affecting the real question in debate.

The real and exact question between myself and the class of persons represented by the speech at the City Hall may be fairly stated thus:

- 1st, Does the United States Constitution guarantee to any class or description of people in that country the right to enslave, or hold as property, any other class or description of people in that country?
- 2nd, Is the dissolution of the union between the slave and free States required by fidelity to the slaves, or by the just demands of conscience? Or, in other words, is the refusal to exercise the elective franchise, and to hold office in America, the surest, wisest, and best way to abolish slavery in America?

To these questions the Garrisonians say Yes. They hold the Constitution to be a slaveholding instrument, and will not cast a vote or hold office, and denounce all who vote or hold office, no matter how faithfully such persons labour to promote the abolition of slavery.

I, on the other hand, deny that the Constitution guarantees the right to hold property in man, and believe that the way to abolish slavery in America is to vote such men into power as well as use their powers for the abolition of slavery. This is the issue plainly stated ...

[A] very eloquent lecturer at the City Hall doubtless felt some embarrassment from the fact that he had literally to give the Constitution a pro-slavery interpretation; because upon its face it of itself conveys no such meaning, but a very opposite meaning. He thus sums up what he calls the slaveholding provisions of the Constitution. I quote his own words:

—"Article 1, section 9, provides for the continuance of the African slave trade for the 20 years, after the adoption of the Constitution.

Art. 4, section 9, provides for the recovery from the other States of fugitive slaves.

Art. 1, section 2, gives the slave States a representation of the three-fifths of all the slave population;

Art. 1, section 8, requires the President to use the military, naval, ordnance, and militia resources of the entire country for the suppression of slave insurrection, in the same manner as he would employ them to repel invasion."

Now any man reading this statement, or hearing it made with such a show of exactness, would unquestionably suppose that he speaker or writer had given the plain written text of the Constitution itself. I can hardly believe that the intended to make any such impression. It would be a scandalous imputation to say he did. Any yet what are we to make of it? How can we regard it? How can he be screened from the charge of having perpetrated a deliberate and point-blank misrepresentation? That individual has seen fit to place himself before the public as my opponent, and yet I would gladly find some excuse for him. I do not wish to think as badly of him as this trick of his would naturally lead me to think. Why did he not read the Constitution? Why did he read that which was not the Constitution? He pretended to be giving chapter and verse, section and clause, paragraph and provision. The words of the Constitution were before him. Why then did he not give you the plain words of the Constitution?

Oh, sir, I fear that the gentleman knows too well why he did not. It so happens that no such words as "African slave trade," no such words as "slave insurrections," are anywhere used in that instrument.

These are the words of that orator, and not the words of the Constitution of the United States. Now you shall see a slight difference between my manner of treating this subject and what which my opponent has seen fit, for reasons satisfactory to himself, to pursue. What he withheld, that I will spread before you: what he suppressed, I will bring to light: and what he passed over in silence, I will proclaim: that you may have the whole case before you, and not be left to depend upon either his, or upon my inferences or testimony. Here then are several provisions of the Constitution to which reference has been made. I read them word for word just as they stand in the paper, called the United States Constitution.

Art. I, sec. 2. "Representatives and direct taxes shall be apportioned among the several States which may be included in this Union, according to their respective numbers, which shall be determined by adding to the whole number of free persons, including those bound to service for a term years, and excluding Indians not taxed, three-fifths of all other persons;

Art. I, sec. 9. The migration or importation of such persons as any of the States now existing shall think fit to admit, shall not be prohibited by the Congress prior to the year one thousand eight hundred and eight, but a tax or duty may be imposed on such importation, not exceeding ten dollars for each person;

Art. 4, sec. 2. No person held to service or labour in one State, under the laws thereof, escaping into another shall, in consequence of any law or regulation therein, be discharged from service or labour; but shall be delivered up on claim of the party to whom such service or labour may be due;

Art. I, sec. 8. To provide for calling for the militia to execute the laws of the Union, suppress insurrections, and repel invasions."

Here then, are those provisions of the Constitution, which the most extravagant defenders of slavery can claim to guarantee a right of property in man. These are the provisions which have been pressed into the service of the human fleshmongers of America.

Let us look at them just as they stand, one by one. Let us grant, for the sake of the argument, that the first of these provisions, referring to the basis of representation and taxation, does refer to slaves. We are not compelled to make that admission, for it might fairly apply to aliens—persons living in the country, but not naturalized. But giving the provisions the very worse construction, what does it amount to? I answer—It is a downright disability laid upon the slaveholding States; one which deprives those States of two-fifths of their natural basis of representation.

A black man in a free State is worth just two-fifths more than a black man in a slave State, as a basis of political power under the Constitution.

Therefore, instead of encouraging slavery, the Constitution encourages freedom by giving an increase of "two-fifths" of political power to free over slave States. So much for the three-fifths clause; taking it at is worst, it still leans to freedom, not slavery; for, be it remembered that the Constitution nowhere forbids a coloured man to vote.

... Men at that time, both in England and in America, looked upon the (international) slave trade as the life of slavery. The abolition of the slave trade (directly from Africa to the Americas) was supposed to be the certain death of slavery. Cut off the stream, and the pond will dry up, was the common notion at the time.

Wilberforce and Clarkson, clear-sighted as they were, took this view; and the American statesmen, in providing for the abolition of the slave trade, thought they were providing for the abolition of slavery. This view is quite consistent with the history of the times. All regarded slavery as an expiring and doomed system, destined to speedily disappear from the country. But, again, it should be remembered that this very provision, if made to refer to the African slave trade at all, makes the Constitution anti-slavery rather than for slavery; for it says to the slave States, the price you will have to pay for coming into the American Union is, that the slave trade, which you would carry on indefinitely out of the Union, shall be put an end to in twenty years if you come into the Union.

Secondly, if it does apply, it expired by its own limitation more than fifty years ago.

Thirdly, it is anti-slavery, because it looked to the abolition of slavery rather than to its perpetuity.

Fourthly, it showed that the intentions of the framers of the Constitution were good, not bad. I think this is quite enough for this point.

Source: A Speech Delivered in Glasgow, Scotland. March 26, 1860. TeachingAmericanHistory.org © 2006 Ashbrook Center for Public Affairs.

26. History of American abolitionism: its four great epochs, embracing narratives of the ordinance of 1787, compromise of 1820, annexation of Texas, Mexican war, Wilmot proviso, negro insurrections, abolition riots, slave rescues, compromise of 1850, Kansas bill of 1854, John Brown insurrection, 1859, valuable statistics, &c., &c., &c., together with a history of the southern confederacy, 1861

F. G. DE FONTAINE

In this critique of American abolitionism after 1787, F. G. De Fontaine focuses on the negative impact of the movement on the South and slavery. He blames fanatic abolitionists for causing dissolution of the Union and for spoiling chances for gradual emancipation in the South. In addition, he gives basic facts and figures on the initial six states of the southern confederacy, including biographies of Jefferson Davis and Alexander Stevens, and the slave and free populations of these states.

INTRODUCTION

The following pages originally appeared in the New York Herald, of February 2d, 1861. By request, they have been reproduced in their present shape, with the view of preserving, in a form more compact than that of a newspaper, the valuable facts embraced.

Without an extensive range of research it is almost impossible to acquire the information which is thus compiled, and, at the present time, especially, it is believed that the publication of these facts will be desirable to the reading community. F.G. DEF.

The Spirit of the Age—Two Classes of Abolitionists—Their Objects—The Sources of their Inspiration—Influences upon Church and State—Proposed Invasions upon the Constitution—Effect upon the Slave States, &c, &c.

One of the commanding characteristics of the present age is the spirit of agitation, collision and discord which has broken forth in every department of social and political life. While it has been an era of magnificent enterprises and unrivalled prosperity, it has likewise been an era of convulsion, which has well nigh upturned the foundations of the government. Never was this truth more evident than at the present moment. A single topic occupies the public mind—Union or Disunion—and is one of pre-eminently absorbing interest to every citizen. Upon this issue the entire nation has been involved in a moral distemper, that threatens its utter and irrevocable dissolution. Union—the child of compact, the creature of social and political tolerance—stands face to face with Disunion, the natural offspring of that anti-slavery sentiment, which has ever warred against the interests of the people and the elements of true government, and struggles for the maintenance of that sacred pledge by which the United States have heretofore been bound in a common brotherhood. Like the marvellous tent given by the fairy Ranou to Prince Achmend, which, when folded up, became an ornament in the delicate hands of women, but, spread out, afforded encampment to mighty armies; so as this question of abolitionism, to which the present overwhelming trouble of our land is to be traced, in its capacity to encompass all things, and its ability to attach itself even to the amenities and refinements of life. It has entered into everything, great and small, high and low, political, theological, social and moral, and in one section has become the standard by which all excellence is to be judged. Under the guise of philanthropic reform, it has pursued its course with energy, boldness and unrelenting bitterness, until it has grown from "a cloud no bigger than a man's hand" into the dimensions of the tempest which is to-day lowering over the land charged with the elements of destruction. Commencing with a pretended love for the black race, it has arrived at stage of restless, uncompromising fanaticism which will be satisfied with nothing short of the consummation of its wildest hopes. It has become the grand question of the day—of politics, of ethics, of expediency, of justice, of conscience, and of law, covering the whole field of human society and divine government.

In this view of the subject, and in view also of the surrounding unhappy circumstances of the country which have their origin in this agitation, we give below a history of abolition, from the period it commenced to exist as an active element in the affairs of the nation down to the present moment.

There are two classes of persons opposed to the continued existence of slavery in the United States. The first are those who are actuated by sentiments of philanthropy and humanity, but are at the same time no less opposed to any disturbance of the peace or tranquility of the Union, or to any infringement of the powers of the States composing the confederacy. Among these may be classed the society of "Friends," one of whose established principles is an abhorrence of war in all its forms, and the cultivation of peace and good will amongst mankind. As far back as 1670, the ancient records of their society refer to the peaceful and exemplary efforts of the sect to prevent the holding of slaves by any of their number; and a quaint incident is related of an eccentric "Friend," who, at one of their monthly meetings, "seated himself among the audience with a bladder of bullock's blood secreted under his mantle, and at length broke the quiet stillness of the worship by rising in full view of the congregation, piercing the bladder, spilling the blood upon the floor and seats, and exclaiming with all the solemnity of an inspired prophet, 'thus shall the Lord spill the blood of those that traffic in the blood of their fellow men.'"

The second class are the real ultra abolitionists—the "reformers" who, in the language of Henry Clay, are "resolved to preserve at all hazards, and without regard to any consequences, however calamitous they may be. With them the rights of property are nothing; the deficiency of the powers of the general government is nothing; the acknowledged and incontestible powers of the State are nothing; civil war, a dissolution of the Union, and the overthrow of a government in which are concentrated the fondest hopes of the civilized world, are nothing. They are for the immediate abolition of slavery, the prohibition of the removal of slaves from State to State, and the refusal to admit any new State comprising within its limits the institution of domestic slavery—all these bring but so many means conducive to the accomplishment of the ultimate but perilous end at which they avowedly and boldly aim—so many short stages, as it were, in the long and bloody read to the distant goal at which they would ultimately arrive. Their purpose is abolition, 'peaceably if it can, forcibly if it must.'"

Utterly destitute of Constitutional or other rightful power; living in totally distinct communities, as alien to the communities in which the subject on which they would operate resides, as far as concerns political power over that subject, as if they lived in Asia or Africa, they nevertheless promulgate to the world their purpose to immediately convert without compensation four millions of profitable and contented slaves into four millions of burdensome and discontended negroes.

This idea, which originated and still generally prevails in New England, is the result of that puritanical frenzy which has always characterized that section of the country, and made it the natural breeding ground of the most absurd "isms" ever concocted. The Puritans of today are not less fanatical than were the Puritans of two centuries ago. In fact, they have progressed rather than retrograded. Their god then was the angry, wrathful, jealous god of the Jews—the Supreme Being now is the creation of their own intellects, proportioned in dimensions to the depth and fervor of their individual understandings. Then the Old Testament was their rule of faith. Now neither old nor new, except in so far as it accords with their consciences, is worth the paper upon which it is written. Their creeds are begotten of themselves, and their high priests are those who best represent their peculiar "notions." The same spirit which, in the days of Robes-pierre and Marat, abolished the Lord's day and worshipped Reason, in the person of a harlot, yet survives to work other horrors. In this age, however, and in a community like the present, a disguise must be worn; but it is the old threadbare advocacy of human rights, which the enlightenment of the age condemns as impracticable. The decree has gone forth which strikes at God, by striking at all subordination and law, and under the specious cry of reform it is demanded that every pretended evil shall be corrected, or society become a wreck— that the sun must be stricken from the heavens if a spot is found upon his disc.

The abolitionist is a practical atheist. In the language of one of their congregational ministers—Rev. Henry Wright of Massachusetts:—

"The God of humanity is not the God of slavery. If so, shame upon such a God. I scorn him. I will never bow to his shrine; my head shall go off with my hat when I take it off to such a God as that. If the Bible sanctions slavery, the Bible is a self-evident falsehood. And, if God should declare it to be right, I would fasten the chain upon the heel of such a God, and let the man go free. Such a God is a phantom."

The religion of the people of New England is a peculiar morality, around which the minor matters of society arrange themselves like ferruginous particles around a loadstone. All the elements obey this general law. Accustomed to doing as it pleases, New England "morality" has usually accomplished what it has undertaken. It has attacked the Sunday mails, assaulted Free Masonry, triumphed over the intemperate use of ardent spirits, and finally engaged in an onslaught upon the slavery of the South. Its channels have been societies, meetings, papers, lectures, sermons, resolutions, memorials, protests, legislation, private discussion, public addresses; in a word, every conceivable method whereby appeal may be brought to mind. Its spirit has been agitation!—and its language, fruits and measures have partaken throughout of a character that is thoroughly warlike.

"In language no element ever flung out more defiance of authority, contempt of religion, of authority to man. As to agency, no element on earth has broken up more friendships and families societies and parties, churches and denominations, or ruptured more organizations, political, social or domestic. And as to measures! What spirit of man ever stood upon earth with bolder front and wielded fiercer weapons? Stirring harangues! Stern resolutions! Fretful memorials! Angry protests! Incendiary pamphlets at the South! Hostile legislation at the North! Underground railroads at the West! Resistance to the Constitution! Division of the Union! Military contribution! Sharpe's rifle! Higher law! If this is not belligerence ongoing, Mohammed's work and the old Crusades were an appeal to argument and not to arms."

What was philanthropy in our forefathers has become misanthropy in their descendants, and compassion for the slave has given way to malignity against the master. Consequences are nothing. The one idea preeminent above all others is abolition!

It is worthy of notice in this connection that most abolitionists know little or nothing of slavery and slaveholders beyond what they have learned from excited, caressed and tempted fugitives, or from a superficial, accidental or prejudiced observation. From distorted facts, gross misrepresentations, and frequently malicious caricatures, they have come to regard Southern slaveholders as the most unprincipled men in the Universe, with no incentive but avarice, no feeling but selfishness, and no sentiment but cruelty.

Their information is acquired from discharged seamen, runaway slaves, agents who have been tarred and feathered, factious politicians, and scurrilous tourists; and no matter how exaggerated may be the facts, they never fail to find willing believers among this class of people.

In the Church, the missionary spirit with which the men of other times and nobler hearts intended to embrace all, both bond and free, has been crushed out. New methods of Scriptural interpretation have been discovered, under which the Bible brings to light things of which Jesus Christ and his disciples had no conception. Assemblings for divine worship have been converted into occasions for the secret dissemination of incendiary doctrines, and thus a common suspicion has been generated of all Northern agency in the diffusion of religious instruction among the slaves. Of the five broad beautiful bands of Christianity thrown around the North and the South—Presbyterian, old school and new, Episcopalian, Methodist and Baptist, to say nothing of the divisions of Bible, tract and missionary societies—three are already ruptured—and whenever an anniversary brings together the various delegates of these organizations, the sad spectacle is presented of division, wrangling, vituperation and reproach, that gives to religion and its professors anything but that meekness of spirit with which it is wont to be invested.

Politically, the course of abolition has been one of constant aggression upon the South.

At the time of the Old Confederation, the amount of territory owned by the Southern States was 647,202 square miles; and the amount owned, by the Northern States, 164,081. In 1783, Virginia ceded to the United States, for the common benefit, all her immense territory northwest of the river Ohio. In 1787, the Northern States appropriated it to their own exclusive use by passing the celebrated ordinance of that year, whereby Virginia and all her sister States were excluded from the benefits of the territory. This was the first in the series of aggressions.

Again, in april, 1803, the United States purchased from France, for fifteen millions of dollars, the territory of Louisiana, comprising an area of 1,189,112 square miles, the whole of which was slaveholding territory. In 1821, by the passage of the Missouri Compromise, 964,667 square miles of this was converted into free territory.

Again, by the treaty with Spain, of February 1819, the United States gained the territory from which the present State of Florida was formed, with an area of 59,268 square miles, and also the Spanish title of Oregon, from which they acquired an area of 341,463 square miles. Of this cession, Florida only has been allowed to the Southern States, while the balance—nearly six-sevenths of the whole—was appropriated by the North.

Again, by the Mexican cession, was acquired 526,078 square miles, which the North attempted to appropriate under the pretense of the Mexican laws, but which was prevented by the measures of the Compromise of 1850. Of slave territory cut off from Texas, there have been 44,662 square miles.

To sum this up, the total amount of territory acquired under the Constitution has been, by the square

Northwest cession	286,081	miles
Louisiana cession	1,189,112	do
Florida and Oregon cession	400,731	do
Mexican cession	526,078	do
Total	2,377,602	do

Of all this territory the Southern States have been permitted to enjoy only 283,713 square miles, while the Northern States have been allowed 2,083,889 square miles, or between seven and eight times more than has been allowed to the South.

The following are some of the invasions that have been from time to time proposed upon the Constitution in the halls of Congress by these agitators:

1. That the clause allowing the representation of three-fifths of the slaves shall be obliterated from the Constitution; or, in other words, that the South, already in a vast and increasing minority, shall be still further reduced in the seal of insignificance, and thus, on every attempted usurpation of her rights, be far below the protection of even a Presidential veto.

Next has been demanded the abolition of slavery in the District of Columbia in the forts, arsenals, navy yards and other public establishments of the United States. What object have the abolitionists had for raising all this clamor about a little patch of soil ten miles square, and a few inconsiderable places thinly scattered over the land—a mere grain of sand upon the beach—unless it be to establish the precedent of Congressional interference, which would enable them to make a wholesale incursion upon the constitutional rights of the South, and to drain from the vast ocean of alleged national guilt its last drop? Does any one suppose that a mere microscopic concession like this would alone appease a conscience wounded and lacerated by the "sin of slavery?"

Another of these aggressions is that which was proposed under the pretext of regulating commerce between the States—namely, that no slave, for any purpose and under any circumstances whatever, shall be carried by his lawful owner from one slaveholding State to another; or, in other words, that where slavery now is there it shall remain forever, until by its own increase the slave population shall outnumber the white race, and thus by a united combination of causes—the fears of the master, the diminution in value of his property and the exhausted condition of the soil—the final purposes of fanaticism may be accomplished.

Still another in the series of aggressions was that attempted by the Wilmot Proviso, by which Congress was called upon to prohibit every slaveholder from removing with his slaves into the territory acquired from Mexico—a territory as large as the old thirteen States originally composing the Union. It appears to have been forgotten that whether slavery be admitted upon one foot of territory or not, it cannot alter the question of its sinfulness in the slightest degree, and that if every nook and corner of the national fabric were open to the institution, not a single slave would be added to the present number, or that, if excluded, their number would not be a single one the less.

We might also refer to the armed and bloody opposition to the Fugitive Slave Law, to the passage of Personal Liberty Bills, to political schemes in Congress and out, and to systematic agitation everywhere, with a view to stay the progress of the South, contract her political power, and eventually lead, at her expense, if not of the Union itself, to the utter expurgation of his "tremendous national sin."

In short, the abolitionists have contributed nothing to the welfare of the slave or of the South. While over one hundred and fifty millions have been expended by slaveholders in emancipation, except in those sporadic cases where the amount was capital invested in self-glorification, the abolitionists have not expended one cent.

More than this: They have defeated the very objects at which they have aimed. When Virginia, Maryland, Kentucky, or some other border State has come so near to the passage of gradual emancipation laws that the hopes of the real friends of the movement seemed about to be realized, abolitionism has stepped in, and, with frantic appeals to the passions of the negroes, through incendiary publications, dashed them to the ground, tightening the fetters of the slave, sharpening authority, and producing a reaction throughout the entire community that has crushed out every incipient thought of future manumission.

Such have been the obvious fruits of abolition. Church, state and society! Nothing has escaped it. Nowhere pure, nor peaceable, nor gentle, nor easily entreated, nor full of mercy and good fruits; but everywhere forward, scowling, noncompromising, and fierce, breaking peace, order and structure at every step, crushing with its foot what would not bow to its will; defying government, despising the Church, dividing the country, and striking Heaven itself if it dated to obstruct its progress; purifying, pacifying, promising nothing, but marking its entire pathway by disquiet, schism and ruin.

We come now to the train of historical facts upon which we rely in proof of the foregoing assertions. The Ordinance of 1787—The Slave Population of 1790—Abolitionism at that time—The Importation of Slaves the Work of Northerners—Statistics of the Port of Charleston, S.C., from 1804 to 1808—Anecdote of a Rhode Island Senator, &c, &c

The first great epoch in the history of our country at which the spirit of abolitionism displayed itself was immediately preceding the formation of the present government. From the close of the Revolutionary War, in 1783, to the sitting of the Constitutional Convention, was a space of only four years. Two years more brings us to the adoption of the Constitution, in 1789. It was in the summer of 1787, and at the very time the Convention in Philadelphia was framing that instrument, that the Congress in New York was framing the ordinance which was passed on the 13th of July, 1787, by which slavery was forever excluded from all the territory northwest of the river Ohio, which, three years before, had been generously ceded to the United States by Virginia, and out of which have since been organised the States of Ohio, Indiana, Illinois, Michigan, Wisconsin, Minnesota and Iowa.

According to the first census, taken in 1790, under the Constitution, when every State in the Union, with one exception, was a slave State, the number of slaves was as follows:

	STATES	NO. OF SLAVES
1	Massachusetts	
2	New Hampshire	158
3	Rhode Island	948
4	Connecticut	2,764
5	New York	21,340
6	New Jersey	11,423
7	Pennsylvania	3,737
8	Delaware	8,887
9	Maryland	103,036
10	Virginia	305,057
11	North Carolina	100,571
12	South Carolina	107,094
13	Georgia	29,264
	Territory of Ohio	3,417
	Total	697,696

In 1820, New York had 10,088 slaves. In 1827, however, by virtue of an Act, passed in 1817, they were declared free, and emancipated, without compensation to their owners. Even in 1830, Rhode Island, Connecticut, New Jersey and Pennsylvania had slaves: New Jersey containing 2,254. Since 1790, the increase of slaves has been at the rate of thirty per cent each decade.

At this period numerous emancipation societies were formed, comprised principally of the Society of Friends, and petitions were presented to Congress, praying for the abolition of slavery. These were received with but little comment, referred, and reported upon by a committee. The reports stated that the general government had no power to abolish slavery as it existed in the several States, and that the States themselves had exclusive jurisdiction over the subject.

This sentiment was generally acquiesced in, and satisfaction and tranquillity ensued, the abolition societies thereafter limiting their exertions, in respect to the black population, to offices of humanity within the scope of existing laws.

In fact, if we carry ourselves by historical research back to that day, and ascertain men's opinions by authentic records still existing among us, it will be found that there was no great diversity of opinion between the North and the South upon the subject of slavery. The great ground of objection to it then was political; that it weakened the social fabric; that, taking the place of free labor, society was less strong and labor less productive; and both sections, with an exhibition of no little acerbity of temper and violence of language, ascribed the evil to the injurious and aggrandizing policy of Great Britain, by whom it was first entailed upon the Colonies. The terms of reprobation were then more severe in the South than the North. It is a notorious fact that some of our Northern forefathers were then the most aggravated slave dealers. They transported the miserable captives from Africa, sold them at the South, and were well paid for their work; and, when emancipation laws forbade the prolongation of slavery at the North, there are living witnesses who saw the crowds of negroes assembled along the shores of the New England and the Middle States to be shipped to latitudes where their bondage would be perpetual. Their posterity toil today in the fields of the Southern planter.

It is a remarkable fact, also, that of the slaves imported into the United States during a period of eighteen years, from 1790 to 1808, not less than nine-tenths were imported for and by account of citizens of the Northern States and subjects of Great Britain—imported in Northern and British vessels, by Northern and British men, and delivered to Northern born and British born consignees.

The trade was thus carried on, with all its historic inhumanity, by the sires and grand sires of the very men and women, who, for thirty years, have been denouncing slavery as a sin against God, and slaveholders as the vilest class of men and tyrants who ever disgraced a civilized community; and the very wealth in which, in a large degree, these agitators now revel, has descended to them as the fruit of the slave trade in which their fathers grew fat.

The following statistics of the port of Charleston, S.C., from the year 1804 to 1808, will more plainly illustrate this remark:—

Imported into Charleston from Jan. 1, 1804, to Jan. 1, 1808 slaves 29,075

BY British subjects	19,649
BY French subjects	1,078
BY Foreigners in Charleston	5,107
BY Rhode Islanders	8,238
BY Bostonians	200
BY Philadelphians	200
BY Hartford, citizens of	250
BY Charlestonians	2,006
BY Baltimoreans	750
BY Savannah, citizens of	300
BY Norfolk, citizens of	387
BY Naw Orleans, citizens of 100	39,075
BY British, French and Northpeople	35,532
BY Southern people 3,543	39,075

CONSIGNEES OF THESE SLAVES

Natives of Charleston	13
Natives of Rhode Island	88
Natives of Great Britain	91
Natives of France	10
Total	202

It is related, that during the debate on the Missouri question, a Senator from South Carolina introduced in the Senate of the United States a document from the Custom House of Charleston, exhibiting the names and owners of vessels engaged in the African slave trade. In reading the document the name of De Wolfe was repeatedly called. De Wolfe, who was the Senator elect from Rhode Island, was present, but had not been qualified. The Caroline Senator was called to order. "Order!" "Order!" echoed through the Senate Chamber. "It is contrary to order to call the name of a Senator," said a distinguished gentleman. The Senator contended he was not out of order, for the Senator from Rhode Island had not been qualified, and consequently was not entitled to a seat. He appealed to the Chair. The Chair replied, "You are correct, sir; proceed," and proceed he did, calling the name of De Wolfe so often, that before he had finished the document, he had proved the honorable gentleman the importer of three-fourths of the "poor Africans" brought to the Charleston market, and the Rhode Island abolitionist bolted, amid the sympathies of his comrades and the sneers of the auditors.

Such was the aspect of affairs with reference to this question at the time of the adoption of the Constitution. The spirit of affection created and fostered by the revolution—the cords binding together a common country in a common struggle and a common destiny—were too strong in the breasts of our revolutionary fathers for them to countenance the feeble efforts even of these prompted by motives of humanity for the immediate emancipation of the slaves, and by almost the entire North of that period they were regarded with general disfavor, as an unwarrantable interference with an already established institution of the country. The consequence was that they sank into disrepute, and the country was blessed with and prospered under their comparative cessation for a number of years. This hostile feeling long lay dormant, and it was not until the year 1818, when Missouri applied for admission into the Union as a State, that the period of quiet was interrupted, and the little streams of abolitionism that had been quietly forming, merged into the foul and noisome current which is now devastating the land, has undermined and destroyed the Union, and is exerting its blighting influence upon every department of the political and social fabric.

History of the Missouri Compromise, 1820—Benjamin Lundy and the *"Genius of Universal Emancipation"*—Resurrection at Charleston, S.C. —The result of agitation in Congress—British Influence and Interference—Abolition in the East and West Indies—Remarkable opinion of Sir Robert Peel—Letter from Lord Brougham on the Harper's Ferry Insurrection.

Probably there has never been in the history of the United States, except at the present time, a more critical moment, arising from the violence of domestic excitement, than the agitation of the Missouri question from 1818 to 1821. On the 18th day of December, 1818, the Speaker of the House of Representatives of the United States presented before that body a memorial of the Legislature of the Territory of Missouri, praying that they might be admitted to form a Constitution and State government upon "an equal footing with the original States." Here originated the difficulty. Slavery existed in the Territory proposed to be erected into an independent State. The proposition was therefore to admit Missouri as a slave State, which involved three very essential and important features. These were:—

1. The recognition of slavery therein as a State Institution by the national sovereignty.
2. The guarantee of protection to the ownership of her slave property by the laws of the United States, as in the original States under the Constitution.
3. That the right of representation in the National Legislature should be apportioned on her slave population, as in the original Sates. This was a recognition of slavery, which at once aroused the interest of the people in every section of the Union.

The petition was received, read and reported upon, and in February, 1819, Mr. Tallmadge, of New York, proposed an amendment "prohibiting slavery except for the punishment of crimes, and that all children born in the said State after the admission thereof into the Union, shall be free at the age of twenty-five years."

This passed the House, but was lost in the Senate. The excitement, not only in Congress, but throughout the Union, soon became intense, and for eighteen months the country was agitated from one extreme to the other. In many of the Northern States meetings were called, resolutions were passed instructing members how to vote, prayers ascended from the churches, and the pulpit began to be the medium of the incendiary diatribes for which it has since become so famous.

In both branches of Congress amendments were passed and rejected without number, while the arguments on both sides brought out the strongest views of the respective champions.

On one hand it was maintained that the compromise of the federal constitution regarding slavery respected only its existing limits at the time; that it was remote from the views of the framers of the Constitution to have the domain of slavery extended on that basis; that the fundamental principles of the American Revolution and of the government; and institutions erected upon it were hostile to slavery; that the compromise of the Constitution was simply a toleration of things that were, and not a basis of things that were to be; that these securities of slavery, as it existed, would be forfeited by an extension of the system; that the honor of the republic before the world, and its moral influence with mankind in favor of freedom, were identified with the advocacy of principles of universal emancipation; that the act of 1787, which established the Territorial government north and west of the river Ohio, prohibiting slavery forever therefrom, was a public recognition and avowal of the principles and designs of the people of the United States in regard to new States and Territories north and west; and that the proposal to establish slavery in Missouri was a violation of all these great and fundamental principles.

On the other hand, it was urged that slavery was incorporated in the system of society as established in Louisiana, which comprehended the Territory of Missouri, when purchased from France in 1803; that the faith of the United States was pledged by treaty to all the inhabitants of that wide domain to maintain their rights and privileges on the same footing with the people of the rest of the country; and consequently, that slavery, being a part of their state of society, it would be a violation of engagements to abolish it without their consent. Nor could the government, as they maintained, prescribe the abolition of slavery to any part of said Territory as a condition of being erected into a State, if they were otherwise entitled to it. It might as well, as they said, be required of them to abolish any other municipal regulation, or to annihilate any other attribute of sovereignty. If the government had made an ill-advised treaty in the purchase of Louisiana, they maintained it would be manifest injustice to make its citizens suffer on that account. They claimed that they received as a slaveholding community on the same footing with the slave States, and that the existence or non-existence of slavery could not be made a question when they presented themselves at the door of the Capitol of the republic for a State charter.

After much bitter and acrimonious discussion, the question was finally, through the exertions of Henry Clay, settled by a compromise, and a bill was passed for the admission of Missouri without any restriction as to slavery, but prohibiting it throughout the United States north of latitude thirty-six degrees and thirty minutes.

Missouri was not declared independent until August 1821. Previous to passage of the bill for its admission, the people had formed a State constitution, a provision of which required the Legislature to pass a law "To prevent free negroes from coming to and settling in the State." When the constitution was presented to Congress, this provision was strenuously opposed. The contest occupied a greater part of the session; but Missouri was finally admitted on condition that no laws should be passed by which any free citizen of the United States should be prevented from enjoying those rights within the State to which he was entitled by the Constitution of the United States.

Such was the Missouri Compromise, and though its settlement once more brought repose to the country and strengthened the bonds of fraternity and union between the States, its agitation in Congress was like the opening of a foul ulcer—the beginning of that domineering, impertinent, ill-timed, vociferous and vituperative opposition which has ever since been the leading characteristic of the abolition movement.

The "settlement" of the question in Congress seemed to be merely the signal for its agitation among the non-slaveholding States. Fanatics sprang up like mushrooms, and, "in the name of God," proclaimed the enormity of slavery and eternal damnation to all who indulged in the wicked luxury.

Among the earliest and most notable of these philanthropic reformers was one Benjamin Lundy, who, in the year 1821, commenced the publication of a monthly periodical called the *"Genius of Universal Emancipation,"* which was successively published at Philadelphia, Baltimore, Washington City, and frequently *en route* during his travels wherever he could find a press. It is related of him that at one time he traversed the free States lecturing, collecting, obtaining subscribers, stirring up the people, writing for his paper, getting it printed where he could, stopping to read the "proof" on the road, and directing and mailing his papers at the nearest post office. Then, packing up in his trunk his column-rules, type, "Heading" and "direction book," he pushed along like a thorough-going pioneer. What this solitary "Friend"—for such he was—in this manner accomplished, he himself states in an appeal to the public in 1830. He says:—

"I have within the period above mentioned (ten years) sacrificed several thousands of dollars of my own hard earnings; I have travelled upwards of five thousand miles on foot and more than twenty thousand in other ways; have visited nineteen States of this Union, and held more than two hundred public meetings—have performed two voyages to the West Indies, by which means the emancipation of a considerable number of slaves has been effected, and I hope the way paved for the enfranchisement of many more."

The year 1822 was marked by one of the most nefarious negro plots ever developed in the history of the country. The first revelation was made to the Mayor of the city of Charleston on the 30th of May, 1822, by a gentleman who had on the morning of the same day returned from the country, and obtained on his arrival an inkling of what was going on from a confidential slave, to whom the secret had been imparted.

Investigations were immediately set on foot, and one of the slaves who was apprehended, fearing a summary execution, confessed all he knew. He said he had known of the plot for some time; that it was very extensive, embracing an indiscriminate massacre of the whites, and that the blacks were to be headed by an individual who carried about him a charm which rendered him invulnerable. The period fixed for the rising was on Sunday, the 16th of June, at twelve o'clock at night.

Through the instrumentality of a colored class-leader in one of the churches, this information was corroborated, and it was ascertained that enlistment for the insurrection was being actively carried on in the colored community of the church. It appeared that three months before that time, a slave named Rolla, belonging to Governor Bennett, had communicated intelligence of the intended rising, saying that when this event occurred they would be aided in obtaining their liberty by people from St. Domingo and Africa, and that if they would make the first movement at the time above named, a force would cross from James Island and land at South Bay, march up and seize the arsenal and guardhouse; that another body would at the same time seize the arsenal on the Neck, and a third would rendez-vous in the vicinity of his master's mill. They would then sweep the town with fire and sword, not permitting a single white soul to escape.

Startled by this terrible intelligence, the military were immediately ordered out and preparations made to suppress the first signs of an outbreak. Finding the city encompassed with patrols and a strict watch kept upon every movement, the negroes feared to carry out their designs, and when the period had passed for the explosion of the plot, the authorities proceeded with vigor to arrest all against whom they possessed information.

The first prisoner tried was Rolla, a commander of one of the contemplated forces. On being asked whether he intended to kill the woman and children, he remarked, *"When we have done with the men we know what to do with the women."* On this testimony he was found guilty, and sentenced to be executed on the 2d of July.

Another was Denmark Vesey, the father of the plot, and a free black man. It was proved that he had spoken of this conspiracy upwards of four years previously. His house was the rendezvous of the conspirators, where he always presided, encouraging the timid by the hopes of success, removing the scruples of the religious by the grossest perversion of Scripture, and influencing the bold by all the savage fascinations of blood, beauty and body. It was afterwards proved, though not on his trial, that he had been carrying on a correspondence with certain persons in St. Domingo—the massacre and rebellion in that island having suggested to him the conspiracy in which he embarked at Charleston. His design was to set the mills on fire, and as soon as the bells began to ring the alarm, to kill every man as he came out of his door, and afterwards murder the women and children, "for so God had commanded in the Scriptures." At the same time, the country negroes were to rise in arms, attack the forts, take the ships, kill every man on board except the captains, rob the banks and stores, and then sail for St. Domingo. English and French assistance was also expected.

Six thousand were ascertained to have been enlisted in the enterprise, their names being enrolled on the books of "The Society," as the organization was called.

When the first rising failed, the leaders, who still escaped arrest, meditated a second one, but found the blacks cowed by the execution of their associates and by the vigilance of the whites. The leaders waited, they said, "for the head man, who was a white man," but they would not reveal his name.

The whole number of persons executed was thirty-five; sentenced to transportation, twenty-one; the whole number arrested, one hundred and thirty-one.

Among the conspirators brought to trial and conviction, the cases of Glen, Billy Palmer and Jack Purcell were distinguished for the sanctimonious hypocrisy they blended with their crime. Glen was a preacher, Palmer exceedingly pious, and Purcell no less devout. The latter made the following important confession:—

"If it had not been for the cunning of that old villain Vesey I should not now be in my present situation. He employed every stratagem to induce me to join him. He was in the habit of reading to me all the passages in the newspapers that related to St. Domingo, and apparently every pamphlet he could lay his hands on that had any connection with slavery. *He one day brought in a speech which he told me had been delivered in Congress by a Mr. King on the subject of slavery. He told me this Mr. King was the black man's friend; that he (Mr. King) had declared he would continue to speak, write and publish pamphlets against slavery to the latest day he lived, until the Southern States consented to emancipate their slaves, for slavery was a great disgrace to the country."*

The Mr. King here spoken of was Rufus King, Senator from New York. This confession shows that the evil which was foretold would arise from the discussion of the Missouri question had been in some degree realized in the course of two or three years.

Religious fanaticism also had its share in the conspiracy at Charleston, as well as politics. The secession of a large body of blacks from the white Methodist church formed a hot-bed, in which the germ of insurrection was nursed into life. A majority of the conspirators belonged to the "African church," an appellation which the seceders assumed after leaving the white Methodist church, and among those executed were several who had been class- leaders. Thus was religion made a cloak for the most diabolical crimes on record. It is the same at this day. The tirades of the North are calculated to drive the negro population of the South to bloody massacres and insurrections.

During all this time, British abolition sentiments and designs were industriously infused into the minds of the people of the North. Looking over their own homeless, unfed, ragged millions, their filthy hovels and mud floors, worse than the common abode of pigs and poultry, crowded cellars, hungry paupers, children at work under ground—a community of wretchedness such as the American slave never dreamed of—British philanthropists wrote, declaimed, and expended untold sums upon a supposed abuse three thousand miles off, with which they have no connection, civil, social or political, and of which they know comparatively nothing. They passed their fellow subjects by who were dying of hunger upon their very door sills, to make long prayers in the market place for the imaginary sufferings of negroes to whose well-fed and happy condition their own wretched paupers might aspire in vain.

Before they indulged in this invective, it would have been wise to have inquired who were the authors of the evil. In the language of an English statesman—

"If slavery is the misfortune of America, it is the crime of Great Britain. We poured the foul infection into her veins, and fed and cherished the leprosy which now deforms that otherwise prosperous country."

Having filled their purses as traders in slaves, they have become traders in philanthropy, and manage to earn a character for helping slavery out of the very plantations of the South they helped to stock. They resemble their own *beau ideal* of a fine gentleman - George IV - who, it is said, drove his wife into imprudences by his brutality and neglect, and then persecuted her to death for having fallen into them; or one of those fashionable philosophers who seduce women and then upbraid them for a want of virtue. Like the Roman emperor, they find no unsavory smell in the gold derived from the filthiest source.

The first abolition society in Great Britain was established in 1823, and it is a fact worthy of note that the first public advocate in England of the doctrine of immediate and unconditional abolition was a woman—Elizabeth Herrick. In 1825, the Anti-Slavery Society commenced the circulation of the Monthly Anti-Slavery Reporter, which was edited by Zacharay Macaulay, Esq., the father of the late Thomas B. Macaulay, the essayist, historian and lord. Petitions began to be circulated, public meetings were held, and the Methodist Conferences took an active part in the movement, exhorting their brethren, "for the love of Christ," to vote for no candidates not known to be pledged to the cause of abolition. Rectors, curates, doctors of divinity, members of Parliament and peers engaged in the work, and converts rapidly increased. Riots and disturbances resulted. In 1832, an insurrection fomented by abolition missionaries, broke out in the island of Jamaica, which was only terminated by a resort to the musket and gibbet—the usual fruit of these incendiary doctrines, wherever they have been circulated. In 1833, a bill was passed by the British government, by which, for a compensation of one hundred millions of dollars, eight hundred thousand slaves in the British West Indies received their liberation. This was followed, in 1843, by the abolition of slavery throughout the British dominions, which emancipated twelve millions more in the East Indies. The cause thus received a new impetus; societies sprang into life all over the United Kingdom; a correspondence was opened in every part of the world where negroes were held in bondage; lectures were sent abroad, especially to the United States, to disseminate their doctrines and stir up rebellion, both among the people and the slaves; earnest endeavors were made to influence the policy of the non- slaveholding States of the North, and create a hatred for the South; and, in short, the abolition movement settled down in a determined warfare against the institution of slavery wherever it existed.

It has been a war in which newspapers, pamphlets, periodicals, tracts, books, novels, essays—in a word, the entire moral forces of the human mind—have been the weapons. England became the champion of anti-slavery, and the United States became the theatre of a crusade, which seemed as if intended to carry out the spirit of the remark of Sir Robert Peel, that *"the one hundred millions of dollars paid for the abolition of slavery in the West Indies was the best investment ever made for the overthrow of American institutions."*

Exeter hall and the Staffed House became the center of this new system, around which revolved all the lights of British abolitionism. The ground of immediate and unconditional emancipation, however, was not taken by the English abolitionists until subsequent years, but these views, when presented, found ready concurrence from Clarkson, Wilberforce and other well known advocates of the cause. Among the English statesmen pledged upon the subject, were Grey, Lansdowne, Holland, Brougham, Melbourne, Palmerston, Graham, Stanley and Baxton, and in the hands of these fervent leaders the cause speedily progressed towards its fruition.

From this time forward the coalesced efforts of British and Northern influence to disturb the institution of slavery in the South, to render slave labor less valuable and incite the negroes to rebellion, have been continued with more or less system, occasionally threatening the stability of the Union; the whole object of Great Britain being, not the welfare of the slave, but the destruction of slave labor, whereby, through a system of conquest and forced labor, she would be able to supplant the United States, by producing her cotton from the fields of the Eastern world. With this end in view, and coupled perhaps with the idea that the abolition of slavery would break down our republican form of government, she resorted to every species of intrigue that promised success. Dissensions have been sown between the North and South; the "underground railroad" system has been established leading to her Canadian possessions; agitation and assault have been perservingly maintained; the country has been flooded with tirades of every hue and kind against the institution; the Northern pulpit has been desecrated in its dedication to the work of stirring up strife; churches have been severed in twain, and Southern Christians denied fellowship with their Northern brethren, until the grand political climax has been reached of secession and revolution. It is safe to say that from the time this plan of operation was digested in England, thirty years ago, there is scarcely a movement that has taken place on the chess-board of American abolitionism, which, under the guise of philanthropy, has not been dictated at Exeter Hall for the purpose of destroying the production of cotton and breaking down the free government of this country.

Among the more far-seeing and practical statesmen of Great Britain, however—men who have ever dissented from the ultra views of abolitionists—there is an evident alarm that this headlong policy that has been pursued will rebound upon the interests of the mother country. Already the subject has become a source of anxious consideration, and the people of England are beginning to look around for some relief from that dependence upon American institutions which has heretofore been the reliance and support of millions of their workers. They find that the example they have set, and the policy they have urged, does not promise to be altogether so beneficial to them as they supposed. In this connection it will be interesting, as a matter of history, to preserve the master rebuke of Lord Brougham to the unconditional abolitionists of Boston, who invited him to be present at the John Brown anniversary of the past year. He says:—

"Brougham, Nov. 20, 1860.

"Sir—I feel honored by the invitation to attend the Boston Convention, and to give my opinion upon the question "How can American Slavery be abolished?" I consider the application is made to me as conceiving me to represent the anti-slavery body in this country; and I believe that I speak their sentiments as well as my own in expressing the widest difference of opinion with you upon the merits of those who prompted the Harper's Ferry expedition, and upon the fate of those who suffered for their conduct in it. No one will doubt my earnest desire to see slavery extinguished, but that desire can only be gratified by Lawful means, a strict regard to the rights of property, or what the law declares property, and a constant repugnance to the shedding of blood. No man can be considered a martyr unless he not only suffers but is witness to the truth; and he does not bear this testimony who seeks a lawful object by illegal means. Any other course taken for the abolition of slavery can only delay the consummation we so devoutly wish, besides exposing the community to the hazard of an insurrection of perhaps less hurtful to the master than the slave."

Progress of Abolition in America—An Era of Reforms—Southern Efforts for Manumission—Various Plans of Emancipation that have been suggested—The first Abolition journal—New York "Journal of Commerce"—William Lloyd Garrison, his Early Life and Association—The Nat. Turner Insurrection in 1832, &c, &c.

Probably no period in the history of the country has been more characterized by the spirit of reform and innovation than that embraced between the years 1825 and 1839. It then seemed as if all the social, moral and religious influences of the community had been gathered in a focus that was destined to annihilate the wickedness of man. Missionary enterprises, though in their youth, were full of vigor. Anniversaries were the occasion of an almost crazy excitement; religion assumed the shape of fanaticism; the churches were thrilled with the sudden idea that the millennium was at hand—the "evangelization of the world" never was blessed with fairer prospects—the "awakenings to grace" were on the most tremendous scale. Peace societies were formed—temperance societies flourished more than ever—Free masonry was attacked, socially and politically—the Sabbath mail question became one of the absorbing topics of the day—theatres, lotteries, the treatment of the "poor Indian" by the general government—all came under the most rigorous religious review—the Colonization Society, established in 1816, enlarged its operations, and, in short, the spirit of reform became epidemic, and the period one of unprecedented moral and political inquiry.

It was a period, too, when in many of the States of the South, and especially those upon the Northern border, the subject was freely discussed of a gradual and healthy emancipation of the slaves, and various plans for this object were presented and entertained. The most valuable agencies were set at work—not by abolitionists, but by Southerners themselves, in whose hearts there had sprung up an embryo reformatory principle simultaneously with the landing upon their shores of the first slaves of their Northern brethren, which would have gone on increasing and fructifying had not the bitterest of denunciation been launched against them and driven the assaulted into an attitude of self- defence, whose defiant spirit now speaks out to the assailant in a bold justification of the institution attacked, as natural and necessary, and which it shall be their purpose to perpetuate forever.

As early as 1816 a manumission society was formed in Tennessee, whose object was the gradual emancipation of the slaves under a system of healthy and judicious State legislation. At a later day, Virginia, Maryland and Kentucky were the theatres of discussion on the same subject, and in all of them the question was agitated, socially and politically, with a freedom and liberty that indicated a general desire to effect the philanthropic object.

Various plans having the same end in view were likewise proposed, some of them evincing a remarkable ingenuity. One of these, in 1817, was to encourage, by all proper means, emancipation in the South; then to make arrangements with the non-slaveholding States to receive the freed negroes, and compel the latter, by law, if necessary, to reside in those States. By this means it was thought that a gradual change of "complexion" could be effected from natural causes, which would not take place unless the blacks were scattered, and that thus, from simple association and adventitious mixtures, the sable color would retire by degrees, and after a few generations a black person would be a rarity in the community.

Another plan proposed in 1819 was to remove the females to the Northern States, where they should be bound out in respectable families; those unmarried, of ten years and upwards, to be immediately free, and all the rest of the stock then existing to become so at ten years of age; the proceeds of the males sold to be appropriated by the party making the purchase to the removal and education of these females. In furtherance of this scheme, it was argued that while negro women would still bear children, though settled among white persons, they would not do so half so rapidly, and thus their posterity would in three or four generations lose the offensive color and have a tint not more disagreeable than the millions who are called white men in Southern Europe and the West Indies, and finally be lost in the common mass of humanity. While it is true that very few people, after fifty or sixty years, could under this rule boast of their fathers and mothers, the grand object would be attained, and the world be satisfied.

Another proposition, which emanated from a distinguished gentleman in one of the Southern States, and filling one of the highest offices in the government of the United States, was that a grade of color should be fixed in all the slaveholding States at which a person should be declared free and entitled to all the rights of a citizen, even if born of a slave. He contended that this act would separate all such persons from the negro race, and present a very considerable check to the progress of the black population, giving them at the same time new interests and feelings. The children thus emancipated, even if the parents should not be wholly fitted for it, would come into society with advantages nearly equal to those of the poorer classes of white people, and might work their way to independence as well, without any counteracting detriment to the public good.

In Virginia, in 1821, it was suggested through the columns of the Richmond Enquirer, that an act should be passed declaring that all involuntary servitude should cease to exist in that State from and after the year 2000; thus, without reducing for one or two generations the value of slave property one cent, affording ample time and opportunity to dispose of or exchange that dead property for a more useful and profitable kind.

In 1825, Hon. Mr. King, of New York, introduced into the Senate of the United States the annexed resolution:—

"That as soon as the portion of the existing funded debt of the United States, for the payment of which the public land is pledged, shall have been paid off, thenceforth the whole of the public lands of the United States, with the net proceeds of al future sales thereof, shall constitute and form a fund which is hereby appropriated to aid the emancipation of such slaves and the removal of any free persons of color in any of the said States, as by the laws of the several States respectively may be allowed to be emancipated, or to be removed to any territory or country without the limits of the United States of America."

This resolution, however, was not called up by the mover, or otherwise acted upon.

Still another plan was to raise money by contribution throughout the Union and elsewhere, and buy all the slaves at $250 each. The value of four million negroes at $500 each, their average market value, would be $2,000,000,000. It is unnecessary to say that none of these propositions were ever adopted in practice. In fact, while abolitionism has pretended to fell for the supposed sufferings of slaves, it has never felt much in its pockets to aid them.

At such a period—when the rampant spirit of reform was attacking every imaginary evil of the times—it is not a matter of wonder that northern abolitionists, yielding to their fanatical prejudices and to the British intrigue that was urging them onward, commenced that acrimonious agitation of the question which has since been its leading characteristic. The negro was pronounced "a man and a brother," and that was the beginning and end of the argument. Tracts, speeches, pamphlets and essays were scattered, "without money and without price." The pulpit vied with the press, and every imaginable form of argument was used to hold up slavery as the most horrible of all atrocities, and the "sum of all villanies." Newspapers began to be an acknowledged element in the land, and falling in the train of the young revolution, or rather growing out of it, wielded immense power among the masses. Among those then devoted to the subject of reform were the National Philanthropist, commenced in 1826; the Liberator, by William Lloyd Garrison, at Boston, in 1831, and the Emancipator, in New York.

The first abolition journal ever published in this city was the present Journal of Commerce, which was commenced September 1, 1827, by a company of stockholders, the principal of whom was the famous Arthur Tappan. The following extracts from its prospectus, issued March 24, 1827, will sufficiently indicate the puritanical character of its authors, and the general tone of the paper:—

"In proposing to add another daily paper to the number already published in this city, the projectors deem it proper to state that the measure has been neither hasty nor unadvisedly undertaken. Men of wisdom, intelligence and character have been consulted, and with one voice have recommended its establishment.

"Believing, as we do, that the theatre is an institution which all experience proves to be inimical to morality, and consequently tending to the destruction of our republican form of government, it is a part of our design to exclude from the columns of the journal all theatrical advertisements. "The pernicious influence of lotteries being admitted by the majority of intelligent men, and this opinion coinciding with our own, all lottery advertisements will also be excluded. "In order to avoid a violation of the Sabbath, by the setting of types, collecting of ship news, &c, on that day, the paper on Monday will be issued at a later hour than usual, but as early as possible after the arrival of the mails. In this way the Journal will anticipate by several hours a considerable part of the news contained in the evening papers of Monday and the morning papers of Tuesday, and will also give the ship news collected after the publication of the other morning papers. With these views we ask all who are friendly to the cause of morality in encouraging our undertaking."

Extract from the Minutes of a Meeting of Merchants and others at the American Tract Society's house, March 24, 1827:

"*Resolved*, That the prospectus of a new daily commercial paper, to be called the 'New York Journal of Commerce,' having been laid before this meeting, we approve of the plan upon which it is conducted, and cordially recommend it to the patronage of all friends to good morals and to the stability of our republican institutions."

"ARTHUR TAPPAN, Chairman."

"ROX LOCKWOOD, Secretary."

In its issue of October 30, 1828, we find the following:—

"It appears from an article in the Journal of the Times, a newspaper of some promise just established in Bennington, Vt., that a petition to Congress for the abolition of slavery in the District of Columbia is about to be put in circulation in that State.

"The idea is an excellent one, and we hope it will meet with success. That Congress has a right to abolish slavery in that District seems reasonable, though we fear it will meet with some opposition, so very sensitive are the slaveholding community to every movement relating to the abolition of slavery. At the same time, it would furnish to the world a beautiful pledge of their sincerity if they would unite with the non-slaveholding States, and by a unanimous vote proclaim freedom to every soul within sight of the capital of this free government. We could then say, and the world would then admit our pretence, that the voice of the nation is against slavery, and throw back upon Great Britain that disgrace which is of right and justice her exclusive property."

Another of its editorials on November 15, 1828:—

"We are all equally interested in demolishing the fabric (of slavery) and we may as well go to work peaceably and reduce it brick by brick as to make it a matter of warfare, and throw our enterprise and industry into the opposite scale."

In the course of time changes were made in the ownership of the paper, but one of its original proprietors is still its senior editor.

About this period William Lloyd Garrison made his appearance upon the stage, and he has been probably one of the most intensely hated, as well as one of the most sternly, severely and vociferously enthusiastic men in the Union. He is a native of Massachusetts, and at a very early age was placed in a printing office in Newburyport by his mother. Shortly after he was twenty- one years of age he set up a paper which he called the Free Press, which was read chiefly by a class of very advanced readers at the North. After this he removed to Vermont, and edited the Journal of the Times. This was as early as 1828. In September, 1829, he removed to Baltimore for the purpose of editing the Genius of Universal Emancipation, in company with

Benjamin Lundy. While performing these duties, a Newburyport merchant, named Francis Todd, fitted out a small vessel, and filled it in Baltimore with slaves for the New Orleans market. Mr. Garrison noticed this fact in his paper, and commented upon it in terms so severe that Mr. Todd directed a suit to be brought against him for libel. He was thereupon tried, convicted and thrown in jail for non-payment of the fine (one hundred dollars and costs). After an incarceration of fifty days, he was released on the payment of his fine, by Mr. Arthur Tappan, of this city, who, and his brother Lewis, before and since that time, have been chiefly celebrated for their efforts in the cause of abolition. In 1831, he wrote a few paragraphs that bear out the idea we have advanced—that there was then more real philanthropy in the South than at the North. He says:—

"I issued proposals for the publication of the *"Liberator"* in Washington City, during my recent tour, for the purpose of exciting the minds of the people on the subject of slavery. Every place I visited gave fresh evidences of the fact that a greater revolution in public sentiment was to be effected in the free States, and particularly in New England, than at the South. I found contempt more bitter, opposition more active, detraction more relentless, prejudice more stubborn and apathy more frozen, than among the slaveowners themselves. I determined at every hazard to lift up the standard of emancipation in the eyes of the nation, within sight of Bunker Hill, and in the birthplace of liberty. I am in earnest; I will not equivocate, I will not excuse, I will not retreat a single inch. I will be heard. The apathy of the people is enough to make every statue lift from its pedestal, and to hasten the resurrection of the dead."

From this time it may be said that the anti-slavery cause took its place among the moral enterprises of the day. It assumed a definite shape, and commenced that system of warfare which has since been unremittingly waged against the South.

During this year—1830—Mr. Tappan, Rev. S. S. Jocelyn, and others, projected the establishment of a seminary of learning at New Haven for the benefit of colored students; but, opposition manifesting itself, it was abandoned.

The first regularly organized convention of colored men ever assembled in the United States for a similar purpose also held a meeting this year, and aided and abetted by the Tappan, Jocelyns and other agitators of the period, attempted to devise ways and means for bettering their condition and that of their race. They reasoned that all distinctive differences made among men on account of their origin was wicked, unrighteous and cruel, and solemnly protested against every unjust measure and policy in the country having for its object the proscription of the colored people, whether state, national, municipal, social, civil or religious. In fact, white men and black seem to have started in the race together, consorting like brothers and sisters together in their aims and projects to accomplish the same end.

About this time publications began to be scattered through the South, whose direct tendency was to stir up insurrection among the slaves. The Liberator found its way mysteriously into the hands of the negroes, and individuals, under the garb of religion, were discovered in private consultation with the slaves. Suddenly, in August, 1831, the whole Union was startled by the announcement of an outbreak among the slaves of Southampton County, VA; and now commences the history of a career of violence and bloodshed that has marked every footstep of the abolition movement.

The leader of this outbreak was a slave named Nat Turner, and from him its name has been derived. Impelled by the belief that he was divinely called to be the deliverer of his oppressed countrymen, he succeeded in fixing the impression upon the minds of two or three others, his fellow slaves. Turner could read and write, and these acquirements gave him an influence over his associates. He was possessed, however, of little information, and, is represented to have been cowardly, cruel, and as he afterwards confessed, "a little credulous." It was a matter of notoriety that "secret agents of abolition had corrupted and betrayed him." However that may be, Nat declared that "he was advised" only to read to the slaves, that "Jesus came not to bring peace, but a sword!" Such a tree produced fitting fruits.

About midnight on the Sabbath of the 21st of August, 1831, Turner, with his confederates, burst into his master's house, and murdered every one of the white inmates. They were armed with knives and axes, and, in order to strike terror into the whites, most shockingly mangled the bodies of their victims. Neither helpless infancy nor female loveliness were spared. They then, by threats of death, compelled all the slaves to join them who would not do it voluntarily, and, exciting themselves to fury by ardent spirits, they proceeded to the next plantation. The happy family were reposing in the sound and quiet slumbers which precede the break of day, as the shouts of the raving insurgents fell upon their ears. It was the work of a moment, and they were all weltering in their gore. Not a white individual was spared to carry the tidings. The blow which dashed the infant left its brains upon the hearth. The head of the youthful maiden was in one part of the room and her mangled body was in another. Here again the number of insurgents was increased by those who voluntarily joined them, and by others who did it through compulsion. Stimulating their passions still more by intoxication, and arming themselves with such guns as they could obtain, some on horseback and others on foot, they rushed along to the next plantation. The morning now began to dawn, and the shrieks of those who fell under the sword and the axe of the negro were heard at a distance, and thus the alarm was soon spread from plantation to plantation, carrying inconceivable terror to every heart. The whites supposed it was a plot deeply laid and widely spread, and that the day had come for indiscriminate massacre. One gentleman who heard the appalling tidings hurried to a neighboring plantation, and arrived there just in time to hear the dying shrieks of the family and triumphant shouts of the negroes. He hastened in terror to his own home, but the negroes were there before him, and his wife and daughter had already fallen victims to their fury. Thus the infuriated slaves went on from plantation to plantation, gathering strength at every step, and leaving not a living white behind. They passed the day, until late in the afternoon, in this work of carnage, and numberless were the victims of their rage.

The population in this country is not dense, and, rapidly as the alarm spread, it was impossible for some time to collect a sufficient number to make a defence. Every family was entirely at the mercy of its own slaves. It is impossible to conceive of more distressing circumstances of apprehension. It is said that most of the insurgent slaves belonged to kind and indulgent masters, and consequently no one felt secure.

Late in the afternoon, a small party of whites, well armed, collected at a plantation for defence. The slaves came on in large numbers, and, emboldened by success, they at first drive back the whites. The slaves pressed on, thirsting for blood, and shouting with triumphant fury as the whites slowly retreated, apparently destined to be butchered, with their wives and children. Just at this awful moment a reinforcement of troops arrived, which turned the tide of victory and dispersed the slaves.

Exhausted with the horrible labors of the day, the insurgents retired to the woods and marshes to pass the night. Early the next morning they commenced their work again. But the first plantation they attacked—that of Dr. Blount—they were driven from by the slaves, who rallied around their master, and fearlessly hazarded their lives in his defence. By this time the whites were collected in sufficient force to bar their further progress. The fugitives were scattered over the country in small parties, but every point was defended, and wherever they appeared they were routed, shot, taken prisoners, and the insurrection quelled. The leader, Nat Turner, for a few weeks succeeded in concealing himself in a cave in Southampton county, near the theatre of his bloody exploits; but was finally taken, and suffered the extreme penalty of the law.

To describe the state of alarm to which this outbreak gave rise is impossible. Whole States were agitated; every plantation was the object of fear and suspicion; free negroes and slaves underwent the most rigid examination; armed bodies of men were held in constant readiness for any emergency which might arise; every slave who had participated in the insurrection were either shot or hung, and for months the entire South remained in a fever of excitement.

All this time the abolition journals of the North were singing their hallelujahs over the event. They circulated through the South then much more freely than at present, and the following extract was read from one of these by a gentleman to his terrified family, in the presence of the gentleman from whom the above particulars were derived:—

"The news from the South is glorious. General Nat is a benefactor of his race. The Southampton massacre is an suspicious era for the African. The blood of the men, women and children shed by the sword and the axe in the hand of the negro is a just return for the drops which have followed the master's lash."

Another extract, of similar rhetoric, from the record of that day, is from a speech by the "Reverend" Mr. Bayley, then of Sheffield, Mass.:—

"It is time that the ice was broken—time that the blacks considered they have the same right to regain their liberties, and even the present property of their owners, as the Hebrews had in despoiling the heathen round about them. The blacks should also know that it is their duty to destroy, if no other means offer conveniently, the monstrous incubuses and tyrants, yelept planters; and I, for one, would gladly lend a helping hand to lay them in one common grave! The country would be all the better for ridding the world of such a nest of vampyres."

Whether the abolitionist of the present time have modified the ideas they promulgated then, we shall see hereafter from a few among the ten thousand specimens that might be adduced.

The effect of these tirades upon the south cannot be well conceived.

Public opinion, just then opening to a free discussion of the question, drew back and shut itself within its castle. The bonds of slavery were bound tighter, the rivets were more strongly fastened, and a reactionary movement commenced that has never yet terminated.

The New England Anti-Slavery Society, 1832—More Newspapers and Tracts—New York City Anti-Slavery Society and the Incident of Its Organization—The American Anti-Slavery Society and its Creed—The Extent and System of their operations—Abolition Rots in New York—An Era of Excitement—Negro Conspiracy in Mississippi—George Thompson, the English Abolitionist—Riot at Alton, Ill., and Death of the Rev. E. P. Lovejoy.

In the year 1832, January 30, the New England or Massachusetts Anti-Slavery Society went into operation, but with limited means. From this society have sprung the American Anti-Slavery Society and all its numerous auxiliaries. It was the first organized body that attacked slavery on the principle of its inherent sinfulness, and enforced the consequent duty of "immediate emancipation." All the events of a historical character which have marked the annals of the last thirty years, may be traced directly to the agitation which this society first set on foot in this country. Men have been forced to throw aside their disguises and stand forth either as the open defenders of slavery or as propagators of the abolition movement. The two great antagonistic parties of the present day are the children of its vile creation. It has excited the very fury of antagonism; it has shaken the pulpit with excummicating thunders; it has indulged in the most bitter invective, deluged the country with invented instances of Southern barbarity, denounced the Constitution as a "league with hell," and scattered its venom in every household of the free States, until men, women and children have become imbued with its contaminating infection. Their discourses have all been tirades; their exordium, argument and peroration have turned on epithets, slanders, innuendoes; Southerners have been reviled as "tyrants," "thieves," "murderers," "atrocious monsters," "violators of the laws of nature, God and man," while their homes have been designated as "the abodes of iniquity," and their land "one vast brothel."

More abolition papers sprang into existence. The New York Evangelist, then conducted by the Rev. Samuel Griswold, espoused the cause. Through the influence of the Tappans, millions of anti-slavery tracts were circulated monthly, and sent by mail to all portions of the country, and especially to clergymen. These publications were likewise scattered through the South, their direct tendency being to stir up the slaves to further insurrection. Recruits of all ages and professions came forward, and the cause numbered amongst its adherents many of the theologians and professional men of the period. On the 2d of October, 1833, a New York City Anti-Slavery Society was organized, though not without some demonstrations of opposition. In fact, a large majority of the most respectable citizens were opposed to the enterprise, and they accordingly determined, if possible, to crush the dangerous project in the bud. The meeting was advertised to be held in Clinton Hall, but during the course of the day the public feeling was excited by the posting through the city of a large placard, of which the following is a copy:

"NOTICE—TO ALL PERSONS FROM THE SOUTH: All persons interested in the subject of a meeting called by J. Leavitt, W. Green, Jr., W. Goodell, J. Rankin and Lewis Tappan, at CLINTON HALL, this Evening, at 7 o'clock, are requested to attend at the same hour and place. "New York, Oct. 2d, 1833. MANY SOUTHERNERS."

Southerners, however, had nothing to do with the meeting. At an early hour people began to assemble in crowds in front of Clinton Hall, but the trustees, or some others, had closed the premises. The throng, however, still increased, and it soon became evident from the execrations mutually indulged in by the people, that the authors of the projected meeting were acting with discreet valor in staying away. William Lloyd Garrison, who had then just returned from England, where he had been engaged in fomenting excitement against this country, traducing its people and institutions, was an especial object of popular abhorrence and disgust, and it is said that many grave and respectable citizens would have gladly assented to his decoration in a coat of tar and feathers. Notwithstanding the notification of "No meeting," Clinton Hall was opened and crowded to suffocation. Speeches were delivered by a number of citizens, and a series of resolutions, prepared by Mr. F. A. Tallmadge, were adopted, deprecating any interference in the question of slavery, and expressing a determination to resist every attempt on the part of the abolitionist to effect their object.

It appears, however, that the purposes for which the meeting was originally called were indirectly attained. Finding it much easier to raise a popular whirlwind than to ride securely upon it, they prudently and privately changed their place of meeting to Chatham street chapel. Here the New York City Anti-Slavery Society was duly organized, having for its object the "total and immediate abolition of slavery in the United States." Its first officers were:—

President—Arthur Tappan

Vice-President—John Rankin

Corresponding Secretary—Elizur Wright, Jr.

Recording Secretary—Rev. Chas. W. Dennison

Managers—Joshua Leavitt, Isaac T. Hopper, Abraham Cox, M.D., Lewis Tappan, William Goodell.

The proceedings of the night appear to have terminated in a broad farce, for after the breaking up of the citizens' meeting, the crowd proceeded to Chatham street Chapel to see what was going on there. They found the doors open and the lights burning, but the meeting had suddenly dispersed. The dignified philosophers, unable to "stand fire," had retreated "bag and baggage," through the back windows. To have the frolic out, a black man was put upon the stage, a series of humorous resolutions were passed, good- natured speeches on the burlesque order were made, and, instead of the angry frowns with which the evening was commenced, the whole affair terminated amid the broad grins of a numerous multitude. Precisely one week after the above occurrence, another meeting of the citizens was held, over which the Mayor of the city presided. Among the orators was Hon. Theodore Frelinghuysen, then United States Senator from New Jersey, afterwards a candidate for Vice-President of the United States on the ticket with Henry Clay, and he directly charged the abolitionists with "Seeking to dissolve the Union," declared that nine-tenths of the horrors of slavery were imaginary, and that "the crusade of abolition was merely the poetry of philanthropy." Chancellor Walworth was likewise in attendance, and denounced their efforts as unconstitutional, and the individuals instigating them as "reckless incendiaries."

On the 4th, 5th and 6th of December, 1833, a National Anti-Slavery Convention was held in the city of Philadelphia, when, pursuant to previous notice, sixty delegates from ten States assembled, viz:—Maine, New Hampshire, Vermont, Massachusetts, Rhode Island, Connecticut, New York, New Jersey, Pennsylvania and Ohio. Beriah Green, President of Oneida Institute, was chosen President, and Lewis Tappan and John G. Whittier, Secretaries. The resolution were prepared in committee by William Lloyd Garrison. This convention organized the American Anti-Slavery Society, of which Arthur Tappan was chosen President; Elizur Wright, Jr., Secretary of Domestic Correspondence; William L. Garrison, Secretary of Foreign Correspondence; A. L. Cox, Recording Secretary, and William Green, Jr., Treasurer. The Executive Committee was located in New York city, the seat of the society's operations, which were not prosecuted with vigor. The Emancipator became the organ of the society. Tracts, pamphlets and books were published and circulated; a large number of agents were employed in different guises to promote the work throughout the country, North and South; State, county and local anti-slavery societies were organized throughout the free States; funds were collected; the New

England Anti-Slavery Society became the Massachusetts State Society, and the whole machinery of agitation was put in thorough working order.

Among the earliest principles adopted by the abolition societies was the following:

"Immediate and unconditional emancipation is eminently prudent, safe and beneficial to all parties concerned.

"No compensation is due to the slaveholder for emancipating his slaves; and emancipation creates no necessity for such compensation, because it is of itself a pecuniary benefit, not only to the slave, but to the master."

So perfect was this system of operations, that in 1836 the society numbered two hundred and fifty auxiliaries in thirteen States. In eighteen months afterwards it had increased to one thousand and six. In one week alone, $6,000 were raised in Boston and $20,000 in the city of New York. To such an extent was the abolition furor carried at this time, that many prominent individuals had their dinner service, plates, cups, saucers, &c, embellished with figures of slaves in chains, and other emblems of the same character.

Similar prints, or pictorial illustrations of the natural equality before God of all men, without distinction of color, and setting forth the happy fruits of a universal acknowledgement of this truth by the exhibition of a white woman in no equivocal relations to a black man, were circulated in the South. The infection also broke out on Northern pocket handkerchiefs made for Southern children, candy wrappers, fans and anti-slavery seals, all being made to represent the prevailing idea. The reaction shortly took place. Laws were passed forbidding the reception or circulation of these incendiary articles in the Southern States. Mobs broke into the post offices and burned all abolition prints that could be found, and rewards were offered for the detection and punishment of any person found tampering with the slave population. Nor was this reaction confined to the Southern section of the country; it was largely developed in the North. Churches soon began to be the theatres of discussions on the subject, and a conservative spirit sprang into life among all the principal religious sects. Merchants began to suffer in their business; manufacturers found their wares of no avail for the Southern market; and, in short, a strong spirit of opposition to the revolutionary doctrines of the abolitionists was manifested throughout the Northern States.

This excited feeling soon culminated in an outbreak. On the 8th of July, 1834, the New York Sacred Music Society attempted to assemble, as was their wont, in Chatham street Chapel, for the purpose of practising sacred harmony. They found the place, however, filled with an audience of whites and blacks who had gathered to listen to an abolition address, and who obstinately refused to remove. But this was not all. The anger of the negroes was aroused in consequence of the request to remove, and they attacked several of the gentlemen with loaded canes and other implements, knocking some down and severely injuring others. The alarm was raised, crowds assembled, a fight ensued in the church, the congregation were expelled, and the building was closed. As Mr. Lewis Tappan was returning to his house, the mob, supposing him to have been instrumental in producing the disorder, followed him home and threw stones at his house.

On the 9th, three more riots occurred. The crowd proceeded to the Bowery Theatre, took possession of the house, and put an end to "Metamora," without waiting the tragic conclusion to which it was destined by the author. A great number then proceeded to the house of Lewis Tappan, in Rose street, broke open the door, smashed the windows and threw the furniture into the street. A bonfire was lighted, and beds and bedding made the flames. Fuel was added to the excitement by publications in the Emancipator, over the signature of Elizur Wright, Jr., in which intimations were thrown out covertly, inviting to a forcible resistance to the laws which authorize the recapture of runaways slaves. Placards were posted through the streets in great numbers, and the demon of disorder appeared to have taken possession of the city.

On the night of the 10th, the crowd again assembled and made their way to Dr. Cox's church, then on the corner of Laight and Varick streets, which they assaulted with stones, breaking the windows and doing a variety of mischief. They then proceeded to Dr. Cox's house, No. 3 Charlton street, but, anticipating an attack, he had packed up and sent away his furniture, and removed with his family into the country on the previous afternoon. The mob commenced the work of destruction by breaking in the two lower windows; but they had scarcely effected an entrance before they were driven from the premises by the police officers and a detachment of horse. They were thence- forward kept at bay, but as far east as Thompson street, the streets were filled with an excited multitude, armed with paving stones, which they smote together, crying "All together." A fence was torn down and converted into clubs, and a barricade of carts was built across the street to impede the horsemen. After a while order was gradually restored and the tumult subsided for the night.

On the 11th, it broke out again, when an attack was made on the store of Arthur Tappan, in Pearl street. The rioters were driven away, however, by the police, without further damage than the smashing of a few windows. A second attack was likewise made on Dr. Cox's church, and also the church of Rev. Mr. Ludlow, in Spring street. The latter was almost completely sacked, nearly the entire interior being torn up and carried into the street to erect barricades against the horse and infantry which had assembled at various rendezvous at an early hour, in compliance with the proclamation of the Mayor. The excitement continued to increase. The bells were rung, and the Seventh (then the Twenty-seventh) regiment, under Col. Stevens, charged upon the rioters, driving them from their position an clearing Spring street. The crowd next proceeded to the residence of Rev. mr. Ludlow, whose family had retired, and after breaking the windows and doors, left the ground. Later in the night an immense riot occurred in the neighborhood of the Five Points. St. Phillip's Episcopal Church (colored), in Center street, was nearly torn down, while several houses occupied by negroes in the vicinity were entirely demolished. Several days elapsed before quiet was effectually restored. Al the military of the city during this time were under arms.

Similar, outbreaks also occurred at Norwich, Conn., Newark, N.J., and other places, where the negroes, under the effect of abolition teachings, grown bold and impudent, were compelled to leave town. In Norwich the mob entered a church during the delivery of an abolition sermon, took the parson from the pulpit, walked him into the open air to the tune of the "Rogue's March," drummed him out of the town, and threatened if he ever made his appearance in the place again they would give him "a coat of tar and feathers."

Similar scenes were enacted in Philadelphia, where a large hall was burned, and other public and private buildings in which the negroes and abolitionists were in the habit of meeting, were either injured or demolished.

On the 28th of June, 1835, it was discovered that the negroes of Livingston, in Madison county, Miss., under the lead of a band of white men, contemplated a general rising. A committee of safety was instantly organized, and two of the white ringleaders were arrested, tried, and, after a confession, forthwith hanged. By this confession, it appeared that the plan was conceived by the notorious John A. Murrel, a well known Mississippi pirate at that time, and that it embraced the destruction of the entire population and liberation of the slaves in the South generally. For two years the disaffection had thus been spreading, and, with few exceptions, adherents existed on every plantation in the county. Arms and ammunitions had been secreted for the purpose, and everything made ready for a general outbreak. The confession involved numerous white men and black, many of whom were arrested and suffered for their diabolical designs. Among these was one Ruel Blake, of Connecticut. The summary proceedings adopted, however, had the desired effect, and in a few months tranquillity was restored to the unsettled and excited district. The year 1835 was one of the most exciting eras of agitation in the early history of anti-slavery. The events of the preceding few months had aroused the entire country to a realizing sense of the dangerous tendency of the abolitionists and the rapid progress of their cause. In Congress the subject had gain begun to be agitated, through petitions presented by various individuals and bodies in the free States, praying the interference of the government in the abolition of slavery, and in society at large a more decided sentiment was evidently being formed pro and con, than had previously been manifested.

In the South, incendiary publications were circulated to such an alarming extent, that the press and people of that section rose en masse to put down the growing evil. Following the insurrection to which allusion has been made above, at a public meeting held in the town of Mississippi, it was unanimously resolved that any "individual who dared to circulate incendiary tracts or publications, likely to excite the slaves to rebellion, was justly worthy, in the sight of God and man, of immediate death." And at a similar meeting in Williamsburg, Va., no less a personage than General John Tyler, afterwards President of the United States, endorsed a resolution to the effect that the circulation of these incendiary documents was an act of treasonable character, and that when offenders were detected in the fact, condign punishment ought and would be inflicted upon them without resort to any other tribunal. In this state of alarm, the allows and stake soon found victims, and within a period of a few months, no less than a dozen individuals, white and black, who were found among the slaves, inciting them to insurrection, receive the just award of their crime. Efforts were also made at this time by several Southern communities to get some of the prominent abolitionists in their power, so that an example might be made of those who were too cowardly to appear in the field of this species of missionary labor themselves. Among others, a reward of five thousand dollars was offered by the Legislature of Georgia for the apprehension of either of ten persons named in a resolution, citizens of New York and Massachusetts, and "one George Thompson, a subject of Great Britain." An offer of ten thousand dollars was likewise made for the arrest of Rev. A. A. Phelps, a clergyman of New York, and fifty thousand dollars was offered to any one who would deliver into their hands the famous Arthur Tappan or Le Roy Sunderland, a well known Methodist minister.

Even the clergymen added their voice to the general cry of indignation that rose from the Southern heart; and when, in July, 1835, a few days after the forcing of the Post office, and the destruction of the abolition publications there found, by a crowd in Charleston, S.C., a public meeting was held for completing measures of protection, the clergy of all denominations attended in a body to lend their sanction to the proceedings. About this time one of the Methodist preachers of South Carolina addressed the following novel letter to Rev. Le Roy Sunderland, editor of Zion's Watchman of New York:—

"If you wish to educate the slaves, I will tell you how to raise the money, without editing Zion's Watchman. You and old Arthur Tappan come out to the South this winter, and they will raise one hundred thousand dollars for you. New Orleans itself would be pledged for it. Desiring no further acquaintance with you, I am, &c. J. C. POSTELL

Laws of the most stringent character were passed by nearly all the Southern States to prevent the further dissemination among the Southern people of abolition doctrines, and an appeal was made to the Legislatures of the North to do the same thing. Indeed, the entire policy of that section as regards the previous license allowed to slaves and free negroes was changed so as to render it difficult, if not impossible, for any future influence of an insurrectionary character to be exerted upon them. Public meetings were also held, at which resolutions were passed declaratory of the determination to put down at all hazards these repeated attempts on the part of abolitionists to deluge their families and firesides in blood. In many of the principal cities a list of all persons arriving and departing was kept, that it might be known who were and who were not to be regarded with suspicion.

The effect upon the North was not less marked, and this prompt action on the part of their Southern brethren found thousands of sympathizers. Indignation was almost universal. The press teemed with articles upon the subject, and among the majority of the order-loving journals of the day, it was generally agreed that if the madmen who were scattering firebrands, arrows and death, could not be persuaded or rebuked to silence, no other alternative was allowed to the slaveholding States to protect themselves, except by the system of passports, examination and punishments, which to some extent they had adopted, and in which they were justified.

The people, too, were smarting under the insults that were poured out upon the nation by the English emissaries and agents who were in the country lending their assistance to the prevailing mischief. Among these individuals was the famous George Thompson, an agent and orator of the British Anti- Slavery Society. Such was the excitement produced by his opprobrious language towards the South, that in many places where he appeared he was greeted with demonstrations of anything but a complimentary character. At Lynn, Mass., he was assaulted by females with rotten eggs and stones, and driven off the ground; and at New Bedford, in the language of the poet,

"When to speak the man essayed, Gods! what a noise the fiddles made."

He was emphatically "sung down." At Boston the matter was still more serious. It having been announced that Garrison and Thompson would speak before a female anti-slavery meeting, the following hand-bill was circulated:—

"THOMPSON THE ABOLITIONIST.—That famous foreign scoundrel, Thompson, will hold forth this afternoon, at the Liberator office, No. 48 Washington Street. The present is a fair opportunity for the friends of the Union to 'snake Thompson out!' It will be a contest between the abolitionists and the friends of the Union. A purse of $100 has been raised by a number of patriotic citizens to reward the individual who shall first lay hands on Thompson, so that he may be brought to the tar-kettle before dark. Friends of the Union, be vigilant."

It is needless to say that Thompson did not appear. Garrison did, however, or rather he was found ensconced, martyr-like, under a pile of shavings in a carpenter's shop. A rope was then fastened around his neck, and he was gently lowered out of a window to the ground. A general exclamation from the assembled crowd, "Don't hurt him," indicated the gentleness of the mob, and, pale and convulsed, he was thus led to the Mayor's office in the City Hall. Afterwards he was conducted to jail, and, as he sank exhausted into his place, he made the remark, "Never was man so rejoiced to get into jail before." The rabble, which by the by, was of an unexceptionable character, soon after dispersed, their object having been effected, and the next morning Garrison was liberated from confinement. In Uttica and Rochester, N.Y., Worcester, Mass., Canaan, N.H., and at various places in the New England States, the abolitionists met with similar treatment. Their assemblages were either disturbed or broken up, and they often found it required a large amount of determination to resist the indignation which their fanaticism had aroused against them. Meetings were also held in every portion of the North, at which influential citizens attended to denounce the policy of the abolitionists as subversive of the Union and Constitution, and to express their sympathy for the South. Several of the postmasters of the North, participating in this reactionary sentiment, on their own responsibility, even refused to allow the incendiary documents to pass through the mails. Such was the activity of the abolitionists, however, that in the month of August alone over 175,000 copies of their publications were circulated through the United States; and their presses, under the direction of the Tappans and Garrison & Co., were employed night and day to foment the excitement. It was said that these individuals had then planned an insurrectionary movement throughout the South, which was to have been developed on a certain day; but the whirlwind they raised in every section of the country rendered this impossible, and they were compelled to change their programme of operations.

Though somewhat modified by the restrictions with which public opinion had surrounded the abolitionists, this state of affairs continued through the year 1836. The subject of excluding from the mails the whole series of publications came under the consideration of government, and the proposition of the President, Andrew Jackson, regarding the propriety of passing a law for this purpose, being acted upon in Congress, resulted in a bill rendering it unlawful for any deputy postmaster to deliver to any person any pamphlet, newspaper, handbill or pictorial representation, touching the subject of slavery, where, by the laws of the State, Territory or District their circulation was prohibited. This healthy measure was defeated, however, on the final vote.

The principal anti-slavery event of the year 1837 was a riot at Alton, Ill. For a long time the community of that town had been agitated by the abolitionists, and finally, on an attempt being made to resuscitate the Alton observer, a newspaper previously edited by the Rev. E. P. Lovejoy, (brother of Owen Lovejoy, the present member of Congress from Illinois,) a journal which, in his hands, had become conspicuous for the violence of its denunciations against the South and its institutions, a terrible riot ensued. It had been announced for several days that a printing press was hourly expected to arrive, intended for the purpose above named. This gave rise to an intense excitement and to open threats, that its landing would be resisted, if necessary, by force of arms. It was landed, however, and placed in a warehouse, under the protection of a guard of twenty or thirty gentlemen who had volunteered for the purpose. Almost immediately there were indications of an attack. The press was demanded by the mob, who insisted that they would not be satisfied with anything less than its destruction. The party in the building determined it should not be given up, and during the angry altercation which ensued, a shot was fired from one of the windows, which mortally wounded a man named Lyman Bishop. The crowd then withdrew, but with the death of Bishop the excitement increased to such an extent that they shortly appeared in greater numbers, armed with guns and weapons of different kinds, more than ever intent upon carrying out their original purpose. A rush was made upon the warehouse with the cries of "Fire the house," "Burn them out," &c. The firing soon became fearful. The building was surrounded, and the inmates threatened with extermination and death in the most frightful form imaginable. Fire was applied, and all means of escape by flight were cut off. The scene now became appalling.

About the time the fire was communicated to the building, Rev. E. P. Lovejoy received four balls in the breast, near the door of the warehouse, and fell a corpse. Several persons engaged in the attack were also severely wounded. The contest raged for more than an hour, when the party in the house intimated that they would abandon the premises and the press, if allowed to pass out unmolested. This was granted, and they made their escape, though several shots were fired in the act. A large number of persons then rushed into the building, threw the press upon the wharf, where it was broken in pieces and thrown into the river. The fire was then extinguished, and without further attempts at violence, the mob dispersed. No further indications of disorder were manifested.

For long time this outbreak served as a check upon the aggressive policy of the abolitionists, and, though not thoroughly cowed, both principals and agents found that the agitation of the subject was like the handling of a sword whose double edges cut in both directions. After this event, with the exception of the burning of a hall in 1838, in which they held their meetings, in Philadelphia, the country for a number of years became comparatively quiet, and the agitators took good care not to give occasion for further public demonstrations.

CHAPTER VI.

The Era of "Gags" and Congressional Petitions—John Quincy Adams; his Petition for Disunion—Legislation from 1835 to 1845—Annexation of Texas—The Liberty Party of 1840, Free Soil Party of 1848, and Republican Party of 1850—Mexican War and Wilmot Proviso.

The decade embraced between the years 1835 and 1845 may be termed the third epoch in the history of this movement. In that period, the grand experiment of the abolitionists was most effectually tried. They had felt the public pulse, developed their power and resources, had the benefit of experience, and ascertained to what extent the public mind could be prejudiced by the course of agitation which they had pursued. It was in fact an era of lessons, as well to the country as to themselves. From a mere handful, the original organization had grown to be a power within itself—a power at the ballot-box—a power for right or wrong, for good or mischief, too self- reliant and too strong to be disregarded. Neither legislative enactments nor riots, nor personal chastisement, nor public opinion, had been able to restrain its rapid advances towards the consummation of its hopes. It lost ground nowhere, and in every non-slaveholding State its friends and funds were greatly multiplied. As an indication of its extraordinary growth, the number of anti-slavery societies in the United States, in the year 1838, may be safely estimated at two thousand, with at least two hundred thousand persons enrolled as members.

These, however, were not all entitled to the suffrages of the party. They were the children and wives of fanatics who learned their lessons of abolition in the Bible classes, Sunday and secular schools, and from their parents and husbands. The sentiment was intruded, indeed, in all the relations of life—social, financial and domestic, and even in the affairs of love, Cupid himself was made subservient to its ascendency. The belles of the day would hardly look upon a suitor who was not as well a worshipper at the shrine of their political passion, as of their beauty, and no youngster's domestic destiny was at all certain of fruition who was not sound upon what was then regarded as the soul-saving question of abolitionism. The youths of 1840 have become the men of 1860, and in the enormous increase of the republican party, we see the result of the early influences thus set at work.

For the first time in its history, the organization began to be regarded as a political element in the land, and worthy of a courtship by those who desired its influence and support. Candidates for office began to be catechised, and such men as William H. Seward, Levi Lincoln, William L. Marcy and others, found time to give lengthy replies to the authors of this new inquisition, setting forth their views. In local politics, it was the moral and political test by which men were measured, and it lay at the foundation of all the subsequent State action of the Northern Legislatures upon the subject of anti-slavery.

In both branches of Congress, also, the question of abolition for the first time occupied a large share of the deliberations, and was discussed under every possible aspect. From 1831, when John Quincy Adams presented fifteen petitions in a single bunch, for the abolition of slavery in the District of Columbia, similar documents, got up and circulated by anti- slavery societies, poured into both branches of the National Legislature in a steady stream. They also called for a prohibition of what was termed an "internal slave trade" between the States, avowing at the same time that their ultimate object was to abolish slavery, not only in the District, but throughout the Union. It was, indeed, the only mode in which the fanatics could agitate the question in Congress, and was a part of the scheme by which they expected to accomplish their purposes. Under the influence of the feelings excited by these causes, the Southern Senators and members declared, almost to a man, that if the Southern States could not remain in the Union without having their domestic peace continually disturbed by the systematic attempts of the abolitionists to produce dissatisfaction and revolt among the slaves and incite their wild passions to vengeance, the great law of self-preservation would compel them to separate from the North. This persistent demand of the abolitionists, through petitions, continued from session to session, until, becoming a nuisance, an effort was made to prevent their farther reception. The effort was, for a time, successful, and resulted in what was called the "era of gags"—these gags being simply a rule of the House, "That all petitions, memorials, resolutions and propositions relating in any way or to any extent to the question of slavery shall, without either being printed or referred, be laid on the table, and no further action whatever shall be had thereon."

This was respectively passed in 1836, 1837 and 1838, and in 1840 it was incorporated into the standing rules of the House—being henceforward known as the "Twenty-first Rule." The vote upon this was—yeas, 128; nays, 78.

The excitement produced in the House on the occasion of these several votes was intense, and speeches were made upon the question by the most distinguished men of the country.

In 1837, the immediate occasion of the contest was the pertinacious effort of Mr. Slade, of Vermont, to make the presentation of abolition petitions the ground of agitation and action against the institution of slavery in the Southern States. Mr. Rhett, of South Carolina, warned him of the consequences of such inflammatory harangues, and his refusal to desist from them was the signal for a general disorder and uproar. The next morning a resolution similar to that above quoted was adopted by a vote of 135 yeas to 60 nays—the full two-thirds and fifteen. "This," says Thomas H. Benton, "was one of the most important votes ever delivered in the House." Upon its issue depended the quiet of the House on one hand, and on the other the renewal and perpetuation of the scenes of the day before—ending in breaking up all deliberation and all national legislation.

Thus were stifled, and in future, for a few years at least, prevented in the House the inflammatory debates on these disturbing petitions. It was the great session of their presentation, being offered by hundreds and signed by hundreds of thousands of persons—many of them women, who forgot their sex and their duties to mingle in the inflammatory work; and some of them clergymen, who forgot their mission of peace to stir up strife among those who should be brethren. After long and protracted efforts by John Quincy Adams, who was then champion of the abolitionists on the floor of the House, this restriction upon the right of petition was removed in December, 1845, by a vote of 108 to 80. Among the acts of this statesman in 1839, was the presentation of a resolution that the following amendments to the Constitution of the United States should be proposed to the several States of the Union:—

"1. From and after the 4th July, 1842, there shall be throughout the United States no hereditary slavery; but on and after that day, every child born in the United States, their territory or jurisdiction, shall be born free."

"2. With the exception of the Territory of Florida, there shall henceforth never be admitted into this union any State, the Constitution of which shall tolerate within the same the existence of slavery."

"3. From and after the 4th July, 1845, there shall be neither slavery nor slave trade at the seat of government of the United States."

This proposition of course received no favor either North or South, and was speedily laid aside. Subsequently he presented a petition praying for a dissolution of the Union—the first of the kind ever offered to the government—whereupon a resolution was submitted to Congress to the effect that Mr. Adams in so doing had offered the deepest indignity to the House and insult to the people of the United States, and that, for thus permitting, through his instrumentality, a wound to be aimed at the Constitution and existence of his country he merited expulsion from the national council and the severest censure. It concluded—"This they hereby do for the maintenance of their own purity and dignity; for the rest, they turn him over to his own conscience and the indignation of all true American citizens."

The resolution was discussed for several days, in which Mr. Adams and his anti-slavery propagandism were handled without gloves; but finally the whole subject was laid upon the table. Another source of discussion, both in and out of Congress, about this time, was the Texas question. As far back as 1829, the annexation of Texas was agitated in the Southern and Western States, being urged on the ground of the strength and extension it would give to the slaveholding interest. This fact at once enlisted opposition from the entire anti-slavery sentiment of the North, in which British abolitionist took part, and every effort was made on the other side of the water to increase the sectional jealousy already known to be exciting. The English press, Parliament and statesmen, all treated the proposed acquisition as one in which they felt called upon to interfere. The famous "Texan plot," which was matured at the "World's Anti-Slavery Convention," held in London in 1840, was one of the results.

The part to be performed by the British government embraced a double object. The large territory claimed by Texas was known to contain most of the remaining cotton lands of North America. A virtual control of these lands would, therefore, be invaluable to British commerce. The country was but thinly settled, and the number of slaves was small enough to render emancipation of essay attainment. Thus, if by a timely interposition of her influence and diplomacy, Great Britain could establish a rival cotton producing country at our very door, and prevent the growth of slavery there, she would partially prevent a growing dependence on the slave products of the United States, and at the same time set up a barrier to the further extension of Southern civilization in that direction. There was but one obstacle in the way. Texas preferred annexation to the United States, and, notwithstanding British assistance, believed to have proffered to Santa Anna in 1842, when he resolved to send an invading army into the territory for the purpose of declaring emancipation, and other objects; notwithstanding the resolutions of Northern Legislatures and acrimonious debates in Congress; notwithstanding every effort, home and foreign, to prevent annexation; through the patriotic efforts to General Jackson, President Tyler, Mr. Calhoun and other statesmen, on the 16th of December, 1845, Texas was admitted into the Union.

Though thus defeated in their immediate designs, one point was gained by the friends of anti-slavery. They succeeded in obtaining a position in Congress which enabled them to agitate the whole Union. From that time their power began to increase, until the infection has diseased the great mass of the people of the North, who, whatever may be their opinion of the original abolition party, which still keeps up its distinctive organization, never fail, when it comes to acting, to cooperate in carrying out their measures.

The year 1840 was marked by two important events, namely, the formation of a distinct political party of abolitionists, and a division in the two leading anti-slavery societies of the country. The Liberty Party arose from the fact that, after a protracted experiment, the candidates of the old parties could not, to any extent, however questioned or pledged, be depended upon to do the work which the abolitionists demanded of them. Such an organization was advocated by Mr. Garrison as early as 1834; but it was not until the annual meeting of the New York Anti-Slavery Society at Uttica, in September, 1838, that a series of resolutions or a platform was adopted, setting forth the principles of political action, and solemnly pledging those who adopted them to vote for no candidates who were not fully pledged to anti-slavery measures. In July, 1839, a National Anti-Slavery Convention was held at Albany, and the mode of political action against slavery, including the question of a distinct party, was fully discussed, but without coming to any definite decision by vote farther than to refer the question of independent nominations to the judgment of abolitionists in their different localities. The Monroe county convention for nominations at Rochester, N.Y., September, 1839, adopted a series of resolutions and an address prepared by Myron Holly, which have been regarded as laying the real cornerstone of the Liberty party. He may, therefore, be regarded, more than any other man, as its founder.

In January, 1840, a New York State Anti-Slavery Convention was held in Genesee county. The traveling at that season of the year was bad, and delegates were in attendance from only six States. Among these were Myron Holly and Gerrit Smith. By this convention, a call was issued for a National Convention, and accordingly, April 1, 1840, it assembled at Albany—Alvan Stuart presiding. After a full discussion, the Liberty party was organized, and James J. Birney and Thomas Earle were nominated for President and Vice President of the United States. At the Presidential election in the autumn of that year, the entire vote of the Liberty party amounted to 7,059. In 1844, the Liberty candidates, James G. Birney and Thomas Morris, received 62,399 votes. These, however, were but a small part of the professed abolitionists of the United States, the great majority voting for the nominees of the old parties—Harrison, Van Buren, Polk and Clay.

The other event of the year 1840, to which we have alluded, was the division in the Massachusetts Anti-Slavery Society in Boston, and a division in the American Anti-Slavery Society of New York, the causes in each case being more or less identified with each other. Without going into the subject, it may be briefly stated that the principal cause in both instances was a difference of opinion on theological jealousies. The most rabid among the abolitionists have been infidels, or little less, from the start, and have absorbed every species of fanaticism, in whatever shape it has appeared since. Another question resulting in the division appears to have been "Woman's Rights," or, in other words, what position females ought to occupy in the society. As early as 1835, these moral hermaphrodites were in the habit of delivering public lectures and scattering publications through the land; but their wagging tongues finally became such a nuisance that several clergymen published a pastoral letter in 1837, strongly censuring all such unwomanly interference. The result was, as has been stated, great excitement and a subsequent separation of the respective opponents.

Shortly after this division, we find the American Anti-Slavery Society, at one of its annual meetings, raising the flag of "No Union with Slaveholders," demanding a dissolution of the Union, and denouncing the federal constitution as pro-slavery— "a covenant with death and an agreement with hell."

To resume the history of the progress of the party. In 1835, a State Convention of abolitionists was held at Port Byron, New York, at which an address was presented embodying the views of a number of individuals, who, while they were abolitionists at heart, were not rabid or ultra enough to be prepared to act with the Liberty party. This was printed, circulated, and gained adherents, and upon its basis, in 1847, a convention assembled at Macedon, New York, when Gerrit Smith and Elhu Burrit were nominated for President and Vice President of the United States; but the latter declining, the name of Charles C. Foote was afterwards substitute. This party was known by the name of the Liberty League. Subsequently its principles became merged into the Buffalo platform of 1847. Gerrit Smith was then again proposed as a candidate for the Presidency; but the course of leading men in the convention required the nomination of a different man. Accordingly, Hon. John P. Hale, of New Hampshire—an "independent democrat," as he termed himself—and Hon. Leicester King, of Ohio, were nominated. This, however, was only temporary;

and another convention was called, and held at Buffalo, August 9, 1848, composed of "the opponents to slavery extension, irrespective of parties," and including, of course, all those committed to the one idea of abolition. It was one of the most remarkable political meetings on record, for it was the beginning of the political drama which has since resulted in a dissolution of the Union. Vast multitudes, from all parts of the non- slaveholding States, of all political parties, came together, and seemed to be melted into one by their common zeal against the aggressions of slavery. Though they looked only to the restraint of slavery within the bounds which they claimed our fathers had erected for its protections, still the opposition sprang from the strong anti-slavery sentiment already pervading the country. It was the springing up of the green blade, and the forming of the ear from the many years sowing of the abolitionists. The nomination of Martin Van Buren and Charles Francis Adams, of Massachusetts, was made with great unanimity and enthusiasm, though by a body composed of original elements of the most extreme contrariety. Messrs. Hale and King, as was expected, withdrew their names. The old Liberty party was absorbed in the new organization, whose platform was broad enough to satisfy any reasonable abolitionist. Mass meetings were held in every village to hear the new word, and within a few months an impulse was communicated to the great mass of the Northern mind which has constituted the basis of its action ever since. The number of votes cast for these candidates in 1848 was 291,263.

The platform was substantially as follows:—That the people propose no interference by Congress with slavery within the limits of any State; that the federal government has no constitutional power over life, liberty or property without due legal progress; that Congress has no more power to make a slave than to make a king—no more power to establish slavery than to establish a monarchy; that Congress ought to prohibit slavery in all the territories; that the issue of the slave power is accepted—no more slave States and no slave territory; no more compromises; and finally, the establishment of a free government in California and New Mexico.

In 1852, this same party nominated John P. Hale and George W. Julian. The number of votes then cast was 155,825. The platform was much the same as that which preceded it four years before, though more progressive and revolutionary in several of its ideas, one of its clauses being "that slavery is a sin against God and a crime against man, which no human enactment nor usage can make right, and that Christianity, humanity and patriotism, alike demand its abolition." Another clause was to the effect that the Fugitive Slave law of 1850, being repugnant to the principles of Christianity and the principles of the common law, had no binding force upon the American people.

The republican party of 1856 was merely an enlargement or extension of the old free soil organization of the preceding eight years. It was modified, it is true, by many of the events of the time, but its foundation was laid upon precisely the same principles that had been enunciated during the previous twelve years. It was emphatically a Northern party, extending only here and there by some straggling outposts over the slave boundary. It was so far anti-slavery as to resent the repeal of the Missouri Compromise, and oppose the introduction of slavery into new territory. As events progressed, the forces combatting on either side of the great question of the day became more concentrated and determined, and more inspired by a single purpose, until the one idea of anti-slavery became distinctly developed and firmly fixed in the Northern mind.

The Republican Convention assembled at Philadelphia, June 18, 1856, when John C. Fremont and Wm. L. Dayton were nominated for President and Vice President of the United States, and in the following November received 1,341,264 votes.

The election for 1869 has only recently terminated in the elevation to the head of the Federal Government of Abraham Lincoln and Hannibal Hamlin, by a purely anti-slavery vote of 1,865,840. The events which preceded it are too fresh to require repetition; but, for the first time in the history of our confederacy, we look upon the spectacle of a sectional party, defiant, unyielding and uncompromising, whose principles aim a blow directly at the annihilation of one of the institutions of the South, in the full flush of victory, singing poeans of glory over its success, with a Union dissolving around it, while another portion of the country is agitated to its very center in preparations for self-protection against the usurpations which, from press and pulpit, and floor of Congress, have been so boldly threatened. Whether as abolition, liberty, free-soil or republican, the party has always shown the cloven hoof, and the best efforts of its more considerate friends have never been able to cover the deformity. Into the masses it has instilled the most unrelenting hatred to slavery, until all other ideas, feelings and passions have, for the time, been swallowed up in this one overwhelming sentiment.

It has dissolved the Union, though formed and cemented in the blood of our fathers, rather than it should tolerate an institution which is older than the Union. It has shed the blood of innocent white men while engaged in the discharge of their sworn duty, and made widows and orphans rather than return an escaped servant to his master and obey the Constitution of the country. Such is the spirit which controls this party, by whatever name it may be known.

Its leaders, claiming to stand by principle, hug to their bosom the most damning political heresies. Pretending to obey God and reverence the Bible, some of them are the most unblushing infidels, who boldly proclaim that the Sacred Word is not, worth the paper upon which it is printed, unless it denounce slavery and applaud abolitionism of every iniquity. Some of them aspire to be the followers of Jesus, but convert their sacred desks into political rostrums, from which are fulminated the falsest denunciations that a diseased mind can conjure into existence. Claiming to be teachers of religion and peace, they prove the authenticity of their holy commission by exhorting to civil war, making collections for Sharpe's rifles, and playing the role of spiritual demagogues among the falling ruins of the republic.

The year 1841 was marked by another attempt at insurrection. On the 22d of July, during a hot night, several negroes were overheard conversing in their quarters, on a plantation, near New Orleans, respecting an insurrection in which they intended to join. An investigation was made the next day, and resulted in tracing out a widely-extended organization among the slaves of the neighborhood, having a general rising in view. This early discovery of the plot of course prevented its consummation, and the execution and punishment of the instigators soon quelled every design of an outbreak.

In 1845 we find Cassius M. Clay mobbed in Lexington, Ky., and his paper, the True American, stopped, the presses, type, &c., being packed up and forwarded to Cincinnati, for advocating the incendiary doctrines of the abolitionists, and thereby producing an excitement among the slaves, and arousing apprehensions in the community lest they should rise in rebellion against the whites.

We have already brought our chronological history down to the year 1845, when Texas was admitted as a State. It was during the progress of annexation that the government of Mexico served a formal notice on the United States that annexation would be viewed in the light of a declaration of war. This notice, however, was of little avail, and before the close of the year 1845, Congress had consummated the act. The war broke out in April, 1846, the second year of Mr. Polk's administration, and on the 11th of May the President issued his proclamation to that effect. A large portion of the western domain of Texas, as now described, was disputed territory, occupied by Mexicans and under Mexican rule at the time of and after annexation. General Taylor was ordered to march from Corpus Christi, and take up his position on the Rio Grande, opposition Matamoras, thus traversing the dispute territory from its eastern to its western border. The Mexican army, on the opposite side of the river, immediately commenced hostilities, and soon after followed the battles of Palo Alto and Resaca de la Palma. How the war was continued and terminated are matters of general history. Peace was at last dictated to Mexico on the 30th of May, 1848, and resulted in a surrender by her of a large belt of her northern territories, extending from the Rio Grande to the Pacific, including California, though at that time its immense wealth and great importance were not fully appreciated. In Congress and among the people of the North the war was not popular. It was said to be a scheme for the acquirement of more slave territory, and this fact of itself excited contention throughout the land.

On the 12th of August, 1846, a bill being under consideration in the Committee of the Whole, making further provision for the expenses attending the intercourse between the United States and Mexico, Mr. David Wilmot, of Pennsylvania, moved the following amendment:—

"Provided, that as an express and fundamental condition to the acquisition of territory from the republic of Mexico, by the United States, by virtue of any treaty which may be negotiated between them, and to the use by the Executive of the moneys herein appropriated, neither slavery nor involuntary servitude shall ever exist in any part of said territory, except for crime, whereof the party shall first be duly convicted."

This amendment was adopted by a vote of yeas 77, nays 58. The bill was not voted on in the Senate, that body adjourning sine die before it reached that stage.

On the 8th of February, the Three Million Bill being under consideration, a similar amendment was offered in the House, and on the 15th was adopted by a vote of 115 yeas and 106 nays. The Senate having passed a similar bill, which came before the House on the 3d of March, 1847, Mr. Wilmot moved to amend the same by adding his proviso thereto; but it was rejected by a vote of yeas 97, nays 102. The Senate bill, without the amendment of Mr. Wilmot, then became a law. This celebrated proviso has been offered, by different senators and representatives, to various bills since. Its popular use, in fact, since that time, constitutes a great chapter in the political history of the country. For a long time it has rung in the ears of the public, and it will never cease until the question of slavery ceases to be a political question in the organization of new Territories and new States.

In 1848, Connecticut, which had never passed a law completely abolishing slavery, and which then contained some eight or ten slaves, through her Legislature enacted its total abolition forever, compelling the masters of the few slaves existing to support them for life. The escape of slaves from the South has been one of the principal practical effects of abolition ever since the idea assumed shape, in 1830. Men and women have been found, North and South, who, either from philanthropic motives or under the pecuniary inducements of abolition societies, have aided in their escape. Among these, New England "schoolmarms" and schoolmasters have played an active part, and several were from time to time arrested.

One Delia Webster suffered for such an interference with other people's affairs by an incarceration in the penitentiary at Lexington, Ky., in 1845, for two years. Another, Rev. Charles Torrey, for similar offences, was sentenced to six years in the Maryland penitentiary, but died before the expiration of the sentence.

Many other instances of a similar nature might be cited; but these are enough to indicate the extent to which fanaticism carried its followers.

The year 1848 was characterized by the usual venom which the anti-slavery societies industriously endeavored to distil into the community. Fred Douglass, Edmund Quincy, Francis Jackson, Abby Kelly, Garrison, Phillips, Pillsbury, Lucy Stone, Theodore Parker, and a retinue of negro orators, escaped slaves and others, regularly held their meetings and indulged in their customary rhodomontades. At the New England Convention, which assembled during this year, a series of one hundred conventions for the purposes of agitating the question of dissolution of the Union was commenced in Massachusetts, and funds were raised for the purpose. Some of these meetings were broken up by indignant mobs, but they were mainly allowed to go on, and accumulated disciples.

We have before given a table of the number of slaves in the United States in 1790. It was then 697,696. The following is a similar estimate for the year 1850, as determined by the seventh census:

1	New Jersey	222
2	Delaware	2,990
3	Maryland	90,368
4	Virginia	472,528
5	North Carolina	.288,548
6	South Carolina	384,984
7	Georgia	386,682
8	Florida	39,309
9	Alabama	342,892
10	Mississippi	.309,878
11	Louisiana	244,809
12	Texas	58,161
13	Arkansas	47,100
14	Tennessee	239,460
15	Kentucky	210,981
16	Missouri	87,422
17	District of Columbia	3,687
18	Utah	26
	Total	3,204,347

Adding to this sum thirty percent, a fair estimate of the increase for the last ten years, and we have in 1860, 3,965,651 slaves in the United States, or *four millions in round numbers*. There were in the United States 347,525 persons owning slaves. Of this number two owned 1,000 each; both resided in South Carolina. Nine only owned between 500 and 1,000, of whom two resided in Georgia, four in Louisiana, one in Mississippi. Fifty-six owned from 300 to 500, of whom one resided in Maryland, one in Virginia, three in North Carolina, one in Tennessee, one in Florida, four in Georgia, six in Louisiana, eight in Mississippi, twenty-nine in South Carolina, one hundred and eighty-seven owned from 200 to 300, of whom South Carolina had sixty-nine, Louisiana thirty-six, Georgia twenty-two, Mississippi eighteen, Alabama sixteen, North Carolina twelve, five other States fourteen, and four States none. Fourteen hundred and seventy-nine owned from 100 to 200. All the slave-holding States, except Florida and Missouri, are represented in this class, Southern Carolina having one-fourth of the whole; 29,733 person owned from ten to twenty slaves each. South Carolina, from this statement, owns more slaves in proportion to her population than any other State in the South.

A few general considerations, and we conclude our narrative. After tracing the course of events recorded in the foregoing pages, the questions naturally arise— What has been the result? what have the abolitionists gained? The answers may be briefly summed up as follows:

1. They have put an end to the benevolent schemes of emancipation which originated among the real philanthropists of the South, and were calculated, in a proper time and manner, beneficent to all concerned, to produce the desired result. In their wild and fanatical attempts they have counteracted the very object at which they have aimed. Instead of ameliorating the condition of the slaves, they have only aroused the district of the master, and led to restrictions which did not before exist. The truth is, the lost of the people of the South is not more implicated in that of the slaves than is the lot of the slaves in the people of the South. In their mutual relations, they must survive or perish together. In the language of another, "The worst foes of the black race are those who have intermeddled in their behalf. By nature, the most affectionate and loyal of all races beneath the sun, they are also the most helpless: and no calamity can befall them greater than the loss of that protection they enjoy under this patriarchal system. Indeed, the experiment has been tried of precipitating them upon a freedom which they know not how to enjoy; and the dismal results are before the world in statistics that may well excite astonishment. With the fairest portions of the earth in their possession, and with the advantage of a long discipline as the cultivators of the soil, their constitutional indolence has converted the most beautiful islands of the sea into howling wastes. It is not too much to say, that if the South should, at this moment, surrender every slave, the wisdom of the entire world, united in solemn council, could not solve the question of their disposal. Freedom would be their doom. Every Southern master knows this truth and feels its power."

2. Touch the negro, and you touch cotton—the mainspring that keeps the machinery of the world in motion. In teaching slaves to entertain wild and dangerous notions of liberty, the abolitionists have thus jeopardized the commerce of the country and the manufacturing interests of the civilized world. They have likewise destroyed confidence. Northern institution are no longer filled with the young men and women of the South, but find rivals springing up in every State south of Mason and Dixon's line. Northern commerce can no longer depend upon the rich placer of wealth it has hitherto found in Southern patronage. Northern men can no longer travel in the South without being regarded as objects of suspicion and confounded with the abolitionists of their section. In short, all the kind relations that have ever existed between the North and the South have been interrupted, and a barrier erected, which, socially, commercially and politically, has separated the heretofore united interests of the two sections, and which nothing but a revolution in public sentiment, a higher sense of the moral obligations due our neighbor, a religious training, which will graft upon our nature a truer conscience and inculcate a purer charity, and finally a recognition of abstract right and justice can ever remove.

3. They have held out a Canadian Utopia, where they have taught the slaves in their ignorance to believe they can enjoy a life of ease and luxury, and having cut them off from a
race of kind masters and separated them from comfortable homes, left the deluded beings
incapable of self-support upon an uncongenial soil, to live in a state of bestiality and misery, and die cursing the abolitionists as the authors of their wretchedness.
4. They have led a portion of the people of the North, as well as of the South, to examine
the question in all its aspects, and to plant themselves upon the broad principle that that
form of government which recognizes the institution of slavery in the United States, is the
best, the condition of the two races, white and black being considered, for the development, progress and happiness of each. In other words, to regard servitude as a blessing to
the negro, and under proper and philanthropic restrictions, necessary to their preservation
and the prosperity of the country.
5. Step by step they have built up a party upon an issue which has led to a dissolution of the
Union. They have scattered the seeds of abolitionism until a majority of the voters of the
free States have become animated by a fixed purpose not only to prevent the further
growth of the slave power, but to beard the lion in his den.

The power of the North has been consolidated, and for the first time in the history of the country it is wielded as a sectional weapon against the interests of the
South. The government is now in the hands of men elected by Northern votes, who
regard slavery as a curse and a crime, and they will have the means necessary to accomplish their purpose.

The utterances that have heretofore come from the rostrum or from irresponsible
associations of individuals now come from the throne. "Clad with the sanctities of
office, with the anointing oil poured upon the monarch's head, the decree has gone
forth that the institution of Southern slavery shall be constrained within assigned
limits. Though Nature and Providence should send forth its branches like the ban-
yan tree to take root in congenial soil, here is a power superior to both, that says it
shall wither and die within its own charmed circle."

If this be not believed, let the following selections from the speeches of the leaders of the Republic party be the proof:—

Hon. Charles Sumner, United States Senator from Mass.:—

"This slave oligarchy will soon cease to exist as a political combination. Its final
doom may be postponed, but it is certain. Languishing, it may live yet longer, but it
will surely die. Yes, fellow citizens, surely it will die—when disappointed in its purposes—driven back within the States, and constrained within these limits, it can no
longer rule the Republic as a plantation of slaves at home; con no longer menace
Territories with its five- headed device to compel labor without wages; can no longer fasten upon the constitution an interpretation which makes merchandise of
men, and gives a disgraceful immunity to the brokers of human flesh, and the butch-
ers of human hears; and when it can no longer grind flesh and blood, groans an
sighs, the tears of mothers and the cries of children into the cement of a barbarous
political power! Surely then, in its retreat, smarting under the indignation of an
aroused people, and the concurring judgment of the civilized world it must die;—it
may be, as a poisoned rat dies, of rage in its hole. (Enthusiastic applause.) Meanwhile all good omens are ours. The work cannot stop. Quickened by the triumph,
now at hand,—with a Republic President in power, State after State, quoting the
condition of a territory, and spurning slavery, will be welcomed into our plural unit,
and joining hands together, will become a belt of fire about the slave States, in
which slavery must die."

Hon. John Wentworth, Editor of the *Chicago Democrat*, and Mayor of Chicago:—

"We might as well make up our minds to fight the battle now, as at any other time. It will have to be fought, and the longer the evil day is put off, the more bloody will be the contest when it comes. If we do not place slavery in the process of extinction now, by hemming it in, where it is, and not suffering it to expand, it will extinguish us, and our liberties. "If the Union be preserved, and if the Federal government be administered for a few years by Republican Presidents, a scheme may be devised, and carried out, which will result in the peaceful, honorable and equitable EMANCIPATION of ALL the SLAVES.

"The States must be made ALL FREE, and if a Republican government is entrusted with the duty of making them FREE, the work will be done without bloodshed, without revolution, without disastrous loss of property. The work will be out of time and patience, but it MUST BE DONE!"

Hon. Wm. II Seward, Secretary of State (his Rochester speech of Oct. 25, 1858):

"Our country is a theatre which exhibits, in full operation, two radically different political systems—the one resting on the basis of servile or slave labor, the other on the basis of voluntary labor of freemen.

* * * * * * *

"The two systems are at once perceived to be incongruous. But never have permanently existed together in one country, and they never can.

* * *These antagonistic systems are continually coming in closer contact, and collins ensues.

"Shall I tell you what the collision means? It is an irreprehensible conflict between opposing and enduring forces, and it means that the United States must, and will, sooner or later, become entirely a slaveholding nation, or entirely a free labor nation. Either the cotton and rice fields of South Carolina, and the sugar plantations of Louisiana, will ultimately be tiled by free labor, and Charleston and New Orleans become marts for legitimate merchandise alone, or else their fields and wheat fields of Massachusetts and New York must again be surrendered by their farmers to the slave culture and to the production of slaves and Boston and New York become once more markets for trade in the bodies and souls of men."

At a later period, in the Senate of the United States, the same Senator uttered the following language:—

"A free Republican government like this, notwithstanding all its constitutional checks, cannot long resist and counteract the progress of society.

"Free labor has at last apprehended its rights and its destiny, and is organizing itself to assume the government of the Republic. It will henceforth meet you boldly and resolutely here (Washington); it will meet you everywhere, in the Territories and out of them, wherever you may go to extend slavery. It has driven you back in California and in Kansas, it will invade you soon in Delaware, Maryland, Virginia, Missouri, and Texas. It will meet you in Arizona, in Central America, and even in Cuba.

* * * * * * * * *

"You may, indeed, get a start under or near the tropics, and seem safe for a time, but it will be only a short time. Even there you will found States only for free labor to maintain and occupy. The interest of the whole race demands the ultimate emancipation of all men. Whether that consummation shall be allowed to take effect, with needful and wise precautions against sudden change and disaster, or be hurried on by violence, is all that remains for you to decide. The white man needs this continent to labor upon. His head is clear, his arm is strong, and his necessities are fixed.

* * * * * * * * *

"It is for yourselves, and not for us, to decide how long and through what further mortifications and disasters the contest shall be protracted before freedom shall enjoy her already secured triumph.

"You may refuse to yield it now, and for a short period, but your refusal will only animate the friends of freedom with the courage and the resolution, and produce the union among them, which alone is necessary on their part to attain the position itself, simultaneously with the impending overthrow of the existing Federal Administration and the constitution of a new and more independent Congress."

Hon. Joshua Giddings, Member of Congress from Ohio:—

"I look forward to the day when there shall be a servile insurrection in the South; when the black man, armed with British bayonets, and led on by British officers, shall assert his freedom, and wage a war of extermination against his master; when the torch of the incendiary shall light up the towns and cities of the South, and blot out the last vestige of slavery. And though I may not mock at their calamity, nor laugh when their fear cometh, yet I will hail it as the dawn of a political millennium."

Hon. Abraham Lincoln, President of the United States:—

"I believe this government cannot endure permanently, half slave, and half free. I do not expect the Union to be dissolved; I do not expect the house to fall, but I do expect that it will cease to be divided. It will become all one thing, or all the other. Either the opponents of slavery will arrest the further spread of it, and place it where the public mind shall rest in the belief, that it is in the course of ultimate extinction, or its advocates will push it forward, until it shall become alike lawful in all the States, old as well as new, North as well as South."

"I have always hated slavery as much as any abolitionist. I have always been an old line Whig. I have always hated it, and I always believed it in a course of ultimate extinction. If I were in Congress, and a vote should come up on a question whether slavery should be prohibited in a new territory, in spite of the Dred Scott decision I would vote that it should."

These are a few only of the extracts of a similar nature which may be selected from multitudes of speeches that have been delivered by the leading men of the party. The same sentiment, however, runs through them all, and abolition, in one way or another, is not less a doctrine of the Republic party of 1860 than it was of the Liberty party of 1840, to which it owes it birth. "Abolitionism is clearly its informing and actuating soul; and fanaticism is a blood-hound that never bolts its track when it has once lapped blood. The elevation of their candidate is far from being the consummation of their aims. It is only the beginning of that consummation; and if all history be not a lie, there will be coercion enough till the end of the beginning is reached, and the dreadful banquet of slaughter and ruin shall glut the appetite."

And now the end has come. The divided house, which Mr. Lincoln boastfully said would not fall, has fallen. The ruins of the Union are at the feet as well of those who loved and cherished it as of those who labored for its destruction. The Constitution is at length a nullity, and our flag a mockery. Fanaticism, too, must have its apotheosis.

THE SIX SECEDING STATES

The Six Seceding States and date of their Separation—Organization of the Southern Congress—Names of Members—Election of President and Vice President, and Sketch of their Lives—The New Constitution—The City of Montgomery, &c, &c.

On Saturday, February 9, 1861, six seceding States of the old Union organized an independent government, adopted a constitution, and elected a President and Vice President. These States passed their respective ordinances of dissolution as follows:—

STATE.	DATE.	YEAS.	NAYS.
South Carolina	Dec. 20, 1860		169—
Mississippi	Jan. 9, 1861	84	15
Alabama	Jan. 11, 1861	61	39
Florida	Jan. 11, 1861	61	7
Georgia	Jan. 19, 1861	208	89
Louisiana	Jan. 25, 1861	113	17

Only two of the seceding States—South Carolina and Georgia—were original members of the confederacy. The others came in the following order:

Louisiana	April 8, 1812
Mississippi	Dec. 10, 1817
Alabama	Dec. 14, 1819
Florida	March 3, 1845
Texas	Dec. 29, 1845

The Convention which consummated this event assembled on the 4th of February, at Montgomery, Alabama. Hon. R. M. Barnwell, of South Carolina, being appointed temporary chairman, the Divine blessing was invoked by Rev. Dr. Basil Manly.

We give this first impressive prayer in the Congress of the new Confederacy below, and further add, as an illustration of the religious earnestness by which the delegates were one and all animated, that the ministers of Montgomery were invited to open the deliberations each day with invocations to the Throne of Grace:

Oh, Thou God of the Universe, Thou madest all things; Thou madest man upon the earth; Thou hast endowed him with reason and capacity for government. We thank Thee that Thou hast made us at this late period of the world, and in this fair portion of the earth, and hast established a free government and a pure form of religion amongst us. We thank Thee for all the hallowed memories connected with our past history. Thou hast been the God of our fathers; oh, be Thou our God. Let it please Thee to vouchsafe Thy sacred presence to this assembly. Oh, Our Father, we appeal to Thee, the searcher of hearts, for the purity and sincerity of our motives. If we are in violation of any compact still obligatory upon us with those States from which we have separated in order to set up a new government—if we are acting in rebellion to and in contravention of piety towards God and good faith to our fellow man, we cannot hope for They presence and blessing. But oh, Thou heart searching God, we trust that Thou seest we are pursuing those rights which were guaranteed to us by the solemn covenants of our fathers and which were cemented by their blood. And now humbly recognise Thy hand in the Providence which has brought us together. We pray Thee to give the spirit of wisdom to Thy servants, with all necessary grace, that they may act with deliberation and purpose, and that they will wisely adopt such measures in this trying condition of our affairs as shall redound to Thy glory and the good of our country. So direct them that they may merge the just for spoil and the desire for office into the patriotic desire for the welfare of this great people. Oh God, assist them to preserve our republican form of government and the purity of the forms of religion, without interference with the strongest form of civil government. May God in tender mercy bestow upon the deputies here assembled health and strength of body, together with calmness and soundness of mind; may they aim directly at the glory of God and the welfare of the whole people, and when the hour of trial which may supervise shall come, enable them to stand firm in the exercise of truth, with great prudence and a just regard for the sovereign rights of their constituents. Oh, God, grant that the union of these States, and all that reign rights of their constituents. Oh, God grant that the union of these States, and all that may come into this union, may endure as long as the sun and moon shall last, and until the Son of Man shall come a second time to judge the world in righteousness. Preside over this body in its organization and in the distribution of its offices. Let truth and justice, and equal rights be secured to our government. And now, Our Father in Heaven, we acknowledge Thee as Our God—do Thou rule in us, do Thou sway us, do Thou control us, and let the blessings of the Father, Son and Holy Spirit rest upon this assembly now and forever. Amen.

A. R. Lamar, Esq., of Georgia, was then appointed temporary secretary, and the deputies from the several seceding States represented presented their credentials in alphabetical order, and signed their names to the roll of the Convention. The following is the list:

ALABAMA

R. W. Walker,
R. H. Smith,
J. L. M. Curry,
W. P. Chiton,
S. F. Hale Colon,
J. McRae,
John Gill Shortor,
David P. Lewis,
Thomas Fearn.

FLORIDA

James B. Owens,
J. Patten Anderson,
Jackson Morton, (not present)

GEORGIA

Robert Toombe,
Howell Cobb,
F.S. Bartow,
M. J. Crawford,
E. A. Nisbet,
B. H. Hill,
A. R. Wright,
Thomas R.R. Cobb,
A. H. Kenan,
A. H. Stephens.

LOUISIANA

John Perkins, Jr.,
A. Declonet,
Charles M. Conrad,
D. F. Kenner,
G. E. Sparrow,
Henry Marshall.

MISSISSIPPI

W. P. Harris,
Walter Brooke,
N. S. Wilson,
A. M. Clayton,
W. S. Barry,
J. T. Harrison.

SOUTH CAROLINA

R. B. Rhett.
R. W. Barnwell,
L. M. Keitt,
James Chesnut, Jr.
C. G. Memminger,
W. Porcher Miles,
Thomas J. Withers,
W. W. Boyce.

The following description is from a Southern paper:

"On the extreme left, as the visitor enters the Hall, may be seen a list of the names of the gallant corps constituting the Palmetto regiment of South Carolina, so distinguished in the history of the Mexican War; next to that is an impressive representation of Washington delivering his inaugural address; and still farther to the left, a picture of South Carolina's ever memorable statesman, John C. Calhoun; and next to that, an excellent portrait of Albert J. Pickett, "the historian of Alabama." Just to the right of the President's desk is the portrait of Dixon H. Lewis, a representative in Congress from Alabama for a number of years. Immediately over the President's desk is the portrait of the immortal General George Washington, painted by Stuart. There are a few facts connected with the history of this portrait which are, perhaps, deserving of special mention. It was given by Mrs. Curtis to General Benjamin Smith, of North Carolina. At the sale of his estate it was purchased by Mr. Moore, who presented it to Mrs. E. E Clitherall (mother of Judge A. B. Cliterall, of Pickens), in whose possession it has been for forty years. It is one of the three original portraits of General Washington now in existence. A second one, pained by Trumbull, is in the White House at Washington, and is the identical portrait that Mrs. Madison cut out of the frame when the British attacked Washington in 1812. The third is in the possession of a gentleman in Boston, Massachusetts. Next to the portrait of Washington is that of the Old Hero, Andrew Jackson; next in order is an excellent one of Alabama's distinguished son, Honorable W. L. Yancey; and next, a picture of the great orator and statesman, Henry Clay; and next to that, a historical representation of the swamp encampment scene of General Marion, when he invited the British officer to partake of his scanty fare; and on the extreme right of the door, entering into the Hall, is another picture of General Washington, beautifully and artistically wrought upon canvas by some fair hand."

The deputies having handed in their credentials, on motion of Mr. Rhett, of South Carolina, Honorable Howell Cobb, of Georgia, was chosen President of the Convention, and Mr. J. J. Hooper, Secretary. This permanently organized, the Convention proceeded with the usual routine of business.

A committee was appointed to report a plan for the Provisional Government upon the basis of the Constitution of the United States, and after remaining in secret session the greater part of the time for five days, the "Congress"—the word "Convention" being entirely ignored on motion of Honorable A. H. Stephens, of Georgia—at half past ten o'clock, on the night of February 8, unanimously adopted a provisional constitution similar in the main to the constitution of the old Union.

The vital points of difference are the following:—*1. The importation of African negroes from any foreign country other than the slaveholding States of the Confederated States is hereby forbidden, and Congress is required to pass such laws as shall effectually prevent the same. 2. Congress shall also have power to prohibit the introduction of slaves from any State not a member of this Confederacy.*

The Congress shall have power—1. To lay and collect taxes, duties, imposts, and excises, for revenue necessary to pay the debts and carry on the government of the Confederacy, and all duties, imposts, and excises shall be uniform throughout the Confederacy.

A slave in one State escaping to another shall be delivered up on the claim of the party to whom said slave may belong by the Executive authority of the State in which such slave may be found; and any case of any abduction or forcible rescue full compensation, including the value of slave, and all costs and expenses, shall be made to the party by the State in which such abduction or rescue shall take place.

2. The government hereby instituted shall take immediate steps for the settlement of all matters between the States forming it and their late confederates of the United States in relation to the public property and public debt at the time of their withdrawal from them, these States hereby declaring it to be their wish and earnest desire to adjust everything pertaining to the common property, common liabilities, and common obligations of that Union upon principles of right, justice, equity and good faith.

In several other features the new constitution differs from the original. The old one commences with the words—"We the people of the United States," &c. The new—"We the deputies of the sovereign and independent States of South Carolina," &c, thus distinctly indicating their sovereign and independent character, and yet their mutual reliance.

Again, the new constitution reverentially invokes "the favor of Almighty God." In the old, the existence of a Supreme Being appears to have been entirely ignored.

In the original, not only was the word "slave" omitted, but even the idea was so studiously avoided as to raise grave questions concerning the intent of the several clauses in which the "institution" is a subject of legislation, while in the new, the word "slaves" is boldly inserted, and the intention of its framers so clearly defined with reference to them that there is hardly a possibility of misapprehension.

Again, contrary to the expectation of the majority of the Northern people, who *have persistently urged that the object of the South in establishing a separate government was to re-open the African slave trade, the most stringent measures are to be adopted for its suppression.*

All this was done with a unanimity which indicated the harmony of sentiment that prevailed among the people of the seceding States, and among the delegates by whom they were represented in the Southern Congress.

The constitution having been adopted, the sixth day's proceedings of the Southern Congress, on Saturday, February 9, were characterized by unusual interest, the galleries being crowded with anxious and enthusiastic spectators.

During the preliminary business several model flags were presented for consideration—one being from the ladies of South Carolina; and a committee was appointed to report on a flag, a seal, a coat of arms and a motto for the Southern confederacy. There were likewise appointed committees on foreign affairs, on finance, on military and naval affairs, on postal affairs, on commerce and on patents.

The Congress then proceeded to the election of a President and Vice President of the Southern confederacy, which resulted, by a unanimous vote, as follows:— President—Honorable Jefferson Davis, of Mississippi. Vice President—Honorable Alexander H. Stephens, of Georgia.

This announcement was received with the grandest demonstrations of enthusiasm. One hundred guns were fired in the city of Montgomery in honor of the event, and in the evening a serenade was given to the Vice President elect, to which he eloquently responded. Messrs. Chesnut and Keitt, of South Carolina, and Conrad, of Louisiana, likewise made appropriate speeches.

A resolution was adopted in Congress appointing a committee of three Alabama deputies to make arrangements to secure the use of suitable buildings for the use of the several executive departments of the Confederacy.

An ordinance was also passed, continuing in force, until repealed or altered by the Southern Confederacy, all laws of the United States in force or use on the first of November last.

The Committee on Finance were likewise instructed to report promptly a tariff for raising revenue for the support of the government. Under this law a tariff has been laid on all goods brought from the United States. The appointment of a committee was also authorized for the purpose of reporting a constitution for the permanent government of the Confederacy.

These are some of the measures thus far adopted by the new government. The legislation has been prompt, unanimous, and adapted to the exigency of the moment, and there is little doubt that when all the necessary laws have been passed, a strong, healthy, and wealthy confederation will be in the full tide of successful experiment.

The Southern Cabinet is composed of the following gentlemen:—

Secretary of State Robert Toombs
Secretary of Treasury C. S. Memminger
Secretary of Interior Vacancy
Secretary of War I. P. Walker
Secretary of Navy John Perkins, Jr.
Postmaster General H. T. Ebett Attorney
General J. P. Benjamin

Few men have led a life more filled with stirring or eventful incidents than Jefferson Davis. A native of Kentucky, born about 1806, he went in early youth with his father to Mississippi, then a Territory, and was appointed by President Monroe in 1822 to be a cadet at West Point. He graduated with the first honors in 1828 as Brevet Second Lieutenant, and at his own request was placed in active service, being assigned to the command of General (then Colonel) Zachary Taylor, who was stationed in the West. In the frontier wars of the time young Davis distinguished himself in so marked a manner that when a new regiment of dragoons was formed he at once obtained a commission as first lieutenant. During this time a romantic attachment sprang up between him and his prisoner, the famous chief Black Hawk, in which the latter forgot his animosity to the people of the United States in his admiration for Lieutenant Davis, and not until his death was the bond of amity severed between the two brave men.

In 1835 he settled quietly down upon a cotton plantation, devoting himself to a thorough and systematic course of political and scientific education. He was married to a daughter of Gen. Taylor.

In 1843 he took the stump for Polk, and in 1845, having attracted no little attention in his State by his vigor and ability, he was elected to Congress. Ten days after he made his maiden speech. Soon the Mexican war broke out, and a regiment of volunteers having been formed in Mississippi, and himself chosen Colonel, he resigned his post in Congress, and instantly repaired with his command to join the *corps d'armee* under General Taylor. At Monterey and Buena Vista he and his noble regiment achieved the soldiers' highest fame. Twice by his coolness he saved the day at Buena Vista. Wherever fire was hottest or danger to be encountered, there Colonel Davis and the Mississippi Rifles were to be found. He was badly wounded in the early part of the action, but sat his horse steadily till the day was won, and refused to delegate even a portion of his duties to his subordinate officers.

In 1848 he was appointed to fill the vacancy in the Senate of the United States occasioned by the death of General Speight, and in 1850 was elected to that body almost unanimously for the term of six years.

In 1851 he resigned his seat in the Senate to become the State Rights candidate for Governor, but was defeated by Governor Foote.

In 1853 he was called to a seat in the Cabinet of President Pierce, and was Secretary of War during his administration. In 1857 he was elected United States Senator from Mississippi for the term of six years, which office he held until his resignation on the secession of Mississippi from the Union.

Personally, he is the last man who would be selected as a "fire-eater." he is a prim, smooth looking man, with a precise manner, a stiff, soldierly carriage and an austerity that is at first forbidding. He has naturally, however, a genial temper, companionable qualities and a disposition that endears him to all by whom he may be surrounded. As a speaker he is clear, forcible and argumentative; his voice is clear and firm, without tremor, and he is one in every way fitted for the distinguished post to which he has been called. This gentleman is known throughout the Union as one of the most prominent of Southern politicians and eloquent orators. His father, Andrew B. Stephens, was a planter of moderate means, and his mother (Margaret Grier) was a sister to the famous compiler of Grier's almanacs. She died when he was an infant, leaving him with four brothers and one sister, of whom only one brother survives.

Mr. Stephens was born in Georgia on the 11th of February, 1812. When in his fourteenth year his father died, and the homestead being sold, his share of the entire estate was about five hundred dollars. With a commendable Anglo-Saxon love of his ancestry Mr. Stephens has since repurchased the original estate, which comprised about two hundred and fifty acres, and has added to it about six hundred more. Assisted by friends he entered the University of Georgia in 1828, and in 1832 graduated at the head of his class. In 1834 he commenced the study of the law, and in less than twelve months was engaged in one of the most important cases in the country. His eloquence has ever had a powerful effect upon juries, enforcing, as it does, arguments of admirable simplicity and legal weight. From 1837 to 1840 he was a member of the Georgia Legislature. In 1842 he was elected to the State Senate, and in 1843 was elected to Congress. He was a member of the whig party in its palmiest days, but since its dissolution has acted with the men of the South, and such has been the upright, steadfast and patriotic policy he had pursued, that no one in the present era of faction, selfishness or suspicion has whispered an accusation of selfish motives or degrading intrigues against him. In the House he served prominently on the most important committees, and effected the passage of the Kansas-Nebraska bill through the House at a time when its warmest friends despaired of success. He was subsequently appointed chairman of the Committee on Territories, and was also chairman of the special committee to which was referred the Lecompton constitution. By his patriotic course of various measures, he has, from time to time, excited the ire of many of the Southern people, but he has always succeeded in coming out of the contest with flying colors, and his recent elevation is a mark of the profound respect entertained for his qualities as a man and a statesman.

Mr. Stephens is most distinguished as an orator, though he does not look like one who can command the attention of the House at any time or upon any topic. His health from childhood has been very feeble, being afflicted with four abscesses and a continued derangement of the liver, which gives him a consumptive appearance though his lungs are sound. He has never weighed over ninety-six pounds, and to see his attenuated figure bent over his desk, the shoulders contracted and the shape of his slender limbs visible through his garments, a stranger would never select him as the "John Randolph" of our time, more dreaded as an adversary and more prized as an ally in a debate than any other member of the House of Representatives. When speaking he has at first a shrill, sharp voice, but as he warms up with his subject the clear tones and vigorous sentences roll out with a sonorousness that finds its way to every corner of the immense hall. He is witty, rhetorical and solid, and has a dash of keen satire that puts an edge upon every speech. He is a careful student, but so very careful that no trace of study is perceptible as he dashes along in a flow of facts, arguments and language that to common minds is almost bewildering. Possessing hosts of warm friends who are proud of his regard, and enlightened Christian virtue and inflexible integrity, such is Alexander H. Stephens, the Vice President elect of the Southern confederacy.

The city of Montgomery, the capital of Alabama, has assumed such a sudden importance as the capital of the Southern Confederacy and the seat of the federal operations of the new government, that we give below a brief sketch of its locality and surroundings. It is situated on the left bank of the Alabama River, 331 miles by water from Mobile, and 830 miles from Washington, D.C. It is the second city in the State in respect to trade and population, and is one of the most flourishing inland towns of the Southern States, possessing great facilities for communications with the surrounding country. For steamboat navigation the Alabama River is one of the best in the Union, the largest steamers ascending to this point from Mobile. The city is also the western termination of the Montgomery and West Point Railroad. It contains several extensive iron foundries, mills, factories, large warehouses, numerous elegant stores and private residences. The cotton shipped at this place annually amounts to about one hundred thousand bales. The public records were removed from Tuscaloosa to Montgomery in November, 1847. The State House was destroyed by fire in 1849, and another one was erected on the same site in 1851. The present population of the city is not far from 16,000, and it is probable that, with all its natural advantages, the fact of its present selection as the Southern capital, will soon place it in the first rank of Southern cities.

The united front and united action of the six States which have thus formed themselves into the pioneer guard, as it were, of the remaining nine, is an earnest that no one of them, in its sovereign capacity, will undertake a conflict with the old United States without the assent of its brethren. What they have thus far done "in Congress assembled," they have done soberly and after mature consideration; and in their past action we may find assurance that no future movements will be undertaken—especially those of a nature likely to involve them in a civil war—without equal deliberation, calmness, and a just regard for the common welfare. If there should be, it will be the fault of the aggressive policy of some of the Legislatures of the North.

It will be observed that, notwithstanding Texas had already passed the ordinance of secession, as that act had not yet been endorsed by the people, at the time of the sitting of the Convention, she was not regarded as one of the new confederacy, and consequently was unrepresented. North Carolina also sent three Commissioners to deliberate with the delegates of the seceding States—namely, Messrs. D. I. Swain, J. L. Bridgers and M. W. Ransom.

The entire movement bears upon its face all the marks of a well developed, well digested plan of government—a government now as independent as were the old thirteen States after the Fourth of July, 1776, and possessing what our ancestors of that date did not fully have—the wealth, ability and power to meet almost any contingency that may arise. Meanwhile, judging from the disposition of republicans in Congress and throughout the country, the ball thus set in motion will not stop. The States already united will undoubtedly remain so, and form the nucleus around which will gather others. The new Union will grow in strength as it grows in age. According to our recent intelligence from England and France, these two nations will rival each other in endeavoring to first secure the favor of the new Power. With them cotton will be the successful diplomat. Ministers and agents will be appointed, postal facilities will be rearranged, a new navy will spring into existence, prosperity will begin to pour into the newly opened lap, and we shall witness at our very side the success of a people who, by the pertinacity of the selfish political leaders and the political domination of the North, have been driven to measures of defence which are destined to redound to their benefit, but to our cost and national shame. *New York Herald, Feb. 11, 1861.*

Source: Originally published in the *New York Herald.* New York: D. Appleton & co., 1861. Library of Congress, Rare Book and Special Collections Division, Daniel A. P. Murray Pamphlets Collection.

27. George Wils to Writer's Sister, March 18, 1861

In this letter, a black man named George Wils writes to his sister to inform her of his political beliefs. He reveals he has an elitist, superior attitude as an educated black man living in the South in the days before the Civil War.

Mosey Creek Academy Virginia March 18th 1861

My Dear Sister

I read yours dated the 13th I had almost concluded that did not intend to write to me anymore or at least you waited very long & then when it came it was only a short note. You must write longer letters (than) you have been in the habit of doing. every one of my correspondents write longer letters than you, with the acception of one or two, So Miss Kattie has left old Woodstock perhaps never to return, to the old place where she has so often enjoyed herself and where she made one person (at least) a happy being, but it may turn out the reverse and it may be said she made him miserable instead of happy. I hope not. They certainly have my best wishes. Miss Sallie I suppose spoke in the [*unclear:* bigest] terms of [*unclear:* milton] , and is still in love with him. I think he must be a very nice boy from what I can learn, and is worthy of the love she gives him, but I think he must beware of me or I might spoil his calculations especially if we all get to Texas to gether , which I hope we will. I am almost confident that I will be there in less than twelve months [*unclear:* From] this time, I want to wether [*unclear:* Pee]] goes or not, for I am asshamed of Va. I don't desire to call her my home I shun the very idea of submitting to Black Republican party, who desire to place the insignificant negro on an equality with us, who will submit none but those who at heart if they would but express themselves are partial to the North I fear Va has too many of them in Convention, how glad I was when I saw that Va wished to present an ordinance of secession to the convention. I thought then if they were all like him we would this moment be honored & loved by our seceding Southern Sisters, who now almost as it were despise us. I am ready at any time to join the southern army although I am not prepared to die but [*unclear:* this] I know Dulce et decorum est pro patria mori

I am sorry to learn that Cousin Pet is going to leave I was in hopes that she was going to stay until I came home and in all possibility would be married. I dont think she ought to go back to Ohio such a mean tale, but I am of your opinion that she will not stay long; but then the [unclear: Dr] is so very fickle. I can scarcely trust him he must certainly be in earnest this time,

Nothing surprised me more then to hear of the death of Uncle [unclear: Hen, Clower] , he was the last person that I expected hear was dead but we know not the hour when we shall be called to give a final account of ourselves, and oh! how many are unprepared to meet the doom & how the words (depart from me [illeg.] [unclear: crossed] [missing section] I think [missing section] Confederacy [missing section] What [missing section] speak to Miss Mary, he often told me he never would speak to [unclear: her] Pass the [unclear: neumurous] [unclear: flundes] over. my love to all home Folks also to Tom [unclear: Prach] tell him I am going to leave this state soon write soon to your fondly attached Brother

George

Source: Augusta County, Virginia, March 18, 1861. The Valley of the Shadow: Two Communities in the American Civil War, Virginia Center for Digital History, University of Virginia (http:valley.vcdh.virginia.edu).

28. "Fighting Rebels with Only One Hand," Douglass' Monthly [*The North Star*], September 1861

In 1861, abolitionist Frederick Douglass wrote one of many newspaper editorials criticizing the United States and its people, suggesting that the government and its people must somehow "covet the world's ridicule" at the same time the nation was rapidly racing to its own demise socially and politically. "What are they thinking about, or don't they condescend to think at all?" the abolitionist asked. As always, Douglass was campaigning against the longstanding acceptance and tolerance of slavery.

Washington, the seat of Government, after ten thousand assurances to the contrary, is now positively in danger of falling before the rebel army. Maryland, a little while ago considered safe for the Union, is now admitted to be studded with the materials for insurrection, and which may flame forth at any moment.—Every resource of the nation, whether of men or money, whether of wisdom or strength, could be well employed to avert the impending ruin. Yet most evidently the demands of the hour are not comprehended by the Cabinet or the crowd. Our Presidents, Governors, Generals and Secretaries are calling, with almost frantic vehemance, for men.—"Men! men! send us men!" they scream, or the cause of the Union is gone, the life of a great nation is ruthlessly sacrificed, and the hopes of a great nation go out in darkness; and yet these very officers, representing the people and Government, steadily and persistently refuse to receive the very class of men which have a deeper interest in the defeat and humiliation of the rebels, than all others.—Men are wanted in Missouri—wanted in Western Virginia, to hold and defend what has been already gained; they are wanted in Texas, and all along the sea coast, and though the Government has at its command a class in the country deeply interested in suppressing the insurrection, it sternly refuses to summon from among the vast multitude a single man, and degrades and insults the whole class by refusing to allow any of their number to defend with their strong arms and brave hearts the national cause. What a spectacle of blind, unreasoning prejudice and pusillanimity is this! The national edifice is on fire. Every man who can carry a bucket of water, or remove a brick, is wanted; but those who have the care of the building, having a profound respect for the feeling of the national burglars who set the building on fire, are determined that the flames shall only be extinguished by Indo-Caucasian hands, and to have the building burnt rather than save it by means of any other. Such is the pride, the stupid prejudice and folly that rules the hour.

Why does the Government reject the Negro? Is he not a man? Can he not wield a sword, fire a gun, march and countermarch, and obey orders like any other? Is there the least reason to believe that a regiment of well-drilled Negroes would deport themselves less soldier-like on the battlefield than the raw troops gathered up generally from the towns and cities of the State of New York? We do believe that such soldiers, if allowed to take up arms in defense of the Government, and made to feel that they are hereafter to be recognized as persons having rights, would set the highest example of order and general good behavior to their fellow soldiers, and in every way add to the national power.

If persons so humble as we can be allowed to speak to the President of the United States, we should ask him if this dark and terrible hour of the nation's extremity is a time for consulting a mere vulgar and unnatural prejudice? We should ask him if national preservation and necessity were not better guides in this emergency than either the tastes of the rebels, or the pride and prejudices of the vulgar? We would tell him that General Jackson in a slave state fought side by side with Negroes at New Orleans, and like a true man, despising meanness, he bore testimony to their bravery at the close of the war. We would tell him that colored men in Rhode Island and Connecticut performed their full share in the war of the Revolution, and that men of the same color, such as the noble Shields Green, Nathaniel Turner and Denmark Vesey stand ready to peril everything at the command of the Government. We would tell him that this is no time to fight with one hand, when both are needed; that this is no time to fight only with your white hand, and allow your black hand to remain tied.

Whatever may be the folly and absurdity of the North, the South at least is true and wise. The Southern papers no longer indulge in the vulgar expression, "free n——rs." That class of bipeds are now called "colored residents." The Charleston papers say:

"The colored residents of this city can challenge comparison with their class, in any city or town, in loyalty or devotion to the cause of the South. Many of them individually, and without ostentation, have been contributing liberally, and on Wednesday evening, the 7th inst., a very large meeting was held by them, and a committee appointed to provide for more efficient aid. The proceedings of the meeting will appear in results hereinafter to be reported."

It is now pretty well established, that there are at the present moment many colored men in the Confederate army doing duty not only as cooks, servants and laborers, but as real soldiers, having muskets on their shoulders, and bullets in their pockets, ready to shoot down loyal troops, and do all that soldiers may to destroy the Federal Government and build up that of the traitors and rebels. There were such soldiers at Manassas, and they are probably there still. There is a Negro in the army as well as in the fence, and our Government is likely to find it out before the war comes to an end. That the Negroes are numerous in the rebel army, and do for that army its heaviest work, is beyond question. They have been the chief laborers upon those temporary defenses in which the rebels have been able to mow down our men. Negroes helped to build the batteries at Charleston. They relieve their gentlemanly and military masters from the stiffening drudgery of the camp, and devote them to the nimble and dexterous use of arms. Rising above vulgar prejudice, the slaveholding rebel accepts the aid of the black man as readily as that of any other. If a bad cause can do this, why should a good cause be less wisely conducted? We insist upon it, that one black regiment in such a war as this is, without being any more brave and orderly, would be worth to the Government more than two of any other; and that, while the Government continues to refuse the aid of colored men, thus alienating them from the national cause, and giving the rebels the advantage of them, it will not deserve better fortunes than it has thus far experienced.—Men in earnest don't fight with one hand, when they might fight with two, and a man drowning would not refuse to be saved even by a colored hand.

Source: Philip S. Foner, *The Life and Writings of Frederick Douglass, Vol.III* p.152. International Publishers Co. Inc.: New York, 1950. Permission of International Publishers/New York.

29. Excerpt from *The Gullah Proverbs of 1861, Down by the Riverside: A South Carolina Slave Community*
CHARLES JOYNER

The Gullah are African Americans whose distinct language and culture was developed in the Low Country regions of North Carolina, South Carolina, Georgia, and parts of Florida. They include the coastal plain and the Sea Islands off the coasts of these states. Historically, the Gullah region once extended north to the Cape Fear area on the coast of North Carolina and south to the vicinity of Jacksonville on the coast of Florida; but by 2007, the Gullah area was confined to the South Carolina (Port Royal and Hilton Head regions) and Georgia Low Country. The Gullah people are also called Geechee, especially in Georgia.

When the U.S. Civil War began, the Union rushed to blockade Confederate shipping. White planters on the Sea Islands, fearing an invasion by the U.S. naval forces, abandoned their plantations and fled to the mainland. When Union forces arrived on the Sea Islands in 1861, they found the Gullah people eager for their freedom, and eager as well to defend it. Many Gullahs served with distinction in the Union Army's First South Carolina Volunteers. The Sea Islands were the first place in the South where slaves were freed, including places such as Port Royal and Hilton Head long before the war ended, Quaker missionaries from Pennsylvania came down to start schools for the newly freed slaves. Penn Center, now a Gullah community organization on Saint Helena Island, South Carolina, began as the very first school for freed slaves.

The Gullah are known for preserving more of their African linguistic and cultural heritage than any other black community in the United States. They speak an English-based Creole language containing many African loanwords and significant influences from African languages in grammar and sentence structure. The Gullah language is related to Jamaican Creole, Bahamian Dialect, and the Krio language of Sierra Leone in West Africa. Gullah storytelling, foodways, music, folk beliefs, crafts, farming and fishing traditions, etc., all exhibit strong influences from African cultures.

GULLAH PROVERBS

Promisin' talk don' cook rice.

Empty sack can't stand upright alone.

Most kill bird don't make stew. (An almost killed bird doesn't make stew.)

Onpossible to get straight wood from crooked timber. (It's impossible to get straight wood from crooked timber.)

Every frog praise its own pond if it dry.

Most hook fish don't help dry hominy. (An almost hooked fish doesn't improve the taste of dry hominy.)

Most kill bird don't make stew. (Almost killed birds don't make a stew.)

Chip don't fall far from the block.

One clean sheet can' soil another. (A clean sheet cannot soil another.)

It takes a thief to catch a thief.

Det wan ditch you ain' fuh jump. (Death is one ditch you cannot jump.)

There are more ways to kill a dog than to choke him with butter.

Put yuh bess foot fo moss. (Put your best foot foremost.)

Burn child dread fire. (A burned child dreads fire.)

Eby back is fitted to de bu'den. (Every back is fitted to the burden.)

Er good run bettuh dan uh bad stan. (A good run is better than a bad stand.)

Heart don't mean ever thing mouth say. (The heart doesn't mean everything the mouth says.)

Ef you hol' you mad e would kill eby glad. (If you hold your anger, it will kill all your happiness.)

Source: Urbana: University of Illinois Press, 1984.

30. Excerpted from The Negroes at Port Royal, report of E. L. Pierce, to the Hon. Salmon P. Chase, U.S. Secretary of the Treasury, 1862

In 1861, the federal government decided to attack the Confederacy in the deep South with a Union fleet of about 60 ships and 20,000 men. They sailed from Fortress Monroe at Hampton Roads, Virginia, on October 29, 1861. They arrived off the coast of Beaufort, South Carolina, on November 3. Fleet forces were under the command of Admiral S. F. DuPont and the Expeditionary Corps troops were under the direction of General T. W. Sherman. The attack on the Confederate Forts Walker (on Hilton Head) and Beauregard (at Bay Point on St. Phillips Island) began on the morning of November 7. By 3 P.M. that afternoon the Union fleet had fired nearly 3,000 shots at the two forts and the Confederate forces retreated, leaving the Beaufort area to Union forces.

This battle was the beginning step Sea Island blacks would take down the long road to freedom. For many slaves in the Port Royal area, the fall of Hilton Head was the single greatest event in their lives.

The Civil War changed the lives of both planters and slaves on Hilton Head Island. Gradually a plan was formulated for the education, welfare, and employment of the blacks, combining both government and missionary efforts. The Department of the South, headquartered on Hilton Head Island, became a "Department of

Experiments," conducting what a modern historian has called a "dress rehearsal for Reconstruction" and is often called the "Port Royal Experiment."

THE NEGROES AT PORT ROYAL:

Dear Sir,

'My first communication to you was mailed on the third day after my arrival. The same day, I mailed two letters to benevolent persons in Boston, mentioned in my previous communications to you, asking for contributions of clothing, and for a teacher or missionary to be sent, to be supported by the charity of those interested in the movement, to both of which favorable answers have been received. The same day, I commenced a tour of the largest islands, and ever since have been diligently engaged in anxious examinations of the modes of culture—the amount and proportions of the products—the labor required for them-the life and disposition of the laborers upon them—their estimated numbers—the treatment they have received from their former masters, both as to the labor required of them, the provisions and clothing allowed to them, and the discipline imposed their habits, capacities, and desires, with special reference to their being fitted for useful citizenship—and generally whatever concerned the well-being, present and future, of the territory and its people. Visits have also been made to the communities collected at Hilton Head and Beaufort, and conferences held with the authorities, both naval and military, and other benevolent persons interested in the welfare of these people, and the wise and speedy reorganization of society here. No one can be impressed more than myself with the uncertainty of conclusions drawn from in experiences and reflections gathered in so brief a period, however industriously and wisely occupied.

Nevertheless, they may be of some service to those who have not been privileged with an equal opportunity. Of the plantations visited, full notes have been taken of seventeen, with reference to number of negroes in all; of field hands; amount of cotton and corn raised, and how much per acre; time and mode of producing and distributing manure; listing, planting, cultivating, picking and ginning cotton; labor required of each hand; allowance of food and clothing; the capacities of the laborers; their wishes and feelings, both as to themselves and their masters. Many of the above points could be determined by other sources, such as persons at the North familiar with the region, and publications. The inquiries were, however, made with the double purpose of acquiring the information and testing the capacity of the persons inquired of. Some of the leading results of the examination will now be submitted. An estimate of the number of plantations open to cultivation, and of the persons upon the territory protected by the forces of the United States, if only approximate to the truth, may prove convenient in providing a proper system of administration.

The following islands are thus protected, and the estimated number of plantations upon each is ... about two hundred in all.

The populous island of North Edisto, lying in the direction of Charleston is still visited by the rebels.

REPORT OF THE GOVERNMENT AGENT

A part near Botany Bay Island is commanded by the guns of one of our war vessels, under which a colony of one thousand negroes sought protection, where they have been temporarily subsisted from its stores. The number has within a few days been stated to have increased to 2300.

Among these, great destitution is said to prevail. Even to this number, as the negroes acquire confidence in us, large additions are likely every week to be made. The whole island can be safely farmed as soon as troops can be spared for the purpose of occupation. But not counting the plantations of this island, the number on Port Royal, Ladies', St. Helena, Hilton Head, and the smaller islands, may be estimated at 200 plantations. In visiting the plantations, I endeavored to ascertain with substantial accuracy the number of persons upon them, without, however, expecting to determine the precise number.

On that of Thomas Aston Coffin, at Coffin Point, St. Helena, there were 260, the largest found on any one visited. There were 130 on that of Dr. J. W. Jenkins, 120 on that of the Eustis estate, and the others range from 80 to 38, making an average of 81 to a plantation. These, however, may be ranked among the best peopled plantations, and forty to each may be considered a fair average. From these estimates, a population of 8000 negroes on the islands, now safely protected by our forces, results. Of the 600 at the camp at Hilton Head, about one-half should be counted with the aforesaid plantations whence they have come. Of the 600 at Beaufort, one-third should also be reckoned with the plantations. The other fraction in each case should be added to the 8000 in computing the population now thrown on our protection. The negroes on Ladies' and St. Helena Islands have quite generally remained on their respective plantations, or if absent, but temporarily, visiting wives or relatives. The dispersion on Port Royal and Hilton Head Islands has been far greater, the people of the former going to Beaufort in considerable numbers, and of the latter to the camp at Hilton Head.

Counting the negroes who have gone to Hilton Head and Beaufort from places now protected by our forces as still attached to the plantations, and to that extent not swelling the 8000 on plantations, but adding thereto the usual negro population of Beaufort, as also the negroes who have fled to Beaufort and Hilton Head from places not yet occupied by our forces, and adding also the colony at North Edisto, and we must now have thrown upon our hands, for whose present and future we must provide, from 10,000 to 12,000 persons—probably nearer the latter than the former number. This number is rapidly increasing. This week, forty-eight escaped from a single plantation near Grahamville, on the main land, held by the rebels, led by the driver, and after four days of trial and peril, hidden by day and threading the waters with their boats by night, evading the rebel pickets, joyfully entered our camp at Hilton Head. The accessions at Edisto are in larger number, and according to the most reasonable estimates, it would only require small advances by our troops, not involving a general engagement or even loss of life, to double the number which would be brought within our lines. A fact derived from the Census of 1860 may serve to illustrate the responsibility now devolving on the Government. This County of Beaufort had a population of slaves in proportion of 82 13 of the whole, a proportion only exceeded by seven other counties in the United States, viz.: one in South Carolina, that of Georgetown; three in Mississippi, those of Bolivar, Washington and Issequena; and three in Louisiana, those of Madison, Tensas and Concordia.

An impression prevails that the negroes here have been less cared for than in most other rebel districts. If this be so, and a beneficent reform shall be achieved here, the experiment may anywhere else be hopefully attempted. The former white population, so far as can be ascertained, are rebels, with one or two exceptions. In January, 1861, a meeting of the planters on St. Helena Island was held, of which Thomas Aston Coffin was chairman.

A vote was passed, stating its exposed condition, and offering their slaves to the Governor of South Carolina, to aid in building earth mounds, and calling on him for guns to place upon them. A copy of the vote, probably in his own handwriting, and signed by Mr. Coffin, was found in his house. It is worthy of note that the negroes now within our lines are there by the invitation of no one; but they were on the soil when our army began its occupation, and could not have been excluded, except by violent transportation. A small proportion have come in from the main land, evading the pickets of the enemy and our own,—something easily done in an extensive country, with whose woods and creeks they are familiar. The only exportable crop of this region is the long staple Sea Island cotton, raised with more difficulty than the coarser kind, and bringing a higher price. The agents of the Treasury Department expect to gather some 2,500,00.0 pounds of ginned cotton the present year, nearly all of which had been picked and stored before the arrival of our forces. Considerable quantities have not been picked at all, but the crop for this season was unusually good. Potatoes and corn are raised only for consumption on the plantations,—corn being raised at the rate of only twenty-five bushels per acre. Such features in plantation life as will throw light on the social questions now anxiously weighed deserve notice.

In this region, the master, if a man of wealth, is more likely to have his main residence at Beaufort, sometimes having none on the plantation, but having one for the driver, who is always a negro. He may, however, have one, and an expensive one, too, as in the case of Dr. Jenkins, at St. Helena, and yet pass most of his time at Beaufort, or at the North. The plantation in such cases is left almost wholly under the charge of an overseer. In some cases, there is not even a house for an overseer, the plantation being superintended by the driver, and being visited by the overseer living on another plantation belonging to the same owner.

The houses for the overseers are of an undesirable character. Orchards of orange or fig trees are usually planted near them. The field hands are generally quartered at some distance eighty or one hundred rods from the overseer's or master's house, and are ranged in a row, sometimes in two rows, fronting each other. They are sixteen feet by twelve, each appropriated to a family, and in some cases divided with a partition. They numbered, on the plantations visited, from ten to twenty, and on the Coffin plantation, they are double, numbering twenty-three double houses, intended for forty-six families. The yards seemed to swarm with children, the negroes coupling at an early age.

Except on Sundays, these people do not take their meals at a family table, but each one takes his hominy, bread, or potatoes, sitting on the floor or a bench, and at his own time. They say their masters never allowed them any regular time for meals. Whoever, under our new system, is charged with their superintendence, should see that they attend more to the cleanliness of their persons and houses, and that, as in families of white people, they take their meals together at a table—habits to which they will be more disposed when they are provided with another change of clothing, and when better food is furnished and a proper hour assigned for meals. Upon each plantation visited by me, familiar conversations were had with several laborers, more or less, as time permitted—sometimes inquiries made of them, as they collected in groups, as to what they desired us to do with and for them, with advice as to the course of sobriety and industry which it was for their interest to pursue under the new and strange circumstances in which they were now placed. Inquiries as to plantation economy, the culture of crops, the implements still remaining, the number of persons in all, and of field hands, and the rations issued, were made of the drivers, as they are called, answering as nearly as the two different systems of labor will permit to foremen on farms in the free States. There is one on each plantation—on the largest one visited, two. They still remained on each visited, and their names were noted. The business of the driver was to superintend the field-hands generally, and see that their tasks were performed fully and properly. He controlled them, subject to the master or overseer. He dealt out the rations.

Another office belonged to him. He was required by the master or overseer, whenever he saw fit, to inflict corporal punishment upon the laborers; nor was he relieved from this office when the subject of discipline was his wife or children. In the absence of the master or overseer, he succeeded to much of their authority. As indicating his position of consequence, he was privileged with four suits of clothing a year, while only two were allowed to the laborers under him. It is evident, from some of the duties assigned to him, that he must have been a person of considerable judgment and knowledge of plantation economy, not differing essentially from that required of the foreman of a farm in the free States. He may be presumed to have known, in many cases, quite as much about the matters with which he was charged as the owner of the plantation, who often passed but a fractional part of his time upon it. The driver, notwithstanding the dispersion of other laborers, quite generally remains on the plantation, as already stated. He still holds the keys of the granary, dealing out the rations of food, and with the same sense of responsibility as before. In one case, I found him in a controversy with a laborer to whom he was refusing his peck of corn, because of absence with his wife on another plantation when the corn was gathered, -it being gathered since the arrival of our army. The laborer protested warmly that he had helped to plant and hoe the corn, and was only absent as charged because of sickness. The driver appealed to me, as the only white man near, and learning from other laborers that the laborer was sick at the time of gathering, I advised the driver to give him his peck of corn, which he did accordingly. The fact is noted as indicating the present relation of the driver to the plantation, where he still retains something of his former authority. This authority is, however, very essentially diminished. The main reason is, as he will assure you, that he has now no white man to back him. Other reasons may, however, concur.

A class of laborers are generally disposed to be jealous of one of their own number promoted to be over them, and accordingly some negroes, evidently moved by this feeling, will tell you that the drivers ought now to work as field hands, and some field hands be drivers in their place. The driver has also been required to report delinquencies to the master or overseer, and upon their order to inflict corporal punishment. The laborers will, in some cases, say that he has been harder than he need to have been, while he will say that he did only what he was forced to do. The complainants who have suffered under the lash may be pardoned for not being sufficiently charitable to him who has unwillingly inflicted it, while, on the other hand, he has been placed in a dangerous position, where a hard nature, or self-interest, or dislike for the victim, might have tempted him to be more cruel than his position required. The truth, in proportions impossible for us in many cases to fix, may lie with both parties. I am, on the whole, inclined to believe that the past position of the driver and his valuable knowledge, both of the plantations and the laborers, when properly advised and controlled, may be made available in securing the productiveness of the plantations and the good of the laborers. It should be added that, in all cases, the drivers were found very ready to answer inquiries and communicate all information, and seemed desirous that the work of the season should be commenced.

There are also on the plantations other laborers, more intelligent than the average, such as the carpenter, the plowman, the religious leader, who may be called a preacher, a watchman or a helper,—the two latter being recognized officers in the churches of these people, and the helpers being aids to the watchman. These persons, having recognized positions among their fellows, either by virtue of superior knowledge or devotion, when properly approached by us, may be expected to have a beneficial influence on the more ignorant, and help to create that public opinion in favor of good conduct which, among the humblest as among the highest, is most useful. I saw many of very low intellectual development, but hardly any too low to be reached by civilizing influences, either coming directly from us or immediately through their brethren. And while I saw some who were sadly degraded, I met also others who were as fine specimens of human nature as one can ever expect to find. Beside attendance on churches on Sundays, there are evening prayer-meetings on the plantations as often as once or twice a week, occupied with praying, singing, and exhortations. In some cases, the leader can read a hymn, having picked up his knowledge clandestinely, either from other negroes or from white children.

Of the adults, about one-half, at least, are members of churches, generally the Baptist, although other denominations have communicants among them. In the Baptist Church on St. Helena Island, which I visited on the 22d January, there were a few pews for the proportionally small number of white attendants, and the much larger space devoted to benches for colored people. On one plantation there is a negro chapel, well adapted for the purpose, built by the proprietor, the late Mrs. Eustis, whose memory is cherished by the negroes and some of whose sons are now loyal citizens of Massachusetts. I have heard among the Negroes scarcely any profane swearing—not more than twice—a striking contrast with my experience among soldiers in the army. It seemed a part of my duty to attend some of their religious meetings, and learn further about these people what could be derived from such a source. Their exhortations to personal piety were fervent, and, though their language was many times confused, at least to my ear, occasionally an important instruction or a felicitous expression could be recognized. In one case, a preacher of their own, commenting on the text, " Blessed are the meek," exhorted his brethren not to be "stout-minded."

On one plantation on Ladies' Island, where some thirty negroes were gathered in the evening, I read passages of Scripture, and pressed on them their practical duties at the present time with reference to the good of themselves, their children, and their people. The passages read were the 1st and 23d Psalms; the 61st chapter of Isaiah, verses 1–4; the Beatitudes in the 5th chapter of Matthew; the 14th chapter of John's Gospel, and the 5th chapter of the Epistle of James. In substance, I told them that their masters had rebelled against the Government, and we had come to put down the rebellion; that we had now met them, and wanted to see what was best to do for them; that Mr. Lincoln, the President or Great Man at Washington, had the whole matter in charge, and was thinking what he could do for them; that the great. trouble about doing anything for them was that their masters had always told us, and had made many people believe, that they were lazy, and would not work unless whipped to it; that Mr. Lincoln had sent us down here to see if it was so; that what they did was reported to him, or to men who would tell him; that where I came from all were free, both white and black; that we did not sell children or separate man and wife, but all had to work; that if they were to be free, they would have to work, and would be shut up or deprived of privileges if they did not; that this was a critical hour with them, and if they did not behave well now and respect our agents and appear willing to work, Mr. Lincoln would give up trying to do anything for them, and they must give up all hope for anything better, and their children and grand-children a hundred years hence would be worse off than they had been. I told them they must stick to their plantations and not run about and get scattered, and assured them that what their masters had told them of our intentions to carry them off to Cuba and sell them was a lie, and their masters knew it to be so, and we wanted them to stay on the plantations and raise cotton, and if they behaved well, they should have wages—small, perhaps, at first; that they should have better food, and not have their wives and children sold off; that their children should be taught to read and write, for which they might be willing to pay something; that by-and-by they would be as well off as the white people, and we would stand by them against their masters ever coming back to take them.

The importance of exerting a good influence on each other, particularly on the younger. men, who were rather careless and roving, was urged, as all would suffer in good repute from the bad deeds of a few. At Hilton Head, where I spoke to a meeting of two hundred, and there were facts calling for the counsel, the women were urged to keep away from the bad white men, who would ruin them. Remarks of a like character were made familiarly on the plantations to such groups as gathered about.

At the Hilton Head meeting, a good-looking man, who had escaped from the southern part of Barnwell District, rose and said, with much feeling, that he and many others should do all they could by good conduct to prove what their masters said against them to be false, and to make Mr. Lincoln think better things of them. After the meeting closed, he desired to know if Mr. Lincoln was coming down here to see them, and he wanted me to give Mr. Lincoln his compliments, with his name, assuring the President that he would do all he could for him. The message was a little amusing, but it testified to the earnestness of the simple-hearted man. He had known Dr. Brisbane, who had been compelled some years since to leave the South because of his sympathy for slaves. The name of Mr. Lincoln was used in addressing them, as more likely to impress them than the abstract idea of government. It is important to add that in no case have I attempted to excite them by insurrectionary appeals against their former masters, feeling that such a course might increase the trouble of organizing them into a peaceful and improving system, under a just and healthful temporary discipline; and besides that, it is a dangerous experiment to attempt the improvement of a class of men by appealing to their coarser nature.

The better course toward making them our faithful allies, and therefore the constant enemies of the rebels, seemed to be to place before them the good things to be done for them and their children, and sometimes reading passages of Scripture appropriate to their lot, without, however, note or comment, never heard before by them, or heard only when wrested from their just interpretation; such, for instance, as the last chapter of St. James's Epistle, and the Glad Tidings of Isaiah: "I have come to preach deliverance to the captive." Thus treated and thus educated, they may be hoped to become useful coadjutors, and the unconquerable foes of the fugitive rebels. There are some vices charged upon these people which deserve examination. Notwithstanding their religious professions, in some cases more emotional than practical, the marriage relation, or what answers for it, is not, in many instances, held very sacred by them. The men, it is said, sometimes leave one wife and take another,—something likely to happen in any society where it is permitted or not forbidden by a stern public opinion, and far more likely to happen under laws which do not recognize marriage, and dissolve what answers for it by forced separations, dictated by the mere pecuniary interest of others. The women, it is said, are easily persuaded by white men,—a facility readily accounted for by the power of the master over them, whose solicitation was equivalent to a command, and against which the husband or father was powerless to protect, and increased also by the degraded condition in which they have been placed, where they have been apt to regard what ought to be a disgrace as a compliment, when they were approached by a paramour of superior condition and race. Yet often the dishonor is felt, and the woman, on whose several children her master's features are impressed, and through whose veins his blood flows, has sadly confessed it with an instinctive blush. The grounds of this charge, so far as they may exist, will be removed, as much as in communities of our own race, by a system which shall recognize and enforce the marriage relation among them, protect them against the solicitations of white men as much as law can, still more by putting them in relations were they will be inspired with self-respect and a consciousness of their rights, and taught by a pure and plainspoken Christianity.

In relation to the veracity of these people, so far as my relations with them have extended, they have appeared, as a class, to intend to tell the truth. Their manner, as much as among white men, bore instinctive evidence of this intention. Their answers to inquiries relative to the management of the plantations have a general concurrence. They make no universal charges of cruelty against their masters. They will say, in some cases, that their own was a very kind one, but another one in that neighborhood was cruel. On St. Helena Island they spoke kindly of "the good William Fripp," as they called him, and of Dr. Clarence Fripp; but they all denounced the cruelty of Alvira Fripp, recounting his inhuman treatment of both men and women.

Another concurrenee is worthy of note. On the plantations visited, it appeared from the statements of the laborers themselves, that there were, on an average, about 133 pounds of cotton produced to the acre, and five acres of cotton and corn cultivated to a hand, the culture of potatoes not being noted. An article of the *American Agriculturist*, published in Turner's Cotton Manual, pp. 132, 133, relative to the culture of Sea Island Cotton, on the plantation of John H. Townsend, states that the land is cultivated in the proportion of 7–12th cotton, 3–12ths corn, and 2–12ths potatoes—in all, less than six acres to a hand—and the average yield of cotton per acre is 135 pounds. I did not take the statistics of the culture of potatoes, but about five acres are planted with them on the smaller plantations, and twenty, or even thirty, on the larger; and the average amount of land to each hand, planted with potatoes, should be added to the five acres of cotton and corn, and thus results not differing substantially are reached in both cases. Thus the standard publications attest the veracity and accuracy of these laborers. Again, there can be no more delicate and responsible position, involving honesty and skill, than that of pilot. For this purpose, these people are every day employed to aid our military and naval operations in navigating these sinuous channels. They were used in the recent reconnoisance in the direction of Savannah; and the success of the affair at Port Royal Ferry depended on the fidelity of a pilot, William, without the aid of whom, or of one like him, it could not have been undertaken. Further information on this point may be obtained of the proper authorities here. These services are not, it is true, in all respects, illustrative of the quality of veracity, but they involve kindred virtues not likely to exist without it. It is proper, however, to state that expressions are sometimes heard from persons who have not considered these people thoughtfully, to the effect that their word is not to be trusted, and these persons, nevertheless, do trust them, and act upon their statements. There may, however, be some color for such expressions.

These laborers, like all ignorant people, have an ill-regulated reason, too much under the control of the imagination. Therefore, where they report the number of soldiers, or relate facts where there is room for conjecture, they are likely to be extravagant, and you must scrutinize their reports. Still, except among the thoroughly dishonest,-no more numerous among them than in other races—there will be found a colorable basis for their statements, enough to show their honest intention to speak truly. It is true also that you will find them too willing to express feelings which will please you. This is most natural. All races, as well as all animals, have their appropriate means of self-defense, and where the power to use physical force to defend one's self is taken away, the weaker animal, or man, or race, resorts to cunning and duplicity. Whatever habits of this kind may appear in these people are directly traceable to the well-known features of their past condition, without involving any essential proneness to deception in the race, further than may be ascribed to human nature.

Upon this point, special inquiries have been made of the Superintendent at Hilton Head, who is brought in direct daily association with them, and whose testimony, truthful as he is, is worth far more than that of those who have had less nice opportunities of observation, and Mr. Lee certifies to the results here presented. Upon the question of the disposition of these people to work, there are different reports, varied somewhat by the impression an idle or an industrious laborer, brought into immediate relation with the witness, may have made on the mind. In conversations with them, they uniformly answered to assurances that if free they must work, "Yes, massa, we must work to live; that's the law"; and expressing an anxiety that the work of the plantations was not going on. At Hilton Head, they are ready to do for Mr. Lee, the judicious Superintendent, whatever is desired. Hard words and epithets are, however, of no use in managing them, and other parties for whose service they are specially detailed, who do not understand or treat them properly, find some trouble in making their labor available, as might naturally be expected. In collecting cotton, it is sometimes, as I am told, difficult to get them together, when wanted for work. There may be something in this, particularly among the young men. I have observed them a good deal; and though they often do not work to much advantage, a dozen doing sometimes what one or two stout and well-trained Northern laborers would do, and though less must always he expected of persons native to this soil than those bred in Northern latitudes, and under more bracing air, I have not been at all impressed with their general indolence.

As servants, oarsmen, and carpenters, I have seen them working faithfully and with a will. There are some peculiar circumstances in their condition, which no one who assumes to sit in judgment upon them must overlook. They are now, for the first time, freed from the restraint of a master, and like children whose guardian or teacher is absent for the day, they may quite naturally enjoy an interval of idleness. No system of labor for them, outside of the camps, has been begun, and they have had nothing to do except to bale the cotton when bagging was furnished, and we all know that men partially employed are, if anything, less disposed to do the little assigned them than they are to perform the full measure which belongs to them in regular life, the virtue of the latter case being supported by habit. At the camps, they are away from their accustomed places of labor, and have not been so promptly paid as could be desired, and are exposed to the same circumstances which often dispose soldiers to make as little exertion as possible. In the general chaos which prevails, and before the inspirations of labor have been set before them by proper superintendents and teachers who understand their disposition, and show by their conduct an interest in their welfare, no humane or reasonable man would subject them to austere criticism, or make the race responsible for the delinquencies of an idle person, who happened to be brought particularly under his own observation. Not thus would we have ourselves or our own race judged; and the judgment which we would not have meted to us, let us not measure to others. Upon the best examination of these people, and a comparison of the evidence of trustworthy persons, I believe that when properly organized, and with proper motives set before them, they will, as freemen, be as industrious as any race of men are likely to be in this climate. The notions of the sacredness of property as held by these people have sometimes been the subject of discussion here. It is reported they have taken things left in their masters' houses. It was wise to prevent this, and even where it had been done to compel a restoration, at least of expensive articles, lest they should be injured by speedily acquiring, without purchase, articles above their condition. But a moment's reflection will show that it was the most natural thing for them to do. They had been occupants of the estates; had had these things more or less in charge, and when the former owners had left, it was easy for them to regard their title to the abandoned property as better than that of strangers.

Still, it is not true that they have, except as to very simple articles, as soap or dishes, generally availed themselves of such property. It is also stated that in camps where they have been destitute of clothing, they have stolen from each other, but the Superintendents are of opinion that they would not have done this if already well provided. Besides, those familiar with large bodies collected together, like soldiers in camp life, also know how often these charges of mutual pilfering are made among them, often with great injustice. It should be added, to complete the statement, that the agents who have been intrusted with the collection of cotton have reposed confidence in the trustworthiness of the laborers, committing property to their charge—a confidence not found to have been misplaced. To what extent these laborers desire to be free, and to serve us still further in putting down the rebellion, has been a subject of examination The desire to be free has been strongly expressed, particularly among the more intelligent and adventurous. Every day, almost, adds a fresh tale of escapes, both solitary and in numbers, conducted with a courage, a forecast, and a skill, worthy of heroes. But there are other apparent features in their disposition which it would be untruthful to conceal. On the plantations, I often found a disposition to evade the inquiry whether they wished to be free or slaves; and though a preference for freedom was expressed, it was rarely in the passionate phrases which would come from an Italian peasant. The secluded and monotonous life of a plantation, with strict discipline and ignorance enforced by law and custom, is not favorable to the development of the richer sentiments, though even there they find at least a stunted growth, irrepressible as they are. The inquiry was often answered in this way: "The white man do what he pleases with us; we are yours now, massa."

One, if I understood his broken words rightly, said that he did not care about being free, if he only had a good master. Others said they would like to be free, but they wanted a white man for a "protector." All of proper age, when inquired of, expressed a desire to have their children taught to read and write, and to learn themselves. On this point, they showed more earnestness than on any other. When asked if they were willing to fight, in case we needed them, to keep their masters from coming back, they would seem to shrink from that, saying that "black men have been kept down so like dogs that they would run before white men." At the close of the first week's observation, I almost concluded that on the plantation there was but little earnest desire for freedom, and scarcely any willingness for its sake to encounter white men. But as showing the importance of not attempting to reach general conclusions too hastily, another class of facts came to my notice the second week. I met then some more intelligent, who spoke with profound earnestness of their desire to be free and how they had longed to see this day. Other facts, connected with the military and naval operations, were noted.

At the recent reconnoisanee toward Pulaski, pilots of this class stood well under the fire, and were not reluctant to the service. When a district of Ladies' Island was left exposed, they voluntarily took such guns as they could procure, and stood sentries. Also at North Edisto, is where the colony is collected under the protection of our gunboats, they armed themselves and drove back the rebel cavalry. An officer here high in command reported to me some of these facts, which had been officially communicated to him. The suggestion may be pertinent that the persons in question are divisible into two classes. Those who, by their occupation, have been accustomed to independent labor, and schooled in some sort of self-reliance, are more developed in this direction; while others, who have been bound to the routine of plantation life, and kept more strictly under surveillance, are but little awakened. But even among these last there has been, under the quickening inspiration of present events, a rapid development, indicating that the same feeling is only latent. There is another consideration which must not be omitted. Many of these people have still but little confidence in us, anxiously looking to see what is to be our disposition of them, It is a mistake to suppose that, separated from the world, never having read a Northern book or newspaper relative to them, or talked with a Northern man expressing the sentiments prevalent in his region, they are universally and with entire confidence welcoming us as their deliverers. Here, as everywhere else, where our army has met them, they have been assured by their masters that we were going to carry them off to Cuba. There is probably not a rebel master, from the Potomac to the Gulf, who has not repeatedly made this assurance to his slaves. No matter what his religious vows may have been, no matter what his professed honor as a gentleman; he has not shrunk from the reiteration of this falsehood. Never was there a people, as all who know them will testify, more attached to familiar places than they. Be their home a cabin, and not even that cabin their own, they still cling to it. The reiteration could not fail to have had some effect on a point on which they were so sensitive.

Often it must have been met with unbelief or great suspicion of its truth. It was also balanced by the consideration that their masters would remove them into the interior and perhaps to a remote region, and separate their families, about as bad as being taken to Cuba, and they felt more inclined to remain on the plantations, and take their chances with us. They have told me that they reasoned in this way. But in many cases they fled at the approach of our army. Then one or two bolder returning, the rest were reassured and came back. Recently, the laborers at Parry Island, seeing some schooners approaching suspiciously, commenced gathering their little effects rapidly together, and were about to run, when they were quieted by some of our teachers coming, in whom they had confidence. In some cases, their distrust has been increased by the bad conduct of some irresponsible white men, of which, for the honor of human nature, it is not best to speak more particularly.

On the whole, their confidence in us has been greatly increased by the treatment they have received, which, in spite of many individual cases of injury less likely to occur under the stringent orders recently issued from the naval and military authorities, has been generally kind and humane. But the distrust which to a greater or less extent may have existed on our arrival, renders necessary, if we would keep them faithful allies, and not informers to the enemy, the immediate adoption of a system which shall be a pledge of our protection and of our permanent interest in their welfare. The manner of the laborers toward us has been kind and deferential, doing for us such good offices as were in their power, as guides, pilots, or in more personal service, inviting us on the plantations to lunch of hominy and milk, or potatoes, touching the hat in courtesy, and answering politely such questions as were addressed to them. If there have been exceptions to this rule, it was in the case of those whose bearing did not entitle them to the civility. Passing from general phases of character or present disposition, the leading facts in relation to the plantations and the mode of rendering them useful and determining what is best to be done, come next in order. The laborers on St. Helena and Ladies' Islands very generally remain on their respective plantations. This fact, arising partially from local attachment and partially because they can thus secure their allowance of corn, is important, as it will facilitate their reorganization. Some are absent, temporarily visiting a wife, or relative, on another plantation, and returning periodically for their rations. The disposition to roam, so far as it exists, mainly belongs to the younger people. On Port Royal and Hilton Head Islands, there is a much greater dispersion, due in part to their having been the scene of more active military movements, and in part to the taking in greater measure on these islands of the means of subsistence from the plantations. When the work recommences, however, there is not likely to be any indisposition to return to them. The statistics with regard to the number of laborers, field hands, acres planted to cotton and corn, are not presented as accurate statements, but only as reasonable approximations, which may be of service. The highest number of people on any plantation visited was on Coffin's, where there are 260. Those on the plantation of Dr. Jenkins number 130; on that of the Eustis estate, 120; and the others, from 80 to 38. The average number on each is 81. The field hands range generally from one-third to one-half of the number, the rest being house servants, old persons, and children. About five acres of cotton and corn are planted to a hand; and to potatoes, about five acres in all were devoted on the smaller plantations, and from twenty to thirty on the larger. The number of pounds in a bale of ginned cotton ranges from 300 to 400—the average number being not far from 345 pounds per bale.

The average yield per acre on fifteen plantations was about 133 pounds. The material for compost is gathered in the periods of most leisure—often in July and August, after the cultivation of the cotton plant is ended, and before the picking has commenced. Various materials are used, but quite generally mud and the coarse marsh grass, which abounds on the creeks near the plantations, are employed. The manure is carted upon the land in January and February, and left in heaps, two or three cart-loads on each task, to be spread at the time of listing. The land, by prevailing custom, lies fallow a year. The cotton and corn are planted in elevated rows or beds.

The next step is the listing, done with the hoe, and making the bed where the alleys were at the previous raising of the crop, and the alleys being made where the beds were before. In this process, half the old bed is hauled into the alley on the one side, and the other half into the alley on the other. This work is done mainly in February, being commenced sometimes the last of January.

Workers live in a barracks that is 105 feet square, and contains twenty-one or twenty-two beds or rows. Each laborer is required to list a task and a half; or if the land is moist and heavy, a task and five or seven beds, say one-fourth or three-eighths of an acre. The planting of cotton commences about the 20th or last of March, and of corn about the same time or earlier. It is continued through April, and by some planters it is not begun till April. The seeds are deposited in the beds, a foot or a foot and a half apart on light land, and two feet apart on heavy land, and five or ten seeds left in a place. After the plant is growing, the stalks are thinned so as to leave together two on high land and one on low or rich land. The hoeing of the early cotton begins about the time that the planting of the late has ended. The plant is cultivated with the hoe and plow during May, June and July, keeping the weeds down and thinning the stalks. The picking commences the last of August. The cotton being properly dried in the sun, is then stored in houses, ready to be ginned. The ginning, or cleaning the fibre from the seed, is done either by gins operated by steam, or by the well-known foot-gins—the latter turning out about 30 pounds of ginned cotton per day, and worked by one person, assisted by another, who picks out the specked and yellow cotton. The steam-engine carries one or more gins, each turning out 300 pounds per day, and requiring eight or ten hands to tend the engine and gins, more or less, according to the number of the gins. The footgins are still more used than the gins operated by steam,-the latter being used mainly on the largest plantations, on which both kinds are sometimes employed. I have preserved notes of the kind and number of gins used on the plantations visited, but it is unnecessary to give them here. Both kinds can be run entirely by the laborers, and after this year, the ginning should be done entirely here—among other reasons, to avoid transportation of the seed, which makes nearly three fourths of the weight of the unginned cotton, and to preserve in better condition the seed required for planting. The allowance of clothing to the field hands in this district has been two suits per year, one for summer and another for winter. That of food has been mainly vegetable—a peck of corn a week to each hand, with meat only in June, when the work is hardest, and at Christmas.

No meat was allowed in June, on some plantations, while on a few, more liberal, it was dealt out occasionally, once a fortnight, or once a month. On a few, molasses was given at intervals. Children, varying with their ages, were allowed from two to six quarts of corn per week. The diet is more exclusively vegetable here than almost anywhere in the rebellious regions, and in this respect should be changed. It should be added, that there are a large quantity of oysters available for food in proper seasons. Besides the above rations, the laborers were allowed each to cultivate a small patch of ground, about a quarter of an acre, for themselves, when their work for their master was done. On this, corn and potatoes, chiefly the former, were planted. The corn was partly eaten by themselves, thus supplying in part the deficiency in rations; but it was, to a great extent, fed to a pig, or chickens, each hand being allowed to keep a pig and chickens or ducks, but not geese or turkeys. With the proceeds of the pig and chickens, generally sold to the masters, and at pretty low rates, extra clothing, coffee, sugar, and that necessary of life with these people, as they think, tobacco, were bought. In the report thus far, such facts in the condition of the territory now occupied by the forces of the United States have been noted as seemed to throw light on what could be done to reorganize the laborers, prepare them to become sober and self-supporting citizens, and secure the successful culture of a cotton-crop, now so necessary to be contributed to the markets of the world. It will appear from them that these people are naturally religious and simple-hearted— attached to the places where they have lived, still adhering to them both from a feeling of local attachment and self-interest in securing the means of subsistence; that they have the knowledge and experience requisite to do all the labor, from the preparation of the ground for planting until the cotton is baled, ready to be exported; that they, or the great mass of them, are disposed to labor, with proper inducements thereto; that they lean upon white men, and desire their protection, and could, therefore, under a wise system, be easily brought under subordination; that they are susceptible to the higher considerations, as duty, and the love of offspring, and are not in any way inherently vicious, their defects coming from their peculiar condition in the past or present, and not from constitutional proneness to evil beyond what may be attributed to human nature; that they have among them natural chiefs, either by virtue of religious leadership or superior intelligence, who, being first addressed, may exert a healthful influence on the rest. In a word, that, in spite of their condition, reputed to be worse here than in many other parts of the rebellious region, there are such features in their life and character, that the opportunity is now offered to us to make of them, partially in this generation, and fully in the next, a happy, industrious, law-abiding, free and Christian people, if we have but the courage and patience to accept it. If this be the better view of them and their possibilities, I will say that I have come to it after anxious study of all peculiar circumstances in their lot and character, and after anxious conference with reflecting minds here, who are prosecuting like inquiries, not overlooking what, to a casual spectator, might appear otherwise, and granting what is likely enough, that there are those among them whose characters, by reason of bad nature or treatment, are set, and not admitting of much improvement. And I will submit further, that, in common fairness and common charity, when, by the order of Providence, an individual or a race is committed to our care, the better view is entitled to be first practically applied. If this one shall be accepted and crowned with success, history will have the glad privilege of recording that this wicked and unprovoked rebellion was not without compensations most welcome to our race. What, then, should be the true system of administration here? It has been proposed to lease the plantations and the people upon them. To this plan there are two objections—each conclusive. In the first place, the leading object of the parties bidding for leases would be to obtain a large immediate revenue—perhaps to make a fortune in a year or two.

The solicitations of doubtful men, offering the highest price, would impose on the leasing power a stern duty of refusal, to which it ought not unnecessarily to be subjected. Far better a system which shall not invite such men to harass the leasing power, or excite expectations of a speedy fortune, to be derived from the labor of this people. Secondly: No man, not even the best of men, charged with the duties which ought to belong to the guardians of these people, should be put in a position where there would be such a conflict between his humanity and his self-interest—his desire, on the one hand, to benefit the laborer, and, on the other, the too often stronger desire to reap a large revenue—perhaps to restore broken fortunes in a year or two. Such a system is beset with many of the worst vices of the slave system, with one advantage in favor of the latter, that it is for the interest of the planter to look to permanent results. Let the history of British East India, and of all communities where a superior race has attempted to build up speedy fortunes on the labor of an inferior race occupying another region, be remembered, and no just man will listen to the proposition of leasing, fraught as it is with such dangerous consequences.

Personal confidence forbids me to report the language of intense indignation which has been expressed against it here by some occupying high places of command, as also by others who have come here for the special purpose of promoting the welfare of these laborers. Perhaps it might yield to the treasury a larger immediate revenue, but it would be sure to spoil the country and its people in the end. The Government should be satisfied if the products of the territory may be made sufficient for a year or two to pay the expenses of administration and superintendence, and the inauguration of a beneficent system which will settle a great social question, ensure the sympathies of foreign nations, now wielded against us, and advance the civilization of the age.

The better course would be to appoint superintendents for each large plantation, and one for two or three smaller combined, compensated with a good salary, say $1,000 per year, selected with reference to peculiar qualifications, and as carefully as one would choose a guardian for his children, clothed with an adequate power to enforce a paternal discipline, to require a proper amount of labor, cleanliness, sobriety, and better habits of life, and generally to promote the moral and intellectual culture of the wards, with such other inducements, if there be any, placed before the superintendent as shall inspire him to constant efforts to prepare them for useful and worthy citizenship. To quicken and ensure the fidelity of the superintendents, there should be a director-general or governor, who shall visit the plantations, and see that they are discharging these duties, and, if necessary, he should be aided by others in the duty of visitation. This officer should be invested with liberal powers over all persons within his jurisdiction, so as to protect the blacks from each other and from white men, being required in most important cases to confer with the military authorities in punishing offences.

His proposed duties indicate that he should be a man of the best ability and character: better if he have already, by virtue of public services, a hold on the public confidence. Such an arrangement is submitted as preferable for the present to any cumbersome territorial government. The laborers themselves, no longer slaves of their former masters, or of the Government, but as yet in large numbers unprepared for the full privileges of citizens, are to be treated with sole reference to such preparation. No effort is to be spared to work upon their better nature and the motives which come from it—the love of wages, of offspring, and family, the desire of happiness, and the obligations of religion. And when these fail,-and fail they will, in some cases, we must not hesitate to resort, not to the lash, for as from the department of war so also from the department of labor, it must be banished, but to the milder and more effective punishments—of deprivation of privileges, isolation from family and society, the workhouse, or even the prison. The laborers are to be assured at the outset that parental and conjugal relations among them are to be protected and enforced; that children, and all others desiring, are to be taught; that they will receive wages; and that a certain just measure of work, with reference to the ability to perform it, if not willingly rendered, is to be required of all.

The work, so far as the case admits, shall be assigned in proper tasks, the standard being what a healthy person of average capacity can do, for which a definite sum is to be paid. The remark may perhaps be pertinent, that, whatever may have been the case with women or partially disabled persons, my observations, not yet sufficient to decide the point, have not impressed me with the conviction that healthy persons, if they had been provided with an adequate amount of food, and that animal in due proportion, could be said to have been overworked heretofore on these islands, the main trouble having been that they have not been so provided, and have not had the motives which smooth labor. Notwithstanding the frequent and severe chastisements which have been employed here in exacting labor, they have failed, and naturally enough, of their intended effects. Human beings are made up of so much more of spirit than of muscle, that compulsory labor, enforced by physical pain, will not exceed or equal, in the long run, voluntary labor with just inspirations; and the same law in less degree may be seen in the difference between the value of a whipped and jaded beast, and one well disciplined and kindly treated.

What should be the standard of wages where none have heretofore been paid, is less easy to determine. It should be graduated with reference to the wants of the laborer and the ability of the employer or Government; and this ability being determined by the value of the products of the labor, and the most that should be expected being, that for a year or two the system should not be a burden on the Treasury. Taking into consideration the cost of food and clothing, medical attendance and extras, supposing that the laborer would require rations of pork or beef, meal, coffee, sugar, molasses and tobacco, and that he would work 300 days in the year, he should receive about forty cents a day in order to enable him to lay up $30 a year; and each healthy woman could do about equally well. Three hundred days in a year is, perhaps, too high an estimate of working days, when we consider the chances of sickness and days when, by reason of storms and other causes, there would be no work. It is assumed that the laborer is not to pay rent for the small house tenanted by him. This sum, when the average number of acres cultivated by a hand, and the average yield per acre are considered with reference to market prices, or when the expense of each laborer to his former master, the interest on his assumed value and on the value of the land worked by him, these being the elements of what it has cost the master before making a profit, are computed, the Government could afford to pay, leaving an ample margin to meet the cost of the necessary implements, as well as of superintendence and administration. The figures on which this estimate is based are at the service of the Department if desired. It must also be borne in mind that the plantations will in the end be carried on more scientifically and cheaply than before, the plough taking very much the place of the hoe, and other implements being introduced to facilitate industry and increase the productive power of the soil. It being important to preserve all former habits which are not objectionable, the laborer should have his patch of ground on which to raise corn or vegetables for consumption or sale. As a part of the plan proposed, missionaries will be needed to address the religious element of a race so emotional in their nature, exhorting to all practical virtues, and inspiring the laborers with a religious zeal for faithful labor, the good nurture of their children, and for clean and healthful habits. The benevolence of the Free States, now being directed hither, will gladly provide these. The Government should, however, provide some teachers specially devoted to teaching reading, writing and arithmetic, say some twenty-five, for the territory now occupied by our forces, and private benevolence might even be relied on for these. The plan proposed is, of course, not presented as an ultimate result: far from it. It contemplates a paternal discipline for the time being, intended for present use only, with the prospect of better things in the future. As fast as the laborers show themselves fitted for all the privileges of citizens, they should be dismissed from the system and allowed to follow any employment they please, and where they please. They should have the power to acquire the fee simple of land, either with the proceeds of their labor or as a reward of special merit; and it would be well to quicken their zeal for good behavior by proper recognitions. I shall not follow these suggestions, as to the future, further, contenting myself with indicating what is best to be done at once with a class of fellow-beings now thrown on our protection, entitled to be recognized as freemen, but for whose new condition the former occupants of the territory have diligently labored to unfit them. But whatever is thought best to be done, should be done at once. A system ought to have been commenced with the opening of the year. Beside that, demoralization increases with delay, The months of January and February are the months for preparing the ground by manuring and listing, and the months of March and April are for planting. Already, important time has passed, and in a very few weeks will be too late to prepare for a crop, and too late to assi useful work to the laborers for a year to come. I imrplore the immediate intervention of your Department to avert calamities which must ensue from a further postponement. There is another precaution most necessary to be take As much as possible, persons enlisted in the army and navy should be kept separate from these people. The association produces an unhealthy excitement in the latter, and there other injurious results to both parties which it is unnecessay to particularize. In relation to this matter, I had an interview with the Flag-Officer, Com. Dupont, which resulted an order that "no boats from any of the ships of the squadron can be permitted to land anywhere but at Bay Point at Hilton Head, without a pass from the Fleet Captain," a requiring the commanding officers of the vessels to give special attention to all intercourse between the men under their command and the various plantations in their vicinity. Whatever can be accomplished to that end by this humane and gallant officer, who superadd to skill and courage in profession the liberal views of a statesman, will not be undone. The suggestion should also be made that, when employment is given to this people, some means should be take to enable them to obtain suitable goods at fair rates, and precautions taken to prevent the introduction of ardent spirit among them.

A loyal citizen of Massachusetts, Mr. Frederick A. Eustis has recently arrived here. He is the devisee in a considerable amount under the will of the late Mrs.

Eustis, who own the large estate on Ladies' Island, and also another at Poctaligo, the latter not yet in possession of our forces. The executors are rebels, and reside at Charleston. Mr. Eustis has as yet received no funds by reason of the devise. The are two other loyal devisees and some other devisees reside in rebellious districts, and the latter are understood to ha received dividends. Mr. Eustis is a gentleman of human and liberal views, and, accepting the present conditio of things, desires that the people on these plantations should be distinguished from their brethren on others, but equally admitted to their better fortunes. The circumstances of this case, though of a personal character, may furnish a useful precedent. With great pleasure and confidence, I recommend that this loyal citizen be placed in charge of the plantation on Ladies' Island, which he is willing to accept—the questions of property and rights under the will being reserved for subsequent determination.

A brief statement in relation to the laborers collected at the camps at Hilton Head and Beaufort may be desirable. At both places, they are under the charge of the Quartermaster's Department.

At Hilton Head, Mr. Barnard K. Lee, Jr., of Boston, is the Superintendent, assisted by Mr. J. D. McMath of Alleghany City, Penn., both civilians. The appointment of Mr. Lee is derived from Captain R. Saxton, Chief Quartermaster of the Expeditionary Corps, a humane officer, who is deeply interested in this matter. The number at this camp are about 600, the registered number under Mr. Lee being 472, of which 137 are on the pay-roll. Of these 472, 279 are fugitives from the main land, or other points, still held by the rebels; 77 are from Hilton Head Island; 62 from the adjacent island of Pinckney; 38 from St. Helena; 8 from Port Royal; 7 from Spring, and one from Daufuskie. Of the 472, the much larger number, it will be seen, have sought refuge from the places now held by rebels; while the greater proportion of the remainder came in at an early period, before they considered themselves safe elsewhere. Since the above figures were given, forty-eight more, all from one plantation, and under the lead of the driver, came in together from the main land. Mr. Lee was appointed November 10th last, with instructions to assure the laborers that they would be paid a reasonable sum for their services, not yet fixed. They were contented with the assurance, and a quantity of blankets and clothing captured of the rebels was issued to them without charge. About December 1st, an order was given that carpenters should be paid $8 per month, and other laborers $5 per month. Women and children were fed without charge, the women obtaining washing and receiving the pay, in some cases in considerable sums, not, however, heretofore, very available, as there was no clothing for women for sale here. It will be seen that, under the order, laborers, particularly those with families, have been paid with sufficient liberality. There were 63 laborers on the pay-roll paid to them for the preceding month. On January 1st, there were for the preceding month 127 on the pay-roll, entitled to $468.59. On February 1st, there were for the preceding month 137 on the pay-roll, entitled to something more than for the month of January; making in all due them not far from $1000. This delay of payment, due, it is stated, to a deficiency of small currency, has made the laborers uneasy, and affected the disposition to work. On January 18th, a formal order was issued by General Sherman, regulating the rate of wages, varying from $12 to $8 per month for mechanics, and from $8 to $4 for other laborers. Under it, each laborer is to have, in addition, a ration of food. But from the monthly pay are to be deducted rations for his family, if here, and clothing both for himself and family. Commodious barracks have been erected for these people, and a guard protects their quarters. I have been greatly impressed by the kindness and good sense of Mr. Lee and his assistant, in their discipline of these people. The lash, let us give thanks, is banished at last. No coarse words or profanity are used toward them. There has been less than a case of discipline a week, and the delinquent, if a male, is sometimes made to stand on a barrel, or, if a woman, is put in a dark room, and such discipline has proved successful. The only exception, if any, is in the case of one woman, and the difficulty there was conjugal jealousy, she protesting that she was compelled by her master, against her will, to live with the man. There is scarcely any profanity among them, more than one-half of the adults being members of churches. Their meetings are held twice or three times on Sundays, also on the evenings of Tuesday, Thursday and Friday. They are conducted with fervent devotion by themselves alone or in presence of a white clergyman, when the services of one are procurable. They close with what is called "a glory shout," one joining hands with another, together in couples singing a verse and beating time with the foot. A fastidious religionist might object to this exercise; but being in accordance with usage, and innocent enough in itself, it is not open to exception. As an evidence of the effects of the new system inspiring self-reliance, it should be noted that the other evening they called a meeting of their own accord, and voted, the motion being regularly made and put, that it was now but just that they should provide the candles for their meetings, hitherto provided by the Government. A collection was taken at a subsequent meeting, and $2.48 was the result. The incident may be trivial, but it justifies a pleasing inference. No school, it is to be regretted, has yet been started, except one on Sundays, but the call for reading books is daily made by the laborers. The suggestion of Mr. Lee, in which I most heartily concur, should not be omitted—that with the commencement of the work on the plantations, the laborers should be distributed upon them, having regard to the family relations and the places whence they come. Of the number and condition of the laborers at Beaufort, less accurate information was attainable, and fewer statistics than could be desired. They have not, till within a few days, had a General Superintendent, but have been under the charge of persons detailed for the purpose from the army. I saw one whose manner and language toward them was, to say the least, not elevating.

A new Quartermaster of the post has recently commenced his duties, and a better order of things is expected. He has appointed as Superintendent Mr. Wm. Harding, a citizen of Daufuskie Island. An enrollment has commenced, but is not yet finished. There are supposed to be about six hundred at Beaufort. The number has been larger, but some have already returned to the plantations in our possession from which they came. At this point, the Rev. Solomon Peck, of Roxbury, Mass., has done great good in preaching to them and protecting them from the depredations of white men. He has established a school for the children, in which are sixty pupils, ranging in age from six to fifteen years. They are rapidly learning their letters and simple reading. The teachers are of the same race with the taught, of ages respectively of twenty, thirty, and fifty years. The name of one is John Milton. A visit to the school leaves a remarkable impression. One sees there those of pure African blood, and others ranging through the lighter shades, and among them brunettes of the fairest features. I taught several of the children their letters for an hour or two, and during the recess heard the three teachers, at their own request, recite their spelling-lessons of words of one syllable, and read two chapters of Matthew. It seemed to be a morning well spent. Nor have the efforts of Dr. Peek been confined to this point. He has preached at Cat, Cane and Ladies' Island, anticipating all other white clergymen, and on Sunday, February 2d, at the Baptist Church on St. Helena, to a large congregation, where his ministrations have been attended with excellent effects. On my visits to St. Helena, I found that no white clergyman had been there since our military occupation began, that the laborers were waiting for one, and there was a demoralization at some points which timely words might arrest. I may be permitted to state, that it was at my own suggestion that he made the appointment on this island. I cannot forbear to give a moment's testimony to the nobility of character displayed by this venerable man. Of mild and genial temperament, equally earnest and sensible, enjoying the fruits of culture, and yet not dissuaded by them from the humblest toil, having reached an age when most others would have declined the duty, and left it to be discharged by younger men; of narrow means, and yet in the main defraying his own expenses, this man of apostolic faith and life, to whose labors both hemispheres bear witness, left his home to guide and comfort this poor and shepherdless flock; and to him belongs, and ever will belong, the distinguished honor of being the first minister of Christ to enter the field which our arms had opened.

The Rev. Mansfield French, whose mission was authenticated and approved by the Government, prompted by benevolent purposes of his own, and in conference with others in the city of New York, has been here two weeks, during which time he has been industriously occupied in examining the state of the islands and their population, in conferring with the authorities, and laying the foundation of beneficent appliances with reference to their moral, educational, and material wants. These, having received the sanction of officers in command, he now returns to commend to the public, and the Government will derive important information from his report. Beside other things, he proposes, with the approval of the authorities here, to secure authority to introduce women of suitable experience and ability, who shall give industrial instruction to those of their own sex among these people, and who, visiting from dwelling to dwelling, shall strive to improve their household life, and give such counsels as women can best communicate to women.

All civilizing influences like these should be welcomed here, and it cannot be doubted that many noble hearts among the women of the land will volunteer for the service. There are some material wants of this territory requiring immediate attention. The means of subsistence have been pretty well preserved on the plantations on St. Helena; so also on that part of Ladies' adjacent to St. Helena. But on Port Royal Island, and that part of Ladies' near to it, destitution has commenced, and will, unless provision is made, become very great. Large amounts of corn for forage, in quantities from fifty to four or five hundred bushels from a plantation, have been taken to Beaufort. On scarcely any within this district is there enough to last beyond April, whereas it is needed till August. On others, it will last only two or three weeks, and on some it is entirely exhausted. It is stated that the forage was taken because no adequate supply was at hand, and requisitions for it were not seasonably answered. The further taking of the corn in this way has now been forbidden; but the Government must be prepared to meet the exigency which it has itself created. It should be remembered that this is not a grain-exporting region, corn being produced in moderate crops only for consumption. Similar destitution will take place on other islands, from the same cause, unless provision is made. The horses, mules and oxen, in large numbers, have been taken to Beaufort and Hilton Head as means of transportation. It is presumed that they, or most of them, are no longer needed for that purpose, and that they will be returned to those who shall have charge of the plantations.

Cattle to the number of a hundred, and in some cases less, have been taken from a plantation and slaughtered, to furnish fresh beef for the army. Often cattle have been killed by irresponsible foraging parties, acting without competent authority. There can be no doubt that the army and navy have been in great want of the variation of the rations of salt beef or pork; but it also deserves much consideration, if the plantations are to be permanently worked, how much of a draught they can sustain. The garden seeds have been pretty well used up, and I inclose a desirable list furnished me by a gentleman whose experience enables him to designate those adapted to the soil, and useful too for army supplies. The general cultivation of the islands also requires the sending of a quantity of ploughs and hoes. It did not seem a part of my duty to look specially after matters which had been safely entrusted to others; but it is pleasing, from such observation as was casually made, to testify that Lieutenant-Colonel William H. Reynolds, who was charged with the preservation of the cotton and other confiscated property, notwithstanding many difficulties in his way, has fulfilled his duties with singular fidelity and success. Since the writing of this report was commenced, some action has been taken which will largely increase the numbers of persons thrown on the protection of the Government. Today, February 10th, the 47th Regiment of New York Volunteers has been ordered to take military occupation of North Edisto Island, which is stated to have had formerly a population of 5000 or 6000, and a large number of plantations, a movement which involves great additional responsibility. Agents for the collection of cotton are to accompany it. Herewith is communicated a copy of an order by General Sherman, dated February 6th, 1862, relative to the disposition of the plantations and of their occupants. It is an evidence of the deep interest which the Commanding General takes in this subject, and of his conviction that the exigency requires prompt and immediate action from the Government. I leave for Washington, to add any oral explanations which may be desired, expecting to return at once, and, with the permission of the Department, to organize the laborers on some one plantation, and superintend them during the planting season, and upon its close, business engagements require that I should be relieved of this appointment.

I am, with great respect, Your friend and servant,

Edward L. Pierce

The Committee on Teachers and on Finance would call the attention of the friends of the Commission to the importance of additional subscription to its funds. There are at Port Royal and other places, many thousands of colored persons, lately slaves, who are now under the protection of the U.S. Government. They are a well-disposed people, ready to work, and eager to learn. With a moderate amount of well-directed, systematic labor, they would very soon be able to raise crops more than sufficient for their own support. But they need aid and guidance in their first steps towards the condition of self-supporting, independent laborers. It is the object of the Commission to give them this aid, by sending out, as agents, intelligent and benevolent persons, who shall instruct and care for them. These agents are called teachers, but their teaching will by no means be confined to intellectual instruction. It will include all the more important and fundamental lessons of civilization, voluntary industry, self-reliance, frugality, forethought, honesty and truthfulness, cleanliness and order. With these will be combined intellectual, moral and religious instruction. The plan is approved by the U.S. Government, and Mr. Edward L. Pierce, the Special Agent of the Treasury Department, is authorized to accept the services of the agents of this Commission, and to provide for them transportation, quarters and subsistence. Their salaries are paid by the Commission. More than one hundred and fifty applications have been received by the Committee on Teachers, and thirty-five able and efficient persons have been selected. Twenty-nine of these sailed for Port Royal in the Atlantic, on the 3d instant. Three were already actively employed at that place, and the others are to follow by the next steamer. Some of these are volunteers, who gratuitously devote their time and labor to this cause. Others receive a monthly salary from the Commission. The funds in the treasury, derived from voluntary and almost unsolicited contributions, are sufficient to support those now in service for two or three months. But the Commission is as yet only on the threshold of its undertaking. It is stated by Mr. Pierce that at least one hundred and fifty teachers could be advantageously employed in the vicinity of Port Royal alone.

Source: Boston: R. F. Wallcut, 1862.

31. The Emancipation Proclamation, 1863

President Abraham Lincoln issued the Emancipation Proclamation on January 1, 1863, as the nation approached its third year of bloody civil war. The proclamation declared "that all persons held as slaves" within the rebellious states "are, and henceforward shall be free."

Despite this expansive wording, the Emancipation Proclamation was limited in many ways. It applied only to states that had seceded from the Union, leaving slavery untouched in the loyal border states. It also expressly exempted parts of the Confederacy that had already come under Northern control. Most important, the freedom it promised depended upon Union military victory.

Although the Emancipation Proclamation did not immediately free a single slave, it fundamentally transformed the character of the war. After January 1, 1863, every advance of federal troops expanded the domain of freedom. Moreover, the Proclamation announced the acceptance of black men into the Union Army and Navy, enabling the liberated to become liberators. By the end of the war, almost 200,000 black soldiers and sailors had fought for the Union and freedom.

Whereas on the 22d day of September in the year of our Lord 1862 a Proclamation was issued by the President of the United States containing among other things the following to wit:

That on the first day of January in the year of our Lord 1863 all persons held as slaves within any State, or designated parts of States, the people whereof shall then be in rebellion against the United States, shall be then thenceforth and forever free, and the Executive Government of the United States, including the military and naval authority thereof, will recognize and maintain the freedom of such persons, and will do no act or acts to repress such persons, or any of them in any effort they may make for their actual freedom.

That the Executive will on the first day of January, aforesaid by proclamation, designate the States and parts of States, if any in which the people therein respectively shall then be in rebellion against the United States, and the fact that any

State or the people thereof shall on that day be in good faith represented in Congress of the United States by members, chosen thereto at elections wherein a majority of the qualified voters of such State shall have participated, shall in the absence of strong countervailing testimony be deemed conclusive evidence, that such State and the people thereof are not then in rebellion against the United States.

Now Therefore, I ABRAHAM LINCOLN, President of the United States, by virtue of the power in me invested as commander in chief of the army and navy in time of actual armed rebellion against the authority and government of the *United States,* and as a fit and necessary war measure for suppressing said rebellion, do on this first day of January, in the year of our Lord one thousand eight hundred and sixty three, and in accordance with my purpose so to do publicly proclaimed for the full period of one hundred days from the day of the first above mentioned order, and designate as the States and parts of States, wherein the people thereof respectively are this day in rebellion against the *United States* the following to wit, Arkansas, Texas, Louisiana, except the parishes of St. Bernard, Plaquemines, Jefferson, St. John, St. Charles, St. James, Ascension, Assumption, Terre Bonne, Lafourche, St. Mary, St. Martin and Orleans including the City of New Orleans, *Mississippi, Alabama, Florida, Georgia, South Carolina, North Carolina,* and Virginia, as *West Virginia* and also the counties of Berkeley, Accomac, Northampton, Elizabeth City, York, Princess, Ann and Norfolk, including the cities of Norfolk and Portsmouth, and which excepted parts are for the present left precisely as if this proclamation were not issued. And by virtue of the power, and for the purpose afore said, I do order and declare, that all persons held as slaves, within said designated States and parts of States, are and henceforward shall be free, and that the executive Government of the *United States,* including the military and naval authorities thereof, will recognize and maintain the freedom of said persons. And I hereby enjoin upon the people so declared to be free, to abstain from all violence unless in necessary self-defense, and I recommend to them that in all cases when allowed, they labor faithfully for reasonable wages. And I further declare and make known, that such persons of suitable condition will be received into the armed service of the *United States* to garrison forts, positions, stations, and other places, and to man vessels of all sorts in said service. And upon this sincerely believed to be an act of justice warranted by the *Constitution* upon military necessity. I invoke the considerate judgment of mankind, and the gracious favor of *Almighty God.*

In Witness whereof, I have hereunto set my hand, and caused the Seal of the United States to be affixed. Done at the City of Washington, this first day of January in the year of our Lord, one thousand eight hundred and sixty three, and of the independence of the *United States* of America the eighty-seventh.

By President Abraham Lincoln
William H. Seward, Secretary of State
Source: U.S. National Archives & Records Administration.

32. William Tell Barnitz to the *Pennsylvania Daily Telegraph,* March 27, 1863

Patriot William Tell Barnitz praises the Union and the defeat of the Copperheads. He presents a perspective of the Civil War that includes a prediction of the inevitable defeat of the Confederacy and the presence of contraband slaves within the

Union camps. He commends the ex-slaves for their interest in education and expresses his support for African American troops.

NEWBERN, N.C. March 27, 1863

Like the tocsin peal of victory the news of the resurrection of Northern patriotism broke upon us a few days ago; and oh! the enthusiasm that burst out in every camp! Every face beamed with gladness, every heart was lightened of its depairing burden. No victory however great and splendid, even to the taking of Richmond, could have occasioned such universal joy and mutual good feeling among the patriotic soldiers. Here and there, to be sure, some sneaking leech, who foisted himself upon the Government, in order to have the opportunity of breeding discontent among the men, the effect of which would redound to the disadvantage of the Government, or, as in a multitude of cases, to insure a living, which the party at home could no longer vouchsafe, would skulk along with hang-dog look and sullen mien, discovering his vicious heart and traitorous feeling; but, generally, there was joy—open, beaming joy—and from ten thousand hearts went up a thankful prayer for the awaking of the patriots so long dormant, or who had been regarding our life struggles with a morbid indifference, though they saw the fabric of our Union shaking on its foundation and almost ready to totter to ruins. Since Beauregard's proclamation, exhorting his hosts to call all Union men Abolitionists, his allies in the North, seeing that thus they could deceive the masses and array them against the Government, spreading discontent and sowing disaffection broadcast, took up the cry, and every true patriot—every one who favored the vigorous prosecution of the war, the confiscation of rebel property, or the subjugation of the rebels, the only possible means of crushing the rebellion—was trumpeted forth as an Abolitionist and execrated as an enemy of liberty. Indeed so utterly blinded were many of their followers—so utterly and hellishly belied, betrayed and deceived—that they would have seen our armies annihilated, and rejoiced, and would have thrown themselves in the way for that arch-traitor, Jeff Davis, to ride over in his triumphal entry to our Capital. But, thank God, the film has fallen from their eyes in good time, the bubble of treachery and deceit has burst, and clearer, brighter skies glow around us; and was it not wonderful that men of substance, self-deluded, tarried so long upon the mine that threatened every day to explode and engulf them and their all in an abyss so deep that all the energies of posterity for ten centuries could not resurrect them! We do not realize the terrors and calamities that anarchy spreads when a nation falls under her rule; neither can we appreciate the struggles and difficulties attendant upon the organization of new institutions, else these hell hounds who have been plotting the destruction of our temple of liberty, cemented by the blood of our fathers and reared at so great a cost of life and agony, would now be hanging on every tree, objects for the execration and loathing of patriots all over the civilized world.

Let the fires of liberty, rekindled, be kept steadily burning; let that patriotic association, the *Union League*, be established in every city, town and township throughout the North, gathering together men of every name and party, where sentiments fresh from the fountains of truth and loyalty may be interchanged, and where, like Marius, true men may pledge themselves upon the altars to freedom, and swear to live or die for their country. Then may the traitor demons plot, and howl, and lie, and hiss, as they see their hopes of agrarianism, dissolution and anarchy scattered to the winds; the army of the Union increased, inspirited, jubilant will march on from victory to victory, crush the last stronghold of rebellion and show to the world that a republic has with in itself a self-sustaining power—that princes were not born to rule, and nations only to obey.

Last night our pickets were again driven in; our brave boys dashed off after the rebs, but in asmuch as we have heard no firing, we presume they have vamosed as usual.

There are about 8,000 contrabands here, working on the railroad, cutting wood, and raising a regiment of volunteers. Philanthropists from the North have opened schools for the instruction of the youth, and the avidity and ease with which they study and learn, is truly surprising; how their eyes glitter with every new discovery, with what satisfaction they enter the school room, how attentive, as if they feared something beautiful would escape their notice; it humbles one to see the efforts these youth put forth to attain knowledge, and it is a grand omen for the amelioration of the race. As soldiers they evince the same traits, attentive, active, quick to learn, ambitious, and, above all, courageous; and I will guarantee when put in the field, they will surprise even the cowardly copperheads, whose superiors they are, in everything constituting manliness, worthiness and honor! The Union is safe! The rebellion will be crushed in six months, and these unchained people, fierce under the stings of recent goads, will dash down before the nabobs, who have kept them in eternal bondage, ignorance and degredation, for their own gratification, to administer to their own selfish wants. What a fearful retribution will be visited upon these traitors, who, like satan, dissatisfied with prosperity, with a government the most benignant ever known, with civil immunities and privileges, unknown to other nations, and with an enslaved race to produce the necessaries of life, to jump at their bidding, to fan them while they slept, and tremble when they woke—who thus favored, thus pampered, attempted at one fell blow to dash down their government, and establish one exclusive as China, proscriptive as Spain, with nigger heads and hearts for foundation, pillar, and dome.

Our regiment, the 158th, is in high, good spirits and health, though deploring the abscence of our gallant Colonel D. B. M'Kibbin, who on the night of our search for the rebs, near White Oak river, while riding through the forest, broke the fibula of his right ankle, his horse having gotten his foot into a port hole and fallen upon him.

Adieu.

WM. Tell Barnitz

Source: The Valley of the Shadow: Two Communities in the American Civil War, Virginia Center for Digital History, University of Virginia (http:valley.vcdh.virginia.edu).

33. Sojourner Truth, The Libyan Sibyl, April 1863
HARRIET BEECHER STOWE

During slavery, one of the names that emerged and was much talked about by readers of abolitionist newspapers was Sojourner Truth. She was frequently asked to speak before abolitionist groups that were formed and met throughout the country during slavery. At one such meeting, author Harriet Beecher Stowe met the woman Sojourner Truth, many of whom called Sibyl. This is Stowe's account of her encounter with Sojourner Truth.

Many years ago, the few readers of radical Abolitionist papers must often have seen the singular name of Sojourner Truth, announced as a frequent speaker at Anti-Slavery meetings, and as travelling on a sort of self-appointed agency through the country. I had myself often remarked the name, but never met the individual. On one occasion, when our house was filled with company, several eminent clergymen being our guests, notice was brought up to me that Sojourner Truth was below, and requested an interview.

Knowing nothing of her but her singular name, I went down, prepared to make the interview short, as the pressure of many other engagements demanded.

When I went into the room, a tall, spare form arose to meet me. She was evidently a full-blooded African, and though now aged and worn with many hardships, still gave the impression of a physical development which in early youth must have been as fine a specimen of the torrid zone as Cumberworth's celebrated statuette of the Negro Woman at the Fountain. Indeed, she so strongly reminded me of that figure, that, when I recall the events of her life, as she narrated them to me, I imagine her as a living, breathing impersonation of that work of art.

I do not recollect ever to have been conversant with any one who had more of that silent and subtle power which we call personal presence than this woman. In the modern Spiritualistic phraseology, she would be described as having a strong sphere. Her tall form, as she rose up before me, is still vivid to my mind. She was dressed in some stout, grayish stuff, neat and clean, though dusty from travel. On her head, she wore a bright Madras handkerchief, arranged as a turban, after the manner of her race. She seemed perfectly self-possessed and at her ease,—in fact, there was almost an unconscious superiority, not unmixed with a solemn twinkle of humor, in the odd, composed manner in which she looked down on me. Her whole air had at times a gloom sort of drollery which impressed one strangely.

"So this is YOU," she said.

"Yes," I answered.

"Well, honey, de Lord bless ye! I jes' thought I'd like to come an' have a look at ye. You's heerd o' me, I reckon?" she added.

"Yes, I think I have. You go about lecturing, do you not?"

"Yes, honey, that's what I do. The Lord has made me a sign unto this nation, an' I go round a'testifyin', an' showin' on 'em their sins agin my people."

So saying, she took a seat, and, stooping over and crossing her arms on her knees, she looked down on the floor, and appeared to fall into a sort of reverie. Her great gloomy eyes and her dark face seemed to work with some undercurrent of feeling; she sighed deeply, and occasionally broke out,—

"O Lord! O Lord! Oh, the tears, an' the groans, an' the moans! O Lord!"

I should have said that she was accompanied by a little grandson of ten years,—the fattest, jolliest woolly-headed little specimen of Africa that one can imagine. He was grinning and showing his glistening white teeth in a state of perpetual merriment, and at this moment broke out into an audible giggle, which disturbed the reverie into which his relative was falling.

She looked at him with an indulgent sadness, and then at me.

"Laws, Ma'am, HE don't know nothin' about it—HE don't. Why, I've seen them poor critters, beat an' 'bused an' hunted, brought in all torn,—ears hangin' all in rags, where the dogs been a'bitin'of 'em!"

This set off our little African Puck into another giggle, in which he seemed perfectly convulsed.

She surveyed him soberly, without the slightest irritation.

"Well, you may bless the Lord you CAN laugh; but I tell you, 't wa'n't no laughin' matter."

By this time I thought her manner so original that it might be worth while to call down my friends; and she seemed perfectly well pleased with the idea. An audience was what she wanted,—it mattered not whether high or low, learned or ignorant. She had things to say, and was ready to say them at all times, and to any one.

I called down Dr. Beecher, Professor Allen, and two or three other clergymen, who, together with my husband and family, made a roomful. No princess could have received a drawing-room with more composed dignity than Sojourner her audience. She stood among them, calm and erect, as one of her own native palm-trees waving alone in the desert. I presented one after another to her, and at last said,—

"Sojourner, this is Dr. Beecher. He is a very celebrated preacher."

"IS he?" she said, offering her hand in a condescending manner, and looking down on his white head. "Ye dear lamb, I'm glad to see ye! De Lord bless ye! I loves preachers. I'm a kind o' preacher myself."

"You are?" said Dr. Beecher. "Do you preach from the Bible?"

"No, honey, can't preach from de Bible,—can't read a letter."

"Why, Sojourner, what do you preach from, then?"

Her answer was given with a solemn power of voice, peculiar to herself, that hushed every one in the room.

"When I preaches, I has jest one text to preach from, an' I always preaches from this one. MY text is, 'WHEN I FOUND JESUS.'"

"Well, you couldn't have a better one," said one of the ministers.

She paid no attention to him, but stood and seemed swelling with her own thoughts, and then began this narration:—

"Well, now, I'll jest have to go back, an' tell ye all about it. Ye see, we was all brought over from Africa, father an' mother an' I, an' a lot more of us; an' we was sold up an' down, an' hither an' yon; an' I can 'member, when I was a little thing, not bigger than this 'ere," pointing to her grandson, "how my ole mammy would sit out o' doors in the evenin', an' look up at the stars an' groan. She'd groan an' groan, an' says I to her,—'"Mammy, what makes you groan so?'

"an' she'd say,—

"'Matter enough, chile! I'm groanin' to think o' my poor children: they don't know where I be, an' I don't know where they be; they looks up at the stars, an' I looks up at the stars, but I can't tell where they be.

"'Now,' she said, 'chile, when you're grown up, you may be sold away from your mother an' all your ole friends, an' have great troubles come on ye; an' when you has these troubles come on ye, ye jes' go to God, an' He'll help ye.'

"An' says I to her,—

"'Who is God, anyhow, mammy?'

"An' says she,—

"'Why, chile, you jes' look up DAR! It's Him that made all DEM!'

"Well, I didn't mind much 'bout God in them days. I grew up pretty lively an' strong, an' could row a boat, or ride a horse, or work round, an' do 'most anything.

"At last I got sold away to a real hard massa an' missis. Oh, I tell you, they WAS hard! 'Peared like I couldn't please 'em, nohow. An' then I thought o' what my old mammy told me about God; an' I thought I'd got into trouble, sure enough, an' I wanted to find God, an' I heerd some one tell a story about a man that met God on a threshin'-floor, an' I thought, 'Well an' good, I'll have a threshin'-floor, too.' So I went down in the lot, an' I threshed down a place real hard, an' I used to go down there every day, an' pray an' cry with all my might, a-prayin' to the Lord to make my massa an' missis better, but it didn't seem to do no good; an' so says I, one day,—

"'O God, I been a-askin' ye, an' askin' ye, an' askin' ye, for all this long time, to make my massa an' missis better, an' you don't do it, an' what CAN be the reason? Why, maybe you CAN'T. Well, I shouldn't wonder ef you couldn't. Well, now, I tell you, I'll make a bargain with you. Ef you'll help me to git away from my massa an' missis, I'll agree to be good; but ef you don't help me, I really don't think I can be. Now,' says I, 'I want to git away; but the trouble's jest here: ef I try to git away in the night, I can't see; an' ef I try to git away in the daytime, they'll see me, an' be after me.'

"Then the Lord said to me, 'Git up two or three hours afore daylight, an' start off.'

"An' says I, 'Thank 'ee, Lord! That's a good thought.'

"So up I got, about three o'clock in the mornin', an' I started an' travelled pretty fast, till, when the sun rose, I was clear away from our place an' our folks, an' out o' sight. An' then I begun to think I didn't know nothin' where to go. So I kneeled down, and says I,—

"'Well, Lord, you've started me out, an' now please to show me where to go.'

"Then the Lord made a house appear to me, an' He said to me that I was to walk on till I saw that house, an' then go in an' ask the people to take me. An' I travelled all day, an' didn't come to the house till late at night; but when I saw it, sure enough, I went in, an' I told the folks that the Lord sent me; an' they was Quakers, an' real kind they was to me. They jes' took me in, an' did for me as kind as ef I'd been one of 'em; an' after they'd giv me supper, they took me into a room where there was a great, tall, white bed; an' they told me to sleep there. Well, honey, I was kind o' skeered when they left me alone with that great white bed; 'cause I never had been in a bed in my life. It never came into my mind they could mean me to sleep in it. An' so I jes' camped down under it, on the floor, an' then I slep' pretty well. In the mornin', when they came in, they asked me ef I hadn't been asleep; an' I said, 'Yes, I never slep' better.' An' they said, 'Why, you haven't been in the bed!' An' says I, 'Laws, you didn't think o' such a thing as my sleepin' in dat 'ar' BED, did you? I never heerd o' such a thing in my life.'

"Well, ye see, honey, I stayed an' lived with 'em. An' now jes' look here: instead o' keepin' my promise an' bein' good, as I told the Lord I would, jest as soon as everything got a'goin' easy, I FORGOT ALL ABOUT GOD.

"Pretty well don't need no help; an' I gin up prayin'.' I lived there two or three years, an' then the slaves in New York were all set free, an' ole massa came to our home to make a visit, an' he asked me ef I didn't want to go back an' see the folks on the ole place. An' I told him I did. So he said, ef I'd jes' git into the wagon with him, he'd carry me over. Well, jest as I was goin' out to git into the wagon, I MET GOD! an' says I, 'O God, I didn't know as you was so great!' An' I turned right round an' come into the house, an' set down in my room; for 't was God all around me. I could feel it burnin', burnin', burnin' all around me, an' goin' through me; an' I saw I was so wicked, it seemed as ef it would burn me up. An' I said, 'O somebody, somebody, stand between God an' me! for it burns me!' Then, honey, when I said so, I felt as it were somethin' like an amberill [umbrella] that came between me an' the light, an' I felt it was SOMEBODY,—somebody that stood between me an' God; an' it felt cool, like a shade; an' says I, 'Who's this that stands between me an' God? Is it old Cato?' He was a pious old preacher; but then I seemed to see Cato in the light, an' he was all polluted an' vile, like me; an' I said, 'Is it old Sally?' an' then I saw her, an' she seemed jes' so. An' then says I, 'WHO is this?' An' then, honey, for a while it was like the sun shinin' in a pail o' water, when it moves up an' down; for I begun to feel 't was somebody that loved me; an' I tried to know him. An' I said, 'I know you! I know you! I know you!'—an' then I said, 'I don't know you! I don't know you! I don't know you!' An' when I said, 'I know you, I know you,' the light came; an' when I said, 'I don't know you, I don't know you,' it went, jes' like the sun in a pail o' water. An' finally somethin' spoke out in me an' said, 'THIS IS JESUS!' An' I spoke out with all my might, an' says I, 'THIS IS JESUS! Glory be to God!' An' then the whole world grew bright, an' the trees they waved an' waved in glory, an' every little bit o' stone on the ground shone like glass; an' I shouted an' said, 'Praise, praise, praise to the Lord!' An' I begun to feel such a love in my soul as I never felt before,—love to all creatures. An' then, all of sudden, it stopped, an' I said, 'Dar's de white folks, that have abused you an' beat you an' abused your people,—think o' them!' But then there came another rush of love through my soul, an' I cried out loud,—'Lord, Lord, I can love EVEN DE WHITE FOLKS!'

"Honey, I jes' walked round an' round in a dream. Jesus loved me! I knowed it,—I felt it. Jesus was my Jesus. Jesus would love me always. I didn't dare tell nobody; 't was a great secret. Everything had been got away from me that I ever had; an' I thought that ef I let white folks know about this, maybe they'd get HIM away,—so I said, 'I'll keep this close. I won't let any one know.'"

"But, Sojourner, had you never been told about Jesus Christ?"

"No, honey. I hadn't heerd no preachin',—been to no meetin'. Nobody hadn't told me. I'd kind o' heerd of Jesus, but thought he was like Gineral Lafayette, or some o' them. But one night there was a Methodist meetin' somewhere in our parts, an' I went; an' they got up an' begun for to tell der 'speriences; an' de fust one begun to speak. I started, 'cause he told about Jesus. 'Why,' says I to myself, 'dat man's found him, too!' An' another got up an' spoke, an I said, 'He's found him, too!' An' finally I said, 'Why, they all know him!' I was so happy! An' then they sung this hymn": (Here Sojourner sang, in a strange, cracked voice, but evidently with all her soul and might, mispronouncing the English, but seeming to derive as much elevation and comfort from bad English as from good):—

'There is a holy city,
A world of light above,
Above the stairs and regions,
Built by the God of Love.

"An Everlasting temple,
And saints arrayed in white

There serve their great Redeemer
And dwell with him in light.

"The meanest child of glory
Outshines the radiant sun;
But who can speak the splendor
Of Jesus on his throne?

"Is this the man of sorrows
Who stood at Pilate's bar,
Condemned by haughty Herod
And by his men of war?

"He seems a mighty conqueror,
Who spoiled the powers below,
And ransomed many captives
From everlasting woe.

"The hosts of saints around him
Proclaim his work of grace,
The patriarchs and prophets,
And all the godly race,

"Who speak of fiery trials
And tortures on their way;
They came from tribulation
To everlasting day.

"And what shall be my journey,
How long I'll stay below,
Or what shall be my trials,
Are not for me to know.

"In every day of trouble
I'll raise my thoughts on high,
I'll think of that bright temple
And crowns above the sky."

Source: The Atlantic Monthly, Vol. XI: 473–481, April, 1863. Courtesy of The University of Virginia Library.

34. The Negro in the Regular Army
OSWALD GARRISON VILLARD

When the Fifty-fourth Massachusetts Regiment stormed Fort Wagner on July 18, 1863, it established for all time the fact that the colored soldier would fight and fight well. This had already been demonstrated in Louisiana by colored regiments under the command of General Godfrey Weitzel in the attack upon Port Hudson on May 27 of the same year.

On that occasion regiments composed for the greater part of raw recruits—plantation hands with centuries of servitude under the lash behind them—stormed trenches and dashed upon cold steel in the hands of their former masters and oppressors. After that there was no more talk in the portion of the country of the "natural cowardice" of the negro. But the heroic qualities of regiment Colonel Robert Gould Shaw, his social prominence and that of his officers, and the comparative nearness of their battlefield to the North, attracted greater and more lasting attention to the daring and bravery of their exploit, until it finally became fixed in many minds as the first real baptism of fire of colored American soldiers.

After Wagner the recruiting of colored regiments, originally opposed by both North and South, went on apace, particularly under the Federal government, which organized no less than one hundred and fifty-four, designated as "United States Colored Troops." Colonel Shaw's raising of a colored regiment aroused quite as much comment in the North because of the race prejudice it defied, as because of the novelty of the new organization. General Weitzel tendered his resignation the instant General B. F. Butler assigned black soldiers to his brigade, and was with difficulty induced to serve on. His change of mind was a wise one, and not only because these colored soldiers covered him with glory at Port Hudson. It was his good fortune to be the central figure in one of the dramatic incidents of a war that must ever rank among the most thrilling and tragic the world has seen. The black cavalrymen who rode into Richmond, the first of the Northern troops to enter the Southern capital, went in waving their sabres and crying to the negroes on the sidewalks, "We have come to set you free!" They were from the division of Godfrey Weitzel, and American history has no more stirring moment.

In the South, notwithstanding the raising in 1861 of a colored Confederate regiment by Governor Moore of Louisiana (a magnificent body of educated colored men which afterwards became the First Louisiana National Guards of General Weitzel's brigade and the first colored regiment in the Federal Army), the feeling against negro troops was insurmountable until the last days of the struggle. Then no straw could be overlooked. When, in December, 1863, Major-General Patrick R. Cleburne, who commanded a division of Hardee's Corps of the Confederate Army of the Tennessee, sent in a paper in which the employment of the slaves as soldiers of the South was vigorously advocated, Jefferson Davis indorsed it with the statement, "I deem it inexpedient at this time to give publicity to this paper, and request that it be suppressed." General Cleburne urged that "freedom within a reasonable time" be granted to every slave remaining true to the Confederacy, and was moved to this action by the valor of the Fifty-fourth Massachusetts, saying, "If they [the negroes] can be made to face and fight bravely against their former masters, how much more probable is it that with the allurement of a higher reward, and led by those masters, they would submit to discipline and face dangers?"

With the ending of the civil war the regular army of the United States was reorganized upon a peace footing by an act of Congress dated July 28, 1866. In just recognition of the bravery of the colored volunteers six regiments, the Ninth and Tenth Cavalry and the Thirty-eighth, Thirty-ninth, Fortieth, and Forth-first Infantry, were designated as colored regiments. When the army was again reduced in 1869, the Thirty-eighth and Forty-first became the Twenty-fourth Infantry, and the

Thirty-ninth and Fortieth became the Twenty-fifth. This left four colored regiments in the regular army as it was constituted from 1870 until 1901. There has never been a colored artillery organization in the regular service.

Source: *The Atlantic Monthly* 91: 721–729, 1903.

35. Our alma mater: Notes on an address delivered at Concert Hall on the occasion of the Twelfth Annual Commencement of the Institute for Colored Youth, May 10th, 1864
ALUMNI ASSOCIATION

Octavius V. Catto, alumnus of the Institute for Colored Youth, delivered an address to 1864 graduates of the Institute in Philadelphia that focused on the training of teachers to educate and provide inspiration for the new-freed slaves from the southern United States.

On Wednesday and Thursday last occurred the Twelfth Annual Commencement exercises of the Institute for Colored Youth. The former student of these days was occupied with the public examination of classes at the Institute Buildings, 716 and 718 Lombard Street. Among the audience we noticed Rt. Rev. Alonzo Potter, Rev. Dr. William Mann, and other eminent persons. The rooms were crowded throughout the entire day. Classes were examined in Greek, Latin, Mathematics, and the higher English studies, and they generally acquitted themselves creditably. Rev. Dr. Mann created considerable interest in the Greek classes by closely questioning them, and by reciting an ode of Anacreon. These classes were led over the Greek Testament, extracts from Homer, Lucian, and Anacreon. The Latin classes showed familiarity with the Latin of Virgil, Cicero, Sallust, and Horace. The Greek and Latin scanning and parsing were well spoken of by competent judges. The classes in mathematics generally did well. The English analysis and mental arithmetic were excellent; so was the spherical trigonometry. The "Bible Lesson" was superb.

Much interest was manifested in the distribution of prizes. A fund, yielding about one hundred dollars annually, was some years ago, given to the corporation from an unknown source for this purpose. Mr. M. C. Cope, Secretary of the Corporation, distributed the prizes as follows: To Thomas H. Boling and Harriet C. Johnson, each $15, for excellence in mathematics; to John Wesley Cromwell and Mary V. Brown, each $15, for superiority in Greek and Latin; to James L. Smallwood and Elizabeth Handy, each $10, the prize for diligence and good conduct and to Theophilus J. Minton and Margaret A. Masten, each $5, an honorary prize.

On Thursday morning the anniversary of the Alumni Association was held in Sansom Street Hall, which was comfortably filled. Mr. B. H. Brewster and other prominent citizens were present. The first address, delivered by John H. Smith, a graduate of the Institute, was on a "Model Statesman." It was very intelligently discussed and well received.

An obituary notice of Mary E. Ayers, written by M. F. Minton, was read next by Caroline R. Le Count, all alumni of the Institute. The composition itself was very creditable, and the reading of it excellent. Then came a political address on the "Aspect of the Times," by John Q. Allen, also a graduate of the Institute. The eloquent young gentleman handled the subject well, and was frequently interrupted by applause.

The Alumni Oration was delivered by E. D. Bassett, the principal of the Institute. His subject was the "Elements of Permanent Governments and Societies," which was discussed at some length, in an able manner. For nearly one hour and a half the undivided attention of the audience was given to this argumentative, humorous, and philosophic oration.

The orator said that neither form, territory, population, commerce, wealth, physical well-being, military nor intellectual greatness, either separately or collectively, was sufficient to constitute permanent governments.

He brought prominently before the audience examples from history, classic and modern, to establish his position: that while all the aforesaid characteristics of well-ordered society were essential, yet there must be added virtue, liberty, and a high moral and religious development.

In the evening occurred the rhetorical and elocutionary exercises of the undergraduates. At an early hour Concert hall was crowded to its utmost capacity. About one-third of the audience were respectable white fellow-citizens. On the platform sat the managers, teachers, alumni, and a portion of the pupils. The orations and essays were, as a whole, highly commendable. One of the young ladies read an essay on John Bright, which was greatly applauded. A little fellow, of about fourteen summers, bearing the suggestive name of Toussaint L'Ouverture Martin, kindled a flame of excitement and applause by reciting a poem of his own composing. There were other meritorious productions, but the interest of the evening centred in an address by Mr. O. V. Catto, who graduated at the Institute in 1858. The scope of the address was to give a history of the Institution, which he did very ably and satisfactorily, indeed.

From this address, it appeared that the Institution was incorporated by the Legislature of Pennsylvania in 1842. The members of the Corporation are exclusively members of the Society of Friends. The object aimed at is to afford gratuitously to colored youth, of both sexes, a good High School education, that they may be qualified to act as teachers among their own people, or in other useful capacities. Thirty-six have pursued the full course of study. These are, generally, in useful callings. The average daily attendance at the Institution is about 100. The teachers, six in number, are all colored. The amount of the fund is now $80,000 and upwards, which has been entirely given by members of the Society of friends, one of whom gave $13,000, another $10,000, &c. The detail of facts was very ingeniously woven together, and the address itself possessed more than ordinary literary merit.

At the conclusion of the exercises the principal, Mr. E. D. Bassett, presented the diploma to the successful candidates, as follows: James M. Baxter, Jr., Thomas H. Boling, John Wesley Cromwell, James L. Smallwood, Mary V. Brown, Elizabeth Handy, Harriet C. Johnson, Margaret A. Masten, and M. Gertrude Offit.

Philadelphia, May 20, 1864.

Mr. Octavius V. Catto.

Sir: The Association of Alumni of the Institute for Colored Youth, regarding the address delivered by you on the occasion of the Twelfth Annual Commencement of the Institute as a document which, not less on account of its literary merits than for the information it contains, is entitled to wide-spread circulation, have instructed the undersigned to request a copy for publication.

Very respectfully, yours,

Jacob C. White,

C. A Jennings

Philadelphia, May 22, 1864

Miss C.A. Jennings

The address to which your polite note refers, was not written with a view to publication; but with the hope, that in a printed form, one, at least, of the interest of our Alma Mater may be promoted, a copy is placed at your disposal.

Accept assurances of my deep interest in the Association you so wisely cherish, and believe me,

Yours, truly,

Octavius V. Catto.

Source: Philadelphia: C. Sherman, Son & Co., printers, 1864. Library of Congress, Rare Book and Special Collections Division, Daniel A. P. Murray Pamphlets Collection.

36. Excerpt reprinted from "A Colored Man's Reminiscences of James Madison"

Paul Jennings was employed by the U.S. Department of the Interior in 1865. Born a slave on the estate of President James Madison in Montpelier, Virginia, in 1799, his father was thought to have been Benjamin Jennings, an English trader in Montpelier; his mother, a slave of Madison's and the granddaughter of a native American from the same region. The younger Jennings was a "body servant" of Madison's. When Madison died, Jennings was owned by Daniel Webster. On January 10, 1865, it was recorded in a book found in the possession of another black man among some books, coins and autographs belonging to Edward M. Thomas, another black man who had been a messenger in the House of Representatives in Washington. It contained an autograph of Daniel Webster with these words: "I have paid $120 for the freedom of Paul Jennings; he agrees to work out the same at $8 per month, to be furnished with board, clothes, washing...."

When Mr. Madison was chosen President, we came ... and moved into the White House; the east room was not finished, and Pennsylvania Avenue was not paved, but was always in an awful condition from either mud or dust. The city was a dreary place.

Mr. Robert Smith was then Secretary of State, but as he and Mr. Madison could not agree, he was removed, and Colonel Monroe appointed to his place. Dr. Eustis was Secretary of War—rather a rough, blustering man; Mr. Gallatin, a tip-top man, was Secretary of the Treasury; and Mr. Hamilton, of South Carolina, a pleasant gentleman, who thought Mr. Madison could do nothing wrong, and who always concurred in every thing he said, was Secretary of the Navy.

Before the war of 1812 was declared, there were frequent consultations at the White House as to the expediency of doing it. Colonel Monroe was always fierce for it, so were Messrs. Lowndes, Giles, Poydrass, and Pope—all Southerners; all his Secretaries were likewise in favor of it.

Soon after war was declared, Mr. Madison made his regular summer visit to his farm in Virginia. We had not been there long before an express reached us one evening, informing Mr. M. of Gen. Hull's surrender. He was astounded at the news, and started back to Washington the next morning.

After the war had been going on for a couple of years, the people of Washington began to be alarmed for the safety of the city, as the British held Chesapeake Bay with a powerful fleet and army. Every thing seemed to be left to General Armstrong, then Secretary of war, who ridiculed the idea that there was any danger. But, in August, 1814, the enemy had got so near, there could be no doubt of their intentions. Great alarm existed, and some feeble preparations for defense were made. Com. Barney's flotilla was stripped of men, who were placed in battery, at Bladensburg, where they fought splendidly. A large part of his men were tall, strapping negroes, mixed with white sailors and marines. Mr. Madison reviewed them just before the fight, and asked Com. Barney if his "negroes would not run on the approach of the British?" "No sir," said Barney, "they don't know how to run; they will die by their guns first." They fought till a large part of them were killed or wounded; and Barney himself wounded and taken prisoner. One or two of these negroes are still living here.

Well, on the 24th of August, sure enough, the British reached Bladensburg, and the fight began between 11 and 12. Even that very morning General Armstrong assured Mrs. Madison there was no danger. The President, with General Armstrong, General Winder, Colonel Monroe, Richard Rush, Mr. Graham, Tench Ringgold, and Mr. Duvall, rode out on horseback to Bladensburg to see how things looked. Mrs. Madison ordered dinner to be ready at 3, as usual; I set the table myself, and brought up the ale, cider, and wine, and placed them in the coolers, as all the Cabinet and several military gentlemen and strangers were expected. While waiting, at just about 3, as Sukey, the house-servant was lolling out of a chamber window, James Smith, a free colored man who had accompanied Mr. Madison to Bladensburg, gallopped up to the house, waving his hat, and cried out, "Clear out, clear out! General Armstrong has ordered a retreat!" All then was confusion. Mrs. Madison ordered her carriage, and passing through the dining-room, caught up what silver she could crowd into her old-fashioned reticule, and then jumped into the chariot with her servant girl Sukey, and Daniel Carroll, who took charge of them; Jo. Bolin drove them over to Georgetown Heights; the British were expected in a few minutes. Mr. Cutts, her brother- in-law, sent me to a stable on 14th street, for his carriage. People were running in every direction. John Freeman (the colored butler) drove off in the coachee with his wife, child, and servant; also a feather bed lashed on behind the coachee, which was all the furniture saved, except part of the silver and the portrait of Washington (of which I will tell you by-and-by).

I will here mention that although the British were expected every minute, they did not arrive for some hours; in the mean time, a rabble, taking advantage of the confusion, ran all over the White House, and stole lots of silver and whatever they could lay their hands on.

About sundown I walked over to the Georgetown ferry, and found the President and all hands (the gentlemen named before, who acted as a sort of body-guard for him) waiting for the boat. It soon returned, and we all crossed over, and passed up the road about a mile; they then left us servants to wander about. In a short time several wagons from Bladensburg, drawn by Barney's artillery horses, passed up the road, having crossed the Long Bridge before it was set on fire. As we were cutting up some planks a white wagoner ordered us away, and told his boy Tommy to reach out his gun, and he would shoot us. I told him "he had better have used it at Bladensburg." Just then we came up with Mr. Madison and his friends, who had been wandering about for some hours, consulting what to do. I walked on to a Methodist minister's, and in the evening, while he was at prayer, I heard a tremendous explosion, and, rushing out, saw that the public buildings, navy yard, and ropewalks were on fire.

Mrs. Madison slept that night at Mrs. Love's, two or three miles over the river. After leaving that place she called in at a house, and went up stairs. The lady of the house learning who she was, became furious, and went to the stairs and screamed out, "Miss Madison! if that's you, come down and go out! Your husband has got mine out fighting, and d_ you, you shan't stay in my house; so get out!" Mrs. Madison complied, and went to Mrs. Minor's, a few miles further, where she stayed a day or two, and then returned to Washington, where she found Mr. Madison at her brother-in-law's, Richard Cutts, on F street. All the facts about Mrs. M. I learned from her servant Sukey. We moved into the house of Colonel John B. Taylor [Tayloe], corner of 18th street and New York Avenue, where we lived till the news of peace arrived.

In two or three weeks after we returned, Congress met in extra session, at Blodgett's old shell of a house on 7th street (where the General Post-office now stands). It was three stories high, and had been used for a theatre, a tavern, and an Irish boarding house, but both Houses of Congress managed to get along in it very well, notwithstanding it had to accommodate the Patent-office, City and General Post-office, committee-rooms, and what was left of the Congressional Library, at the same time. Things are very different now.

The next summer, Mr. John Law, a large property-holder about the Capitol, fearing it would not be rebuilt, got up a subscription and built a large brick building (now called the Old Capitol, where the secesh prisoners are confined), and offered it to Congress for their use, till the Capitol could be rebuilt. This coaxed them back, though strong efforts were made to remove the seat of government north; but the southern members kept it here.

It has often been stated in print, that when Mrs. Madison escaped from the White House, she cut out from the frame the large portrait of Washington (now in one of the parlors there), and carried it off. This is totally false. She had no time for doing it. It would have required a ladder to get it down. All she carried off was the silver in her reticule, as the British were thought to be but a few squares off, and were expected every moment. John Suse [Jean-Pierre Sioussat] (a Frenchman, then door-keeper, and still living) and Magraw, the President's gardener, took it down and sent it off on a wagon, with some large silver urns and such other valuables as could be hastily got hold of. When the British did arrive, they ate up the very dinner, and drank the wines, &c., that I had prepared for the President's party.

When the news of peace arrived, we were crazy with joy. Miss Sally Coles, a cousin of Mrs. Madison, and afterwards wife of Andrew Stevenson, since minister to England, came to the head of the stairs, crying out, "Peace! peace!" and told John Freeman (the butler) to serve out wine liberally to the servants and others. I played the President's March on the violin, John Suse and some others were drunk for two days, and such another joyful time was never seen in Washington. Mr. Madison and all his Cabinet were as pleased as any, but did not show their joy in this manner.

After he retired from the presidency, he amused himself chiefly on his farm. At the election for members of the Virginia Legislature, in 1829 or '30, just after General Jackson's accession, he voted for James Barbour, who had been a strong Adams man. He also presided, I think, over the Convention for amending the Constitution, in 1832.

After the news of peace, and of General Jackson's victory at New Orleans, which reached here about the same time, there were great illuminations. We moved into the Seven Buildings, corner of 19th street and Pennsylvania Avenue, and while there, General Jackson came on with his wife, to whom numerous dinner-parties and levees were given. Mr. Madison also held levees every Wednesday evening, at which wine, punch, coffee, and ice-cream were liberally served, unlike the present custom.

While Mr. Jefferson was President, he and Mr. Madison (then his Secretary of State) were extremely intimate; in fact, two brothers could not have been more so. Mr. Jefferson always stopped over night at Mr. Madison's, in going and returning from Washington.

I have heard Mr. Madison say, that when he went to school, he cut his own wood for exercise. He often did it also when at his farm in Virginia. He was very neat, but never extravagant, in his clothes. He always dressed wholly in black—coat, breeches, and silk stockings, with buckles in his shoes and breeches. He never had but one suit at a time. He had some poor relatives that he had to help, and wished to set them an example of economy in the matter of dress. He was very fond of horses, and an excellent judge of them, and no jockey ever cheated him. He never had less than seven horses in his Washington stables while President.

He often told the story, that one day riding home from court with old Tom Barbour (father of Governor Barbour), they met a colored man, who took off his hat. Mr. M. raised his, to the surprise of old Tom; to whom Mr. M. replied, "I never allow a negro to excel me in politeness." Though a similar story is told of General Washington, I have often heard this, as above, from Mr. Madison's own lips.

Source: This excerpt is reprinted from "A Colored Man's Reminiscences of James Madison," *White House History* (Collection Set 1), 2004, p. 51–55. *White House History* is a semi-annual journal published by the White House Historical Association, www.whitehousehistory.org.

37. What the Black Man Wants: a speech delivered by Frederick Douglass at the Annual Meeting of the Massachusetts Anti-Slavery Society in Boston, April 1865

In the spring of 1865, abolitionist Frederick Douglass attended an annual meeting of the Massachusetts Anti-Slavery society in Boston. He arrived as an observer and listener, he said, hoping to avoid confrontations over the differing opinions over slavery and a fear that his words would be misconstrued, or would disturb the proceedings of these meetings. Therefore, his appearance was a rare one.

[In staying away, I] have thus been deprived of that educating influence, which I am always free to confess is of the highest order, descending from this platform. I have felt, since I have lived out West [of Boston, in Rochester, NY], that in going there I parted from a great deal that was valuable; and I feel, every time I come to these meetings, that I have lost a great deal by making my home west of Boston, west of Massachusetts; for, if anywhere in the country there is to be found the highest sense of justice, or the truest demands for my race, I look for it in the East, I look for it here. The ablest discussions of the whole question of our rights occur here, and to be deprived of the privilege of listening to those discussions is a great deprivation.

I do not know, from what has been said, that there is any difference of opinion as to the duty of abolitionists, at the present moment. How can we get up any difference at this point, or any point, where we are so united, so agreed? I went especially, however, with that word of Mr. Phillips, which is the criticism of Gen. Banks and Gen. Banks' policy. Gen. Banks instituted a labor policy in Louisiana that was discriminatory of blacks, claiming that it was to help prepare them to better handle freedom. Wendell Phillips countered by saying, "If there is anything patent in the whole history of our thirty years' struggle, it is that the Negro no more needs to be prepared for liberty than the white man." I hold that that policy is our chief danger at the present moment; that it practically enslaves the Negro, and makes the Proclamation [the Emancipation Proclamation] of 1863 a mockery and delusion. What is freedom? It is the right to choose one's own employment. Certainly it means that, if it means anything; and when any individual or combination of individuals undertakes to decide for any man when he shall work, where he shall work, at what he shall work, and for what he shall work, he or they practically reduce him to slavery. [Applause.] He is a slave. That I understand Gen. Banks to do—to determine for the so-called freedman, when, and where, and at what, and for how much he shall work, when he shall be punished, and by whom punished. It is absolute slavery. It defeats the beneficent intention of the Government, if it has beneficent intentions, in regards to the freedom of our people.

I have had but one idea for the last three years to present to the American people, and the phraseology in which I clothe it is the old abolition phraseology. I am for the "immediate, unconditional, and universal" enfranchisement of the black man, in every State in the Union.

[Loud applause.]

Without this, his liberty is a mockery; without this, you might as well almost retain the old name of slavery for his condition; for in fact, if he is not the slave of the individual master, he is the slave of society, and holds his liberty as a privilege, not as a right. He is at the mercy of the mob, and has no means of protecting himself.

It may be objected, however, that this pressing of the Negro's right to suffrage is premature. Let us have slavery abolished, it may be said, let us have labor organized, and then, in the natural course of events, the right of suffrage will be extended to the Negro. I do not agree with this. The constitution of the human mind is such, that if it once disregards the conviction forced upon it by a revelation of truth, it requires the exercise of a higher power to produce the same conviction afterwards. The American people are now in tears. The Shenandoah has run blood—the best blood of the North. All around Richmond, the blood of New England and of the North has been shed—of your sons, your brothers and your fathers. We all feel, in the existence of this Rebellion, that judgments terrible, wide-spread, far-reaching, overwhelming, are abroad in the land; and we feel, in view of these judgments, just now, a disposition to learn righteousness. This is the hour. Our streets are in mourning, tears are falling at every fireside, and under the chastisement of this Rebellion we have almost come up to the point of conceding this great, this all-important right of suffrage. I fear that if we fail to do it now, if abolitionists fail to press it now, we may not see, for centuries to come, the same disposition that exists at this moment.

[Applause.]

Hence, I say, now is the time to press this right.

It may be asked, "Why do you want it? Some men have got along very well without it. Women have not this right." Shall we justify one wrong by another? This is the sufficient answer. Shall we at this moment justify the deprivation of the Negro of the right to vote, because some one else is deprived of that privilege? I hold that women, as well as men, have the right to vote ... [applause] ... and my heart and voice go with the movement to extend suffrage to woman; but that question rests upon another basis than which our right rests. We may be asked, I say, why we want it. I will tell you why we want it. We want it because it is our right, first of all. No class of men can, without insulting their own nature, be content with any deprivation of their rights. We want it again, as a means for educating our race. Men are so constituted that they derive their conviction of their own possibilities largely by the estimate formed of them by others. If nothing is expected of a people, that people will find it difficult to contradict that expectation. By depriving us of suffrage, you affirm our incapacity to form an intelligent judgment respecting public men and public measures; you declare before the world that we are unfit to exercise the elective franchise, and by this means lead us to undervalue ourselves, to put a low estimate upon ourselves, and to feel that we have no possibilities like other men. Again, I want the elective franchise, for one, as a colored man, because ours is a peculiar government, based upon a peculiar idea, and that idea is universal suffrage. If I were in a monarchial government, or an autocratic or aristocratic government, where the few bore rule and the many were subject, there would be no special stigma resting upon me, because I did not exercise the elective franchise. It would do me no great violence. Mingling with the mass I should partake of the strength of the mass; I should be supported by the mass, and I should have the same incentives to endeavor with the mass of my fellow-men; it would be no particular burden, no particular deprivation; but here where universal suffrage is the rule, where that is the fundamental idea of the Government, to rule us out is to make us an exception, to brand us with the stigma of inferiority, and to invite to our heads the missiles of those about us; therefore, I want the franchise for the black man.

There are, however, other reasons, not derived from any consideration merely of our rights, but arising out of the conditions of the South, and of the country—considerations which have already been referred to by Mr. Phillips—considerations which must arrest the attention of statesmen. I believe that when the tall heads of this Rebellion shall have been swept down, as they will be swept down, when the Davises and Toombses and Stephenses, and others who are leading this Rebellion shall have been blotted out, there will be this rank undergrowth of treason, to which reference has been made, growing up there, and interfering with, and thwarting the quiet operation of the Federal Government in those states. You will se those traitors, handing down, from sire to son, the same malignant spirit which they have manifested and which they are now exhibiting, with malicious hearts, broad blades, and bloody hands in the field, against our sons and brothers. That spirit will still remain; and whoever sees the Federal Government extended over those Southern States will see that Government in a strange land, and not only in a strange land, but in an enemy's land. A post-master of the United States in the South will find himself surrounded by a hostile spirit; a collector in a Southern port will find himself surrounded by a hostile spirit; a United States marshall or United States judge will be surrounded there by a hostile element. That enmity will not die out in a year, will not die out in an age. The Federal Government will be looked upon in those States precisely as the Governments of Austria and France are looked upon in Italy at the present moment. They will endeavor to circumvent, they will endeavor to destroy, the peaceful operation of this Government. Now, where will you find the strength to counterbalance this spirit, if you do not find it in the Negroes of the South? They are your friends, and have always been your friends. They were your friends even when the Government did not regard them as such. They comprehended the genius of this war before you did. It is a significant fact, it is a marvellous fact, it seems almost to imply a direct interposition of Providence, that this war, which began in the interest of slavery on both sides, bids fair to end in the interest of liberty on both sides.

[Applause.]

It was begun, I say, in the interest of slavery on both sides. The South was fighting to take slavery out of the Union, and the North was fighting to keep it in the Union; the South fighting to get it beyond the limits of the United States Constitution, and the North fighting to retain it within those limits; the South fighting for new guarantees, and the North fighting for the old guarantees;—both despising the Negro, both insulting the Negro. Yet, the Negro, apparently endowed with wisdom from on high, saw more clearly the end from the beginning than we did. When Seward said the status of no man in the country would be changed by the war, the Negro did not believe him. [Applause.] When our generals sent their underlings in shoulder-straps to hunt the flying Negro back from our lines into the jaws of slavery, from which he had escaped, the Negroes thought that a mistake had been made, and that the intentions of the Government had not been rightly understood by our officers in shoulder-straps, and they continued to come into our lines, threading their way through bogs and fens, over briers and thorns, fording streams, swimming rivers, bringing us tidings as to the safe path to march, and pointing out the dangers that threatened us. They are our only friends in the South, and we should be true to them in this their trial hour, and see to it that they have the elective franchise.

I know that we are inferior to you in some things—virtually inferior. We walk about you like dwarfs among giants. Our heads are scarcely seen above the great sea of humanity. The Germans are superior to us; the Irish are superior to us; the Yankees are superior to us [Laughter]; they can do what we cannot, that is, what we have not hitherto been allowed to do. But while I make this admission, I utterly deny, that we are originally, or naturally, or practically, or in any way, or in any important sense, inferior to anybody on this globe.

[Loud applause.]

This charge of inferiority is an old dodge. It has been made available for oppression on many occasions. It is only about six centuries since the blue-eyed and fair-haired Anglo-Saxons were considered inferior by the haughty Normans, who once trampled upon them. If you read the history of the Norman Conquest, you will find that this proud Anglo-Saxon was once looked upon as of coarser clay than his Norman master, and might be found in the highways and byways of Old England laboring with a brass collar on his neck, and the name of his master marked upon it. You were down then!

[Laughter and applause.]

You are up now. I am glad you are up, and I want you to be glad to help us up also.

[Applause.]

The story of our inferiority is an old dodge, as I have said; for wherever men oppress their fellows, wherever they enslave them, they will endeavor to find the needed apology for such enslavement and oppression in the character of the people oppressed and enslaved. When we wanted, a few years ago, a slice of Mexico, it was hinted that the Mexicans were an inferior race, that the old Castilian blood had become so weak that it would scarcely run down hill, and that Mexico needed the long, strong and beneficent arm of the Anglo-Saxon care extended over it. We said that it was necessary to its salvation, and a part of the "manifest destiny" of this Republic, to extend our arm over that dilapidated government. So, too, when Russia wanted to take possession of a part of the Ottoman Empire, the Turks were an "inferior race." So, too, when England wants to set the heel of her power more firmly in the quivering heart of old Ireland, the Celts are an "inferior race." So, too, the Negro, when he is to be robbed of any right which is justly his, is an "inferior man." It is said that we are ignorant; I admit it. But if we know enough to be hung, we know enough to vote. If the Negro knows enough to pay taxes to support the government, he knows enough to vote; taxation and representation should go together. If he knows enough to shoulder a musket and fight for the flag, fight for the government, he knows enough to vote. If he knows as much when he is sober as an Irishman knows when drunk, he knows enough to vote, on good American principles. [Laughter and applause.]

But I was saying that you needed a counterpoise in the persons of the slaves to the enmity that would exist at the South after the Rebellion is put down. I hold that the American people are bound, not only in self-defense, to extend this right to the freedmen of the South, but they are bound by their love of country, and by all their regard for the future safety of those Southern States, to do this—to do it as a measure essential to the preservation of peace there. But I will not dwell upon this. I put it to the American sense of honor. The honor of a nation is an important thing. It is said in the Scriptures, "What doth it profit a man if he gain the whole world, and lose his own soul?" It may be said, also, What doth it profit a nation if it gain the whole world, but lose its honor? I hold that the American government has taken upon itself a solemn obligation of honor, to see that this war—let it be long or short, let it cost much or let it cost little—that this war shall not cease until every freedman at the South has the right to vote. [Applause.] It has bound itself to it. What have you asked the black men of the South, the black men of the whole country to do? Why, you have asked them to incure the enmity of their masters, in order to befriend you and to befriend this Government. You have asked us to call down, not only upon ourselves, but upon our children's children, the deadly hate of the entire Southern people. You have called upon us to turn our backs upon our masters, to abandon their cause and espouse yours; to turn against the South and in favor of the North; to shoot down the Confederacy and uphold the flag—the American flag. You have called upon us to expose ourselves to all the subtle machinations of their malignity for all time. And now, what do you propose to do when you come to make peace? To reward your enemies, and trample in the dust your friends? Do you intend to sacrifice the very men who have come to the rescue of your banner in the South, and incurred the lasting displeasure of their masters thereby? Do you intend to sacrifice them and reward your enemies? Do you mean to give your enemies the right to vote, and take it away from your friends? Is that wise policy? Is that honorable? Could American honor withstand such a blow? I do not believe you will do it. I think you will see to it that we have the right to vote. There is something too mean in looking upon the Negro, when you are in trouble, as a citizen, and when you are free from trouble, as an alien. When this nation was in trouble, in its early struggles, it looked upon the Negro as a citizen. In 1776 he was a citizen. At the time of the formation of the Consitution the Negro had the right to vote in eleven States out of the old thirteen. In your trouble you have made us citizens. In 1812 Gen. Jackson addressed us as citizens—"fellow-citizens." He wanted us to fight. We were citizens then! And now, when you come to frame a conscription bill, the Negro is a citizen again. He has been a citizen just three times in the history of this government, and it has always been in time of trouble. In time of trouble we are citizens. Shall we be citizens in war, and aliens in peace? Would that be just?

I ask my friends who are apologizing for not insisting upon this right, where can the black man look, in this country, for the assertion of his right, if he may not look to the Massachusetts Anti-Slavery Society? Where under the whole heavens can he look for sympathy, in asserting this right, if he may not look to this platform? Have you lifted us up to a certain height to see that we are men, and then are any disposed to leave us there, without seeing that we are put in possession of all our rights? We look naturally to this platform for the assertion of all our rights, and for this one especially. I understand the anti-slavery societies of this country to be based on two principles,—first, the freedom of the blacks of this country; and, second, the elevation of them. Let me not be misunderstood here. I am not asking for sympathy at the hands of abolitionists, sympathy at the hands of any. I think the American people are disposed often to be generous rather than just. I look over this country at the present time, and I see Educational Societies, Sanitary Commissions, Freedmen's Associations, and the like,—all very good: but in regard to the colored people there is always more that is benevolent, I perceive, than just, manifested towards us. What I ask for the Negro is not benevolence, not pity, not sympathy, but simply justice.

[Applause.]

The American people have always been anxious to know what they shall do with us. Gen. Banks was distressed with solicitude as to what he should do with the Negro. Everybody has asked the question, and they learned to ask it early of the abolitionists, "What shall we do with the Negro?" I have had but one answer from the beginning. Do nothing with us! Your doing with us has already played the mischief with us. Do nothing with us! If the apples will not remain on the tree of their own strength, if they are wormeaten at the core, if they are early ripe and disposed to fall, let them fall! I am not for tying or fastening them on the tree in any way, except by nature's plan, and if they will not stay there, let them fall. And if the Negro cannot stand on his own legs, let him fall also. All I ask is, give him a chance to stand on his own legs! Let him alone! If you see him on his way to school, let him alone, don't disturb him! If you see him going to the dinner table at a hotel, let him go! If you see him going to the ballot-box, let him alone, don't disturb him!

[Applause.]

If you see him going into a work-shop, just let him alone,—your interference is doing him a positive injury. Gen. Banks' "preparation" is of a piece with this attempt to prop up the Negro. Let him fall if he cannot stand alone! If the Negro cannot live by the line of eternal justice, so beautifully pictured to you in the illustration used by Mr. Phillips, the fault will not be yours, it will be his who made the Negro, and established that line for his government.

[Applause.]

Let him live or die by that. If you will only untie his hands, and give him a chance, I think he will live. He will work as readily for himself as the white man. A great many delusions have been swept away by this war. One was, that the Negro would not work; he has proved his ability to work. Another was, that the Negro would not fight; that he possessed only the most sheepish attributes of humanity; was a perfect lamb, or an "Uncle Tom;" disposed to take off his coat whenever required, fold his hands, and be whipped by anybody who wanted to whip him. But the war has proved that there is a great deal of human nature in the Negro, and that "he will fight," as Mr. Quincy, our President, said, in earlier days than these, "when there is reasonable probability of his whipping anybody." [Laughter and applause.]

Source: Philip S. Foner, *The Life and Writings of Frederick Douglass, Vol. IV*: p.157–165. International Publishers Co. Inc.: New York, 1950. Permission of International Publishers/New York.

38. 14th Amendment, 1866

The 14th Amendment creates a broad definition of citizenship in the United States. It requires the states to provide equal protection under the laws to all persons (not only to citizens) within their boundaries. The significance of the Fourteenth Amendment was exemplified when the U.S. Supreme Court later interpreted it to prohibit racial segregation in public schools and other facilities in *Brown v. Board of Education*.

Section 1. All persons born or naturalized in the United States, and subject to the jurisdiction thereof, are citizens of the United States and of the State wherein they reside. No State shall make or enforce any law which shall abridge the privileges or immunities of citizens of the United States; nor shall any State deprive any person of life, liberty, or property, without due process of law; nor deny to any person within its jurisdiction the equal protection of the laws.

Section 2. Representatives shall be apportioned among the several States according to their respective numbers, counting the whole number of persons in each State, excluding Indians not taxed. But when the right to vote at any election for the choice of electors for President and Vice President of the United States, Representatives in Congress, the Executive and Judicial officers of a State, or the members of the Legislature thereof, is denied to any of the male inhabitants of such State, being twenty-one years of age, and citizens of the United States, or in any way abridged, except for participation in rebellion, or other crime, the basis of representation therein shall be reduced in the proportion which the number of such male citizens shall bear to the whole number of male citizens twenty-one years of age in such State.

Section 3. No person shall be a Senator or Representative in Congress, or elector of President and Vice President, or hold any office, civil or military, under the United States, or under any State, who, having previously taken an oath, as a member of Congress, or as an officer of the United States, or as a member of any State legislature, or as an executive or judicial officer of any State, to support the Constitution of the United States, shall have engaged in insurrection or rebellion against the same, or given aid or comfort to the enemies thereof. But Congress may by a vote of two-thirds of each House, remove such disability.

Section 4. The validity of the public debt of the United States, authorized by law, including debts incurred for payment of pensions and bounties for services in suppressing insurrection or rebellion, shall not be questioned. But neither the

United States nor any State shall assume or pay any debt or obligation incurred in aid of insurrection or rebellion against the United States, or any claim for the loss or emancipation of any slave; but all such debts, obligations and claims shall be held illegal and void.

Section 5. The Congress shall have power to enforce, by appropriate legislation, the provisions of this article.

Source: Primary Documents in American History, Library of Congress.

39. Letter from Amelia [Unknown family name] to brother Eddie, December 11, 1869

This letter was written during the Reconstruction era by a young school teacher named Amelia, who writes to her brother Eddie, telling him about her African American students in Virginia.

Staunton [Va.] Dec 11. /69

Dear Brother Eddie

I am sorry to know you have been so sick and suffered so much. However I hope you are better now and able to read this letter. Do not wonder if I put in many things wrong as the girls seem to be possessed with a talking mania to-night. We have been so quiet before that it makes more difference with me than I thought possible. I have my scholars all to myself now and like it first rate. I have not whipped any yet and dont think I shall as Amelia has given me permission to send all unruly ones to her to deal with. They are going to have compositions next Wednesday. Some of them have never written any before and I expect they will be funny enough. I will send you in this; a specimen of some poetry one of my young boys tried to write. The other day an Indian visited our school. He was seven feet high and just as straight and erect as could be. He was eighty years old. His hair was white as snow as stood up all over his head. He had a fur cap bag slung across his shoulder. We did not know who he was and felt rather frightened when we saw him walking in. He introduced himself as the father of some of our best scholars. He is a kind of doctor among the colored people. He was formerly a slave from Florida: but travelled with his master nearly all over the Union. He is very entertaining telling hunting stories as well as stories of the war. I wished you could go with me some day to the cabin they live in out by the great fire place filled with blazing logs and hear him tell stories. One of his boys is very smart only nine years old and reading nicely in the fourth reader. I am quite proud of my scholars I can tell you, they are getting on so well. The night school is just as amusing as ever, and I cannot help laughing. The colored people here are going to have an exhibition next week. They have got it all up themselves. They are going to have some tableaux, too. I expect it will be as good as going to the minstrel and better too as that is all sham and this will be the real article. I have picked out three pieces for some of my boys to speak and that is all I have had to do with it. I wrote a letter to Roland to-day and am going to try and write him oftener in the future as I shall have more time now. Mr Cristy wote me a nice long letter the other day telling me all about Albert's conversion. They must be very glad and I hope he will make a true earnest christian. Here is the poetry James Tynell had in his composition. The "title" of the composition was this, where he got it from I am sure I do not know, "Who ought to have the credit Columbus or Washington? Columbus for settling discovering it or Washington for settling it." He took the side of Columbus, I copied the whole thing and will bring it home with me, it is a great curiousity. Here is the poetry I will write it on the top of the first page. Try and get well and write me a nice long letter,

Love to all From
Amelia.

"When floating me the mile deep
Not a tree was to be seen
And when the men all grumble
It would make any mans heart humble

But just think of this great carnage
That was on that long voyage
Who was that great man? C. Columbus
Columbus
Beat that if you can, you [*unclear*]

Source: The Valley of the Shadow: Two Communities in the American Civil War, Virginia Center for Digital History, University of Virginia (http:valley.vcdh.virginia.edu).

40. First Annual Address to the Law Graduates of Allen University, class 1884, given by D. Augustus Straker, June 12, 1884

In this address to law graduates in Columbia, South Carolina, Professor Straker, Dean of the Law Department, inspired his audience with his precise references to their historical past and culture. He advised these new law graduates to maintain character in their professional lives and to rely on ancient rhetorical devices for effective expression in the courtrooms.

Mr. President, Ladies and Gentlemen, and young gentlemen, graduates:

At the closing moments of your departure from the law department of Allen University, your Alma Mater, in which you have pursued and completed a course of legal study, entitling you to the usual degree of Bachelor of Laws, and by subsequent examination before the Supreme Court of the State, admitting you to practice in all the courts of the State, it is my duty to present you with a few words of parting advice. Before doing so, let us take a retrospect upon mutual labors.

In October, 1882, the Law Department of Allen University was opened, I was chosen by the trustees Dean and Law Professor in this department. This meant more than I conceived. It did not have its usual meaning, that is a teacher of some legal branch of knowledge, to which I must devote my attention and give instruction, but it meant, by force of circumstances, I should be required to teach all the legal topics prescribed by the curriculum of the university, which are, in a great degree, identical with those prescribed by the 23d rule of the Supreme Court of our State. I was not wanting in diffidence of my ability to perform so herculean a task in which was involved so grave responsibilities. My duty was to educate in the law, colored youth, of a race declared to be inferior in capacity with all others. If I failed I certified to both your and my incapacity. My responsibility then was, the maintenance of an entire race's fitness and capacity. I consoled myself in the belief that I had a heart and will determined enough to commence the work, putting my trust in God, the Father of us all, and believing that he had made of one blood all nations upon the face of the earth. I concluded that he had made them all of like susceptibilities, to glorify him in the comprehension of his handiwork, and the laws of the same. Thus I began my labors. You young gentlemen entered the law school. You did not enter as those of the Caucasian race usually do, with the prestige of a wealthy parentage, a pocket full of gold, and the equal facilities belonging of right, to a common brotherhood in man. At the threshold of the temple, wherein you were to drink deep and full from the fountain of legal knowledge, running from time immemorial in the streamlets of tradition, custom and usage, until, beginning with the Jewish Theocracy to the Justinian age, the confluence was commenced with the fathers of English Common Law, Coke, Littleton, and Sir William Blackstone, and the mighty stream, began to flow down the course of civilization, purified by Christianity.

You were met by the common inquisitor of social life, so frequent at the door of the commencement of the pursuit of knowledge by every young man and woman. He inquired of you, "are you laden with the passport to this world's honors—money? Have you an ancestry of boasted Anglo-Saxon renown, which for more than ten hundred years have made easy the pathway of eminence and fame to that race of people?" To these questions you replied, "none." But, continuing, you were further asked: "Have you a heart full of the desire for knowledge and wisdom—a soul inspired with the truth of the Fatherhood of God and the brotherhood of man, despite a long suffering and oppression of your race? Do you believe in your equal capacity under equal facilities and opportunities with all other men?" To which you eagerly replied: "Aye, and forever aye." Then in clarion voice you were bade enter and be strong, and in the face of poverty and innumerable obstacles you commenced your labors. In the autumn you beheld the sere and yellow leaf falling and decomposing, and testifying, if not to total annihilation, to decay and change, typifying man's mortality. Yet you did not falter, though in some cases, after more than twelve hours of manual as well as mental labor in the engagement of a livelihood you would appear at your recitations and lectures with faces lined with marks of toil and fatigue; but with a cheerful eye, a determination and a will, gladening the heart of your professor and teaching him and yourself how to learn "to labor and to wait." In the spring time joyous nature clad in floral garb with her hill tops carpeted with green, and her valleys resonant with the music of the rippling brooks, gave new life to your studies which strengthened and made you strong. As the summer, the joyous summer of your life of study advanced and ripened into the fruition of your labors on the 24th day of April, your *alma mater* welcomed her sons to her bounty and conferred upon you your degrees, and on the 27th of May last you entered upon the stage of a lawyer's life, to play your part in the arena of struggle for fame and name and wealth, and I trust, usefulness, by virtue of your diploma and the certificate of your efficiency in examination before the Supreme Court of the State. In this arena of lawyer's life there are several stages. Below is the multitude of pettifoggers struggling for filthy lucre only and degrading the profession of law from the height of its great eminence and glory into the mire of selfishness, lying and trickery. The next stage is where you will find a goodly crowd devoted simply to money-making, and utter strangers to the upbuilding of their fellow man. I bid you tarry not in these paths, but strive for the upper-story in your profession—remembering in the language attributed to Daniel Webster, when asked by a despondent young lawyer how he should rise to greatness in his profession amidst the struggles of the pettifogger below, and the competition just above, replied to him, "young man, there is room enough up stairs."

An experience of not more than ten years as a lawyer myself, gives me but little ability to teach you the ways to great height, but such as I have observed I offer you. First, in order to achieve great eminence in your profession you must fully realize and comprehend the width and the depth and the height of law; you must fully comprehend the extent of the word itself. Not only does law mean a rule of action prescribed by a superior to an inferior which he is bound to obey, as found in constitutions, in statutes and in the ordinances of every civilized government, but it is also co-extensive with every known branch of learning. Ascend the heights of science— it is there; traverse the mutifarious avenues of art—it is there too. Go among the poets and philosophers, converse with the healing art—it is there. Investigate the pyramids of Egypt and translate the hieroglyphics of her sons—it is there. Go down into the bowels of the earth and seek for wealth in minerals, or try to prove that every stratum, as shown in geology, is truly the antitype of its prototype, the history of the creation recorded in the first book of Genesis. Enter the halls of legislatures, construe their statutes at the former and there you will find the consummation drawn from history as of necessity. A lawyer has no bounds to the requisite acquirement of knowledge. Beginning with the true source of human law—human necessity—you must continue to erect a superstructure upon the foundation of wisdom, as found revealed in the Bible. You may then adorn the edifice as it should be with the lights of poetry, science, art, established upon the foundation of morality and religion. The lawyer that barely knows the statutes of his State or country is like unto the man who is placed in charge of a locomotive, but has only a superficial knowledge of its several parts, their names and their purposes. He is never safe when danger or emergency arises. He is all right so long as the engine runs smoothly, but should some contesting force appear he soon finds how ignorant he is of that general knowledge of the machinery, its origin and the laws governing its application. In such a condition he wishes he had engaged in some calling of which he was thoroughly the master. You must not only be equipped in general knowledge, but you must be strong of nerve and full of energy. In courts of justice you will encounter some judges who will in some instances endeavor to hold the scales of justice so high as not to be able to see the object weighed in the balance. In such instances you need nerve. You must never cease argument and proof until you have made him bring down his scales before his eyes, or close them shut against any prejudice towards your client. Be never guilty of contempt of court, nor be wanting in courage to show proper contempt for a contemptuous court, nevertheless be not highminded. Let your humility and good conduct secure the favor of bench and bar.

Be of good character—character is that which we really are. When we labor to gain reputation we are not even taking the first step towards the acquisition of character. In reputation you gain favor by something which pleases your neighbor apart frequently from the virtue of the acts. A wisely trained character never stops to ask what will society think of me if I do this thing or leave it undone. It tests the quality of an action by ascertaining whether it is just when judged by the laws of eternal right. Cultivate the good will of all men—politeness is a branch of good character, and remember that your juries come from the county of which county frequently *you* are. For while I would have you brave and courageous in battle for the right, be not puffed up so as to secure the ill will of men, for it is better to be a "living dog than a dead lion," said the prophet. Have due respect for the patience of juries and remember that they are men having feelings to enjoy pleasure and to suffer pain. Do not let it be ever said of you as it is reported in a late number of the *Central Law Journal* of a young lawyer in his maiden speech. It says "he was florid rhetorical, scattering and windy. For four weary hours he talked at the Court until every body felt like lynching him; when he got through his opponent arose and said "your Honor" I will follow the example of my friend and submit the case without argument." This position frequently arises when the young lawyer disregards plain Saxon in his speech and seeks to illumine his argument with rhetorical flashes, so dazzling as to totally obscure the sight of his point and drive away judgement therefrom. Emulate in your profession, those who as lawyers have handed down to us examples at the forum worthy of emulation. As citizens and sons of South Carolina, you will find among her annals lawyers, judges and jurists who have ennobled the profession by their unparalleled ability. I cite you to o'Neil, McDuffie, Parker, Hunt, and Legare; but it was not only in the field of legal contest that they strove and conquered, but they were in the full sense of the term patriots, an attribute indispensable to the immortal honor and glory of a truly great man. It was more than legal ability which enabled lord Mansfield, in his decision in the celebrated Somerset case brought before him under writ of Habeas Corpus, to try the right of an American master to withdraw his alleged slave from the shores of England to say "that the instant a slave landed in England he became a freeman, as the air of England is too pure for a slave to breathe in." If you would combine that noble virtue, patriotism, with an efficiency in law and thus live for the good you can do, I would point you to a standard the highest achieved in English or American lines aye, the highest the world has ever seen. I point you to an American statesman and lawyer in whose patriotism this continent saw the noblest virtue, the greatest daring for good, the sublimest achievements for love of country and the unparalleled philanthropy of any human age. I point you to Charles Sumner, the American Socrates, Cicero and Demosthenes combined. He whose life as a lawyer was chiefly devoted to the enfranchisement, amelioration and elevation of a race of people oppressed for ages by a cruel bondage.

The basis of all his actions at the forum, in the halls of legislation, on the rostrum, everywhere, was equality, which is true equity, the principles of which you have already listened to this evening from one of your number. He denounced all laws in which the equality of all men was not the primal reason. Never more conspicuously was this virtue seen in Charles Sumner than in his celebrated defense in the United States Senate in 1874 against the unjust annexation of the Black Republic of Havti to the United States. His keen eye and fierce legal acumen quickly saw the political assassin's hand at the throat of the young Republic, and with the eloquence of a Demosthenes, the legal knowledge of a Grotius, Vattel, or Puffendorf he exclaimed. "Foremost among admitted principles of international law is the axiom that all nations are equal without distinction of population, size or power. Nor does international law know any distinction of color. Do unto others as you would have them do unto you, is the plan of law for all nations as for all men."

Thus did he plead for the Black Republic, showing his love and his sympathy, not only for the American negro, but for him and for all men wherever found upon the face of the globe where the strong seek to oppress the weak. He would have done the same for the China-man or the Indian. His law extended to humanity at large, and was found, not in text books, but in the wants of man.

Another good and great lawyer, whose knowledge of law shone forth in principles and not mere abstract theories, was Wendell Phillips. He knew no constitutions, laws, customs, traditions, nor usages which did not recognize the equality of rights for all men. Amidst the persecutions of a cruel slaveocracy which threatened his life, he bore onwards and upwards the banner of freedom for all men, and demanded from the American slave-holder the unconditional surrender of the constitutional and natural right of liberty to the slave. He was but a young lawyer when he commenced battle against slavery and for human rights.

I point you to these men as the noblest and purest embodiment of what the lawyer should be. They have died and are no more with us, but their works and their lives are the brightest example for you. You are the legitimate fruit of the tree planted by them. Then, young gentlemen graduates, "Let all thou aim'st at be thy country, thy God's and truth."

In this struggle you will find conflict, false friends, a want of appreciation of your labors by the prejudiced and narrow-minded, nevertheless continue to battle for the right, and learn "to labor and to wait," a lesson no less a virtue because most willingly taught by those for whom you labor most.

"Lives of great men remind us
We can make our lives sublime,
And departing leave behind us
Footsteps on the sands of time."
"Footprints that perchance another
Sailing o'er life's troubled main,
A forlorn and shipwrecked brother
Seeing, shall take heart again."

You will encounter, as I have, and others of my profession and your profession, among our own race, prejudice, hostility and cold cheer, so that you will often feel like abandoning the law and seeking fields of labor more lucrative and congenial. But remember that money perishes with the life that made it, and fortune changes with the changes of time, but good works, built upon the pedestal of truth, will be more enduring than brass or marble. Prejudice once existed, to a great extent, among the white brethren of your profession, owing, as it is said, chiefly to our ignorance. As we grow by education and in knowledge the legal maxim, *cessante ratione cessat lex* applies. This is my experience among my white brethren in this city and elsewhere I have been. I have only asked for and demanded my privilege and my clients' rights. Industry must form a chief feature—seek. "He who seeks shall find, and to him that knocks the door shall be opened." Now that you are about to commence active practice, let me beseech you to be industrious. Action is the soul of life; sympathy is its lever in action. Is there any citizen in this audience who purposes to chill the energy of these young men by refraining to give them their patronage, because they are afraid that they cannot obtain justice through a colored lawyer, thus aiding the very wrong you complain against? If so, let him stand and show his cowardly face, and then be banished as a traitor to his race. I trust there is none.

"His be the praise who, looking down on scorn, consults his own clear heart, and nobly dares to be, not to be thought, an honest man."

It is the boast of the legal profession that it is equally capable of doing work in the elevation of humanity, with any other known calling. It is woven into the fabric of every civilization. Progress must be your watchword; the universe your field. The doctrines taught in Blackstone and Kent will not fully teach you human nature nor human wants. You must read the works of great authors in order to broaden your ideas and enrich your thoughts. Read Dante for depth of conception; Milton for sublimity of idea; Macaulay for force of expression, Charles Dickens and Shakespeare for knowledge of the inner human nature and the Bible for wisdom and understanding."

> "Not enjoyment, and not sorrow,
> Is our destined end or way—
> Put to act that each to-morrow
> Finds us farther than to-day."

Agitate! Agitate! Agitate is the surest course for securing right and conquering wrong. But I must warn you, if success attend your labors in any department of intellectual life—be not vain of your learning. Learning or knowledge is only excellent when it is useful to others. Let it be said of you, "His learning savors not the school-like gloss that most consists in echoing words and terms, and soonest wins a man an empty name." Be it said of you, too, as a lawyer in your works of humanity, your love of justice, your conduct in struggling for the honor of your *alma mater*.

Whereof you are a well-deserving pillar, remember that of the profession you have chosen the great ecclesiastic Hooker has said: "Her seat is in the bosom of God, her voice the harmony of the world; all things in heaven and earth do her homage—the very least as feeling her care, the greatest as not exempt from her power, both angels and men and creatures of what condition soever, through each in different sort and manner; yet all with uniform consent, admiring her as the mother of their peace and joy." Noble profession! Is it any wonder that of one of the most learned of its votaries, Sir William Blackstone, it is said that in his public line of life he approved himself an able, upright, impartial judge? That he was ever an active and judicious promoter of whatever he thought useful or advantageous to the public in general, or to any particular society or neighborhood he was connected with? That he was a believer in the great truths of Christianity from a thorough investigation of its evidence? Attached to the Church of England from conviction of its excellence, his principles were those of its genuine members—enlarged and tolerant. His religion was pure and unaffected, and his attendance upon its public duties regular, and those always performed with seriousness and devotion. His earliest wish was that he should die:

> "Untainted by the guilty bribe,
> Uncursed amidst the harpy tribe—

No orphan's cry to wound my ear—
My honor and my conscience clear.
Thus may I calmly meet my end,
Thus to the grave in peace descend."

And so did Sir William Blackstone live and die, and so likewise, young gentlemen, may your lives be and terminate; for, remember, young gentlemen, the term of life is short. To spend that shortness basely, 'twere too long. Though life did ride upon a dial's point—still ending at the arrival of an hour. And as you go forth into the world in the pursuit of your profession, I bid you farewell and God speed.

Source: At Bethel A.M.E. Church, Columbia, S.C. Atlanta, Georgia: Jas. P. Harrison & Co., printers and publishers, 1885. Library of Congress, Rare Book and Special Collections Division, Daniel A. P. Murray Pamphlets Collection.

41. Emigration to Liberia, Report of the Standing committee on emigration of the Board of directors of the American colonization society, unanimously adopted, Washington D.C.: January 20, 1885

The American Colonization Society (ACS) movement began sometime in the nineteenth century. From the start, colonization of free blacks in Africa was an issue that divided both whites and blacks. Some blacks supported immigration because they thought that black Americans would never receive justice in the United States. Others believed African Americans should remain in the United States to fight against slavery and for full legal rights as American citizens. Some whites saw colonization as a way of ridding the nation of blacks, while others believed black Americans would be happier in Africa or elsewhere, where they could live free of racial discrimination. Still others believed black American colonists could play a central role in Christianizing and civilizing Africa.

The ACS was formed in 1817 to send free African Americans to Africa as an alternative to emancipation in the United States. In 1822, the society established a colony on the west coast of Africa, and in 1847 it became the independent nation of Liberia. By 1867, the society had sent more than 13,000 immigrants to Liberia.

The society was attacked by abolitionists, who tried to discredit colonization as a slaveholder's scheme. And, after the Civil War, when many blacks wanted to go to Liberia, financial support for colonization had waned. This is a report from the Standing Committee on Emigration of the Board of Directors of the American Colonization Society, unanimously adopted January 20, 1885.

The times are changed! Wondrous events combine to turn the world's thought at this moment to the "Dark Continent." The Congo is drawing to itself the activities of nations as never before since the pyramids were built.

As a spider builds his web, beginning with a single thread here and there, attaching the ends to various objects, so does a power in mankind's history weave the texture of human vicissitude. It is a marvelous chapter in this human story which has been written in America. Slaves torn from home and kindred were forced into this country by cruel European greed. From these slaves, then, the most miserable, have sprung nearly seven millions of the colored race, long held here in bondage, but at the same time brought into contact with Christian civilization, finally emancipated, enfranchised, and beginning to be educated. This is one thread.

About seventy years ago a few philanthropists, with far-seeing vision, organized for the purpose of creating a home on the Western coast of Africa for such of these people as could and would return to the Fatherland. The Republic of Liberia has been the result. There is now a focus of light from which the rays may spread across the whole breadth of that long darkness. This is another thread.

England, the same Power that so long winked at "the middle passage" while the forefathers were dragged across the seas and bound in chains in her colonies here, is to-day hovering on the northwestern borders of the infant nation, having within two years past torn from its grasp a large territory, and, if all signs do not fail, is preparing to repeat the act on the southeast borders. Here is a strip of country ready for occupation, and inviting immigrants to come and possess the virgin soil, with all the richness of its productions. This is another thread.

Social and political equality, however fair in name and theory, is difficult in practice as between races so distinct as African and Caucasian. Twenty years of trial here has been sufficient to convince large numbers of the colored people who at first spurned the idea of going to Africa that their proper home is there, and there the fitting field for working out their destiny. This is another thread. And so the loom of Providence weaves on! Amazing threads they all are, but the pattern is from an Omnipotent hand!

Here stands the old Colonization Society alive to-day, while many thought it dead, and as yet about the only ear to listen at the telephone call and gather up the cry which comes from all parts of the land where these African people dwell; and the cry is louder and more intense and multitudinous month by month. Consider the appeals which roll in upon the Society almost every day in proof of the singular truth. The last month illustrates what has been going on for some time past, but now apparently there more earnestly than ever:

December 1st, 1884, Landsford, S. C., one of them writes: Tell us how to get to Liberia—to Africa; our people are sick and tired of this country, and want to go home; 500 men and women of whom I am the teacher are ready to go at once.

December 8th, 1884, Denison, Texas, another writes: I wrote you about seven years ago, and received a few papers. The mass of our people are poorer than they were eight years ago. We want now to go to Africa. What is the latest news? Can you tell us all about it? What can you do for sending us? How and when can we get there, and what are the conditions? All early answer will confer a favor "on a great crowd of us."

We do not give the exact language, but the substance.

December 12th, 1884, from the same place, another writes: A great many of us are making preparations to go to Liberia, and we want direct information in regard to the whole affair. He asks these questions:

1st. How many families must we collect before we can be sent?

2d. Can we go on shipboard at Galveston?

3d. Do we send any money, and to whom?

The same day, Darlington, S. C., J. P. Brockenton, pastor of Macedonia Baptist Church, of more than 1,000 members, 48 years old, with wife and children, writes, applying for passage to Liberia. From his own accounts he must be an important man. He is President of the South Carolina State Baptist Convention, Moderator of the District Association, Trustee of the free School Board of Darlington County, and Life Director of the Home Mission Society. He wants to go to Africa, he says—

1st. Because I want to continue my good work for the Master.

2d. Because I think my Christian influence is more needed there than here.

3d. Because the harvest in Africa is great, but the laborers are few.

4th. Because my children are trained teachers or mechanics, and as such can assist in building up our Fatherland.

5th. Because my condition as a *man* will be better established and my work as a *minister* better appreciated.

Pretty sound and sensible reasons. He says he is poor, and if the Society can aid him he will he thankful.

December 21st, 1884, Waco, Texas, a correspondent, who is a superintendent, writes:

We have organized a Bureau of Home and Foreign Missions in our Baptist State Convention. (The Baptists appear to be plentiful.) They are collecting money to send two messengers to Liberia to obtain information. He is now making up a colony to leave for Liberia in 1886. It will be from 1,500 to 2,000 strong. If they can get sufficient information from the American Colonization Society they will not send the two messengers. He says we may see what they are doing in the South to get to the Fatherland. He wants all kinds of information about the matter. He says they are raising about $500 per month; that it costs the Society $100 per head to take them out and support them for six months. "I mean business. If we come to you 2,000 strong, can't you make it less than that? Help us all you can, and let me know at once how many can go in one ship at a time."

December 24th, 1884, one writes again from Denison, Texas: There are 62 already in our company. What are your lowest terms? We have 35 farmers, 4 school-teachers, 1 cabinet-maker, 6 ministers, 4 hotel and steamboat cooks, 2 brick-makers, 4 blacksmiths, 4 carpenters, 2 well-diggers, and a good many laborers. Please don't get impatient at our asking questions, for we want to be all right when we get to the ship.

December 27th, 1884, Homer, Louisiana, another writes, saying he seeks a home for a poor black man; he wants to know all about Liberia; he wants to get where he can be free; says he is not free here by a long ways. What will it take to put me and my wife over?

December 31st, 1884, from Darlington, S. C., again from our friend Brockenton, who now signs himself Secretary of the Club. He acknowledges receipt of books, papers, &c. Says he can't be ready to go till October; that a colony will go with him. He gives quite a description of the *personnel* of his colony; says they expect to be organized into a church before sailing. He predicts great good from this company. They are in all 43 persons, with more to be added.

The same day, from Lynchburg, S. C., a bright man writes of the progress the colored people are making there and elsewhere in the South for emigration. He says there is the greatest unrest among them ever known. Large numbers are going to the West, but the best portion are preparing to make their way to Liberia. The Clarendon Club wants information, and he writes at their request. He says they will plant large crops of cotton, so as to raise money in the fall. He is Secretary of the Clarendon and Williamsburg Clubs. He is without means to travel as he wishes, to stimulate the people; and in view of this, wants circulars and documents from us to spread ABROAD.

The same day, from Waco, Texas, another writes that the people of his county wish to send him to Liberia to bring back a report of the land. He wants to know if he can go. He says the condition of his people is deplorable; that he learns that a whole county of them are going to Kansas; that hundreds are coming from North Carolina to Arkansas—out of the pan, into the fire. What do horses and cows cost in Liberia? Could you send over my piano? My house is worth $1,000; I was offered $600 for it. He wants to sell and get away; says himself and wife are at our service if we can make any use of them.

January 1st, 1885, Chambersburg, Pa., a colored woman writes: We are now really preparing to leave this country. She has lost a former letter, and wants to hear again; says there are eight of them ready to go in May. "Will they be crowded out?" "We have been a long time getting ready, but the Spirit says, Go! and we must abide God's will." Several other families wish to go, especially one that comes from Alabama, where times are hard for colored people.

January 3d, 1885, Kansas City, Mo., a prudent man writes: Would I be safe to start for Liberia with $100 and five children? A great many people here would be glad to go, but they have no information. I am a kalsominer by trade. Would I be of any use when I get there?

The same day, from Denison, Texas, a sharp man writes, asking for full information about emigration to Liberia. He and several others wish to go there. He says they "are very well equipped, with wealth and literature enough to get there and straighten up and straighten out. Write soon, and let us know."

January 7th, 1885, Forestville, N. C., another writes that he is making preparation to go to Liberia. He sees so many colored people awaking to the project of going, because of their oppressions in this country. "We want to reach Africa, the home of the free. Is there any chance for me?"

Such is the burden of the cry from all quarters of the land. What does it mean? Our Society has absolutely done nothing to awaken this intense longing for Africa among the colored people. No means have been employed by us to stir up so deep and general a feeling, unless our circulars and documents for the spread of information may have contributed to it; otherwise, not a whisper from us has been heard. The cry is spontaneous. One of the correspondents above cited seems to have expressed the secret—"The Spirit says, Go!" What other conclusion can we reach? God's hand is in it, weaving the web of His Providence for Africa.

But we would not just now encourage a wholesale exodus. The vast preparation must no doubt be gradual, as all great things are. In the ancient exodus *from* Africa the people were held for forty years in the wilderness prior to their possession of the Promised Land. The first emigrants to Liberia were sent by this Society in 1820, and we have not failed to send some each year since. The last company of forty-seven was sent last October—in all nearly 16,000 persons, exclusive of 5,722 recaptured Africans—at the cost of $3,000,000—the munificent gift of American Christian philanthropy. At the present time there are on the soil of Liberia about 25,000 souls, comprising the American immigrants and their children, with the recaptured Africans who have settled there, and one million of the native population, enjoying the advantages of the Republic and amenable to its laws, while remoter tribes are pressing down towards the infant Republic as to a centre of brighter hope. There is a coast-line of 500 miles—extending indefinitely inland. This was recently diminished 40 miles by the arbitrary power of England; and about the same extent is coming into dispute on the southeast. It is believed that Liberia could now absorb and assimilate 10,000 persons, especially immigrants from the mother Republic versed in the customs, manners, and laws of a Republican Christian Government. If this population could be transferred to Liberia in the next two years it would probably settle the boundary question now in dispute, besides being of incalculable advantage in many other ways.

They would hardly be missed among us out of a colored population rapidly multiplying, and which by natural increase has nearly doubled during the last score of years, but immense good might flow through them to Liberia and the whole continent.

That many are waking up to this idea, and are ready to leave this country for the land of their forefathers, is evinced, as we have seen, from the constantly-increasing applications for aid to this end. These come in upon us from all quarters and through all channels—through the correspondence of private individuals, members and officers of churches, clubs, and various organizations, and even through Government Departments and through the Christian agencies of our great commercial cities.

The one fact we would emphasize is this: The only hope of lifting Africa up to continental equality and prominence lies not merely in National diplomacy and the jealousy of States, nor in the greed of misers, nor in the craft of unprincipled traders and sharpers who pour out upon the soil, which their touch pollutes, all the vices and wrongs and refuse of modern civilization, but it is mainly in the Christian colony, which is in some sense a Christian mission among stranger tribes of men. This is the voice of history—certainly of modern history. America was redeemed at last by the Christian pilgrims of Europe, who imbued its growing life with the spirit of Christian civilization, and stamped upon its institutions the impress of morality and of Christian faith. Such a power as this is alone adequate to build another Republic like our own from the Atlantic to the Indian Oceans.

It is a marvelous fact that now, simultaneously with the opening of that Continent, such a general desire among our colored people to go to it should spring up so intensely. What a wonderful thread this is in the stupendous web of Providence! And into our hands the grand mission of opening Africa to the splendid realizations of the future is in a very special sense committed, since we are the only Nation on the face of the earth outside of Africa herself that has the fitting material in our colored population; and all signs point to our duty in this respect. The times are ripe for a powerful onward movement in this direction. The two thrilling reports rendered by the Committee on Emigration—one of a year ago and one of the year preceding—were as a bugle blast, calling mankind to action. No form of words could be more eloquent or piercing than the language of those reports. They state the case to the American people with all the cogency of logic, the fire of poetry, and the pathos almost of inspiration. They have been widely circulated; and this seed, so scattered, may yield—Heaven grant it—a rich and plentiful harvest.

But at the opening of another year in the history of this Society we stand confronted with one great necessity, one specific work, which ought to be immediately taken up and accomplished; this is, to put 10,000 of our choicest colored population into Liberia as soon as it is found to be practicable. It will cost a million dollars!

What are our resources—what our means of doing it? The abundance of our own country, the thousands and millions of money in the hands of prosperous capitalists and churchmen, and the everplethoric Treasury of the Government itself. But how shall we open these mighty coffers? What key can unlock our way to the hoarded treasure? We have tried commissioned agents, but the effort has been practically a failure. What, then, is left us?

1. Personal appeals to well-known rich philanthropists.
2. Concise, comprehensive, pointed, specific appeals through the religious and secular press of the country.
3. The same kind of appeal to the Christian clergy, and through them to the entire membership of the churches.
4. An earnest, temperate, emphatic appeal to Congress and the Government.

They have loaned a million dollars to the New Orleans Exposition. Great as that is or ought to be, is it any more; on the welfare of mankind than it would be for the same sum to secure the future of the daughter Republic, and through her the Christian civilization of the entire Continent? This would indeed be a glorious consummation! Everything calls for it—everything incites to it. A million dollars in two years for the redemption of that vast territory with its hundred and fifty or two hundred millions of people—what a splendid golden thread would this be in the mighty loom of Providence; in this Divine pattern of human destiny; this august design of the Infinite Reason; this lofty work of the hands of the Eternal!

B. SUNDERLAND, CHARLES C. NOTT, JAMES SAUL,

Committee. Washington, D. C., *January 20th,* 1885.

Source: Library of Congress, Rare Book and Special Collections Division, African American Pamphlet Collection.

42. The Future of the Colored Race, May 1886
FREDERICK DOUGLASS

In this essay, abolitionist Frederick Douglass discusses the assimilation of the Africans into the American society.

It is quite impossible, at this early date, to say with any decided emphasis what the future of the colored people will be. Speculations of that kind, thus far, have only reflected the mental bias and education of the many who have essayed to solve the problem.

We all know what the negro has been as a slave. In this relation we have his experience of two hundred and fifty years before us, and can easily know the character and qualities he has developed and exhibited during this long and severe ordeal. In his new relation to his environments, we see him only in the twilight of twenty years of semi-freedom; for he has scarcely been free long enough to outgrow the marks of the lash on his back and the fetters on his limbs. He stands before us, today, physically, a maimed and mutilated man. His mother was lashed to agony before the birth of her babe, and the bitter anguish of the mother is seen in the countenance of her offspring. Slavery has twisted his limbs, shattered his feet, deformed his body and distorted his features. He remains black, but no longer comely. Sleeping on the dirt floor of the slave cabin in infancy, cold on one side and warm on the other, a forced circulation of blood on the one side and chilled and retarded circulation on the other, it has come to pass that he has not the vertical bearing of a perfect man. His lack of symmetry, caused by no fault of his own, creates a resistance to his progress which cannot well be overestimated, and should be taken into account, when measuring his speed in the new race of life upon which he has now entered. As I have often said before, we should not measure the negro from the heights which the white race has attained, but from the depths from which he has come. You will not find Burke, Grattan, Curran and O'Connell among the oppressed and famished poor of the famine-stricken districts of Ireland. Such men come of comfortable antecedents and sound parents.

Laying aside all prejudice in favor of or against race, looking at the negro as politically and socially related to the American people generally, and measuring the forces arrayed against him, I do not see how he can survive and flourish in this country as a distinct and separate race, nor do I see how he can be removed from the country either by annihilation or expatriation.

Sometimes I have feared that, in some wild paroxysm of rage, the white race, forgetful of the claims of humanity and the precepts of the Christian religion, will proceed to slaughter the negro in wholesale, as some of that race have attempted to slaughter Chinamen, and as it has been done in detail in some districts of the Southern States. The grounds of this fear, however, have in some measure decreased, since the negro has largely disappeared from the arena of Southern politics, and has betaken himself to industrial pursuits and the acquisition of wealth and education, though even here, if over-prosperous, he is likely to excite a dangerous antagonism; for the white people do not easily tolerate the presence among them of a race more prosperous than themselves. The negro as a poor ignorant creature does not contradict the race pride of the white race. He is more a source of amusement to that race than an object of resentment. Malignant resistance is augmented as he approaches the plane occupied by the white race, and yet I think that that resistance will gradually yield to the pressure of wealth, education, and high character.

My strongest conviction as to the future of the negro therefore is, that he will not be expatriated nor annihilated, nor will he forever remain a separate and distinct race from the people around him, but that he will be absorbed, assimilated, and will only appear finally, as the Phoenicians now appear on the shores of the Shannon, in the features of a blended race. I cannot give at length my reasons for this conclusion, and perhaps the reader may think that the wish is father to the thought, and may in his wrath denounce my conclusion as utterly impossible. To such I would say, tarry a little, and look at the facts. Two hundred years ago there were two distinct and separate streams of human life running through this country. They stood at opposite extremes of ethnological classification: all black on the one side, all white on the other. Now, between these two extremes, an intermediate race has arisen, which is neither white nor black, neither Caucasian nor Ethiopian, and this intermediate race is constantly increasing. I know it is said that marital alliance between these races is unnatural, abhorrent and impossible; but exclamations of this kind only shake the air. They prove nothing against a stubborn fact like that which confronts us daily and which is open to the observation of all. If this blending of the two races were impossible we should not have at least one-fourth of our colored population composed of persons of mixed blood, ranging all the way from a dark-brown color to the point where there is no visible admixture. Besides, it is obvious to common sense that there is no need of the passage of laws, or the adoption of other devices, to prevent what is in itself impossible.

Of course this result will not be reached by any hurried or forced processes. It will not arise out of any theory of the wisdom of such blending of the two races. If it comes at all, it will come without shock or noise or violence of any kind, and only in the fullness of time, and it will be so adjusted to surrounding conditions as hardly to be observed. I would not be understood as advocating intermarriage between the two races. I am not a propagandist, but a prophet. I do not say that what I say *should* come to pass, but what I think is likely to come to pass, and what is inevitable. While I would not be understood as advocating the desirability of such a result, I would not be understood as deprecating it. Races and varieties of the human family appear and disappear, but humanity remains and will remain forever. The American people will one day be truer to this idea than now, and will say with Scotia's inspired son:

"A man's a man for a' that."

When that day shall come, they will not pervert and sin against the verity of language as they now do by calling a man of mixed blood, a negro; they will tell the truth. It is only prejudice against the negro which calls every one, however nearly connected with the white race, and however remotely connected with the negro race, a negro. The motive is not a desire to elevate the negro, but to humiliate and degrade those of mixed blood; not a desire to bring the negro up, but to cast the mulatto and the quadroon down by forcing him below an arbitrary and hated color line. Men of mixed blood in this country apply the name *"negro"* to themselves, not because it is a correct ethnological description, but to seem especially devoted to the black side of their parentage. Hence in some cases they are more noisily opposed to the conclusion to which I have come, than either the white or the honestly black race. The opposition to amalgamation, of which we hear so much on the part of colored people, is for most part the merest affectation, and, will never form an impassable barrier to the union of the two varieties.

Source: Editor James Russell Lowell. *North American Review*, 142. Boston, MA: May 1886. Copyright © 1999, by the Rector and Visitors of the University of Virginia. Courtesy of The University of Virginia Library.